COINAGE AND HISTORY IN THE SEVENTH CENTURY NEAR EAST
6

Edited by
TONY GOODWIN

Proceedings of the 16th Seventh Century Syrian Numismatic Round Table

Held at The Hive Worcester on 6th and 7th April 2019

Published in 2020 for the Seventh Century Syrian Numismatic Round Table

© 2020: Copyright is held by the individual authors

Produced and distributed by:
Archetype Publications
1 Birdcage Walk
London, SW1H 9JJ
www.archetype.co.uk

ISBN: 978-1-909492-73-8

Cover design by Steve Lloyd
Front Cover illustration: see p. 99, coin image courtesy of Leu Numismatik
Title Page illustration: see p. 148
Rear Cover illustration: see p. 99

CONTENTS

Preface	v
Anastasius I at Theopolis – Real or Imagined? *Steve Mansfield*	1
Using the iconography and inscriptions on Heraclean Dynasty coins to construct an historical narrative of the 7th century Byzantine Empire *Stephen Maxfield*	19
A New Coin Type from the mid-seventh century? *Maria Vrij*	35
An Overview of the Phase 1 Byzantine-Arab Coinage *Andrew Oddy*	47
The Lazy S Workshop: Coin Production in Early Arab Syria *Andrew Oddy*	77
A very peculiar group of early Pseudo-Byzantine coins *Tony Goodwin*	97
Greek Monograms and Countermarks in Seventh-Century Syria *David Woods*	101
What can we learn from 'Transitional' coins? *Tony Goodwin*	121
Yet again on Justinian II's gold coinage, 'Abd al-Malik's monetary reform, and the 'War of images' *Federico Montinaro*	133
Die Chains and Die Links with the Mint Name Ḥalab *Ingrid Schulze*	143
The Standing Caliph Coins with the Mint Name Qūrus (قُوْرس) A new Die and a new Die Link *Wolfgang Schulze*	165
From Scythopolis to Baysān: A Glimpse at the Coins of The Hebrew University's Excavations at Beth Shean *Nitzan Amitai-Preiss*	169
The Umayyad Coins excavated during the Danish-German Jerash Northwest Quarter Project 2012–2016 *Ingrid and Wolfgang Schulze*	175

Coins and Papyri in 6th/7th Century Egypt　　　　　　　　　　　　　　　　181
Tasha Vorderstrasse

The weight standard of copper coins as a means for understanding　　　191
the Syrian tradition of the seventh century
Dietrich Schnädelbach

From Ancient to Medieval: The Significance of Fixed Die Axes　　　　　203
Marcus Phillips

PREFACE

The Syrian Arab-Byzantine coinage has been intensively studied over the last 25 years, perhaps more so than any other Islamic coin series. It might therefore be expected that the amount of research would now be diminishing and that new discoveries would be made only occasionally. However, the contents of this volume amply demonstrate that this is not the case; in fact my impression from editing the papers is quite the opposite; the volume abounds with new research, new discoveries and, perhaps surprisingly, new questions.

The volume contains 16 papers presented at a two-day conference held in Worcester in April 2019. Seven of these papers deal solely with Arab-Byzantine coinage and I think that two clear trends can be discerned in this area of research. Firstly the increasing importance of detailed and meticulous die studies (see particularly Oddy and I. Schulze) and secondly the realisation that the administrative structure of Arab-Byzantine minting is more complex than used to be thought only a few years ago. It is now clear that there was considerable delegation of the responsibility for minting; so for example Oddy writes of 'workshops' rather than 'mints', Schulze of 'secondary mints' and I use the term 'contracting out'. At present all we can be sure of is that a number of different types of authority were involved in minting and that this varied over time, but the precise nature of these authorities (governors, moneyers, city councils, bishops etc.?) remains an open question. An eighth paper (Vrij) describes an intriguing new seventh century coin type which may be either Byzantine or Arab-Byzantine.

Two further papers use both contemporary documents and coins to explore historical questions. Montinaro sheds new light on the 'war of images' and Maxfield demonstrates that there is considerable evidence for a continuing Byzantine military presence in Syria/Palestine well into the 650s. This goes against conventional scholarship, but it would certainly help to explain a number of features of Constans II's coinage which have long puzzled numismatists.

A considerable problem in researching Arab-Byzantine coinage has been the lack of relevant excavation publications. This situation is now steadily improving and two short papers give interesting details of recent excavations at Jerash and Beth Shean, although for fuller details we must await the official excavation reports.

Outside the strictly Arab-Byzantine field we have one paper on an emergency Byzantine coinage from Antioch, one on weight standards, one on coin circulation in Egypt in the 6th and 7th century and finally a discussion of the significance of die-axis in medieval numismatics, along with a timely plea for Islamic numismatists to properly record die-axis (Phillips).

Tony Goodwin   November 2019

Anastasius I at Theopolis – Real or Imagined?

S J Mansfield[1]

This paper deals with an emergency coinage minted at Antioch in the years 540 – 542. A Catalogue of 31 examples can be found at the end of the paper along with an Annex of other non-Imperial coins which are possibly related. An example of one of these anomalous coins first entered my collection more than 30 years ago although some of the issues they raise had been the subject of discussion almost 50 years before that. Some of the coins, at least, belong in my opinion to an emergency coinage issued in Antioch during CE 540-542 when the city was occupied by the Persians and thus represent a gap in the "Imperial" Byzantine coinage of the city. Since earlier attempts to provide a historical context for the coins they have been the subject of further recent examination, both directly and in a more oblique way and it the time seems right for a recapitulation[2].

The different elements of the paper are: to provide an outline of the historical study of the coins from 1943 to 2016 and onwards – this may be called the chronology of a numismatic idea; to summarise my own conclusions first published in 2011[3] and to explain how they may have changed; and to update the corpus of known coins. The excuse for a bibliographic history is that my two existing papers on this subject were published in 2011, and then in 2013, in the Journal of the Oriental Numismatic Society (JONS) which seldom addresses Byzantine topics and enjoys only a fairly limited circulation. It is interesting to note that in 2016, in a paper, presumably peer reviewed, on the Byzantine coinage of Antioch, published by the prestigious Royal Brill academic publishing house, referred to later, there was no reference to the two JONS articles and thus to any coinage at Antioch between 540 and 542.

Figure 1. The hybrid "Theopolis" follis.

This is a typical example of the emergency coinage in which an obverse, apparently of Anastasius I (498-522), is muled with a reverse that is traditionally associated with the output of the Antioch mint only after 528 or 529. Here it is the mint mark, an abbreviation (this is signified by the stroke

---

[1] Steve Mansfield is an unaffiliated scholar; sandkmansfield@aol.com.
[2] I owe a debt of gratitude to Dr Timothy Crafter who, in particular, alerted me to a number of the historical references contained herein.
[3] S. Mansfield, *An Emergency Coinage in Antioch: A. D. 540-542*, Journal of the Oriental Numismatic Society (JONS): no. 207 (2011), pp. 6-10; and *An Emergency Coinage in Antioch: A. D. 540-542, Some Additional Evidence*, JONS no. 216 (2013), pp. 8-9.

above the first two letters) of the Greek form of THEOPOLIS (the "City of God"), a name by which Antioch was certainly known in the first half of the sixth century, that is especially significant:

ΘΥΠΟΛS

The story opens in 1987 although there is more than one earlier scene. By 1988 the library of the Royal Numismatic Society, then housed in the Warburg Institute, possessed the first edition of the Bulgarian numismatic journal "Numismatika"[4] in which one of these coins appeared. In the Abstract, the author, G. Jekov, terms the coin "an imitation" noting that it names Anastasius but implying that it was struck post-528.

RESUME

DEUX IMITATIONS DE MONNAIES BYZANTINES DE CUIVRE DU VI s.
G. Jekov

L'auteur publie deux imitations de follissis byzantins du VIe s. découverts en Bulgarie. Sur le droit de la première monnaie est gravé le nom de l'empereur Anastasius I (491—518) et sur le revers — les letteres initiales de l'atelier de Théopolis (Antioche) Antioche a reçu le nom de Théopolis après le grand tremblement de terre en 528.
L'inscription sur le droit de la seconde imitation est analphabète. Sur le revers elle porte les lettres initiales de l'ateiler de Cyzique et à la place des chiffres de l'officine est gravée une étoile.

Figure 2. Numismatika issue 1.

The plates were of poor quality but it was clear enough that Jekov's coin was die-linked to one of my own[5].

The idea formed that coins of this kind were struck at Antioch between 540 and 542 – a period marked by the Persian conquest of the city in June 540, its sack, and forced depopulation. But assuming that some currency might still have been needed (hence use of the terms "emergency" or "necessity" issue) it seemed possible that whoever ordered the coins to be made also instructed the die-makers not to depict the Emperor currently reigning at Constantinople – Justinian I (527-565), but the long dead ruler Anastasius, an inscription for whom would be less likely to attract Persian attention – their armies still being in the neighbourhood. If this sounds fanciful, place yourself in the sixth century, in the precarious situation of the issuers, and bear in mind that the disguising of a coinage forms one of the features that underpin the 20-year operation of the seventh century "Syrian mint" during the "last great war of antiquity" (610-630) between the Byzantine and Sasanian Persian Empires. It has been suggested that the emergency mint served as a forerunner for the Syrian mint, if not a model.

This, then, is an emergency coinage at Antioch 540-542. But there are coins related to that illustrated above that allow for alternative, or perhaps additional, interpretations. The debate has quite a long history – both before and after the encounter in the RNS library.

Coins of this type were known before 1987. Alfred Bellinger published one in Volume 1 of the Dumbarton Oaks (DO) catalogue[6] with the comment *"this is a surprising mule of what looks like a*

---

[4] G. Jekov, ***Deux Imitations de Monnaies Byzantines de Cuivre du VIs***; Numismatika issue 1, pp. 22-25 (1987).
[5] S. J. Mansfield, ***Early Byzantine Copper Coins (EBCC)***, Ex Officio Books, Manchester (2016), p. 60, 6.3. It is worth mentioning that the coin was acquired from the extremely knowledgeable Byzantine numismatist Peter Donald who noted its anomalous nature.
[6] A. Bellinger, ***Catalogue of Byzantine Coins in the Dumbarton Oaks and Whittemore Collections*** (DOC), Volume 1, Anastasius I to Maurice, 491-602, Washington DC, 1966 (p. 140, note 213).

perfectly genuine reverse of Class IV with an obverse of Anastasius with the name so garbled that it must surely be a contemporary forgery". He did not speculate on its origin.

In 1969 the Turkish numismatist Yilmaz Izmirlier illustrated a further example[7] pointing out the obverse die-link with the DO specimen. Reversing the chronology (it adds little to the study of the coins but the circumstances are intriguing): at a meeting of the Société Française de Numismatique held on 3 October 1942 the eminent Byzantinist Henry Longuet exhibited a follis of Anastasius apparently with the mint signature Theopolis.

> M. le Dʳ Longuet présente un *follis* au nom d'Anastase portant, à l'exergue du revers, la marque d'atelier ΘΕΟΥΠΟΛIC. Or, Anastase est mort le 1ᵉʳ juillet 518 et ce n'est qu'après le tremblement de terre du 29 novembre 528, soit plus de dix ans plus tard, qu'Antioche prit le nom de
>
> ΘΕΟΥΠΟΛIC. Le changement du nom de l'atelier ne permet pas d'admettre qu'il s'agit d'une simple immobilisation, mais bien plutôt, pour une monnaie de l'empire d'Orient, de l'expression d'une tendance à prolonger au delà du terme de leur règne le monnayage de certains empereurs, tendance qui s'est manifestée, entre autres, dans le monnayage de certains peuples barbares qui avaient succédé à l'empire d'Occident.

Figure 3. Minutes of the Société Française de Numismatique.

The minutes say that Longuet regarded the coin as a posthumous issue and they record his comment that naming the Emperor Anastasius was "*not a simple immobilization but rather ... the expression of a tendency to extend beyond the term of their reign the coinage of certain Emperors*". There was no other explanation. Assuming that the meeting was held in Paris, then under German occupation, the discussion might perhaps have hit more decisively on the idea of a necessity coinage in disguise and produced in circumstances not wholly unlike that of France at the time.

An emergency coinage.

The first JONS paper of 2011 described what happened at Antioch during the two years in question – drawing, obviously, on Procopius[8]. The Persian army successfully assaulted Antioch's city walls in June 540. The Persians got into the middle of the city and fought with the civilian population slaughtering many (page 335); the survivors were captured and enslaved; the Persian army, except for a small number of men ordered to fire the entire city, withdrew back to its encampment; in the ensuing fire many houses at the extremity of the city were not in fact destroyed; the whole army went to Apamea; all the captives from Antioch were resettled in a new city close to the Persian capital at Ctesiphon.

---

[7] Y. Izmirlier, **Some Unpublished Byzantine Copper Coins**, Numismatic Circular 77 (1969), pp. 318-322, no. 10.
[8] Procopius, **History of the Wars**, Books 1 and 2, Loeb Classical Library, 1914.

Are these events consistent with the possibility of an unofficial mint located in Antioch issuing an emergency coinage? Parts of the city were left standing and the Persian army withdrew. It is quite possible that people still remained in Antioch. On the other hand, Procopius says that the entire population was removed. Is this likely though? The deportation of entire populations requires the mobilisation of enormous resources even by modern standards and ancient authors often appear unreliable about numbers; for example, the obviously exaggerated number of 300,000 given by Procopius for the extent of the earthquake death toll[9]. If there was some kind of residual population a necessity coinage facilitating local trade may well have been needed. But with the Persians at Apamea (the modern Syrian town of Qalaat al-Madiq about 85 miles SSE) it would have been foolhardy for this coinage to have been overtly Imperial in sentiment.

More recently, the 2016 paper mentioned earlier[10], which draws heavily on the unpublished Protonotarios collection, identifies the incidence of missing letters from the names of Emperors in the obverse legends of copper coins struck at Antioch under Justin I and Justinian I. By contrast, the author, Pavla Drapelova, notes that Justin's Constantinople coinage was usually struck *"without any mistakes in legends and in mintmarks"*. She concludes that the Antioch mint may have been subject to less rigorous controls than at Constantinople and elsewhere and attributes this to a variety of factors, including the difficult political and economic situation (in 1961 a historian of Antioch, G. M. Downey, suggested that social unrest lead to the end of the local Olympic games at Antioch and an important source of revenue), natural occurrences such as earthquake and plague, man-made disasters such as the successful Persian siege in the summer of 540 and even the possibility that its population, distanced by reason of ethnicity, language and theological leaning from the mass of the Eastern Empire, required, in essence, a local coinage. On the situation during and just after the Persian conquest she merely states that there was *"a break in minting in 540–542 caused by the sack of the city by the Persians"*.

Much of Drapelova's thinking lies outside the narrower confines of this paper, however. But the year before, Gabriela Bijovsky had examined other aspects of the Antiochene coinage including the emergency issue. Before addressing this, it is time to say more about the coins themselves and why they may be what is claimed.

The Imperial issues and the emergency coins: comparison of obverses/reverses.

For a start, can the necessity coins actually be Imperial issues? The coin on the right is a regular issue of Antioch in the collection of the Bibliothèque Nationale in Paris[11]. Comparing the obverses leaves us in little doubt that the die used to strike the coin on the left was not the work of an experienced die-cutter. The form of many of the letters is idiosyncratic and we will see it repeated as we look at further examples.

---

[9] Procopius, op. cit., Book II, xiv, page 383.
[10] P. Drapelova, *Province in Contrast to City*, in *From Constantinople to the Frontier, The City and the Cities*, Koninklijke Brill NV (2016).
[11] C. Morrisson, *Catalogue des Monnaies Byzantines de la Bibliothèque Nationale*, Paris (1970).

Anomalous legend   Regular legend
                       B. N. Ae/21

Figure 4. Comparison of ΘΥΠΟΛS *coins from the emergency mint (left) and the Imperial mint (right).*

The type of emergency coinage with the denomination mark flanked by two eight-pointed stars is the most common. In 2011 this was designated Type 1a of which the fourth officina predominates[12]. In fact the reverses present more of a difficulty. Bellinger pronounced the DO specimen to be from a genuine die and this was also Donald's opinion back in 1988. In both cases the dies were competently cut and some similarities may be observed - one characteristic common to both the emergency and regular coinage is the tendency for the Greek P (Π) to appear with an extended, and often asymmetrical top line. I am inclined to accept that many of the reverse dies used at the emergency mint came from the Imperial mint.

De civitate Dei.

Why do the coins say "city of God"? The earliest coins of Justinian struck at Antioch have the mintmark ANTIX[13]. This was changed to THEUP – in Latin letters between two stars. All the numismatic works appear to date the change to 528-529, probably early in 529. This was in the middle of the first five year lustrum[14] (that is, a subdivision of the 15 year indictional system of dating) of 527-532 so another reason, more than a purely administrative one, is sought.

The traditional explanation for the change is that it reflects the formal renaming of the city to Theopolis. The sixth century Byzantine chronicler John Malalas says *"In that year Antioch was renamed Theopolis by order of the Emperor"*[15]. Malalas is a very unreliable source for periods prior to his adult life (one historian has called him "the world's worst chronicler"[16]), although it does

---

[12] As pointed out later in the paper, these officina letters are almost certainly meaningless.
[13] W. Hahn, *Money of the Incipient Byzantine Empire (Anastasius – Justinian I, 491-565)*, Veröffentlichungen des Instituts für Numismatik und Geldgeschichte, Vienna (2000), Pl. 24, 125. The coin is dated to 527-529.
[14] Regarding the significance of this - "Dr Hahn's strikingly original insight is that the designs and secret-marks of the coins were changed at regular intervals corresponding with the fifteen-year indictional system of dating, or (in the case of the copper folles) at shorter intervals, namely the five-year subdivisions of the indictions, which are termed lustra." D. M. Metcalfe, *New Light on the Byzantine Coinage System, Numismatic Chronicle LXXXii* (1974), pp. 14-15.
[15] *The Chronicle of John Malalas, A Translation*, Byzantina Australiensia 4, trans. Elizabeth Jeffreys et al., Australian Association for Byzantine Studies, Melbourne, 1986, p. 258.
[16] A. T. Olmstead, *The Mid Third Century of the Christian Era*, in *Classical Philology, Volume 37, no. 4*, October 1942.

seem that he was living in Antioch during the year in question[17]. But as an Imperial bureaucrat (he may well have worked in the office of the Count of the East) he would presumably be anxious to give credit to the Emperor for a decision and may have delivered simply the "official version".

Antioch was an unlucky city. Earthquakes occurred in May 526 and again in November 528[18], it was close enough to the badlands between the Byzantine and Persian Empires to be threatened both by the latter's armies and by its Lakhmid Arab allies, and the plague struck devastatingly in 542 and for a year or so following resulting, apparently, in another break in the issue of coins[19]. The change in name following the second earthquake presumably represented confidence in future Divine intervention – sadly not borne out by events.

In any case, Bijovsky provides other possible reasons for the change. In a paper on the Oboda hoard, in a Festschrift in honour of Wolfgang Hahn, she suggests a different approach to the question of the possible emergency coinage and also to the broader issue of when the mint of Antioch began to employ the name Theopolis[20].

The numismatic evidence is provided by the Oboda hoard of 72 folles of Anastasius I through Justin II. A single coin of the latter provides some idea of the *terminus post quem* but its condition – the regnal year is illegible – makes providing a precise date for the tpq impossible. Most of the Oboda coins are in poor condition but one of them (number 16 - a follis of Anastasius) is particularly interesting since it has the mint mark ΘΥΠΟΛS and an obverse which is certainly distinct from most of the coins attributed to the emergency mint. Is it, in fact, a regular product of the Imperial mint at Antioch? If so, the change of name for the city might have to be taken back at least to the period 512 to 518 at the beginning of which an issue of heavy reformed folles was instituted at Antioch[21].

Bijovsky continues her argument by examining what John Malalas has to say in a wider context. Given the various misfortunes suffered by Antioch and the obvious sentiment expressed in the name Theopolis it seems quite possible that it was used informally well before 528-9. This possibility certainly cannot ruled out in reading Malalas – not only because he cannot be counted a particularly reliable source but because the purpose of his writing seems to have been to entertain the ordinary people – whose views, including their superstitions – he might be expected to reflect[22] even while he keeps to the official version for the change.

We should now turn to the coinage and the possibility that there was a mint called Theopolis under Anastasius as proposed by Bijovsky.

The coins and their mint signatures.

Significantly more of these anomalous coins are now known than was the case in 2011. While obviously providing more data, this also complicates analysis. While coins resembling that in

---

[17] It is possible that he had already moved to Constantinople at this time, however. G. Downey, *A History of Antioch in Syria*, Princeton (1961).
[18] Sbeinati, Darawcheh and Mouty, **The Historical Earthquakes of Syria**, in *Annals of Geophysics*, volume 48, no. 3 (June 2005).
[19] A. Bellinger, **The Antiochene Copper of Justinian**, American Numismatic Society - *Museum Notes 12* (1966), p. 95.
[20] G. Bijovsky and N. Benovitz, *A Hoard of Folles from Oboda and the Mint of Antioch/Theopolis*, in **TOYTO APECH TH XWPA, Festskrift für Wolfgang Hahn zum 70**, Vienna (2015), p. 58.
[21] P. Grierson, *Byzantine Coins*, Methuen (1982), p. 66.
[22] A. D. Momigliano, *Oxford Classical Dictionary* (1970), p. 641 – "Malalas preserves many otherwise unknown facts .. .. His popular language, his interest in local traditions, and his desire to appeal to the semi-educated Christians .. .. are significant".

Figure 1[23] continue to dominate, the corpus of coins has become, overall, more heterogeneous in nature. What implications might this have for the suggestions put forward by Drapelova and Bijovsky as well as for the idea of the emergency mint? In addition, are there implications for the scheme for the etymological evolution of the Antiochene mint signature, first addressed in detail by Bellinger in 1966 in Museum Notes 12[24]?

Before addressing these points, it is useful to reiterate the typology for the coins proposed in the 2011 and 2013 JONS articles and in EBCC even if this may no longer be fully fit for purpose. It was based on a combination of obverse legend (that is the Emperor named) and reverse design, including the mint signature, as follows:

Type 1a: Two stars/Theopolis (Greek form): Naming Anastasius I

Type 1b: Two stars/Theopolis (Greek form): Naming Justin I

Type 2: Two crosses on globes/Theopolis (Greek form): Naming Anastasius I

Type 3: Two stars/CON: Naming Anastasius

Type 4a: Two stars/Theopolis (Latin form): Naming Anastasius I

Type 4b: Two stars/Theopolis (Latin form): Naming Justin I

Mule: type 1a/type 4a

Figure 5. Basic typology for the Emergency Coinage at Antioch.

The larger number of coins now known means that criteria such as accuracy in the engraving of individual letters and of the complete obverse legend should also be considered. Thus in the catalogue of 31 specimens I have identified some additional attributes of the coins using brief descriptors such as "accurate legend", etc.

The sequence of mint signatures at Antioch.

Can a much earlier usage of the mint mark Theopolis be satisfactorily dovetailed into such a sequence? In fact, can it be accommodated in an expansion of Bellinger's scheme incorporating the reigns of both Anastasius I and Justin I as well as the brief joint reign of Justin I and Justinian I of four months in 527? It is helpful to focus on several coins that do not, particularly easily, make a fit with the emergency mint.

A starting point is the coin in the Oboda hoard. I agree with Bijovsky that that its obverse, at least in respect of the lettering of the legend, is quite unlike the coin shown in Figure 1 but there are problems in attributing the coin to the reign of Anastasius I. The only known folles struck by Anastasius at Antioch are to a heavy standard. They are quite rare but the four examples at DO weigh 15 or 16 grams. The Oboda coin weighs only 9.87 grams – quite a difference even allowing

---

[23] About half of the known coins are stylistically similar. They are from two obverse dies and are termed the "majority" and "minority" obverse die sub-groups.
[24] Bellinger, *Antiochene Copper* (ibid).

for its worn condition[25]. The other problem is that, in my opinion, the coin appears to form part of a curious obverse die-chain:

Type 1a (ΘΥΠΟΛS * *)   Type 4a (+THEBC+ **)   Type 1a (ΘΥΠΟΛS **)

Donald/Princeton; Cat. 20   Ebay 2012; Cat. 21   Oboda 16; Cat. 19

Figure 6: Obverse die-link possibly incorporating Oboda no. 16.

In all three cases the images are poor and I do not have sizes or weights for the first two coins. But Donald still had access to the Princeton specimen when he identified the first link in the chain – that is between two coins with reverses Theopolis (in Greek) and Theopolis, albeit blundered, in Latin. Is it possible that all three coins belong to a hitherto unknown light issue of Anastasius at Antioch-Theopolis? It stretches the imagination since, if so, both Greek and Latin mint signatures would seem to be involved.

That said, the Bijovsky theory is supported (even if the overall situation then becomes even more complex) by a more recent discovery (catalogue no. 18).

17.40 g: The Central Forum of Numismatists of the USSR; Cat. 18

Figure 7: "Heavy" Type 1a follis naming Anastasius.

---

[25] The earliest small module reformed folles at Constantinople, while they vary considerably in weight, are generally around 8-9 grams.

The obverse of this coin is die-linked to the Oboda specimen. The reverses were struck from different dies. The difference in their weights (9.87 g and 17.40 g) is hard to explain.

If the Greek form of mint signature can then be traced back to 512 (or even 507 when the bulk of the light series was initiated at Nicomedia) then this would also accommodate a coin in the name of Justin I (Type 1b; catalogue no. 24) that, in 2011, I said I was unable to explain. As far as I am aware, this type existed uniquely in the Fairhead collection until I acquired a second specimen.

4th officina – Fairhead collection (MIB 3 N 131, 2); Cat. 24   5th officina - Mansfield collection; Cat. 22

Figure 8: Justin I with ΘΥΠΟΛS.

The coins are well made and of accomplished style. They are not from the same dies. They may well be regular issues.

A difficulty, nevertheless, with both these coins and with the Oboda/"Soviet" coin is the rarity of all four, both in the numismatic trade and, as far as I am aware, in archaeological reports, if they are the products of the Imperial mint at Antioch - the output of which was enormous[26]. And bear in mind that I have been looking out for them for 30 years.

More scientifically, acceptance of a scheme in which use of the ΘΥΠΟΛS mint signature began under Anastasius (even perhaps with the small module issue of 507) is that it plays merry hell with any obviously rational etymological evolution of the mint signature, particularly that suggested by Bellinger in 1966[27], the final stage of which was the long-lasting Theopolis version that, in one form or another, became the standard at Antioch in 528 or 529 and continued through the currency reform initiated by the Comes Sacrarum Largitionum in 538/9 to the closure of the mint in 610.

Nevertheless, the evolution of the Antioch mint signature from 507 to 565 could conceivably be constructed in the following way.

---

[26] Grierson, ***Byzantine Coins*** (ibid), p. 65.
[27] Bellinger, **Antioch Copper,** *ANS Museum Notes* (ibid).

	Imperial	Non-imperial		
Anastasius I	ϴVΠOΛS/ANTX/AN		507-518	Both light & heavy series
Justin I	ANTIX/ANTX/AN/ϴVΠOΛS		518-527	
Justin I and Justinian I	ANTIX/ANTX		527	
Justinian I	ANTIX		527-529	
Change to *City of God*	THEUP		529-537	
	ANTOΛS/ ϴVΠOΛS		537-539	
Coinage reform	ϴVΠO		539-540	RY 13
Persian occupation of Antioch		ϴVΠOΛS/THEBC/ "CON"	540-542	Emergency Coinage
	THEUPO		542-543	RY 16
Gap in coinage				Plague
	9HUΠ		546-551	RYs 20-24
	ZHUΠ		551-556	RYs 25-29
	ZHUP		554-561	RYs 28-34
	THEUP		561-565	RYs 35-39

Figure 9: Possible evolution of the Antioch mint signature; RY – regnal year (after Hahn).

Anybody who knows even a little about the pre-Justinian Antioch coppers might conclude that this is all rather odd. The mint signatures between 542 and 565 may well also appear random in the preference for Latin letters over Greek (and vice-versa) but at least they attempt to spell out Theopolis. To judge by the coinage under Anastasius and Justin the city seemed uncertain about what to call itself. Then it is not, perhaps, an unreasonable leap to Drapelova's suggestion that Antioch (even though it had claims to be the second city of the Empire) produced a local coinage.

There is a further possible consequence not actually referenced in Bijovsky's Oboda paper. In Hahn's Money of the Incipient Byzantine Empire[28] the case is stated for a sophisticated system whereby privy marks, including mint signatures, were used to indicate a change in the copper coinage in line with the indictional system of dating and with the shorter lustral periods – what he calls in the volume *the Antiochene rule of lustral variations*. What are the implications of dropping a coin marked ϴVΠOΛS with two stars, which formerly had its place in a relatively short period just prior to the reform of 538/9, into the period 512-517, or even into 507-512? Indeed what do the rapid changes in mintmarks shown in that Figure 9 imply? It begins to look like a dismantling of "the rule", or at least a challenge to it.

The corpus of "anomalous hybrid" folles.

This kind of coin appears on the market reasonably regularly but is seldom correctly identified by sellers. They are not particularly rare – 32 examples are known to me, 31 of which are catalogued here[29]. As indicated earlier, they are not a homogeneous group. The "quality" of production varies a

---

[28] Hahn *MIBE* (ibid).
[29] In 1986 I observed a specimen at the London coin dealers Baldwins and noted that it was die-linked to D. O. 213. But Bijovsky pointed out an inconsistency in my reporting in that I described it as being marked with the symbol of the first

great deal as evidenced by the accuracy of the inscriptions, the elegance (or mostly otherwise) of the portraits, and the preparation of the flans. For these reasons the catalogue groups the coins by attribute as well as by typography. About half of the coins belong to the majority or minority obverse die sub-groups. With some confidence these can be attributed to the emergency mint. With the remainder there is less certainty. Some may have been made up to 30 years before. Neither Bijovsky's view that some Imperial coins of Anastasius may have borne the mint mark of Theopolis nor Drapelova's that a purely local coinage may have been struck can be discounted.

Die-links.

It seems likely that many of the reverse dies used to strike the coinage are regular artefacts of the Antioch mint that had escaped destruction. If official dies for Anastasius were found and used, this reinforces the idea that the necessity coins were made in the city itself - perhaps under the auspices of an interim municipal authority[30]. Apart from the majority and minority obverse die sub-groups only two short obverse die chains need to be examined.

Figure 10: Die-linked ΘΥΠΟΛS and CON (1) – majority/minority obverse die sub-groups.

Figure 11: Die-linked ΘΥΠΟΛS and CON (2) – other dies.

---

officina. It seems safer to regard the coin as one of the majority obverse die sub-group from the fourth officina. I do not have an image in any case and the coin is omitted from the catalogue.

[30] It will be obvious that the reverse dies have not received much attention here. Establishing die-links between the Emergency and Imperial coinages could prove helpful in the future. Coins that are clearly the ordinary product of the Imperial Antioch mint are, in fact, little more common than those of the emergency mint.

Officinas and metrology.

Three "officina letters" appear (A; B; Δ) but these are clearly meaningless and were probably inserted by the workers at the emergency mint solely to provide an element of familiarity.

Comment on weights, in any case somewhat limited in nature, is only possible in respect of the dominant group of coins within type 1a (the majority and minority sub-groups - catalogue nos. 4-13 and 14-17 respectively) that are clearly the work of the same hand. While they number 17 coins I only know the weights of 12. They vary between 19.49 g and 10.28 g. Excluding the heaviest coin they show a pattern similar to the weights of the Imperial coins. But I find it hard to believe that the emergency coins were struck to any predetermined weight standard.

Conclusions.

What has the last five years meant for the idea of the emergency mint? The discovery of additional coins, together with Bijovsky's identification of a coin with the Greek form of Theopolis that may be part of an issue as early as 507, mean that the parameters of the problem have expanded and that it is not as simple as I believed in 2011.

Outside of the 2011 scheme there are a number of coins that for the present evade easy conclusion. The condition of some prevents any convenient arrangement in respect of dies in common that might tell us more. Other coins appear to be regular but their rarity poses a problem.

Whether these coins all belong to the emergency mint or some are Imperial in origin remains unresolved. There is a tension between the possibility that official coins bearing the Theopolis mint mark exist for Anastasius and Justin and the problems that this poses for a logical evolution of the mint signature. There is also the possibility of a challenge to Hahn's careful construction of the Antioch lustral rule.

We have two scenarios I think. One suggests an extended period of issue of the ΘVΠOΛS marked coins (just short of 60 years), albeit interspersed with other forms of the mint signature, and the other a much shorter period of only 14-15 years. Both can accommodate the emergency mint as a defined stage when the Imperial mint was non-operational. They are not mutually exclusive.

Whichever may prove, in the future, to be the case we are still left with an anomalous and diverse coinage at Antioch - struck over a long period and displaying a pattern of mint signatures that do not make immediate or obvious sense.

As to the emergency mint, I find it hard, now, to attribute all these coins, that vary so much in style, to a single point of production during 540-542. The existence of a reasonably wide range of specimens that we might otherwise casually write off as sixth century counterfeits makes it possible, as Drapelova suggested, that some coins were produced in Antioch for purely local distribution.

This is speculation, however. In the future, it may be for historians rather than numismatists to engage further with the sources in search of an explanation as to what the people of Antioch actually called their own city.

Emergency Coinage in Antioch 540-542: Catalogue of 31 specimens.

Type 1a (Anastasius) – obverse die majority group: inaccurate legends (ΘΥΠΟΛS)

Cat. 1
15.10 g
Officina B
OD2.1/RD2.1
Private collection
Russian Federation

Cat. 2
13.47 g
Officina B
OD2.2/RD2.2
NCirc. 10

Cat. 1-3: three die-linked coins

Cat. 3
Weight not known
Officina B
OD2.3/RD2.3
Donald/Princeton

Cat. 4
15.66 g
Officina Δ
OD2.4/RD3.1
Mansfield collection

Cat. 5
14.67 g
Officina Δ
OD2.5/RD3.2
Mansfield collection

Cat. 4 – 13 die duplicates

Cat. 6
13.46 g
Officina Δ
OD2.6/RD3.3
DOC 213

Cat. 7
11.99 g
Officina Δ
OD2.7/RD3.4
Mansfield collection

Cat. 8
11.92 g
Officina Δ
OD2.8/RD3.5
Mansfield collection

Cat. 9
10.28 g
Officina Δ
OD2.9/RD3.6
Mansfield collection

Cat. 10
10.03 g
Officina Δ
OD2.10/RD3.7
Private Collection
Italy

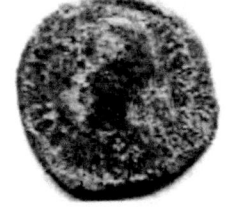 

Cat. 4 – 13 die duplicates

Cat. 11
Weight not known
Officina Δ
OD2.11/RD3.8
Numismatika 1.1

Cat. 12
Weight not known
Officina Δ
OD2.12/RD3.9
Donald/Princeton

Cat. 13
Weight not known
Officina Δ
OD2.13/RD3.10
MIB 131-1 (Handel)

Type 1a (Anastasius) – Obverse die minority group: inaccurate legends (ΘΥΠΟΛS)

Cat. 14
15.66 g
Officina Δ
OD3.1/RD3.11
Mansfield collection

Cat. 15
13.90 g
Officina Δ
OD3.2/RD3.12
CNG 446 lot 439

Cat. 14-17 die duplicates

Cat. 16
11.01 g
Officina Δ
OD3.3/RD3.13
Private Collection USA

Cat. 17
Weight not known
Officina Δ
OD3.4/RD3.14
Ebay 2017 (Savoca)

Type 1a/Type 4a (Anastasius): accurate legends (ΘΥΠΟΛS and THЄUP)

Cat. 18
17.40 g
Officina A
OD1.2/RD4.1
Central Numismatic Forum USSR

Cat 18 & 19 have same obverse die but obverse die link to Cat 20 & 21 is not certain (Figs. 6 & 7)

Cat. 19
9.87 g
Officina A
OD1.3/RD5.1
Oboda hoard no. 16

Cat. 20
Weight not known
Officina A
OD1.1/RD1.1
Donald/Princeton

Cat 20 & 21 from obverse die but obverse die link to Cat 18 & 19 is not certain (Figs. 6 & 7)

Cat. 21
Weight not known
Officina A
OD1.4/RD6.1
Ebay 2012

Type 1b (Justin) – elegant portraits and accurate legends (ΘΥΠΟΛS)

Cat. 22
10.92 g
Officina Є
OD4.1/RD7.1
Mansfield collection

Cat. 23
13.20 g
Officina A
OD5.1/RD8.1
Mansfield collection

Cat. 24
Weight not known
Officina A
OD6.1/RD9.1
MIB131-2 (Fairhead)

Type 2 (Anastasius): accurate legends (ΘΥΠΟΛS)

Cat. 25
9.94g
Officina A
OD7.1/RD10.1
Mansfield collection

Cat. 26
Weight not known
Officina A
OD7.2/RD10.2
Rafah hoard 51

Type 3 (Anastasius) – part of obverse die minority group: inaccurate legends/CON

Cat. 27
12.27 g
Officina Δ
OD3.5/RD11.1
Mansfield collection

See Fig. 10

Type 1a (Anastasius): accurate legend/blundered mint marks (ΘΥΠΟΛS and CON)

Cat. 28
10.33 g
Officina Δ
OD8.1/12.1
Mansfield collection

Same obverse die (Fig. 11)

Cat. 29
10.40 g
Illegible officina
OD8.2/RD13.1
Private collection
Russian Federation

Type 4b (Justin I): elegant portrait and accurate legend (THЄUP)

Cat. 30
Weight not known
Officina Δ
OD9.1/RD14.1
MIB N126 (Fairhead)

Type 1a, var. (Anastasius): apparently accurate legends/portrait unclear (ΘΥΠΟΛS)

Cat. 31
8.80 g
Officina A
ODUncertain/RD15.1
(uncertain)
Private collection Russian
Federation

Annex. Emergency Coinage in Antioch 540-542: Some related anomalous coins.

1. MIB pl. 24, V131 (PC)   2. Ex Leimonstoll collection.

3. Mansfield collection (2558.18)   4. Unknown provenance

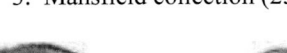

5. Roma Numismatics list (October 2018)   6. Unknown provenance

7. Private collection Russian Federation

All these coins bear legends for Justinian I with the ΘΥΠΟΛS mint mark.

1. Mint mark an "erroneous mixture" (MIBE p. 60) dated to 537-539. Weight not known. A further example is in the Rafah hoard (no. 294).

2. Presumably a well made sixth century counterfeit. 13.42 g.

3. The coin may be Imperial but is relatively light and the legend is garbled. 10.45 g.

4. Barbarous sixth century counterfeit. Weight not known.

5. Barbarous sixth century counterfeit. Weight not known.

6. A well made coin with unusual lettering in the mint mark. Perhaps Imperial. Weight not known.

7. Probably Imperial but note the distinctive Greek form of A in the legend. Weight not known.

Using the iconography and inscriptions on Heraclean Dynasty coins to construct an historical narrative of the 7th century Byzantine Empire

Stephen Maxfield[1]

The genesis of this paper derived from a paper presented by Steve Mansfield in 2016[2]. His paper covered the different coins of **Constantine IV** thoroughly and I would refer readers to that paper for information on those coins. My aim here is to consider whether the iconography of the Heraclean Dynasty coins – and the inscriptions - can help to give substance to our understanding of Byzantine history in the 7th century.

This study has, for reasons of space, had to be confined to coins generally ascribed to Constantinople. It is also limited to copper coins with passing reference to those of precious metal. It was **copper** coins that were in general circulation and used on a day to day basis by most of the citizens of the Eastern Roman Empire. Coins from other mints, Sicily, Carthage, Alexandria and so on need further study but it is not my belief that there is anything in their iconography or production that contradicts the substance of this paper.

What follows is based on two principles:-

The first principle is that coins are a primary historical source.
The second principle is that the coins of the Byzantine (Eastern Roman Empire) were based on a closed fiduciary system. So the gold (and silver) coins had an international value while the **copper** coins were tokens with a value dictated by the government. How this worked is explained in Hendy[3] (1985) but briefly the government made forced purchases of gold, paying in base metal coins at a rate determined by the government. It may also be that in the 7th century the population were required to pay taxes in gold or perhaps silver. If the amount owed resulted in a fraction of a solidus the taxpayer paid in gold and received change in **copper**[4]. There were money changers who would collect in **copper**, and exchange for gold and so the system repeats. Hendy also points out that large numbers of **copper** coins are associated with places of military activity[5]. One may suppose that not only the soldiers but also the victuallers, masons, labourers, mule drivers etc. were paid in **copper** folles, conceivably on a piece-work basis. Again, when sufficient were collected these could be exchanged for gold or used in general day to day commerce. Two points derive from this principle. First, that for the **copper** coins to have any commercial value at all, it was necessary for those using the coins to be sure that they could eventually exchange them for gold. So in an area where there were no Byzantine military or civil officials they were without value. Second that the size, weight and design of the coins were irrelevant to their value, only the mark of value i.e. M (40 nummi), K (20 nummi), I (10 nummi), etc. was important.

---

[1] Protopresbyter Stephen Maxfield is parish priest of the Greek Orthodox parish, Shrewsbury. He also teaches Liturgy, Church History and Canon Law at the Thyateira Midlands Ecclesiastical Seminary. holy.fathers@gmail.com.
[2] Mansfield 2017.
[3] Hendy 1985 p. 285ff.
[4] ibid. p. 286. A note of caution however. The evidence here is based in a 12th century document. It cannot be assumed that this system applied in the 7th century.
[5] ibid. p. 659ff (for example). Also the coins of Heraclius struck at peripatetic mints while he was on campaign: Seleucia; Isaura; Constantia and Jerusalem.

That the principle designs on coins were not arbitrary, but a means whereby the emperor communicated with his people cannot be questioned. The problem is what was he intending to say, and to whom?

During the 6th century Eastern Roman coins conform to a standard design with some differences, but broadly they are of similar size and design whatever the mint[6]. To use modern parlance I am describing this as the "default" design. The emperor is shown as a stylised profile or facing bust, (except for Justin II who had himself and his wife enthroned), with inscriptions that give the titles of the emperor and his name.

a.   *b.*   *c.*   *d.*

*Figure 1: "Default design" Left to Right, folles of: **a.** Tiberius II, **b.** Maurice, **c.** Heraclius (Class 1), **d.** Constans II showing the facing bust of the emperor. This design was in itself a 6th century innovation. Up to that time emperors had normally been shown in profile. For certain denominations of coins the emperor was shown in profile to the end of the 7th century.*

Coins of the Heraclean Dynasty are notable for several distinct features. The size, weight, and accuracy of production were very variable. The first copper coins of Heraclius (folles), Class 1[7] weigh around 11g, Class 4 about 6g, Class 6 around 5g while the first coins of Constans II weigh 4g dropping even to 3g later in the reign[8] (See figure 2). The reduction in weight reflects a shortage of copper. All these coins are folles with identical notional values. They were subject to a considerable amount of over-striking (though this aspect is not unique to this period) and the coins exhibit a very wide range of designs - distinct from any other period in the Byzantine series in the First Millennium.

Designs: Heraclius

The design could be characterised as "God is in his heaven, the emperor is on his throne, all is well in the empire, pay your taxes!" However with the arrival of Heraclius the designs and sizes of the coins started to change very considerably. The initial coins of Heraclius, in the first three years of his reign, conform to those of his predecessors, (Class 1). In year three however there is a new

---

[6] Grierson 1968, p. 226.
[7] Class numbers for folles of Heraclius follow the Dumbarton Oaks Catalogue system.
[8] Michael Decker 2016 p.158, asserts that *"Heraclius, however, due to the war emergency, issued about twice the number of coins annually as was the peacetime norm"*. While I accept this as a reasonable conjecture, I need some concrete evidence: why not three times?

design (Class 2). This shows the emperor standing with his son Heraclius Constantine to his left. Both are in ceremonial dress and both are named. Heraclius was a usurper, who had usurped the throne from another usurper: Phocas. The empire was at war with the Persians which it was losing[9]. Maintaining stability was crucial so the presence of a junior emperor implied continuity of government, stressed stability of the ruling house to preserve confidence and discourage rebels. Evidently it was not considered that this design gave sufficient signs of stability for in year 6 a new design was introduced with Heraclius, his son and the empress Martina on the left. (Class 3 & 4) The inscription disappears for lack of room. That stability needed to be emphasised is not surprising as the emperor himself was away on campaign. It is worth remembering that Roman empresses were crowned *before* they were married so they exercised power in their own right; an important consideration given that Heraclius Constantine was a boy. These coins are generally smaller than the previous class.

Once Heraclius had comprehensively defeated the Persians in year 20 (629) a new design was inaugurated which shows Heraclius in military dress with Heraclius Constantine in civil dress as before (Class 5)[10] initially there was an increase in the weights of these coins to around 11g in year 22 but they declined to 4.5g in year 30[11]. It is perfectly possible to imagine that the lacklustre performance of the Roman troops in Syria was due to the simple fact that Heraclius had run out of money to pay them. Finally at the end of his life there is a new design where Heraclius still in military costume is flanked by his two sons Heraclius Constantine and Heraclonas intending to demonstrate that the succession is secure.

a.   *b.*   *c.*   *d.*   *e.*

Figure 2. The different classes of coins struck during the reign of the Emperor Heraclius. D.O. Classes 1, 2, 3, 5 & 6. (Class 4 differs from Class 3 only in a minor details and average weight – they are lighter by about 2g).
a. Class 1, 30mm, 11.45g, 7h; ***b.*** *Class 2, 30mm, 13.14g, 7h (Mansfield collection EBCC, 2016, 17.35);* ***c.*** *Class 3, 22mm, 4.72g, 2h;* ***d.*** *Class 5 (large type) 29mm, 9.58g, 6h;* ***e.*** *Class 6, 20mm 5.35g, 6h (CNG e-auction 382 lot 478) .*

Constans II
In fact, of course, the succession was not secure at all, and after two very short reigns with no known copper coins, the grandson of Heraclius by Heraclius Constantine came to the throne as a 10 year old boy[12]. He took the name Constantine but is universally known as Constans II. The coins

---

[9] A new silver coin, the hexagram, introduced in 615, has the added inscription of "God help the Romans".
[10] Grierson 1968 Part 1, p. 228.
[11] ibid.
[12] In fact he was only a few days away from his 11th birthday. See Theophanes p. 465 and note 6.

now become very interesting indeed. On the obverse the emperor is shown in ceremonial robes holding a long cross (though this sometimes changes to a Chi Rho)[13] in his left hand and a *globus cruciger* in his right. This is not the only cross on the coins. The emperor has a cross on his crown, there is a cross on the globus cruciger and there is a cross above the cursive M on the reverse. The inscription on the obverse is *En Touto Nika* referring to the vision that Constantine the Great had before his great victory over Maxentius at the battle of the Milvian Bridge on 28th October 312. This links Constans II to Constantine the Great but without mentioning his name and suggests that he is a conquering emperor set apart by God. The reverse designs, of which, there are many, vary slightly but the denominational M is surrounded by a date, a letter of the *officina* and by the word ANA NEOς meaning "restoration".

Given that the emperor was himself but a boy these designs are about as belligerent as one could get. Something is to be restored, presumably the empire, and restored through the conquering power of the cross. This is a theme that is evident throughout Byzantine and indeed Orthodox history, to this day[14]. There are however two other important features about these coins that should be noted. First they are small (generally about 4 – 5 g later dropping to around 3g), atrociously struck from year 3 onwards - often because the dies were engraved for coins larger than the flans supplied. Second the flans themselves are crude and misshapen and many are over-struck. There seem to have been a very large number struck. They are to this day extremely common.

a.   *b.*   *c.*

Figure 3. Typical examples of folles from the beginning of the reign of Constans II. Hurriedly prepared flans, hastily struck with little attention to detail. x 1.25
a. Callot 1, (D.O. Class 1) Constantinople, year 2, Off. Δ, 4.17g, 24mm, 1h.
b. Callot 4, (D.O. - MIB.165) year 3, Off. B; 4.73g, 22mm, 1h.
c. Callot 1; (D.O. Class 1)Constantinople, year 1?, Off. ?, 4.41g, 23mm.7h.

See table 1. This shows the year of the reign, the officina and the Class number as given by Callot and Sear. Callot is currently the most exhaustive presentation of these coins but I will be surprised if they do not need to be re-classified in the future. Where the number is in bold italics it shows the first year that this particular type came into production, where in plain type it shows that production of this particular type continued in that year. So for instance Callot class 1 was first struck in year 1 but went on to be struck in years 2, 3, and 4.

The table comes with a caveat. C. 6 is not a coin of the type described above (See Figure 1). These coins are "default" coins – bust of emperor with the title IhPER COhST on the obverse with an upper case M (etc) on the reverse. They have been subject to a considerable amount of controversy amongst numismatists which seems likely to continue. What is clear is that they are coins of Constans II[15].

---

[13] In the very earliest coins of Constans the emperor is shown holding a labarum and his crown has pendilia a detail that had been absent for 30 years. See Goodwin 2012.

[14] For example on Greek postage stamps.

[15] Grierson believed they were struck in Constantinople, but they do not seem to have circulated in the capital or in Anatolia but they are common in Syria, Cyprus and Rhodes. (I am grateful to Marcus Phillips for pointing this out to me, see also Phillips 2012). To add to the complexity there are coins similar to these with a cursive M on the reverse and the letters SC for Sicily. Were these struck in Constantinople for Sicily as Grierson suggests or were they struck in

Emperor	Year of reign	Constantinople mint officina	Callot[16] and DO[17] Classes
641/2 Constans II	1	ABΓΔE	*1 DO1*
	2	ABΓΔE	1 DO 1
		ABΓΔE	*2[18] DO 2*
	3	BE	1 DO 1
		AΓE	2 DO 2
		ABΓΔE	*3 DO 3*
		ABΓΔE	*4 DO -*
		ABΓΔE	*6 DO -*[19]
	4	ABΓΔE	1 DO 1
	5	ABΓΔ	*5 DO 4*
	6	ABΓΔE	5 DO 4
	7	ABΓΔE	5 DO4
	8,9,10,		No coins struck

Table 1

Be that as it may the table demonstrates that at the beginning of Constans II reign, when he was a minor, large numbers of different patterns of coins were struck. In year 3 for instance there were five different styles of coin being minted probably by all five officinae – even if examples have yet to be discovered for two of the officinae. Everything about these coins suggests haste and I would suggest an enormous number were struck[20]. The dies are too big for the flans, the flans are cut with extreme crudity and the dies are often worn. It is also clear that the shortage of copper evident at the end of Heraclius' reign is now even more severe. We are dealing with a high volume of miserable little coins.

But the most significant thing about these coins is that they are found in numerous hoards and as individual specimens all over Syria[21]. So much so that they became ubiquitous and were copied by

---

Sicily itself? If Grierson is correct in his belief it could be that the IhPЄR COhST coins were struck in Constantinople but specifically for military use.

[16] Callot 1980.

[17] Dumbarton Oaks 1968.

[18] These coins have a peculiar arrangement of the inscription on the reverse. To the left of the 'M' are the letters OΦA, above the 'M' are the letters ANA and to the right the letters NEOS. OΦA is not a Greek word so this must be a contraction, but of what? Grierson (1968) suggests that they represent the Latin word 'Officina'. Given that the Roman authorities were very concerned about the inscriptions in this period, to use a word that would have no relevance whatever to the users of these coins seems to me to be highly unlikely. So what could these letters be a contraction of? A word that perhaps answers the question is "Οφειλημα" meaning a debt or obligation. The word is used twice in the Lord's Prayer but for some unaccountable reason it was translated into English as "trespasses" in the 16th century. Could these coins have been struck to redeem some obligation: back pay perhaps for soldiers owed money in the empire?

[19] Present in the DO catalogue but ascribed to Heraclonas. This has been refuted. These are coins of Constans II.

[20] To demonstrate this there would need to be a study of the Constans II coins found in a variety of ways but relating to a particular place either in the war zone or on the lines of communications. That such a study might exist seemed problematic until my attention was drawn to just such a work: *Coins in Rhodes: From the monetary reform of Anastasius I until the Ottoman Conquest (458 – 1522)* by Dr Anna-Maria Kasdagli (2018). This shows a sample of 122 Rhodian coins of Constans II from 19 years. Of these no less than half are from years 1 – 7 and of these, 35 are from year 3. Rhodes was of course directly on the sea lane and on the lines of communication between Constantinople and Syria. This work demonstrates my contention in a most gratifying manner!

[21] See Clive Foss, Arab-Byzantine Coins 2008 who notes their occurrence in Antioch (48), Apamea (15), Assur (2), Dehes (20), Epiphania (30?), Hama hoard (144), Qalat Siman (4), Tell Rifaat (3), Balis Raqqa (7), Resafa (4), Bethany

Syrian mints. This is absolutely extraordinary, because their very existence implies value, and if they had value it must have been possible for those using the coins to exchange them relatively easily for silver or gold. Several explanations have been given for their existence in Syria but none of these explanations can be supported by the fiduciary principle explained above. There can in fact be only one possible solution to the problem and that is that for the first five years of Constans II reign the empire was conducting a war throughout Syrian territory and that these coins were struck in order to finance this war. That such a war took place is not particularly difficult to envisage and it may be that its course could be approximated by mapping hoard sites. That the Byzantines lost, and that Syria was conquered eventually by the Arabs is not in dispute. The problem is that historians of 7th century Syria, and indeed of the Arab conquests have used and continue to use late Arab chronicles as their principle sources, and these sources claim that Syria was entirely conquered by the Arabs by the end of the reign of Heraclius. These Arab sources are very late – often 200 years late – and they simply cannot be supported by the numismatics, hence the first principle stated at the outset of this paper. Mark Whittow in his work *The Making of Orthodox Byzantium 600 – 1025*,[22] demonstrates the extreme unreliability of Arab sources, leading to the conclusion that while they may well record events, the loading and dating placed upon those events renders them largely worthless as sources.

However what of non-Arab primary sources? Are they closer to events? Do they give any insight into the putative Syrian campaigns of 641 – 645? They do! But before referring to these there are certain fundamental questions that need to be considered:-
1) After Heraclius had defeated the Persians in 627 he returned the Holy Cross[23] that he had recovered to Jerusalem, marching through what had been territory conquered by the Persians and administered by them for about 20 years. The Persian army was supposed to have returned home at the conclusion of the war, but did they and did their administrators? - for there is evidence[24] that suggests that they did not.
2) The sources refer to Arabs and Saracens[25] but who do they mean? There were Arabs living in, or close to Syria who were one time allies or client kings of the emperor: the Ghassanids. Can we be sure what Arabs are being referred to? Arabs from Arabia or Ghassanids?
3) Syria was a stronghold of Monophysitism. The Byzantines made strenuous efforts to come to a rapprochement with the monophysites, but was this for purely religious reasons or was there more to it? Were the Byzantines fighting local monophysites rather than Arabian Arabs?

It is outside the scope of this paper to consider any of these questions further but they should be born in mind when looking at the written sources. These must be read with caution because the dating is often awry or contradictory between one source and another and sometimes the sources are basing their information on an Arab source. The following may here be noted:

Dionysios of Tel Mahre[26] *When Theodoric reached Edessa, however, the Persians there turned a deaf ear to his proclamation. Their reply was, "We do not know Sh|roe (sic. Shīrōē) and we will not surrender the city to the Romans"…… This provoked him* (i.e. Theodoric) *to an all out attack on the city, which he subjected with his catapults to a hail of rocks. The Persian resistance was crushed and they accepted an amnesty to return to their country.* **(circa 626/7)**

---

(3), Capernaum (2), Emmaus (2) Jerusalem (6), Lachish hoard (2) Scythopolis (3) Tel Jezreel (2) Amman (2) Jerash (26), Pella (3).
[22] Whittow 1996 p. 82ff.
[23] Nikephoros 1989 p.15.
[24] Theophanes p. 458 n.2 The Persian garrison of Edessa had to be expelled by force.
[25] Theophanes p. 466 a reference to Arab soldiers in Byzantine pay.
[26] Dionysios reconstituted in *The Seventh Century in West-Syrian Chronicles* p.139.

This passage demonstrates that the Persians did not leave Syria without a struggle. Because it is not recorded, it cannot be assumed that this did not happen elsewhere. There are notable accounts of the taking of two cities in 640/1 in Michael the Syrian and in the Chronicle of 1234:-

Michael the Syrian[27] *The Arabs ravaged Caesarea in Palestine.....From the beginning of December until May, by day and night, he (Muʿāwiya) waged war against it. They did not obtain a guarantee for their lives. Seventy-two siege engines continuously hurled stones, but the wall was not penetrated on account of its solidity. Finally they made a breach and some of them entered through it while others scaled the wall by ladders. They fought and were fought for three days, after which the Arabs overwhelmed the Romans. Of the 7000 of them who were guarding it some escaped by boat.*
Chronicle 1234[28] *... When he (Muʿāwiya) subdued it by the sword he fought and killed all who were found in it. He seized and plundered vast quantities of gold and silver and then abandoned it to its grieving and lamentation. Those who settled there afterwards he made pay tribute.*
These texts describing the taking of Caesarea do not describe a conquest, where the victors occupy and re-garrison a conquered city. It is, rather, a successful raid.

There is a most interesting account of the taking of Euchaita[29] in the Chronicle of 1234:-
Chronicle 1234[30] *From there (i.e. Caesarea) Muʿāwiya determined to go to the heartland of the Romans. He ravaged, enslaved and pillaged his way as far as Euchaita... No one in it noticed them. The Euchaitans were scattered about the fields and vineyards.* <u>*When they saw the troops, they thought they were Christian Arabs, from those allied to the Romans.*</u> *So no person fled or moved away.... Then they entered and took possession of the city and plundered it.... They seized the women, boys and girls to lead into captivity.... Thus they returned, exulting to their own country.*

Demonstrating that even at this date Syria was subject to raids rather than conquest, on the principle that if a country is conquered the inhabitants may be enslaved but they are not removed, for to do so destroys the area conquered. In the light of this evidence it cannot be asserted that Syria was at this time – 640/1 - ruled by the Arabs.

It is also clear that the Roman Empire was taking counter measures. The following text comes from the Chronicle of Zuqnin. The Chronicle is a list of dates and events with names of rulers and bishops and their successors. There are a small number of historical events which the editor believes date from a source from about 653 - a mere decade away from the coins we are considering. The account is all too brief but nevertheless crucial:-

Chronicle of Zuqnin[31] AD 644 "*AG 953 The patrikios Valentine, the Roman general, came to make war on the Arabs, but he became afraid at their approach and ran away, leaving behind all the money he had with him for the Arabs to take.*
The same year Procopius and Theodore marched out and invaded Batnon da-Serugh[32] *in a great fury: they pillaged and plundered it, taking as many captives as they wanted before returning to their own territory.*"

---

[27] Michael the Syrian in *Theophilus of Edessa's Chronicle*, p.124.
[28] Chronicle of 1234 in *Theophilus of Edessa's Chronicle*, p.124.
[29] David Woods pointed out at the Round Table Conference, that Euchaita is a highly improbable destination for this raid and is scribal interference with the original source *Dionysios of Tel Mare*. Given the sheer logistical problem of getting an Arab army this far north of the Taurus mountains and back in the time, I am certain he is right and I would like to express my gratitude for his intervention. We must assume therefore that this raid was to a town in northern Syria not far from Caesarea.
[30] Chronicle of 1234 p.125.
[31] Chronicle of Zuqnin in *The Seventh Century in West-Syrian Chronicles* p.57.
[32] Batnon da-Serugh or Markopolis a city in Northern Syria.

This would seem to coincide with the death of Umar and the start of an Arab civil war. Such campaigns would have to be financed giving credence to the enormous number of coins being struck in year 3 for these campaigns. It is reasonable to assume that these campaigns had several elements both on land and sea. Several of the Chronicles (Theophanes, Agapius, Michael the Syrian and the Chronicle of 1234 mention that in the year 650/1 there was peace between the Arabs and the Byzantines. For example *"The Emperor Constans sent a certain Prokopios as ambassador to Mauias to ask for peace, which was concluded for two years."*[33]

Possibly this should be dated a year earlier but, if the military significance of Constans' copper coins is accepted, it explains why there were apparently no coins struck for three years (8, 9 & 10). The coins were not now needed as there was peace and plenty of coins left over for domestic use. The Romans would pay tribute in gold (and possibly silver) to the Arab authorities.

In year 11 hostilities are resumed and coins are struck with a new depiction of the emperor. Constans is now depicted with extensive whiskers, presumably intending to demonstrate that an adult was now in power with an effort at a portrait. These coins occur with variants up to year 17.

Date	Reign year	Indiction	Officina	Callot[34] and DO[35] Classes
651/2	11	10	BΓΔ	7 DO – note 20 **8A DO 5a** Long Beard
652/3	12	11	BΓΔE	**8B DO 5b**
653/4	13	12	ABΓΔE Δ	8B DO 5b 9 DO -
654/5 Constantine IV becomes joint Emperor	14	13	ABΓΔE	8B DO 5B Con IV on Solidus
655/6	15	14	ABΓΔE ABΓΔE ABΓΔE ABΓΔE	8B DO 5b **10 DO 6** **11 DO 7** **12 DO 8** first military issue Constans + Con.IV
656/7	16	15	ABΓΔE Δ ABΓΔE	10 DO 6 11 DO 7 12 DO 8
657/8	17	1	AΓ BΓΔE	11 DO 7 12 DO 8
658/9	18	2		

Table 2

It will be seen from the table 2 above that there is suddenly a new flourishing of **copper** coins. In years 11 to 14 these may be associated with a considerable amount of military activity most of

---

[33] Theophanes p.479.
[34] Callot 1980.
[35] Dumbarton Oaks 1968.

which did not go well for the Byzantines. Cyprus and Rhodes were taken and the Arabs invaded Armenia. In year 15 an entirely new design emerges (C.12). Constans, suitably bearded is depicted in military costume with his son Constantine IV now a co-emperor on his right (as you look at the coin) in civilian dress. The design is, with minor details, almost identical to that issued by Heraclius in year 20 when he returned from having defeated the Persians. These coins of Constans II must relate to this and be intended to proclaim a similar military triumph. But what could this be?

a.   *b.*   *c.*   *d.*

Figure 4. Comparison of the coins of Heraclius celebrating his defeat of the Persians (a. & b.) and Constans II after the defeat of the Arabs before Constantinople. (c. & d.) The pattern is almost identical though slightly more elaborate in the coins of Heraclius. x 1.25

a. *Heraclius, Follis, Constantinople D.O. Class 5 (Large type), yr. 20, 6.91g; 23mm; 6h.*
b. *Heraclius, Follis, Constantinople D.O. Class 5, yr. 25, 5.58g, 22mm, 7h.*
c. *Constans II, Follis, Constantinople Callot Class 12, (D.O. 8), yr.16, 4.90g, 20mm, 6h.*
d. *Constans II, Follis, Constantinople Callot Class 12, (D.O. 8), yr.16/7, 5.05g, 20mm, 6h.*

There may be such a triumph which might well fit the circumstances but it is only recorded in Sebeos[36]. In this year 654 Sebeos records that a huge fleet set off for Constantinople with an army travelling by land to Chalcedon.

Sebeos[37] *When they were about two stades distance from the dry land, then one could see the awesome power of the Lord. For the Lord looked down from heaven with the violence of a fierce wind, and there arose a storm, a great tempest, and the sea was stirred up from the depths below. Its waves piled up high like the summits of very high mountains, and the wind whirled over them; it crashed and roared like the clouds and there were gurgling from the depths. The towers* (on the ships) *collapsed, the ships broke up, and the host of soldiers were drowned in the depths of the sea... Cast hither and thither in the tossing of the waves, they perished... When the Ishmaelites saw the fearsome hand of the Lord, their hearts broke. Leaving Chalcedon by night, they went to their own land...*

The difficulty is that none of the other chroniclers mention this Arab disaster. However Shaun O'Sullivan[38] in an article on the subject has demonstrated that in this respect the account of

---

[36] Sebeos 1999 p.144.
[37] ibid. p.146.
[38] O'Sullivan 2004.

Sebeos[39] is probably correct and I believe the coins give further substance to his argument. There are two things which need consideration. The first is that all the Chroniclers had a very low opinion of Constans II who could do no right. It may well be therefore that this was more of a military victory, with Constans in command, than Sebeos suggests. Second the events only make obvious sense if the sequence is:- Byzantine forces defeated by Arabs at Phoenix – Arabs strike while the iron is hot and march on Constantinople - where they are defeated.

It should also be noted that in year 15 Constans felt sufficiently secure to commence military operations against the Slavs in the Balkans[40].

a. *b.* *c.* *d.*

Figure 5. Examples of the later coins of Emperor Constans II struck in Constantinople. These are very small coins where every small scrap of copper has been used by the mint. Despite the poor quality of the coins the engraving is rather charming. x1.5
a. Obv. shows Constans in military costume with his three sons in court dress on the reverse. Callot 13 (D.O. Class 9), Yr 19, 21mm, 4.91g, 12h. The denominational M is on the obverse.
b. as above - Callot 13 (D.O. Class 9), yr. ?, 21mm, 4.87g, 12h.
c. Obv. shows Constans in military dress with Constantine IV in court dress beside him. The rev. shows the two younger sons in court dress with the M between them. Above is a cross and below is CON. Callot 14 (D.O. Class 10), yr. 25, 21mm, 4.10g, 12h.
d. Obv. shows facing bust of Constans in military dress. The rev. shows the busts of the three sons arranged around the denominational M. There is no year given for these coins. Callot 15 (D.O. Class 11), 21mm, 4.42g, 12h.

There is a gap in coin production in year 18 but they resume in year 19. Constans is now alone in military costume on the obverse with his three sons Constantine IV, Heraclius and Tiberius on the reverse. This coincides with Constans making his way overland to Italy. The date of his arrival in Italy is disputed and the sources, such as Theophanes, find this move to Italy incomprehensible. One suspects that the Italians found it all too comprehensible.

---

[39] Sebeos. I have considerable reservations with Sebeos as a historian. His history is a mixture of ecclesiastical politics, contradictory theology and historical events. The work jumps backwards and forwards taking up part of the narrative and then moving on to a different subject. This raises three difficulties: 1) The author himself may have written a confusing account: 2) Subsequent scribes may have confused events: 3) The nature of the writing is an open invitation for subsequent scribes to "embroider" the text. Nevertheless as far as the incident above is concerned I have no reservations. I believe the coins!
[40] Theophanes p.484.

Liber Pontificalis[41] *In his time... (Pope Vitalian) the emperor Constantine [Constans II] came from the imperial city along the coast to Athens (see Asclepeion hoard IBC), thence to Tarentum, and then to Beneventum and Naples in the 6th indiction [663]. Afterwards he came to Rome, on 5th day of July, a Wednesday, in the same indiction.... He stayed in Rome twelve days, he dismantled all the city's bronze decorations; he removed the bronze tiles from the roof of the church of St Mary ad martyres, [The Pantheon or rotunda] and sent them to the imperial city with various other things he had dismantled.*

Clearly Constans was seriously short of money to finance the empire and more particularly to prosecute war against the Arabs. He badly needed bronze and he went to Rome to collect some. In the following year he made his base at Syracuse in Sicily. The written sources were appalled by this, but presumably they had never been there. Strategically there were several important advantages. The island is extremely fertile and had not been much affected by the recent wars. Syracuse stands on an island in a magnificent natural harbour and is geographically well placed for a fleet to defend Italy and North Africa and mount naval expeditions to the Middle East. And significantly for the administration of an empire, Syracuse is the only place in Europe where Papyrus grows on a commercial scale. (It is in fact further to the south than parts of North Africa).

Constans II, commenced a rapacious collection of taxes:-
Liber Pontificalis[42] *Entering Sicily in the 7th indiction he lived in Syracuse. He imposed such afflictions on the people, occupiers, and proprietors of the provinces of Calabria, Sicily, Africa, and Sardinia for years on end by registrations of land and persons and by imposts on shipping as had never before been seen, and such as even to separate wives from their husbands and sons from their parents; so much else unheard of did they suffer that no one expected them to survive. They even took away all the sacred vessels and equipment from God's holy churches, leaving nothing behind.*

It seems likely that he was raising funds in order to commence a new campaign against the Saracens. Whatever his intention however, according to the near contemporary *Liber Pontificalis* he was murdered in his bath on *"the 15th July in the 12th indiction (669)*[43]. Thus his eldest son Constantine IV came to the throne. The Chronicles at this point are in disagreement. **Theophanes**[44] states:-
When Constantine had heard of his father's demise, he arrived in Sicily with a great fleet and, having captured Mizizios *(a usurper) put him to death together with his father's murderers. After establishing order in the West he hastened to Constantinople...*

The Liber Pontificalis[45] however reports the matter thus:-
In his time (i.e. Pope Adeodatus) Mezezius, who was in Sicily with the eastern army rebelled and seized the kingship. The army of Italy made their way, some through the districts of Histria, some through the districts of Campania; others, those of Africa, made their way through the districts of Sardinia. In this way they all came to Sicily and Syracuse, and with God's help the unspeakable Mezezius was killed. Many of his judges were taken mutilated to Constantinople along with the rebel's head.

One may presume that this concentration of Italian troops was organised by the Exarch of Ravenna. Given that the *Liber Pontificalis* was written much closer to the events than the eastern Chronicles,

---
[41] Liber Pontificalis *The Lives of the eighth-Century Popes (Liber Pontificalis)*, p.73.
[42] Liber Pontificalis p.74.
[43] ibid.
[44] Theophanes p.491.
[45] Liber Pontificalis p.74.

being almost a contemporary account, it is reasonable to suggest that the *Liber Pontificalis* account is more accurate.

Figure 6. ***a.*** *Follis of Emperor Constantine IV. with Heraclius and Tiberius. Off Æ 36mm, 19.26 g, 7h. Constantinople mint, 1st officina. Struck circa 669-674. d N CONStAN τINЧS PP AЧ, helmeted and cuirassed beardless bust facing, holding globus cruciger in right hand / Large M between standing figures of Heraclius, on left, and Tiberius, on right, each wearing crown and holding globus cruciger in right hand; cross above DOC 28a (CNG e-auction 90 lot 1906)*
b. *Follis of Emperor Constantine IV. As **a.**. Off Æ 31mm, 14.82g, 6h. Constantinople mint, 1st officina. Struck circa 669-674., helmeted and cuirassed, short beard, bust facing, holding spear in right hand / Large M between standing figures of Heraclius, on left, and Tiberius, on right, each wearing crown and holding globus cruciger in right hand; cross above DOC 30 (CNG e-auction 90 lot 1906)*

Constantine IV

The coins of Constantine IV are almost as extraordinary as those of his father. The entire copper coinage from Constantinople was radically revised with major increase in weights taking the coins back to weights similar to that of Justinian I. Sadly these coins are quite rare but fifteen folles were offered for sale by Sotheby's from the William Herbert Hunt Collection which varied in weight from 15.25g to 21.42g. None of these coins were dated. The implication must be that Constantine had ambitions for the restoration of the empire and plenty of copper. Presumably this came from his father's efforts in Italy[46]. But why reform the coinage in this manner? Taking the second principle – the fiduciary system, it would seem to be entirely unnecessary. There may be two reasons, both of which may be true. First of all given the vast number of Constans II coins in circulation – both regular and copies, Constantine may have intended to withdraw these to restore some kind of fiscal order. This reason may account for the confusing lettering on these coins[47]. The other possible reason was that they were intended to make a point - a statement about the status of the empire. The folles may be divided into three types. The emperor is shown in military dress but with globus cruciger (Class 1)[48] – a "default" pattern. These coins are relatively scarce implying that they were soon superseded by subsequent patterns. The second type shows Constantine with a raised shield and a spear over his shoulder. His co-emperor brothers are depicted on the on the reverse (Classes 2, 3 and 4) and the third with no co- emperors on the reverse (Class 5). If, in the type showing

---

[46] Apart from the Pantheon we do not know if Constans II removed the roofs of any other churches. The Liber Pontificalis mentions that Heraclius gave Pope Honorios permission to remove the bronze tiles from a pagan temple in order to re-roof the Lateran. It is rather odd therefore that Pope Gregory II (715 – 731) needed to repair so many churches in Rome. Several are mentioned in the Liber Pontificalis but the author concludes with "He renewed various basilicas which were collapsing which it would take too long to list". Had Constans removed their roofs as well?
[47] see S. J. Mansfield above.
[48] Dumbarton Oaks Catalogue classes.

Constantine with a spear and shield, he is following his great-grandfather's example (see above) it would suggest that he is celebrating a notable victory. Is this possible?

The point at issue here is the putative siege of Constantinople which could indeed have been a truly decisive victory over the Arab forces. Whether or not this siege did or did not take place, and when, has been aired at the Round Table and elsewhere, some scholars suggesting that it did not happen at all principally because several of the Chronicles do not mention it. Other more traditional scholars are content that there was indeed a siege, but there is controversy about its date and length. As the reform of the coinage may well have a bearing on this siege the case for the siege needs to be re-stated.

First of all Theophanes[49] and Nikephoros[50] mention the siege and record that it lasted seven years. A seven year siege is highly improbable, particularly so far from the besieger's base. However there are other sieges which Chroniclers record as lasting seven years for instance the siege of Caesarea as reported by Theophanes[51]. So we may be dealing with a kind of Topos. An event recorded in an account to give colour. These are all too common in hagiography:
"What do saints do?"
"They raise people from the dead!"
" Ah! so St George must have done this, so it may be added to his miracles".

If I am right here, the dialogues goes like this.
"What happens at a long siege?"
"They last for seven years."
"Why?"
"Because the siege of Troy lasted for seven years!"

Should this be the case we may **not** conclude that either Nikephoros is dependent on Theophanes or vice versa, nor that they are dependent on a common source, nor even that they wrote seven years – it could have been inserted by a scribe at a much later date.

Nevertheless Theophanes and Nikephoros record the following details.
1) It is stated that in the first year, the siege lasted from April until October (which interestingly is seven *months*)[52].
2) It is recorded that the Arab forces over-wintered at Kyzikos[53]
3) The siege resumed in the following Spring.
4) This campaign ended in a major naval victory for the Byzantines with the remnants of the Arab fleet being destroyed in a storm at Syllalion[54].
5) A battle took place where Souphion (Sufyan b. Awf) was defeated by three Byzantine generals (Florus, Petronas & Cyprian). 30,000 Arabs were killed.

There is some circumstantial evidence to corroborate these details.

First there is the synodical letter made by Thomas, the late patriarch of Constantinople, to Vitalian the Pope of Rome, which, he was unable to send when he wanted because of *"the long-lasting*

---

[49] Theophanes p. 493.
[50] Nikephoros p.23.
[51] Theophanes p. 475.
[52] Theophanes p. 494.
[53] ibid. p.494.
[54] Nikephoros p.24.

incursion by the godless Saracens and their presence throughout the two years when he was a bishop"[55].

These synodical letters are sent by Patriarchs to each other when they are elected. The purpose is so that each Patriarch may commemorate each of his brother Patriarchs at the Divine Liturgy thus demonstrating the unity of the Church.

Vitalian was Pope from 30th July 657 to 27th January 672. Thomas II was Patriarch of Constantinople between 17th April 667 and 15th November 669. This therefore dates the siege to the very beginning of Constantine's reign. A case could surely be made that there was collusion between the Saracens and the rebels in Sicily and makes it most unlikely that Constantine was in any position to lead a fleet against the rebel Mezezios in Syracuse. A date for the siege of 668 – 669 seems probable. Nikephorus states that the siege took place *"At the beginning of his reign"*[56].

Second there is the matter of Kyzikos. In the next reign – that of Justinian II, the emperor re-founded this city with immigrant Cypriots[57] calling it Nea Justinianea (new Justinianopolis). Canon 39 of the Quinisext Council refers to this:-
Since our brother and fellow worker, John, bishop of the island of Cyprus, together with his people in the province of Hellespont, both on account of the barbarian incursions,... have emigrated from the said island,....: viz that new Justinianopolis shall have the rights of Constantinople... the existing bishop of the city of Kyzikos being subject to the Metropolitan of the aforesaid Justinianopolis...[58]
etc.
It seems that many of the Cypriots were not happy with their new home and returned[59] but this evidence is corroborated in the Canon of the Quinisext Council 685. To this day the Archbishop of Cyprus is titled Archbishop of Nea Justiniana and All Cyprus.

Third there is the matter of the Sixth Ecumenical Council at Constantinople in 680-681. An Œcumenical Council was an enormously expensive undertaking particularly if delegates were to attend from Rome, Antioch, Jerusalem, North Africa and Alexandria as was the case with this Council - certainly at the later sessions. It involved housing and paying for numerous bishops with their advisers, servants and beasts for several months. Such a council was inconceivable except in a period of peace. It has been pointed out that there is little evidence for travel around the Eastern Empire.[60] This is uncertain negative evidence. Unless it is actually stated that travel was rare it could be that travel was so frequent that it was a commonplace. Historians do not record commonplace.

It is also worth noting that the 6th Œcumenical Council was followed by a further Council in 692 known variously as the Quinisext, Penthekte or Council in Trullo. This council only promulgated Church canons but it would have been as expensive to organise as that in 680-681[61].

The evidence therefore suggests a siege: a failed siege is often catastrophic for the besieging army. An outcome could include a long peace and in this instance, a peace during which a Council could be called. This is the account of Nikephoros[62]:-

---

[55] ACO, ser. sec.II, pp. 612–614.
[56] Nikephoros p.23.
[57] Theophanes p.509.
[58] The Seven Ecumenical Councils p.383.
[59] Theophanes p.509.
[60] Jankowiak 2011.
[61] It is a curious but remarkable fact that neither the Sixth Ecumenical Council nor the Quinisext Council mention Islam, the Quran or Muhammad.
[62] Nikephoros p.24.

When the King of the Saracens learned of his fleet's failure, he sent ambassadors to Constantine to conclude a treaty with annual tribute. After receiving them and learning of their offer, Constantine dispatched the Patrician John Pitzigaudios who was both skilled and prudent in these matters) to arrange terms of peace. In accordance with Saracen custom, peace was secured by oaths for thirty years with the proviso that the Saracens give the Romans 3,000 pounds of gold, fifty hostages, and fifty thoroughbred horses annually ...Henceforth, peace and calm prevailed in both the East and the West.

If this was the case here, the optimistic and triumphant coins of Constantine IV are comprehensible. They celebrated a notable triumph and the successful prosecution of a war even into putative Arab territory. This latter idea may have support in some very remarkable pseudo-Byzantine ? Arab Byzantine coins of very similar design to coins of Constantine IV struck in Sicily. However they have Pahlavi inscriptions! These have been discussed at previous Round Tables[63].

Justinian II

As far as copper coins are concerned those struck in Constantinople have little to add. The folles are of the "default" type, and some are dated. The half folles are made from generally carefully quartered folles of Constantine IV overstruck as half folles: an excellent example of an emperor doubling his money. They are significantly smaller suggesting that the supply of copper was now much reduced.

Conclusion

The coins of the Heraclian Emperors are a rich source of interest for numismatists. They also, through their weights, iconography and distribution are able to inform us of the political, military and fiscal situation in the eastern part of the empire allowing us to state that the Arab conquest of Syria was nothing like as straight forward as some historians have led us to believe. They point to significant Byzantine victories in the reigns of emperors Constans II and Constantine IV. This point is made by James Howard-Johnston (2010 p.304) "*'Abd al Malik could not do much in response, merely sending forces to occupy Antioch (so it had not yet been permanently annexed by the Arabs)..*" And this was 685, more than 40 years after the Arabs were supposed to have conquered Syria!

Thanks: *I have considerable help in preparing this paper from Tony Goodwin, Andrew Oddy, Steve Mansfield and Luke Treadwell. Dennis Onions and Alice Skinner have been a great help with the photography and illustration. I am very grateful to all of you.*

Bibliography

Primary Sources
Chronicle of 1234 in ***Theophilus of Edessa's Chronicle***, 2011 translated by Robert Hoyland, Liverpool University Press
Chronicle of Zuqnin in ***The Seventh Century in West-Syrian Chronicles*** 1993 translated by Andrew Palmer, Liverpool University Press
Dionysios reconstituted, in ***The Seventh Century in West-Syrian Chronicles*** 1993 translated by Andrew Palmer, Liverpool University Press
Liber Pontificalis, ***The Book of Pontiffs (Liber Pontificalis),*** 2000, translated by Raymond Davis, Liverpool University Press
Liber Pontificalis, ***The Lives of the eighth-Century Popes (Liber Pontificalis),*** 1992,

---
[63] Oddy 2010.

translated by Raymond Davis, Liverpool University Press

Michael the Syrian in *Theophilus of Edessa's Chronicle*, 2011 translated by Robert Hoyland, Liverpool University Press

Nikephoros, *An Eyewitness to History, The short history of Nikephoros our Holy Father the Patriarch of Constantinople*, 1989, Translated by Norman Tobias & Anthony R. Santoro, Hellenic College Press

Sebeos, *The Armenian History attributed to Sebeos*, 1999 translated by R.W. Thompson, Liverpool University Press

The Seven Ecumenical Councils of the Undivided Church their Canons and Dogmatic Decrees, reprint 1983, Editor: Henry R. Percival, Eerdmans.

Theophanes, *The Chronicle of Theophanes the Confessor*, 1999, Translated by Cyril Mango & Roger Scott, Clarendon Press

Other Primary sources consulted

The Acts of the Lateran Synod of 649, 2014, Translated by Richard Price, Liverpool University Press

Chronicon Paschale 284 – 628 AD, 2007, Translated by Michael Whitby and Mary Whitby, Liverpool University Press

John of Nikiu, *The Chronicle of John of Nikiu*, 1913 Translated from Zotenberg's Ethiopic Text by R.H.Charles, London

Secondary Sources consulted include

Callot, Olivier and others, *Salamine de Chypre, XI, Une residence Byzantine "L'Huilerie"*, 1980, Brocard, Paris

Decker, Michael J *The Byzantine Dark Ages*, 2016, Bloomsbury (Debates in Archaeology Series).

Foss, Clive *Arab-Byzantine Coins: An Introduction with a Catalogue of the Dumbarton Oaks Collection* 2008 Dumbarton Oaks

Goodwin Tony, 'The Early Folles of Constans II' in *Numismatic Circular* April 2012

Grierson, Philip *Catalogue of the Coins in the Dumbarton Oaks Collection Volume 2 Parts 1 & 2*, 1968, Dumbarton Oaks

Hendy, Michael F. *Studies in the Byzantine Monetary Economy c.1300-1450*, 1985, Cambridge.

Howard-Johnston, J, *Witnesses to a World Crisis*, 2010, Oxford

Hoyland, R.G. *In God's Path, The Arab Conquests and the Creation of an Islamic Empire*, 2015, Oxford

Hoyland, R.G. *Seeing Islam as others saw it*, 1997, The Darwin Press

Jankowiak, M., 'Travelling Across Borders' in *Arab-Byzantine Coins and History*, 2012

Jankowiak, M., 'The First Arab Siege of Constantinople', 2013 in *Constructing the Seventh Century*, 2013, edited by Constantin Zuckerman, Association des Amis du Centre d'Histoire et Civilisation de Byzance

Kasdagli A-M., *Coins in Rhodes: From the monetary reform of Anastasius I until the Ottoman Conquest (458 – 1522)* 2018, Archaeopress Publishing Ltd.

Mansfield, S., 'Constantine IV embattled – what can his coins tell us?' in *Coinage and History in the Seventh Century Near East 5*, 2017

Oddy, A., 'Constantine IV as a Prototype for Early Islamic Coins' in *Coinage and History in the Seventh Century Near East 2*, 2010

O'Sullivan, S., *Sebeos' account of an Arab attack on Constantinople in 654*, in *Byzantine and Modern Greek Studies 28* (2004) 67-68

Phillips, Marcus, 'The Import of Byzantine Coins to Syria Revisited' in *Arab-Byzantine Coins And History* 2012

Sear, David R. *Byzantine Coins and their Values*, 1987, Spink & Sons

Whittow, Mark, *The Making of Orthodox Byzantium, 600-1025*, 1996, Macmillan Press

A New Coin Type from the mid-seventh century?

Maria Vrij[1]

Introduction[2]

This short piece intends to bring to light what appears to be a new type of follis. When this paper was originally given as an oral piece to the seventh century Syrian numismatic Round Table, it was the author's opinion that the type probably belonged to the early part of the reign of Constans II and was probably produced somewhere in North Africa. Following feedback and further reflection, however, it seems that it is likely a part of the Arab-Byzantine corpus. What therefore follows is a full consideration of the features of the type, and the possible permutations of a tentative attribution.

Two 'non-identified' coins

Unusually, the two coins which led this paper to exist were not highlighted during the course of excavations, but rather found in a tray of the coin collection housed at the Barber Institute of Fine Arts in Birmingham. Both coins were both found by the author in a tray marked 'non-identified' in the Barber Institute's coin collection.[3] Since the Barber's coin collection derives principally from the collection of Philip Whitting, it may come as a surprise to the reader (as it did to the author) that Whitting, a prolific writer of numismatic publications, had not written about some of the oddities in his collection.[4] The tray must have been at least moved, if not compiled, in 1999-2000, when the collection was rehoused in climate-controlled cabinets after conservation; and the 'non-identified' group was likely compiled in the period 1979-1985, when the collection was being renumbered during Whitting's own lifetime, though it is unclear what input the collector had in that process. I have been unable to locate identifiable records of these coins among the records of these two shifts. This may be explicable in that the renumbering records amount to a catalogue which begins with the Roman Republic and ends with Justinian I – though the entire collection was renumbered, only this section was recorded. For the conservation records, it seems more likely that nothing in this tray went away for conservation. They are further unrecorded in the digital records compiled for the collection during the first decade of the 21st century.

---

[1] Maria Vrij is curator of coins at The Barber Institute of Fine Arts in Birmingham and is affiliated to the Centre for Byzantine, Ottoman and Modern Greek Studies at the University of Birmingham. Email: m.c.vrij@bham.ac.uk.
[2] I would like to thank and acknowledge the feedback and advice given by attendees of the Round Table, which have greatly contributed to this improved form of the paper I presented on 6th April 2019 under the title 'Two Puzzling Coins from the Barber Institute of Fine Arts'.
[3] Readers interested in the Arab-Sasanian base metal coinage may also wish to note that the second specimen of type 86 in R. Gyselen *Arab-Sasanian Copper Coinage* (Vienna, 2000, revised edition 2009) from an untraced collection was also found in this tray at the Barber Institute. Its dimensions are: weight, 1.67g; diameter at the widest point, 27.02mm; axis, 10 o'clock; thickness, 0.69mm. Image available on request.
[4] The Barber Institute collection includes just over 10,000 coins, mainly Byzantine, from Whitting's collection, plus over 4,000 coins, mainly Roman, from the collection of Geoffrey Haines, and nearly 500 Hungarian coins from the collection of Edgar Guest, the remainder were bought by the Barber Institute after the opening of the collection in 1970.

Thus these two coins (see figures 1 and 2 below) have remained unremarked upon, even in curatorial records, for at least 50 years. The coins themselves had no provenance tickets located with them, and a thorough search of Whitting's extensive records and notes has yielded nothing.[5] Nevertheless, these coins, clearly Byzantine or imitative Byzantine, match closely Philip Whitting's pattern of collecting – his fondness for unusual or overstruck base metal coins, and his tendency to acquire more than one sample of each type or feature.[6]

Features of the coins

Fig. 1. UI0017 (scale: X1.8)[7] *Fig. 2. UI0018 (scale: X1.8)*

The obverses both show the bust alongside a *globus cruciger*, although on both specimens the *globus* does not appear to be held by the bust. On both examples the hair on the bust is about ear-length, and on both examples there is an exergue under the bust.

Fig. 3. Features visible on the obv. of UI0017. *Fig. 4. Features visible on the obv. of UI0018.*

Where the obverses differ, however, is that the bust on UI0017 appears to be crowned with a simple cross-surmounted diadem, while there is no evidence that the bust on UI0018 was crowned at all, though this could be due to wear on the coin. The bust on UI0017 also looks to be dressed in a *chlamys*, where the dress of the bust on UI0018 is not readily identifiable, it may be that he holds a cross before him, or that, unlike any other imperial issue coin I am aware of, his clothing is decorated with a cross.

---

[5] It is worth noting, however, that Whitting's records for his Indian and imitative Sasanian coins either do not exist, never came to the Barber, or have been lost, and his notes on these two coins may be experiencing a similar problem.

[6] A note on terminology: I prefer to use the term 'base metal' to describe coins often labelled 'bronze' or 'copper', following the precedent of M. Hendy ***Studies in Byzantine Monetary History, c.300-1450*** (Cambridge 1985), on the grounds that there is no systematic study of the composition of Byzantine base metal coins across the empire and its mints to ascertain what particular base metal alloy these coins are.

[7] All coin images are from the Barber Institute of Fine Arts collection at Birmingham, unless otherwise stated.

Fig. 5. Features visible on the rev. of UI0017. *Fig. 6. Features visible on the rev. of UI0018.*

The reverses both have the more common angular 'M' denomination mark at the centre, and both display a cross above the M. Neither specimen appears to have an exergual line beneath the M, however, as might be expected on most folles of the period. Both have lettering beneath, which is clearest on UI0017, and this appears to read N–K. On both specimens, the M is flanked by the ligatured *nomina sacra* of Christ: $\overline{\text{IC}}$ $\overline{\text{XC}}$.

The two specimens appear to be from different obverse and reverse dies, which, combined with their worn state, adds to the sense that these are not modern forgeries. That they are not imitating an otherwise known type in addition to the different dies would also seem to indicate that they are not contemporary counterfeits.

Dating

The appearance of the M denomination should limit the estimation of the date for the production of the coins to between 498 and 867.[8] However, the first otherwise recorded appearance of the *nomina sacra* on Byzantine coins is on the class A of the Anonymous Follis series of the tenth and eleventh centuries (see either side of the bust of Christ in figure 7). Even the earlier depictions of Christ on Byzantine coins (all on gold or silver) give his name in full, rather than use his *nomina sacra*. It is interesting to note, however, that the *nomina sacra* $\overline{\text{MP}}$ $\overline{\text{ΘV}}$ for the Theotokos appears earlier than that of Christ, from her first appearance on official Byzantine coinage during the reign of Leo VI (886-912) (see figure 8). Nevertheless, *nominae sacrae* on recorded official Byzantine coins all post-date the removal of the M denomination mark.

Fig. 7. Obv. of an Anonymous Follis class A, B5015. *Fig. 8. Obv. of a nomisma of Leo VI, B4807.* *Fig. 9. Rev. of a miliaresion of Leo III and Constantine, B4518.*

---

[8] 498 being the date of the introduction of denominational marks under Anastasius I (491-518), and 867 the end of the reign of Michael III (842-867), whose Sicilian issue folles were the last thought to bear the M denomination mark, even though they had been removed by Theophilos (829-842) in the 830s at the Constantinople mint.

The dissonance between the dating for these two reverse features causes no small problem in determining the date of the new type presented in this paper. Either these coins are the earliest examples of the use of the *nomina sacra* on Byzantine coinage, or they represent a sudden return, on one type, to a redundant denomination mark.

The N–K, which may represent the word *nika*, is similar in its ligatured rendering to the countermarks highlighted by David Woods in this volume from the reign of Herakleios.[9] The word *nika* also appears (with attendant religious symbolism) on the most common type of Constans II early reign follis types: the EN TϒTO NIKA type and its Arab-Byzantine derivatives. The phrase itself appears in full (IhSϒS XRISTϒS hICA) on all Byzantine silver miliaresia from the denomination's introduction under Leo III between 720 and 741 (figure 9) until Basil II introduced a new type focussed on the Theotokos rather than Christ sometime between 976 and 1025.

It is at this point that we must focus on the features of the obverse. With no vestiges of an inscription it is only possible to work with the style, features and module of the coins. That the bust is facing, not profile, that neither have any signs of pendilia, and the small size and weight of the module seems to rule out a date in the sixth century. In terms of style, the bust seems to be more reminiscent of the first three-quarters of the seventh century. On both examples, the face is more round than long, and the hair terminated by the ears, rather than at the bottom of the jaw, as is more common on the longer faces of the later seventh to early ninth-century coins. Figure 10 shows some examples of the change in bust style between 602 and 867, though it is, of course, not comprehensive. That the bust also looks to be of a younger emperor would seem to indicate the early part of the reign of Constans II.

Fig. 10. Obv. of folles from 602 to 867: B2626 (Phocas); B3097 (Herakleios alone); B3479 (Herakleios and Herakleios Constantine); B3957 (Constans II); B4293 (Constantine IV); B4403 (Justinian II); B4497 (Anastasios II); B4526 (Leo III); B4594 (Leo IV and Constantine); B4616 (Nikephoros I); B4662 (Michael II and Theophilos); B4756 (Michael III).

There is, however, one other very unusual coin type which may provide parallels, MIB III type X28, supposed to be an unofficial issue from Jerusalem during the Persian occupation (figure 11).[10]

---

[9] See David Woods's article in this volume. As a note on spelling, I use Latinised spellings for all emperors after Herakleios (inclusive) and any individuals after 629 (the replacement of Latin with Greek in the promulgation of novels) and Latinised spelling for all emperors before Phocas (inclusive) and any individuals before 629.

[10] S. Bendall 'The Byzantine Coinage of the mint of Jerusalem' **Revue Numismatique** 159 (2003), pp. 307-322.

On this type, the mint mark is XC NIKA. Though not the full I̅C̅ X̅C̅, it is by far the closest parallel to the new type. Unlike the bust on the new type, however, the bust on X28 is clearly imitating a combination of Phocan and 610-613 Herakleian features. Also unlike the new type, X28 has an inscription around the bust, and is on a larger module. Nevertheless, X28 provides the precedent and context for the new type to be from around the 640s/650s. To further contextualise the appearance of the *nomina sacra* on Byzantine coinage and its derivatives, it is important to, briefly, consider the *nomina sacra* in wider artistic trends.

Fig. 11. MIB III type X28 follis of Herakleios, Jerusalem mint, CNG sale 102, lot 1150

The nomina sacra in other artforms

Images of Christ in Greek Christianity before the Iconomachy (c.680-850) never seem to have used the *nomina sacra*, so its use on this coin type predates its use in other artforms, too.[11] However, this pertains only to images of Christ, and this coin type does not contain an image of Christ. Breadstamps containing I̅C̅ X̅C̅ certainly exist, however, dating them is deeply problematic.[12]

In manuscript caligraphy, *nomina sacra* in Christian contexts can be traced back in form to the second century, and in probable meaning to the fourth century.[13] To suggest that these coins could date from the first half of the seventh century (alongside X28) is therefore plausible and not wholly anachronistic, especially since the *nomina sacra* on these coin types appears away from the bust of Christ. In this way, the coin is perhaps more a document, with its functional denomination mark and ecclesiastical exhortation, than a piece of artwork.

Mint

Without a mint mark, this type is both unusual for the period and problematic for determining where it might have been made. At this point it may be instructive to consider the other two unusual features of the obverse as yet undiscussed.

---

[11] K. Boston 'The Power of Inscriptions and the Trouble with Texts' in A. Eastmond and L. James eds. ***Icon and Word: The Power of Images in Byzantium. Studies Presented to Robin Cormack.*** (Aldershot, 2003) pp. 35-57, pp. 36-37. In dating the Iconomachy to c.680-850, I am following L. Brubaker and J. Haldon ***Byzantium in the Iconoclast Era c. 680-850*** (Cambridge, 2011) viewing the Council of Trullo (691/2) as the first manifestation of a Byzantine struggle over religious images, rather than the traditional 726-843.

[12] G. Galavaris ***Bread and the Liturgy. The Symbolism of Early Christian and Byzantine Bread Stamps.*** (Madison WI, 1970), p. 70.

[13] J. Heath ''Nomina Sacra' and 'Sacra Memoria' Before the Monastic Age.' ***The Journal of Theological Studies*** 61 (2010) pp. 516–549.

The exergue under the obverse bust is unusual but not entirely unprescedented. There are no examples I have found from the reign of Constans II, though there are a handful from the reign of Herakleios.[14] In Hahn's typology, the presence of an exergual line has no bearing on the assignment of a type, while Grierson only notes the exergual line as part of the type for 187 and notes exergual lines for individual examples of types which do not include the exergual line as part of the typology.

On the gold, mint provenance is problematic due to the ubiquitous 'CONOB', but there are examples of solidi and lightweight solidi with an exergual line under the busts for the mints of Constantinople and an 'Eastern' mint identified either as a military mint, Alexandria, Cyprus or Jerusalem.[15] These are all of the broad obverse type with a small Herakleios Constantine and the more complex jewelled crowns, as demonstrated in figures 12-14. On the silver, there is an example commonly assigned to the mint of Carthage (see figure 15) though, again, this is beneath two busts, this time Herakleios Constantine and Epiphania Eudokia.[16] Neither Hahn nor Grierson list the exergual line as part of the type, though there seem to be no examples that lack the line.[17]

Fig. 12. Solidus of Herakleios and Herakleios Constantine, Constantinople mint, B2762.

Fig. 13. Lightweight solidus of Herakleios and Herakleios Constantine, B2998.

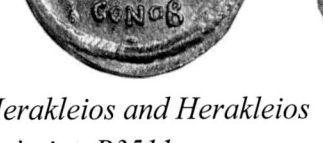

Fig. 14. Solidus of Herakleios and Herakleios Constantine, 'eastern' mint, B3511.

Fig. 15. 1/3 siliqua of Herakleios, Herakleios Constantine and Epiphania Eudokia, B3607.

---

[14] Here I follow Hahn in not making a distinction for the arguable coinages of Constantine III and Heraklonas. For Hahn's reasoning see W. Hahn *Moneta Imperii Byzantini 3. Teil* (Vienna 1981), p. 123; for the author's reasoning on the subject see M. Vrij *The Numismatic Iconography of the Period of Iconomachy (610-867)* (University of Birmingham PhD thesis 2016), pp. 72-77.

[15] Constantinople solidi: MIB III 8a and 10, and DOC II.1 8 include examples with an exergue under the busts. Constantinople lightweight solidi: MIB III 55, 59 and 60 include examples with an exergue under the busts. Cyprus/Eastern military mint solidi: MIB III 77 and 78 include examples with an exergue under the busts. Alexandria solidi: DOC II.1 187 includes the exergue as part of the type. On the various attributions of the 'eastern' mint: for Alexandria, DOC II.1, p. 220. For the military mint or Cyprus, MIB III, pp. 89-90. For Jerusalem, S. Bendall 'The Byzantine Coinage of the mint of Jerusalem' *Revue Numismatique* 159 (2003), pp. 307-322. See also, D. Woods 'Once more on the Solidi of an Eastern Military Mint under Phocas and Heraclius' in *Revue Numismatique* 173 (2016) pp. 359-372.

[16] The female figure is often identified as Martina, the niece and second wife of Herakleios, but Constantin Zuckerman put forward a coherent proposal that she should be identified as Herakleios's eldest daughter, Epiphania Eudokia, on the grounds of the dated folles and understood chronology for the reign of Herakleios in: C. Zuckerman. 'La petite Augusta et le Turc. Epiphania-Eudocie sur les monnaies d'Héraclius', *Revue Numismatique* 150 (1995), pp 113-26. See also the responses of Henri Pottier, Paul Speck and Cécile Morrisson in *Revue Numismatique* for 1997.

[17] MIB III 149 or DOC II.1 233.

For the base metal coins, where mint provenance can be reasonably assumed to be more accurate, while there appear to be no other examples from this period with an exergual line below the bust(s), there are examples of busts truncated noticeably before the die border at the mint of Rome, Alexandria and Seleukia in Isauria. Like the gold examples, the truncated busts are not noted as a part of the type, but there are a few examples from each. Figures 16-18 show an example from each. Also like the gold examples, all of the base metal examples are from the period of Herakleios with the child Herakleios Constantine. None of any of the examples are for a lone emperor.

Fig. 16. Half follis of Herakleios and Herakleios Constantine, mint of Rome, B3683.

Fig. 17. Dodekanummion of Herakleios and Herakleios Constantine, mint of Alexandria, B3526.

Fig. 18. Follis of Herakleios and Herakleios Constantine, mint of Seleukia in Isauria, B3478.

Fig. 19. Dodekanummion of Herakleios and Herakleios Constantine, Alexandria mint, B3541.

The other unusual feature is the placement of the globus cruciger beside the bust of the emperor, rather than it being held by him. The only similar precedent I can find here is on the dodekanummia of Alexandria, where the cross potent on steps appears unheld between the truncated busts of Herakleios and Herakleios Constantine, as demonstrated in figure 19 above.

Finally, it is worth noting that there is a third example of this type of coin, which I have been made aware of in the time between presenting this work as a paper and writing this article, which was found in Egypt.

While Egypt appears to be a likely attribution in terms of iconographic features alone, there is one glaring problem: Egyptian base metal coins are marked by their distinctively thick flan. The coins under discussion here are of a very different module. Their measurements are given in the table below.

Table 1 – measurements of the two coins

Coin	Diameter (mm)	Thickness (mm)	Weight (g)	Axis (clockface)
UI0017	22.5	1.7	3.36	6h
UI0018	23.6	2.2	5.08	6h

It is of course plausible, perhaps even probable, that, given the lack of an official mint mark, these coins represent a small, non-imperial issue from an area near to Egypt, especially since Alexandrian dodekanummia are often found outside of Egypt. Given the Jerusalemite precedent for XC NIKA on a 40-nummi piece, it seems most likely that the coin was produced somewhere in the south eastern mediterranean.[18] The presence of an almost certainly imperial figure (note the cross crown) on a provincial or unofficial issue would not be unprecedented – see here the on-going work of the Roman Provincial coinage project. In order to fully appreciate the array of possibilities for identifying these coins, however, it is now important to contextualise them in the *probable* period and place of production.

The coins in the context of mid-seventh century North Africa

While a number of the features discussed in support of identifying a production location seem to find their only parallels in the coinage of Herakleios, it seems to me that the new coin type cannot be of the reign of Herakleios, as the bust on the type that is the focus of this article is very different from the lone bust from the reign of Herakleios (compare figures 20 and 21).

Fig. 20. Obv. of a follis of Herakleios alone, B3097.   *Fig. 21. Obv. of UI0017 and UI0018.*   *Fig 22. Obv. of the INPER CONST type, B3957.*

By contrast, the similarities of the bust of the new type to a number of those from the early years of the reign of Constans II are much more striking. The folles from the early reign of the child Constans II also demonstrate a varied and experimental corpus, with Christianising tendencies, which fits the features of this new coin type well. The introduction of EN T8TO NIKA in place of the name of the Emperor, the replacement of the ANNO plus regnal year with ANA NEO, the sudden re-emergence of the title imperator over *dominus* and Augustus, these are all fairly major changes, and the first is innovatively Christianising.[19] Visually, the bust on the new coin type also seems to be most reminiscent of the INPER CONST type (compare figures 20 and 21).

---

[18] The module difference between the two examples of the new type and X28 being much more readily explicable by the passage of time: folles of the early part of the reign of Herakleios being much larger than those of the early years of the reign of Constans II.

[19] These are also sometimes interpreted as emulating the legacy of Constantine I rather than simple Christianising: see J. W. Drijvers 'Heraclius and the Restitutio Crucis, Notes on Symbolism and Ideology' in G. J. Reinink and B. H. Stolte eds. ***The Reign of Heraclius (610-641). Crisis and Confrontation.*** (Leuven, 2002), pp. 175-190.

It is also worth addressing the suggestion given to me in responses to the paper as delivered to the Round Table that the coin might be of the revolt against Phocas, however, the coins of the revolt consistently have two figures, with only two exceptions: the possibility that the coins naming Herakleios but bearing the bust of Phocas are of the revolt period, and the silver and base metal coins produced at Carthage. To the first exception it can be said that this new type has a much rounder, probably unbearded, face and no pendilia. The second exception, the products of the mint of Carthage, does provide a possible parallel. Unlike the coins of the reign of Herakleios, the silver and base metal coins of the revolt of Herakleios from Carthage show the emperor with ear-length hair instead of pendilia (since he is without the trappings of imperial power) as can be seen in figures 23 and 24. The apparent crown with cross worn by example UI0017 of the new type could be explained in this context as the cross that appears above Herakleios's head on these pieces. Furthermore, the mint of Carthage had a history of striking overtly religious types unique among the output of other mints at the same time, with phrases such as LVX MVNDI, SALVS MVNDI and AMENITAS DEI, or symbols like the A and ω either side of the cross.[20] It is to be noted, however, that these are all on the silver coinage, and that all the revolt coins contain an inscription, probably for the purposes of propaganda.[21]

Fig. 23. 1/3 siliqua of the Herakleian revolt, B2708.

Fig. 24. Dekanummion of the Herakleian revolt B2709.

The combination of all of the features and their parallels outlined above lead me to consider the coin type to belong to one of 6 groups:

1) An official issue from the early years of the reign of Constans II (641-648).
2) An unofficial issue from the early years of the reign of Constans II (641-648).
3) An official issue from the reign of either Constantine III or Heraklonas (641).
4) An unofficial issue from the reign of either Constantine III or Heraklonas (641).
5) A revolt coin of the Exarch Gregory (645-647).
6) A part of the Arab-Byzantine series.

Identifying which of the coins apparently of the last years of the reign of Herakleios and the first years of the reign of Constans II should actually, if at all, be attributed to either of the short reigns of Constantine III (Herakleios Constantine) or Heraklonas (Constantine Herakleios) is a problem

---

[20] *Lux mundi*: MIBE II Tiberius II type 20; *salus mundi*: MIBE II Maurice types 57 and 58; *amenitas Dei*: MIBE II Maurice type 60; A - ω: MIBE II Maurice types 61 and N61 and Phocas type 56.
[21] On revolt coinage and propaganda: V. Penna and C. Morrisson 'Usurpers and rebels in Byzantium: image and message through coins', in D. Angelov and M. Saxby eds. ***Power and Subversion in Byzantium*** (Farnham, 2013) pp. 21-42.

that has long vexed numismatists and historians of the seventh century. Grierson's case for reattributing a number of coins from the early part of the reign of Constans to Constantine III and Heraklonas has been disputed convincingly by Hahn through reasonable doubt and overstrikes in the case of the folles and fractions.[22] The suggestion that some of the unnamed three figure solidi of the end of the reign of Herakleios may be of Constantine III, Heraklonas and David Tiberios, then of Heraklonas, Constans II and David Tiberios is also subject to reasonable doubt.[23] It is worth pointing out that it is perfectly possible for there to be no coins produced for a period of time – the example *par excellence* is that of the first 24 years of the reign of Michael III, when there appear to have been no folles produced at the Constantinople mint – and this may well be the case for the short and fraught reigns of the sons of Herakleios. That said, it is possible that this young unnamed imperial bust is that of the child-emperor Heraklonas, less likely that it could be of the adult Constantine III, who had a clear beard already on the coins of his father. If it were from this short period, it would explain why this type seems to have been produced by multiple obverse and reverse dies, yet are apparently so scarce that they are only now being discussed. There are, however, other good explanations for why these coins are so scarce. Though the administration around Heraklonas was almost certainly very different from that around Constans II, both administrations would have been producing coins in the context of the Christianising of the coinage under Herakleios. It is into this tradition as much as that of the succeeding Christianising coinage of the reign of Constans II that this new type is being produced.[24]

Given the lack of an inscription identifying the depicted emperor and the lack of an official mint mark, it seems unlikely, though not impossible, that this coin represents an official Byzantine issue. While there are precedents for emperors without an identifying inscription, and coins without mint marks on post-498 base metal coins, these only occur either when the coin is excessively small or there are multiple figures, and thus always appears to be an issue of space. There is ample space in the field around the lone figure on this new type. There also exist base metal coins without mint marks, however, these are almost all fractions of the follis, rather than the follis itself. Of course, although most of the folles of Constans II do contain an inscription, these do not necessarily give the name of the emperor, but rather allude to it.

Rather than coins, it may be that these objects were tokens made by a monastery, or a bishop, to keep institutions running in what must have been a very chaotic period, though the use of the M denomination mark makes a coin intended for local or general circulation in the monetary system based on multiples of the nummus more likely than a token issue for alms or similar purposes. Certainly this explanation would best explain the presence of the liturgical *Iesous Christos Nika* in a format pertaining to manuscript tradition and *possibly* Eucharistic bread stamps rather than wider artistic trends.

---

[22] P. Grierson *Byzantine Coins in the Dumbarton Oaks Collection and in the Whittemore Collection. Volume II.2* (Washington D.C., 1968), pp. 386-7 for Constantine III, pp. 391-4 for Heraklonas; W. Hahn *Moneta Imperii Byzantini 3. Teil* (Vienna 1981), p. 123.
[23] W. Hahn *Moneta Imperii Byzantini 3. Teil* (Vienna 1981), pp. 87-88.
[24] On the differing administrations around the child-emperors Heraklonas and Constans II: J. Haldon *The Empire that would not Die. The Paradox of Eastern Roman Survival, 640-740* (Cambridge MA, 2016), pp.32-3.

Equally closely linked to Church concerns in the middle of the seventh century is the revolt of Gregory, the exarch of North Africa in 645-647.[25] In 645, Gregory had presided over a debate between the monothelite former Patriarch Pyrrhos, and Saint Maximos the Confessor, who would later be mutilated for his adherence to dyophisitism.[26] When Gregory declared himself emperor in opposition to the child Constans, who was under the regency of the monothelite Valentinos, it was apparently for both military and religious reasons.[27] Given that the time of the revolt is also the likely period of production for this new type, the iconographic links of the new type to the mint of Carthage, and the use of IC XC NIKA over XC NIKA, which links human nature Jesus and divine nature Christ to the dyophisitism of Gregory and many North Africans at the time, this is a possibility that ought to be at least mentioned.[28] However, as the possible Herakleian revolt coinage attribution was considered doubtful for its lack of inscription and because there are no other identified revolt coins of Gregory in other metals – like gold for his supporters – this seems a less likely possibility.

The coins of the early part of the reign of Constans II were also widely copied and adapted in the early Caliphate as 'Pseudo-Byzantine' or 'Phase I' of the Arab-Byzantine coinage.[29] While the appearance of new coin types for these phases usually amount to variants of already known types, or suggested reattributions between the corpus of the coinage of Constans and that of the Pseudo-Byzantine series, it is within the realms of possibility that this new coin type, in combining features of the coinages of both Herakleios and Constans II is a part of the Arab-Byzantine corpus.[30] Even though the new type contains an innovative, overtly Christian feature that is not simply copied from a known Byzantine model, this does not discount the possibility of the type belonging to the series, rather, this series of coinage even provides further parallels.

The Arab-Byzantine coinage presents the historian with two faces. The first is that of official local control within the administrative area – the mints of Damascus, Ba'albek, and Manbij present a fairly consistent series of coins, suggesting a controlled mint. The second is one of individualism, so much so that the very existence of the Pseudo-Damascus and *al-wafā' lillah* mints as mints have been questioned.[31] While it has been proven that these latter mints were producing coins on the same site through die link chains, they exhibit such individualism and artistic flourishes on the part of the die engravers that they give the appearance of a group of moneyers loosely connected rather

---

[25] R.-J. Lilie et al. *Prosopographie der mittelbyzantinischen Zeit* (Berlin, 2000), Gregory: #2345.
[26] R.-J. Lilie et al. *Prosopographie der mittelbyzantinischen Zeit* (Berlin, 2000), Pyrrhos: #6386; Maximos: #4921.
[27] R.-J. Lilie et al. *Prosopographie der mittelbyzantinischen Zeit* (Berlin, 2000), Valentinos: #8545. On the revolt of Gregory more generally: J. Haldon *Byzantium in the Seventh Century* (London, 1997) pp. 306-307.
[28] On Maximus's teachings on the human and divine natures of Christ against the Monothelites: P. M. Blowers *Maximus the Confessor: Jesus Christ and the Transfiguration of the World* (Oxford, 2016), especially pp. 146-165.
[29] The best current introduction to the phases of the Arab-Byzantine coin series is R. Gyselen and T. Goodwin *Coins of the Irbid Hoard. With a New Introduction to the Arab-Byzantine Series* (London, 2015), chapter 1. On copies of early Constans II coin types during Phase I of the Arab-Byzantine coinage, see Andrew Oddy's two articles elsewhere in this volume; or S. Album and T. Goodwin *Sylloge of Islamic Coins in the Ashmolean. Volume 1: The Pre-reform Coinage of the Early Islamic Period* (Oxford, 2002) pp. 77-80.
[30] For some of the problems of whether to assign coins to the Arab-Byzantine series see Andrew Oddy's 'An Overview…' elsewhere in this volume.
[31] A good recent summary of the issues around Arab-Byzantine mint attributions and practice: A. Walmsley 'Coinage and the Economy of Syria-Palestine in the Seventh and Eighth Centuries CE' in J. Haldon ed. *Money, Power and Politics in Early Islamic Syria. A Review of Current Debates.* (London, 2010), pp. 21-40.

than a controlled mint.[32] Some of these mints are even thought to be under ecclesiastical control, which would certainly provide an explanation for the appearance of the *nomina sacra* on this type.

It seems to me extremely probable that the type could both be the product of one of these ecclesiastical Arab-Byzantine mints.[33] By 641 most of Egypt and Palestine were part of the young Caliphate, so if this coin type was produced in the 640s or 650s and somewhere in the southwest Mediterranean, it would likely have been in a place within the Caliphate. A particularly pertinent example here is the ΠAN type from transitional Egypt, which contains the overtly Christian (though not innovative) A ω. It has even further been suggested that the ΠAN may stand for *Pantokrator*, an epithet of Christ.[34] Moreover, this type, despite being clearly Egyptian in origin (not only are they disproportionately found there, but moulds for casting them have also been excavated), they do not usually exhibit the typical thick flan common to Egyptian coins.[35]

Fig. 25. ΠAN type of Egyptian dodekanummion, A-B0049.

Conclusions

It is the author's view that this coin type was probably forms part of the Arab-Byzantine series of coinage, and was probably produced by an ecclesiatically-controlled mint somewhere along the North African coast between Cathage and Jerusalem. While this conclusion is the author's own opinion on the coin type, readers may well draw different conclusions and, to that end, all of the suggestions I am able to provide, and those which have so far been suggested to me, are given in the article. It is hoped that this piece will form the beginning of an academic conversation. A conversations that will, hopefully, encompass new specimens of this type being proffered from the unidentified and forgeries trays of other museum collections, interested private collectors long unsure what to do with such pieces, and dealers and sales rooms alike. A conversation that will, ultimately, lead to a more conclusive resolution to this little puzzle.

---

[32] T. Goodwin and R. Gyselen *Arab-Byzantine Coins from the Irbid Hoard. Including a New Introduction to the Series and a study of the Pseudo-Damascus Mint.* (London, 2015), chapter 3.

[33] On these sorts of mints, and Arab-Byzantine mints in general: A. Walmsley 'Coinage and the Economy of Syria-Palestine in the Seventh and Eighth Centuries CE' in J. Haldon ed. *Money, Power and Politics in Early Islamic Syria. A Review of Current Debates.* (London, 2010) pp. 21-40, in particularly pp. 27-29.

[34] D. Woods 'Deciphering the Dodecanummia of Heraclius and Constans II' in *Israel Numismatic Research* 13, 2018 pp. 195-207, particularly 204-206.

[35] T. Goodwin 'The Egyptian Arab-Byzantine Coinage' in A. Oddy, I Schulze and W. Schulze eds. *Coinage and History in the Seventh Century Near East 4* (London, 2015), pp. 205-214, particularly 211-212.

An Overview of the Phase 1 Byzantine-Arab Coinage

Andrew Oddy[1]

Research over the past 30 years has made it abundantly clear that very soon after the conquest of Greater Syria,[2] known to the Arabs as *Bilād al-Shām*,[3] coins, whose imagery was derived initially from the official issues of Heraclius, and subsequently from those of Constans II, began to be struck in a number of towns and cities in the area. The understanding of this coinage is relatively recent and John Walker's 1956 British Museum Catalogue of the Umayyad coinage [4] makes no mention of it, although Warwick Wroth had been aware of the existence of "Syrian imitations" of Constans II coppers as early as 1908.[5] Even as late as 1980, although William Metcalf recognised that large numbers of imitations of Byzantine coins were struck in Greater Syria between the Arab conquest and the start of a definitely Umayyad minting, he regarded them as purely local issues with a random typology.[6]

In fact the earliest significant publications of groups of these coins were by Alec Kirkbride in 1948,[7] Michael Metcalf in 1964,[8] Cécile Morrisson in 1980,[9] and Wolfgang Hahn in 1981.[10] Then in 1992 Steve Mansfield made the first numismatic analysis of these coins by die-linking some of those with a facing bust on the obverse and the date XX on the reverse. This group of coins have become known as the Year 20 Mint.[11]

These 'imitations of Byzantine coins' became variously known as 'Arab copies' or 'Arab imitations' and then 'Pseudo-Byzantine', a term which was previously used to describe the Byzantine imitations struck by the emerging post-Roman kingdoms in Western Europe.[12]

---

[1] Andrew Oddy is an independent scholar   waoddy@googlemail.com
[2] Caesarea Maritima fell in 640/641 after a long siege. It held out as it could be supplied by sea. Modern historians are not in agreement about the date of the final capture.
[3] Literal meaning "land on the left-hand" relative to someone in the Hejaz facing east – in other words "land to the north".
[4] J Walker, *A Catalogue of the Arab-Byzantine and Post-Reform Umaiyad Coins* [in the British Museum], British Museum, London, 1956.
[5] W Wroth, *Catalogue of the Imperial Byzantine Coins in the British Museum* (2 vols.), British Museum, London, 1908.
[6] W E Metcalf, Three Seventh Century Byzantine Gold Hoards, *ANSMN* 25 (1980) 87-109 at page 101, note. 9. I am grateful to Marcus Phillips for this reference.
[7] A S Kirkbride, Coins of the Byzantine-Arab Transition Period, *Quarterly of the Department of Antiquities of Palestine* 13 (1947-8) 59-63. It is noteworthy that Kirkbride used the logical 'Byzantine-Arab' but this was not followed by Walker whose use of 'Arab-Byzantine' has become ubiquitous.
[8] D M Metcalf, Some Byzantine and Arab-Byzantine Coins from Palaestina Prima, *Israel Numismatic Journal* 2 (3-4) (1964) 32-46.
[9] C Morrisson, Les Monnaies, pp.267-287, in J P Sodini *et al*. Déhès (Syrie du Nord) Campagnes 1976-1978, *Syria* 57 (1980) 1-310.
[10] W Hahn, *Moneta Imperii Byzantini: Band 3 - Von Heraclius bis Leo III. / Alleinregierung (610-720)*, Vienna, 1981.
[11] S J Mansfield, A Byzantine Irregular Issue of 'Year 20 ', *Numismatic Circular* 100 (3) (April 1992) 81- 82. The Year 20 coinage was brought up to date by W A Oddy and S J Mansfield, The 'Year 20 Mint' Revisited, *Journal of the Oriental Numismatic Society* 214 (Winter 2013) 4-11.
[12] Andrew Oddy seems to have been the first to use the term 'Pseudo-Byzantine' publicly in a paper about the Byzantine-Arab coinage (Another Group of Die-Linked Pseudo-Byzantine Coins - What do they mean?) delivered at the third **Seventh Century Syria Numismatic Round Table** held at the British Museum in December 1995. 'Pseudo-Byzantine' seems to have been first used in print in this context by Luke Treadwell in 2000 (The Chronology of the Pre-

Then, in 2012, a new nomenclature was proposed.[13] This suggested the term 'Phase 1' to replace Pseudo-Byzantine. This coinage, which was struck in greater Syria from about 638 to about 670,[14] started to trickle onto the European market in the middle 1970s, and this trickle became a flow in the 1980s and a flood in the 1990s and subsequently.[15]

In recent years the name most associated with the study of the Phase 1 coinage is that of Tony Goodwin who, in April 1992, gave a paper entitled 'Imitations of Constans II' at the very first meeting of what has become the *Seventh Century Syria Numismatic Round Table*. This was subsequently published as Occasional Paper no. 28 by the Oriental Numismatic Society in 1993.[16] Twenty five coins were illustrated, five of which have a facing bust on the obverse and the rest a standing figure with either m or M on the reverse. All appear to be derived from the regular coinage of Constans II. Two pairs of coins were die-linked via their reverses and it is interesting to note that in both cases one of the obverses is a 'single standing figure' and the other is a 'facing bust' (see appendix 2 below). This was the first paper of a series in which Goodwin developed a system of classification for the phase 1 coinage which emerged in its (more or less) final form in 2002.[17] *En route*, however, the classification system inevitably underwent a number of changes as understanding of the coinage developed.

In 1994, Goodwin was able to extend his work to Phase 1 coins with a 'three standing figures' obverse when he had the good fortune to have access to 30 coins which appear to be from a hoard (see appendix 2).[18] These are derived from the regular coinage of Heraclius minted in Cyprus ('three standing figures' obverse) as well as from the regular coinage of Constans II ('single standing figure', 'two standing figures' and 'facing bust' obverses). The diversity of coins in this hoard led to them being divided into five categories based on the different Byzantine coins from which they appeared to be derived stylistically.

In 1995, Goodwin published more comments on the Phase 1 coinage and drew attention to three groups which were connected both stylistically and by die-links (see appendix 1).[19] One of these groups he called 'Lazy B' because of the recumbent B (ie ⌒⌒) above the m on the reverse.[20] Two other die-linked groups were noted; one connecting a 'single standing figure' obverse with a 'two standing figures' obverse, and the other a die-linked group of three coins which were said to be "part of an extensive group which freely mixes dies which copy a number of different Heraclius and Constans prototypes" (see appendix 1). This paper is important as it recognises the existence of more 'mints' or 'workshops' which must have served the same purpose as the Year 20 mint.

Reform Copper Coinage of Early Islamic Syria, supplement to the *Oriental Numismatic Society Newsletter* **162** (2000) 1-14.

[13] W Schulze and A Oddy, Terminology for the Transitional Coinage Struck in 7th Century Syria after the Arab Conquest, in T Goodwin (ed.) *Arab-Byzantine Coins and History*, London, 2012, pp. 187-200

[14] H Pottier, I Schulze and W Schulze, Pseudo-Byzantine Coinage in Syria under Arab Rule (638-c.670): Classification and Dating, *Revue Belge de Numismatique*, **CLIV** (2008) 87-155.

[15] Phase 2 is the name given to the coinage of the Umayyads before the introduction of the 'Standing Caliph' type by 'Abd al-Malik, which is Phase 3.

[16] T Goodwin, *Imitations of the Folles of Constans II*, Occasional Paper no. 28, Oriental Numismatic Society, April, 1993.

[17] S Album and T Goodwin, *Sylloge of Islamic Coins in the Ashmolean: Volume 1: the Pre-Reform Coinage of the Early Islamic Period*, Ashmolean Museum, Oxford, 2002, pp. 78-9.

[18] T Goodwin, A Hoard of Imitative Byzantine Folles, *Numismatic Circular* **CII** (8) (October 1994) 357-9.

[19] T Goodwin, 7th century Arab imitations of Byzantine Folles, *Numismatic Circular* **CIII** (9) (November 1995) 336-7.

[20] A paper on the Lazy B Workshop, to be renamed The Lazy BZ Workshop, is in preparation.

Two years later Tony Goodwin and Marcus Phillips published another hoard which contained 73 Phase 1 coins, with one die-link (see appendix 4), along with regular Byzantine issues.[21] This hoard demonstrated the breadth of designs and styles of the imitative Byzantine coinage, which was soon to become widely-known as 'Pseudo-Byzantine'.

More recently, studies of Phase 1 have been published by Foss,[22] and by Pottier, Schulze and Schulze,[23] and studies of individual Phase 1 mints or workshops have been published by Oddy,[24] Goodwin,[25] and Schulze.[26]

---oOo---

In his very first paper on the 'imitations' of coins of Constans II in 1993,[27] Tony Goodwin suggested classifying them on the basis of their stylistic relationship to the regular Byzantine prototypes:

    A   passable imitations
    B   crude imitations with vestigial legends
    C   free adaptions of good Byzantine style
    D   free adaptions with new stylistic components

He used the same classification again in 1995 [28] when developing his discussion of the 'Arab Imitations'.[29]

Meanwhile, in 1994,[30] he had proposed a different approach to classifying the contents of a hoard of what were then described as 'Imitative Byzantine Folles', but are now recognised as part of the Phase 1 coinage. These coins mainly had obverses with three standing figures, but also a few with two standing figures, or with a single standing figure, or with a facing bust. Goodwin divided the coins into five categories by using the regular Byzantine coins that it was assumed were being copied as the basis for grouping the contents of the hoard:

---

[21] M Phillips and T Goodwin, A Seventh–Century Syrian Hoard of Byzantine and Imitative Copper Coins, **Numismatic Chronicle 157** (1997) 61-87.
[22] C Foss, ***Arab-Byzantine Coins: an Introduction, with a Catalogue of the Dumbarton Oaks Collection***, Washington DC, 2008, Chapter 4.
[23] H Pottier, I Schulze and W Schulze, Pseudo-Byzantine Coinage in Syria under Arab Rule (638-c.670): Classification and Dating, **Revue Belge de Numismatique, CLIV** (2008) 87-155.
[24] A Oddy, Imitations of Constans II Folles of Class 1 or 4 Struck in Syria, **Numismatic Circular CIII** (4) (May 1995) 142-3; A Oddy, The Christian Coinage of Early Muslim Syria, **ARAM 15** (2003) 185-192; A Oddy, Whither Arab-Byzantine Numismatics? A Review of 50 Years' Research, **Byzantine and Modern Greek Studies 28** (2004) 121-152; A Oddy, Constantine IV as a Prototype for Early Islamic Coins, in A Oddy (ed.), ***Coinage and History in the Seventh Century Near East 2***, London, 2010, pp. 95-109; A Oddy, A Die-Chain in the Phase 1 Arab-Byzantine Coinage of Greater Syria, in J-M Doyen and C Morrisson (eds.) ***Mélanges de numismatique et d'archéologie de Byzance offerts à Henri Pottier***, Cercle d'études numismatiques, Bruxelles, 2019, pp. 277-292.
[25] T Goodwin, Pseudo-Byzantine Coinage from Seventh Century Syria, **The Celator** (September 2000) 18-27; T Goodwin, The Dating of a Series of Early Arab-Byzantine Coins, **Oriental Numismatic Society Newsletter** no. 181 (Autumn 2004) 5-9; T Goodwin, A Mint Striking Early Dated (?) Arab-Byzantine Coins, **Numismatic Circular CXIX** (1) (March 2011) 8-11; T Goodwin, An enigmatic early Arab-Byzantine coin type, in J-M Doyen and C Morrisson (eds.) ***Mélanges de numismatique et d'archéologie de Byzance offerts à Henri Pottier***, Cercle d'études numismatiques, Bruxelles, 2019, pp. 137-150.
[26] I Schulze, Ugly Square Flan Coins: Another Consistent Group within the Byzantine-Arab Transitional Coinage, in T Goodwin (ed.), ***Arab-Byzantine Coins and History***, London, 2012, pp. 81-87.
[27] T Goodwin, ***Imitations of the Folles of Constans II***, Occasional Paper no. 28, Oriental Numismatic Society, April 1993.
[28] T Goodwin, 7th century Arab imitations of Byzantine Folles, **Numismatic Circular CIII** (9) (November 1995) 336-7.
[29] The term 'Pseudo-Byzantine' had still not come into general use in print. See footnote no. 12 above.
[30] T Goodwin, A Hoard of Imitative Byzantine Folles, **Numismatic Circular CII** (8) (October 1994) 357-9.

Category I.	Reasonably close copies of Heraclius folles of Cyprus
Category II.	Anomalous obverses [based on both Heraclius and Constans II prototypes] coupled with Cyprus year 17 … reverses
Category III.	Three figure obverses coupled with reverses which do not closely copy the Cyprus prototype
Category IV.	Imitations of class 5 folles of Heraclius
Category V.	Imitations of a follis of Phocas with standing figures of Phocas and … Leontia

Then, in 2002, Goodwin proposed a classification for the whole of the Phase 1 coinage in which he modified the above categories and extended the classification to nine 'groups'. The categories/groups were now given titles which reflect the appearance of the *actual coins* rather than those of the Byzantine prototypes. Each group (A to I) has a short title which makes it easy to refer to them:

A	Two Figure Phocas
B	Three Standing Figures
C	Two Standing Figures, one wearing Military Dress
D	Single Figure in Military Dress
E	Standing Emperor with cursive m reverse
F	Standing Emperor with capital M reverse
G	Imperial Bust
H	Bearded Imperial Bust
I	Constantine IV Bust

In 2004, Andrew Oddy presented a survey of research on Arab-Byzantine numismatics over the 'last fifty years' in which he suggested that some of the 'three figure' **imitations** of folles of Heraclius with the Cyprus mintmark might be an 'emergency' coinage struck in Syria for payment to the Byzantine army. However, he also made the point that "the same type of three figure imitations continued to be struck after the [Arab] conquest."[31] In order to demonstrate that many of the 'three standing figures' imitations had to be post-conquest and could not have been struck by the military, Tony Goodwin wrote about those imitations struck on 'oval' flans made by bisecting older Byzantine folles and arranged them using a more detailed division by obverse type:[32]

1	Two standing figures copying folles of Phocas and Leontia,
2	Three standing figures with Martina differentiated,
3	Three standing figures with the left-hand figure not differentiated,
4	Two standing figures with the left one in military dress,
5	Three standing figures with the left-hand figure smaller and the central figure bearded,
6	Three standing figures with the centre figure in military dress,
7	One standing figure,
8	Beardless bust,
9	Bearded bust.

As the 'oval' coins are all part of Phase 1, the difference between this system (2004) and that of 2002 is inevitably somewhat confusing. This new classification in effect sub-divides the 'three standing figures' obverses, coalesces the 'single standing figure' obverses, and omits the 'single standing figure' in military dress and the Constantine IV bust because these varieties do not occur on 'oval' flans.

---

[31] A Oddy, Whither Arab-Byzantine Numismatics? A Review of 50 Years' Research, ***Byzantine and Modern Greek Studies 28*** (2004) 121-152, esp. p. 127.
[32] T Goodwin, The Dating of a Series of Early Arab-Byzantine Coins, ***Oriental Numismatic Society Newsletter*** no. 181 (Autumn 2004) 5-9.

However, in 2005 Tony Goodwin returned to the 2002 classification (with minor changes to the titles) and this has remained his 'standard':[33]

Type A.	Phocas and Leontia
Type B.	Three Imperial figures
Type C.	Two Imperial figures
Type D.	Single figure in military dress
Type E.	Standing Emperor with cursive m reverse
Type F.	Standing Emperor with capital M reverse
Type G.	Imperial bust
Type H.	Bearded Imperial bust
Type I.	Constantine IV bust

Thus he has recently used the 2002/2005 system of classification in a book about the Irbid hoard [34] but omitted the short titles in bold letters leaving only the detailed description defining nine groupings. Although this does not present a material change to the classification, the absence of the short titles does make for less easy reference.

For example Type A becomes:
Two Standing Figures, copying the obverse of folles of Phocas (602-10) and his Empress Leontia

and Type C becomes
Copying two figure folles of Heraclius class 5 (or sometimes perhaps the similar class 8 folles of Constans II) where the left-hand figure is wearing military dress.

The list is also brought up to date with the recent discoveries:
Type J	Two Imperial Busts probably copying a solidus of Heraclius
Type K	A relatively recent discovery with a palm branch on the obverse and a cursive m or capital M on the reverse

--oOo--

Now, in looking again at how to organise the Phase 1 coinage it seems, on the face of it, inappropriate to include Type K, with a palm branch obverse (fig. 1), as this has no prototype in the official Byzantine coinage [35] and the fabric is very different from the mass of Phase 1 coinage, being thicker and quadrilateral in shape rather than approximately round.

---

[33] T Goodwin, *Arab-Byzantine Coinage*, The Nour Foundation, London, 2005, pp. 16-17.
[34] T Goodwin and R Gyselen, *Arab Byzantine Coins from the Irbid Hoard*, Royal Numismatic Society Special Publication no. 53, London, 2015, pp. 14-15.
[35] A Palm Branch appears on the obverse of Phase 2 coins of Damascus (see A Oddy, Symbolism and Design in the Early Umayyad Coinage, in T Goodwin (ed.), *Arab-Byzantine Coins and History*, London 2012, pp. 109-123 esp.118-9) and on the obverse and reverse of a few Pseudo-Damascus coins, although not as a principal feature of the design (see T Goodwin and R Gyselen, *Arab Byzantine Coins from the Irbid Hoard*, Royal Numismatic Society Special Publication no. 53, London, 2015).

Figure 1. Palm branch on obverse. 8.05g, 10.00h, maximum diameter 21mm, flan thickness 4.5mm.   Magnification c.x2.

Figure 1 probably has the same obverse die as Schindel no.3.[36] Of the twelve specimens whose weights have been recorded, the mean is 4.22g and the median is 5.32g. The coin illustrated in figure 1, at 8.05g, is the heaviest of those known, but one of the others weighs 7.23 g. The coin illustrated in figure 1 is also, at 4.5mm, the thickest, the others ranging from "1.7mm to more than three mm,"[37] but whereas Schindel records that the coins he had examined all appeared to have been cut into approximately square shapes from other bronze objects (probably not coins), this coin has clearly been broken off a larger piece of metal. As Coptic Egypt is well known at this period for the production of cast bronze vessels made of highly alloyed bronze which is more brittle than normal coinage alloy,[38] the flan for coin 1 may be made of a similar alloy, i.e. a high-tin bronze.

In this respect, the 'palm branch' coin illustrated above may be compared with the coins illustrated in figures 2 and 3 which also appear to have flans made by breaking an approximately square piece of bronze from a larger piece of metal. These, however, clearly fit into Phase 1 even though the flans are not approximately round.

Figure 2. Standing figure on obverse with long cross and globus cruciger. 5.24g, 7.00h, max diam 23mm, flan thickness 3mm.   Magnification c.x1.5.

Figure 3. Standing figure on obverse with long cross and globus cruciger. 4.88g, 4.00h, max diam 22mm, flan thickness 3mm.   Magnification c.x1.5.

Arab-Byzantine coins struck on small quadrilateral flans are well known and some of them have Arabic legends reading *Muhammad* on the obverse to the left of a 'single standing facing figure' and

---

[36] N C Schindel. A New Arab-Byzantine Coin Type, ***Oriental Numismatic Society Newsletter*** no. 182 (Winter 2005) 7-11, no. 3 on p. 10.
[37] N C Schindel (2005) *op. cit*. p. 8.
[38] W A Oddy and P T Craddock, Scientific Examination of the Coptic Bowl and Related Coptic Metalwork Found in Anglo-Saxon Contexts, in A C Evans (ed), ***The Sutton Hoo Ship-Burial*** (volume 3 part 2), The British Museum, London, 1983, pp. 753-7.

either *ba'ḍ* or *sa'id* or, occasionally, *Muhammad* on the reverse below the m.[39] These coins are also difficult to place. Because of the Arabic legends they would normally be regarded as Phase 2. However, although no die studies have been published, these *Muhammad / ba'ḍ / sa'id* coins bear a close physical relationship to coins of a similar size but without the Arabic legends. These, in turn, may be related to coins of the type illustrated in figures 2 and 3. One group of square coins, identified stylistically by the pose of the standing figure on the obverse, has been described by Ingrid Schulze.[40] It should be noted, however, that among the die-linked coins identified by Ingrid Schulze, most of them are quadrilateral but some are approximately round and are indistinguishable from normal Phase 1 coins.

What, if any, meaning can be attributed to the 'palm branch' obverse? In pre-Islamic times it was a symbol of victory, triumph, peace, and eternal life originating in the ancient Near East and Mediterranean world. The palm *(Phoenix)* was sacred in Mesopotamian religions, and in ancient Egypt represented immortality. A palm branch was awarded to victorious athletes in ancient Greece, and a palm frond or the tree itself is one of the most common attributes of Victory personified in ancient Rome. It therefore seems reasonable to postulate that the palm branch on these coins represents victory and that these are the first coins to be struck specifically under Arab authority after the conquest. The unknown question is whether they were struck by Muʿawiya in the 660s when he probably introduced the Phase 2 coinage in a number of named towns, or whether they could have been struck before then.

It seems possible that all (or at least most) of the quadrilateral coins are inter-related and may well bridge the boundary between Phases 1 and 2. Hence, for the purposes of this paper, they will not be considered further until a consensus emerges how they should be treated.[41]

---oOo---

In a paper published in 2008, Henri Pottier, Ingrid Schulze and Wolfgang Schulze considered the Phase 1 coinage from a metrological point of view and proposed a dating scheme related to changes in weight.[42] This placed the various 'classes' of Phase 1 coins in a different order from the arrangement published by Tony Goodwin in 2002.[43]

The scheme proposed by Pottier *et al* is essentially that used by Clive Foss in his book on Arab-Byzantine Coins.[44] It (the Pottier *et al* classification) has been extended here to take account of more recent research on the Phase 1 coinage.[45]

---

[39] Different readings are proposed by different authors. These coins are discussed in N C Schindel, A New Arab-Byzantine Coin Type, **Oriental Numismatic Society Newsletter** no. 182 (Winter 2005) 7-11; and in C Foss, **Arab-Byzantine Coins: an Introduction, with a Catalogue of the Dumbarton Oaks Collection**, Washington DC, 2008, p. 34.

[40] I Schulze, Ugly Square Flan Coins: Another Consistent Group within the Byzantine-Arab Transitional Coinage, in T Goodwin (ed.), **Arab-Byzantine Coins and History**, London, 2012, pp. 81-87.

[41] There is another workshop that die-links 'one standing figure' and 'two standing figures' Phase 1 coins to 'facing bust' coins derived from the Constantine IV coinage of Syracuse, but with a Pahlavi legend on the obverse. (A Oddy, Constantine IV as a prototype for Early Islamic Coins, in A Oddy (ed.), **Coinage and History in the Seventh Century Near East 2**, London, 2010, pp. 95-109.) It is not obvious whether this workshop should be placed in Phase 1 or Phase 2. It has not hitherto been given a 'name' so, as the use of the name Constantine IV would be misleading, it is proposed to call it The Pahlavi Workshop.

[42] H Pottier, I Schulze and W Schulze, Pseudo-Byzantine Coinage in Syria under Arab Rule (638-c.670): Classification and Dating, **Revue Belge de Numismatique**, CLIV (2008) 87-155.

[43] S Album and T Goodwin, **Sylloge of Islamic Coins in the Ashmolean: Volume 1: the Pre-Reform Coinage of the Early Islamic Period**, Ashmolean Museum, Oxford, 2002, pp. 78-9; T Goodwin and R Gyselen, **Arab Byzantine Coins from the Irbid Hoard**, Royal Numismatic Society Special Publication no. 53, London, 2015, pp. 14-15.

[44] C Foss, **Arab-Byzantine Coins: an Introduction, with a Catalogue of the Dumbarton Oaks Collection**, Washington DC, 2008.

[45] In the original publication, Pottier *et al* gave the Imperial names from the coins which were being copied to identify the obverse images in this list. These personal names have been dropped here as the coins were struck when the

Class I obverse with three figures	I.1a	Mintmark KYΠP (sometimes blundered) dated 17
	I.1b	Mintmark CON (sometimes blundered) dated 17
	I.1c	Mintmark THEUP (sometimes blundered) dated 17
	I.1d	Mintmark OEC(P) dated 17
	I.1e	Uncertain mintmark sometimes dated 17
	I.2	Middle figure in military dress
Class II obverse with two figures	II.1	Two figures wearing chlamys [46]
	II.2a	One figure in military dress and one in chlamys, rev. M
	II.2b	One figure in military dress and one in chlamys, rev. m
	II.3	Male and female figures
Class III obverse with bust	III.1a	Bust with a usually blundered legend sometimes recognisably based on the IhPER COhST legend of folles of Constans II with a facing bust.
	III.1b	Bust without legend
	III.1c	A star and crescent on the obverse[47]
	III.2	The Year 20 Mint[48]
Class IV obverse with one standing figure	IV.1a	M on reverse
	IV.1b	m on reverse
	IV.1c	The LITOIE Mint
	IV.1d	The Lazy S Mint,[49] with ∽ below the m
	IV.1e	The Lazy B Mint, with ⌒ or S above the m

And to these must now be added:

Class V obverse with two busts [50]

This arrangement of the Phase 1 (Classes I-V) coinage will now be discussed to see how well this classification serves ten years 'down the line'. However, it is first necessary to look at the prototype for Class I which was the official Byzantine coinage minted in Cyprus by Heraclius.[51]

Byzantine emperors no longer ruled in this area. The figures, standing or as busts, are better seen as features of the design rather than representations of real people.

[46] A 'chlamys' is a large square cloak worn as an outer garment. It is normally pinned with a large brooch on the right shoulder. It is much more visible on the Byzantine copper coinage of Constans II than on that of Heraclius where the only indication that it is being depicted is the loop on the right shoulder representing a brooch. The imagery of the 'chlamys' is often misunderstood on the Arab-Byzantine coinage derived from the bronze issues of Constans. This paper uses the term 'long robe' to describe the dress of most standing figures unless they are in military costume.

[47] T Goodwin, An enigmatic early Arab-Byzantine coin type, in J-M Doyen and C Morrisson (eds.), *Mélanges de numismatique et d'archéologie offerts à Henri Pottier*, Cercle d'études numismatiques, Bruxelles, 2019, pp. 137-150.

[48] S J Mansfield, A Byzantine Irregular Issue of 'Year 20', *Numismatic Circular* **100** (3) (April 1992) 81- 82. The 'Year 20' coinage was brought up to date by W A Oddy and S J Mansfield, The 'Year 20 Mint' Revisited, *Journal of the Oriental Numismatic Society* **214** (Winter 2013) 4-11.

[49] A Oddy, Imitations of Constans II Folles of Class 1 or 4 Struck in Syria, *Numismatic Circular* **CIII** (4) (May 1995) 142-3. Since this paper was published in 1995 a visit to Ajloun in northern Jordan produced five of these coins, perhaps suggesting that they were struck in Ajloun or its vicinity. See a separate paper in this volume.

[50] T Goodwin, A New Type of Seventh Century Syrian Pseudo-Byzantine Coin, *Journal of the Oriental Numismatic Society* **187** (Spring 2006) 46-47.

[51] All the illustrated coins are from the author's collection unless otherwise indicated.

The Cyprus Mint under Heraclius

Figure 4. Folles of Heraclius struck in Cyprus in years 17 (626-7), 18 (627-8) and 19 (628-9) (a) 5.64g 5.30h; (b) 5.60g 5.30h; (c) 6.15g 7.30h. Scale: 1:1.

The most common mintmark, KYΠP, on Phase 1 Class I coins is that for Cyprus and indicates that the Class 1 coinage was inspired by the coinage of Heraclius struck in Cyprus in the regnal years 17, 18, and 19 (626-629) illustrated in figure 4. The coins always have Martina on the right of Heraclius (ie to the left when looking at the coins) and are always from officina Γ. The lettering A/N/N/O to the left and the dates X/Ч/II, X/ЧI/II or X/ЧI/III to the right are always vertically aligned and do not follow the curve of the flan. The reverses occasionally have an exergual line below the M and always have the monogram ᚱ above.

The opening of an official Byzantine mint in Cyprus by Heraclius in his regnal year 17 (AD 626/7), which struck coins for three regnal years, is usually assumed to be connected with providing coins for the army in the final stages of the war against the Persians.[52] This led Oddy in 2004 to suggest that the 'three standing figures' imitations (ie Class I) were the product of a Byzantine military mint.[53] Goodwin refuted this suggestion by pointing out that the central figure on some of the coins is bearded and that the left hand figure – originally the empress Martina – has usually become indistinguishable from the other two.[54] Goodwin does concede, however, that the army may have taken minting equipment to the mainland and initially produced coins there.[55]

If the best quality 'Cyprus' coins were actually struck at an official Byzantine mint in Cyprus, how much of the gradually increasingly barbarous 'three standing figures' coinage was struck by the army in the northern part of *Bilād al-Shām* (Greater Syria)?

---

[52] P Whitting, ***Byzantine Coins***, London, 1973, p. 132. Whitting writes "…in the years 17,18 and 19, there was a mint in Cyprus, probably … in connection with military operations …" However, Grierson is more circumspect and writes in P Grierson, ***Byzantine Coins***, London, 1982, p.121 ".. a mint was called into existence in Cyprus … for the striking of folles, though once again we are ignorant of the precise circumstances." More recently, Michael Metcalf has written: "Their unusual occurrence [in Syria/Lebanon rather than Cyprus] is best understood in a political or military context. The exact circumstances are conjectural, but we may imagine that troops raised in Cyprus to take part in Heraclius's campaigns on the mainland were supported by a military chest of newly-minted folles." D M Metcalf, ***Byzantine Cyprus 491-1191***, Cyprus Research Centre Texts and Studies in the History of Cyprus LXII, Nicosia, 2009, p. 163.
[53] A Oddy, Whither Arab-Byzantine Numismatics? A Review of 50 Years' Research, ***Byzantine and Modern Greek Studies 28*** (2004) 121-152, esp. p. 127.
[54] T Goodwin, The Dating of a Series of Early Arab-Byzantine Coins, ***Oriental Numismatic Society Newsletter*** no. 181 (Autumn 2004) 5-9
[55] Goodwin (2004) *op. cit.* wrote "the army quickly moved on to the mainland with its minting equipment and supply of coinage, but retained the Cyprus mintmark".

A Heraclian Military Mint in Greater Syria in c. 630?

The vast majority of the 'three standing figures' imitations are struck on oval flans made by halving older Byzantine folles and cutting off the corners to make an approximately oval shaped flan. However there are some undoubted imitations that were struck on approximately round flans but on these the lettering is larger than usual and often less neat. In addition, the Heraclian monogram ℞ over the M on the reverse of the regular Cyprus Mint coins has sometimes been replaced by a ✠, or, on one die, a ✱. All have the 'officina'[56] letter Γ. It is now suggested that these coins, three of which are illustrated in figure 5, were the product of a Heraclian military mint in Greater Syria in the final stages of the war against the Persians. These are not, by definition, Arab-Byzantine Phase 1 coins as they were not struck under Arab authority.

A few of these approximately round imitations have the 'mintmark' CON, or a derivative, in the exergue on the reverse instead of KYΠP (for Cyprus). Where legible, 'officina' letters are [A], Γ and Є. It is suggested that these may have also been struck by the military in Syria and it is not difficult to see why the pseudo-mintmark has been changed to CON by an army serving the Emperor.

Figure 5. Folles with 'mintmark'[57] KYΠP possibly struck at a Military Mint in Syria in the final stages of the war with the Persians; c. 630.
(a) 5.95g 6.00h; (b) 2.51g 5.30h; (c) 4.07g 5.30h   Scale: 1:1.

Figure 6. Folles with 'mintmark' CON possibly struck at a Military Mint in Syria near the end of the war with the Persians; c. 630
(a) 4.29g 6.00h; (b) 4.93g 5.00h; (c) 3.09g 4.30h.   Scale: 1:1

---

[56] Where the word officina refers to a non-official Byzantine mint it is written 'officina'.
[57] Where the word mintmark refers to a non-official Byzantine mint it is written 'mintmark'.

Less common are approximately round coins with blundered 'mintmarks' and the 'officina' letters A or Δ, or without an 'officina' letter at all. Examples are illustrated in figure 7.

Figure 7. Round folles with blundered 'mintmarks' and 'officina' letters (L to R) A, Δ *and 'blank'. (a) 3.24g 8.00h; (b) 3.60g 6.30h; (c) 3.86g 11.00h.* Scale: 1:1

Whether the coins illustrated in figures 5, 6 and 7 really were minted by the army must remain a hypothesis for the moment. There is no unifying design feature which would mark them out as having a common origin. It boils down to the fact that they are approximately round and have three standing figures on the obverse and an M on the reverse.

The opening of this Military Mint, if that is what it is, must have taken place soon after year 17 (626/7) as the imitations do not copy years 18 and 19. Presumably the mint did not last for long as hostilities with the Persians were essentially over by 630.

This paper will now discuss the Phase 1 Byzantine-Arab coinage using the classification system of Pottier *et al* as laid out above. They use the notation 'Class' to define the different obverse types and in what follows the use of 'Class' refers to this notation unless it is clear from the context that it is alluding to another publication, such as the Dumbarton Oaks Catalogue.

Byzantine-Arab Phase 1; Class I.1a-e   {Goodwin Type B}

Pottier, Schulze and Schulze arranged Class I according to the 'mintmark' KYΠP, CON, THEUP, and OEC(P). However the above suggestion about a possible military mint removes most of the Class I.1b coins with the 'mintmark' CON as these coins are rare and appear to be (almost) always approximately round. Poitier *et al* illustrate two examples with a CON 'mintmark', one of which is a die duplicate of figure 6b.[58] The other [59] is an oval coin with the 'mintmark' OƆ, which should now be regarded as Class I.1e, having an uncertain or illiterate 'mintmark'.

As pointed out above, the vast majority of Classes I.1a to I.1e have an oval flan created by hammering out earlier Byzantine bronze coins, cutting them in half with a chisel, and cutting off the two sharp corners. The 'oval' coins, then, become the first Phase 1 Byzantine-Arab coins struck in *Bilād al-Shām* by surviving local authorities - bishops, magistrates, or men with power and influence on a local level - to provide 'small change' after the Arab conquest of 633-640. Pottier *et al* have postulated, on the basis of countermarks,[60] that this coinage started to be struck before A.D. 640 and

---

[58] H Pottier, I Schulze and W Schulze, Pseudo-Byzantine Coinage in Syria under Arab Rule (638-c.670): Classification and Dating, ***Revue Belge de Numismatique***, **CLIV** (2008) 87-155, plate 3 no. 6.
[59] Pottier *et al* (2008) *op. cit.* plate 3 no. 5.
[60] Pottier *et al* (2008) *op. cit.* p. 96.

they suggest that the 'three standing figures' Phase 1 coinage (Class I) was struck in the period c.638 to c.645. Whether these local workshops [61] were, in any way, heirs to the Military Mint after an interval of about eight years, can only be determined if a die-link is found. Otherwise it must be assumed that the start of the Class I coinage will have resulted from a shortage of small change and the ability of some local 'authority' to strike coins. Whether this date is c. 638 or slightly later is impossible to determine. What is clear is that the 'three standing figures' Class I coinage of Phase 1 was produced in large quantities in a significant number of towns in the northern part of Greater Syria.

Examination of a large number of the oval 'three standing figures' Class I coins of Phase 1 shows that they can be divided into two groups according to whether the figures on the obverse are clean shaven (beardless) or whether the central figure is wearing a beard (bearded). The majority of the clean-shaven coins have blundered, illegible, or missing 'mintmarks'. Most of them have the 'officina' letter Γ or ꓶ but a very few have A, B, Δ, or Є. The following 'mintmarks' and 'officina' letters occur in a very small number of cases:

mintmark	officina	mintmark	officina	mintmark	officina
KYΠP	Γ	NIK	//	KYZ	Δ
THЄ//	A	CON	Γ		

It is noticeable that on some of the KYΠP coins the figure of Martina is still distinguishable by her special crown (see figure 10a below). Examples of beardless 'three standing figures' Class I coins are illustrated in figures 8, 9 and 10.

Examination of a random collection of 'three standing figures' Phase 1 coins suggests that those on which the central figure has a beard are more common than the clean-shaven ones. Strangely, die-linking is much more common among the bearded coins than the clean-shaven ones.

Figure 8. Beardless Class I folles with blundered or absent 'mintmarks' and 'officina' letters Γ or ꓶ (a) 3.40g 6.00h; (b) 4.39g 1.00h; (c) 4.80g 6.00h; (d) 6.86g 5.30h; (e) 5.04g 6.30h

Scale: 1:1

---

[61] In referring to the local production of Phase 1 coinage in greater Syria after the Arab conquest, the word 'workshop' is used here in preference to 'mint' as the latter usually implies a government authority in the production of coin.

Figure 9. Beardless Class I folles. (a)-(d) with blundered or absent 'mintmarks' and 'officina' letters Γ, A, B, Є . *(e) with 'mintmark'* KY[ΠP] *and 'officina'* Γ.
(a) 3.83g 7.00h; (b) 5.98g 12.30h; (c) 3.54g 7.30h; (d) 6.01g 12.30h; (e) 4.61g 6.00h. Scale: 1:1

As with the beardless coins, the great majority of the bearded coins have a blundered or absent or missing 'mintmark' and bear the 'officina' letters Γ or Ⴢ, or, very occasionally, A, B or Δ. The only recognisable 'mintmarks' are KYΠP, COИ and OЄCP.

Examples of bearded 'three standing figures' Class I coins of Phase 1 are illustrated in figures 11 and 12.

Figure 10. Beardless Class I folles with 'mintmarks', 'officina' letters, weights and die axes as follows: (a) KVΠPI Γ *4.66g 7.00h; (b)* NIK Γ *5.64g 5.30h; (c)* KYZ Δ *8.98g 12.00h; (d)* THE A *4.47g 1.00h; (e)* [C]ON Γ *4.14g 5.00h. On (a) the left hand figure (Martina) has her distinctive crown.* Scale: 1:1

Figure 11. Bearded Class I folles; (a)-(d) with blundered or missing 'mintmarks' and 'officina' letters Γ; *(e) with 'officina'* A. *(a) 5.52g 6.00h; (b) 2.85g 5.00h; (c) 5.12g 6.00h; (d) 4.06g 5.00h; (e) 5.32g 6.30h.* Scale: 1:1

Figure 12. Bearded Class I folles; (a) and (b) with missing 'mintmarks' and 'officina' letters B *and* Δ *respectively; (c), (d) and (e) with 'officina' letters* Γ *and 'mintmarks'* OECP, COИ *and* KYΠPI *respectively* Scale: 1:1

The impression left by an overall view of the Class 1 'three standing figures' coins is that legible 'mintmarks' are unusual and the area below the M is either blundered or off the flan. Where meaningless 'mintmarks', such as KYΠPI, OECP, CON, COИ, KYZ, THE// and NIK, do occur they merely reflect the fact that regular Byzantine coins struck at these mints were still in circulation and would be known to the die cutters.

Pottier *et al* have subjected the Class I coinage to a very thorough investigation based on metrology and aspects of the design and have concluded that there is no distinction to be made between the 'three standing figures' coins with respect to the various pseudo-mintmarks. In fact, they have published a die-link between class I 'three standing figures' coins with 'mintmarks' KYH (presumably for KYZ) and THP (presumably for THEUP) [62] (see appendix 3 below), and another die-link between coins reading OECP and KYꝗ is illustrated in figure 13. The anecdotal provenances of Class I coins are most commonly in modern Syria and Lebanon (ie the northern part of *Bilād al-Shām*).

---

[62] H Pottier, I Schulze and W Schulze, Pseudo-Byzantine Coinage in Syria under Arab Rule (638-c.670): Classification and Dating, ***Revue Belge de Numismatique***, **CLIV** (2008) 87-155, plate 4 nos. 6 and 7.

Figure 13. Bearded Class I folles; (a) 4.12g 5.30h OECP B*;*
(b) 3.81g 6.00h KYq 7 *Scale: 1:1*

The division of the 'three standing figures' Class I coins of Phase 1 into Classes I.1a to I.1e by Pottier *et al* was a method of arranging the coins for further scrutiny. However die-linking between different pseudo-mintmarks makes this arrangement less useful, particularly as Class Ie, having a blundered or missing 'mintmark', is far larger than all the other classes put together. The way forward, then, is the identification of die-linked coins which can be attributed to a single workshop. This is no mean task; Tony Goodwin has written that "there are quite large numbers of [these 'three standing figures'] dies; certainly 200 obverses and may be considerably more."[63] In fact, since this comment was published fifteen years ago the steady flow of 'three standing figures' Phase 1 coins onto the market, particularly via the www, suggests that this *is* probably a low figure.

In his paper of 1994,[64] Goodwin drew attention to three short die chains (see appendix 3) where two reverse dies share a common 'three standing figures' obverse. Ten years later,[65] he illustrated a fourth short chain and extended one of the chains by the inclusion of a coin where the obverse has two standing figures, one of which wears military dress.[66] Another reverse die has been added to this chain from a private collection (see appendix 3).

Pottier *et al* [67] also mention die-links among coins with the 'three standing figures' obverse and draw attention to the fact that in some cases coins with different pseudo-mintmarks are die-linked, confirming the results of the metrological analysis which failed to find any significant weight differences between the coins with the various 'mintmarks'. They have illustrated two short die chains on plate IV (see appendix 3).[68]

Recent work by this author has now identified 25 die chains within the 'three standing figures' group (i.e. Pottier *et al* Class I), eight chains being for beardless coins and seventeen chains for bearded coins. Another die-chain, with two obverse dies and six reverse ones, links 'three standing figures' and 'two standing figures' obverses and is illustrated in figure 14. It is proposed that this should be known as The Alpha Workshop because of the prominent a on the reverse of figures 14e and f.

---

[63] T Goodwin, The dating of a series of early Arab-Byzantine coins, ***Oriental Numismatic Society Newsletter*** no. 181 (Autumn 2004) 5-9, esp. fn. 19 on p. 7
[64] T Goodwin, A Hoard of Imitative Byzantine Folles, ***Numismatic Circular*** CII (8) (October 1994) 357-9.
[65] T Goodwin, The Dating of a Series of Early Arab-Byzantine Coins, ***Oriental Numismatic Society Newsletter*** no.181 (Autumn 2004) 5-9.
[66] Goodwin (2004) *op. cit.* nos. 4 & 9. See also H Pottier, I Schulze and W Schulze, Pseudo-Byzantine Coinage in Syria under Arab Rule (638-c.670): Classification and Dating, ***Revue Belge de Numismatique***, CLIV (2008) 87-155, pl. V nos. 3 and 4.
[67] Pottier *et al* (2008) *op. cit.* pp. 92-3.
[68] Pottier *et al* (2008) *op. cit.* pl. IV.

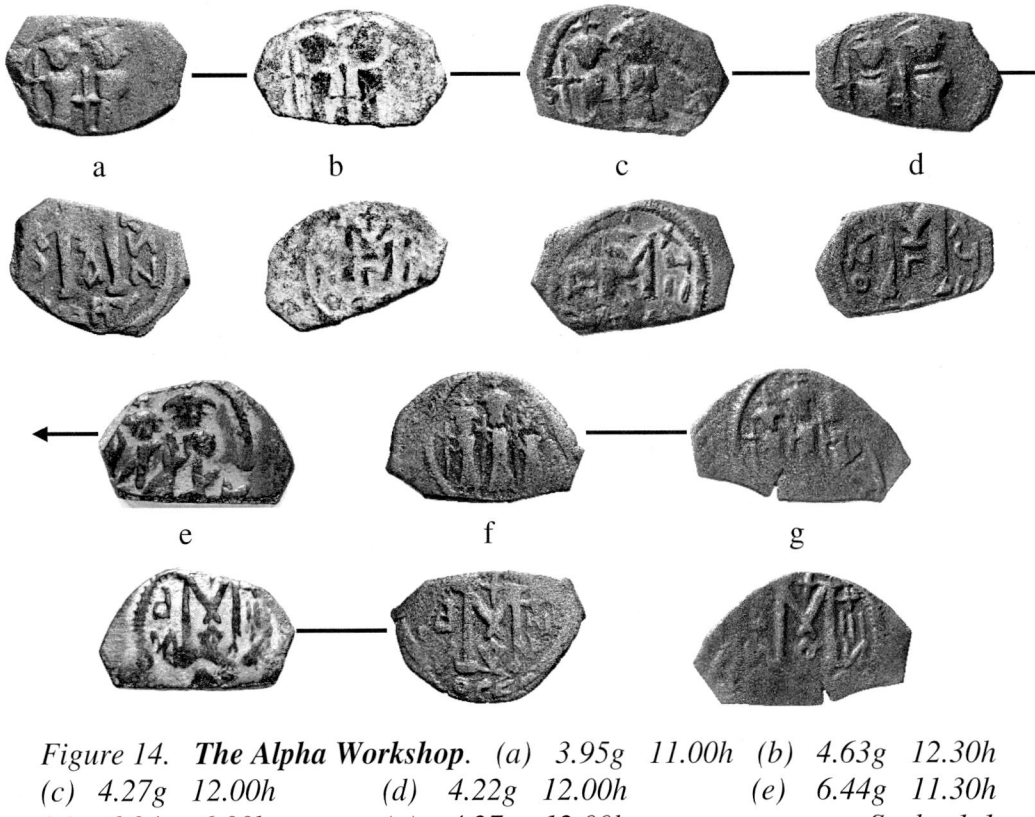

*Figure 14. **The Alpha Workshop.** (a) 3.95g 11.00h (b) 4.63g 12.30h
(c) 4.27g 12.00h (d) 4.22g 12.00h (e) 6.44g 11.30h
(e) 6.04g 6.00h (g) 4.27g 12.00h Scale: 1:1*

Another recently published die-chain which links different types of obverses has 10 obverse dies and 11 reverse dies.[69] One of the obverse dies has 'three standing figures' and two have a 'single standing figure' and the other seven have a 'facing bust'. It has to be said that there are gaps in the chain but the similarities in design strongly indicate that the coins all originate from the same workshop. It is even possible that the dates on the reverses are 'real' and Goodwin suggests 646/7 to 649/650. It is proposed that this 'mint' be called The Years 7 and 9 Workshop.

Most of the unpublished 'three standing figures' die-chains so far identified have very few dies (either one obverse connecting two reverse dies or vice versa), but they are indicative of what could be achieved if many more specimens were available. The longest unpublished chain has two obverse dies and four reverse dies. Such a number of die-chains suggest that there was a significant number of workshops in the area of what is now Lebanon and Syria in the years immediately after the Arab conquest. Much work on die-chains remains to be done.

Byzantine-Arab Phase 1; Class I.2

A rather rare variety of 'three standing figures' Phase 1 coins have the central figure wearing military dress. These are derived from the Class 6 coinage of Heraclius [70] struck between 639 and the end of his reign in January 641. Above the M (or very occasionally m) on these imitations are a ✶ (or possibly a ⚹) or a + or the Heraclian monogram ₱ℏ. The 'officina' letters are A or Γ.

Examples of Class I.2 are illustrated in figure 15. Unfortunately there are no stylistic traits running through all six coins which might indicate that they are from the same workshop. In fact, some 'three

---

[69] T Goodwin, A Mint Striking Early Dated (?) Arab-Byzantine Coins, *Numismatic Circular* **CXIX** (1) (March 2011) 8-11.
[70] P Grierson, ***Catalogue of the Byzantine Coins in the Dumbarton Oaks Collection: Volume 2: Phocas to Theodosius III 602-717***, Washington DC, 1968, pp. 305-6.

standing figures' obverses with the central figure in military dress die-link with other classes of obverse.

Figure 15. Class I.2 Byzantine-Arab Phase 1 folles with the middle figure in military dress. (a) 4.43g 6.00h; (b) 3.47g 6.00h; (c) 3.20g 1.00h; (d) 4.10g 6.00h; (e) 4.55g 6.00h; (f) 4.72g 5.00h. Scale: 1:1.

Byzantine-Arab Phase 1; Class II {Goodwin Types A and C}

The Class II of Pottier *et al* has two standing figures on the obverse and has been arranged thus:

Class II.1 two figures wearing long robes (figure 16)

Class II.2a one figure in military dress and one in a long robe, rev. M (figure 17)

Class II.2b one figure in military dress and one in a long robe, rev. m (figure 18)

Class II.3 male and female figures (figure 19).

All are uncommon and are very variable in design indicating that they are probably from several different workshops. Compared with Class I, reverses with an m are more common.

The two standing figures usually hold long crosses or *globus crucigers*, and in one case, apparently, a crozier (figure 16c) and it is possible that this coin is proclaiming that it was a Bishop who organised the emergency coinage in one particular, so-far-unknown, town or city.[71] Against this is the fact that the figure holding the 'crozier' is recognisably derived from images of Heraclius wearing military costume and a crown with a cross and having a pointed beard and prominent moustache.[72]

Examples of Pottier *et al* Class II are illustrated in figures 16 to 20.

Figures 16a and b have a distinctive obverse which is known with two different reverses. The obverse and one of the two different reverses (figure 16b) have strange symbols in the right field. Very superficially these might be taken as Arabic but Goodwin thinks they are incompetently copied Byzantine monograms.[73]

---

[71] Croziers also appear on the obverses of coins now associated with The Lazy S Workshop. (See a separate paper by Oddy in this volume.)

[72] This is not true of the Lazy S crozier types where the standing figures are anonymous silhouettes without crowns or regalia and holding a long cross in the right hand and a crozier in the left hand (see a separate paper in this volume).

[73] T Goodwin, Imitative 7th Century Byzantine Folles with a Single Figure in Military Dress, *Numismatic Circular* **CI** (4) (May 1993) 112-113.

Figure 16. Class II.1 Byzantine-Arab Phase 1 folles with two standing figures wearing long robes, rev. M *(a) 2.55g 6.00h; (b) 2.88g 6.00h; (c) 4.06g 12.00h; (d) 4.30g [74] (e) 4.28g [75] (f) 3.76g 6.00h. Scale: 1:1*

Figure 17. Class II.2a folles with one figure in military dress and one in a long robe, rev. M*; (a) 5.90g[76] (b) 3.91g[77] (c) 2.97g 5.00h (d) 3.49g 6.00h (e) 2.71g 0.30h (f) 2.97g 3.00h   Scale: 1:1*

Figure 17a belongs to a short die-chain (see appendix 5) published by Pottier *et al*,[78] to which another reverse die can now be added.[79] Figure 17b belongs to a die-chain connecting 'two standing figures' obverses with 'facing bust' obverses. There are two different 'facing bust' obverse dies and three different 'two standing figures' obverse dies which are linked to ten reverse dies.[80] The 'mint' was not given a name in the original publication; it is suggested that it be called The CON Workshop as most of the reverse dies have the meaningless letters CON in the exergue on the reverse.

The rest of figure 17 and figure 18 demonstrate the variety of the 'two standing figures' obverses to be found with M or m reverses.

---

[74] Image from www.
[75] Image from www.
[76] Image from www.
[77] Album 19, 15th May 2014, lot 158.
[78] Pottier *et al* (2008) *op. cit.* plate VI nos. 1-3.
[79] Author's collection.
[80] A Oddy, A Die-Chain in the Phase 1 Arab-Byzantine Coinage of Greater Syria, in J-M Doyen and C Morrisson (eds.), ***Mélanges de numismatique et d'archéologie offerts à Henri Pottier***, Cercle d'études numismatiques, Bruxelles, 2019, pp. 277-291.

Figure 18. Class II.2b Reverse m *Two standing figures, one wearing a long robe and the other military dress (a and b) or both wearing long robes (c and d) (a) 2.36g 6.00h; (b) 3.90g 6.00h; (c) 3.75g* [81] *(d) 3.57g 1.30h.*   Scale: 1:1

Figure 19 illustrates a 'two standing figures' obverse, re-published by Pottier *et al*,[82] in which one figure represents Phocas (according to the legend reading ...FOOC...) and the other is female. Whether this can have had any particular significance for those striking these Phase 1 coins seems unlikely and there is no real reason to separate Class II.3 from Class II.1 apart from the fact that both figures hold a *globus cruciger*.

Figure 19. Class II.3 Two standing figures each holding a globus cruciger, one male & the other female (Phocas & Leontia) 4.20g 6.00h Scale: 1:1

Figure 20 illustrates another short die chain with one obverse and two reverses. The obverse die is close to figures 16a and 16b and they may be from the same workshop. This suggestion is reinforced by the symbol in the reverse left field of figure 20a which appears to be a monogram. The pseudo-mintmarks in figure 20 are CON and NIKA and those on figure 16a and 16b are KY⋝ and ИYK.

Figure 20.   Class II.2a folles with one figure in military dress and one in a long robe, rev. M *(a) 6.42g 7.00h (b) 3.45g 6.30h   Scale: 1:1*

With all the variety in the design of Pottier *et al* Class II coins illustrated in figures 16 to 20, there is no doubt that the 'two standing figures' coins were struck at numerous workshops like the 'three standing figures' obverses discussed above. Comprehensive die studies are long overdue!

---

[81] Image from www
[82] Pottier *et al* (2008) *op. cit.* plate VI, no. 7 taken from T Goodwin, A Hoard of Imitative Byzantine Folles, ***Numismatic Circular* CII** (8) (October 1994) 357-9 no. 29.

Byzantine-Arab Phase 1; Class III   {Goodwin Types G and H}

Pottier *et al* Class III coins have a bust on the obverse and the authors have arranged them as follows:

- III.1a   Bust with a usually blundered legend sometimes recognisably based on the IhPER COhST legend of folles of Constans II with a facing bust. These may be beardless or have a short beard.
- III.1b   Bust without legend
- III.1c   A star and crescent [and S] on the obverse [83]
- III.2   The Year 20 Mint [84]

As with previous classes, coins with a bust on the obverse (figures 21 to 24) are very variable in style. Many of those obverses that show a clean shaven face and are derived from the IhPER CONST issues of Constans II, dated year 3 (AD 643/4) (figure 21f) which are assumed to have been struck at Constantinople.[85] Some Class III.1a coins are bearded and these may copy a reissue by Constans of the IhPER CONST type, but with a bearded portrait, in his year 11 (AD 652/3) (figure 22f).

The die study by Goodwin [86] has die-linked 'facing bust' coins to 'single standing figure' and 'three standing figures' obverses. Similarly, a die study by Oddy,[87] has linked 'facing bust types' to 'two standing figures' types of obverse. Goodwin has also published two short chains each consisting of a 'single standing figure' and a 'facing bust' linked via the same reverse (see appendix 2).[88]

---

[83] T Goodwin, An enigmatic early Arab-Byzantine coin type, in J-M Doyen and C Morrisson (eds.), *Mélanges de numismatique et d'archéologie de Byzance offerts à Henri Pottier*, Cercle d'études numismatiques, Bruxelles, 2019, pp. 137-150.

[84] S J Mansfield, A Byzantine Irregular Issue of 'Year 20 ', *Numismatic Circular* C (3) (April 1992) 81- 82. The year 20 coinage was brought up to date by W A Oddy and S J Mansfield, The 'Year 20 Mint' Revisited, *Journal of the Oriental Numismatic Society* 214 (Winter 2013) 4-11.

[85] Attributed by P Grierson (*Catalogue of the Byzantine Coins in the Dumbarton Oaks Collection and in the Whittemore Collection* Volume 2 Part Two, Washington DC, 1968, p.396-7) to Heraclonas, but now shown by George Bates ('Constans II or Heraclonas', *Museum Notes* 17 (of the ANS) (1971) 141-161) to belong to Constans II. However a 'bust type', dated to year three, does not fit comfortably into the sequence of folles issued by Constans II at Constantinople. Perhaps some lateral thinking is required here. As the 'year 3 bust type' coins of Constans II are found in large numbers in the northern part of *Bilād al-Shām*, could they have been specially struck in Constantinople to be sent in bulk to the areas of Greater Syria recently conquered by the followers of Mohammad – along with batches of the regular Constans II coppers? The IhPER COhST coins would proclaim to the people in Greater Syria, now living under Arab Rule, that their **legitimate** ruler was Constantine (Constans II) in a way that the 'regular' coinage of Constans (without name or 'portrait') did not. It has to be remembered that from c.611 to 640 Byzantine authority was virtually totally lacking in Greater Syria and a whole generation had grown up **not** being subject to the Byzantine Emperor. The last emperor that they knew from the coinage, and from military activity between 633 and 636, was Heraclius. A similar issue with facing bust was struck by Constans II in year 11 (652-3), but on this the facing bust is bearded and this image also gave rise to Phase 1 Arab-Byzantine imitations. These regular 'facing bust' coins of Constans II struck in year 11are much less common than those of year 3. The same argument can apply that they were minted for export in bulk to northern Syria, although by 653 the main bulk export of copper coins of Constans II to the Arab-occupied areas of the former Byzantine Empire had ceased. (See M Phillips, The Import of Byzantine Coins to Syria Revisited, in T Goodwin (ed.) *Arab-Byzantine Coins and History*, London, 2012, pp. 39-72).

[86] T Goodwin, A Mint Striking Early Dated (?) Arab-Byzantine Coins, *Numismatic Circular* CXIX (1) (March 2011) 8-11.

[87] A Oddy, A Die-Chain in the Phase 1 Arab-Byzantine Coinage of Greater Syria, in J-M Doyen and C Morrisson (eds.), *Mélanges de numismatique et d'archéologie de Byzance offerts à Henri Pottier*, Cercle d'études numismatiques, Bruxelles, 2019, pp. 277-291.

[88] T Goodwin, *Imitations of the Folles of Constans II*, Occasional Paper no.28, Oriental Numismatic Society, April 1993, coins 1 and 3 and coins 10 and 12.

Figure 21 (a-e) are Class III.1a folles with a beardless facing bust. (f) is a regular coin of Constans year 3 with a beardless bust   (a) 3.79g 6.00h;   (b) 4.59g 6.00h;   (c) 4.80g 6.00h; (d) 3.56g 12.00h;   (e) 2.90g 5.00h;   (f) 6.75g 6.00h.   Scale: 1:1

*Figure 22 (a-e) are Class III.1a folles with a bearded facing bust. 22a unusually has an **m** reverse. (f) is a regular coin of Constans year 11 with a bearded bust.   (a) 3.26g 12.00h   (b) 6.17g [89] (c) 2.79g [90] (d) 9.78g 12.00h (e) 4.86g [91] 7.00h (f) 3.35g [92] 7.00h   Scale: 1:1*

Figure 23. Class III.1b folles with a facing bust, sometimes bearded, but without a legend.   (a) 3.87g 6.00h;   (b) 2.91g 11.00h;   (c) 3.50g 1.00h; (d) 4.80g 12.00h;   (e) 5.11g 1.00h [93]   (f) 3.51g 1.00h.   Scale: 1:1

---

[89] Album 19, 15th May 2014, lot 190.
[90] Album 19, 15th May 2014, lot 194.
[91] Leu web auction 4, 25th June 2018, lot 1339.
[92] Album 19, 15th May 2014, lot 196.
[93] Leu web auction 5, 23rd September 2018, lot 1327.

However, unlike Classes I and II, Class III contains two sub-sets, III.1c and III.2, (figure 24) which each represent a single workshop. The first of these to have been published is represented by figures 24b and 24c which are coins of the so-called 'Year 20 Mint' because the coins are invariably dated on the reverse X/X.[94] With the passage of time, more specimens have become available and the paper was revised in 2013.[95] This revision explored the possibility that the Year 20 Mint may have issued 'single standing figure' and 'three standing figures' obverses, but without being able to prove the connection via die-links.

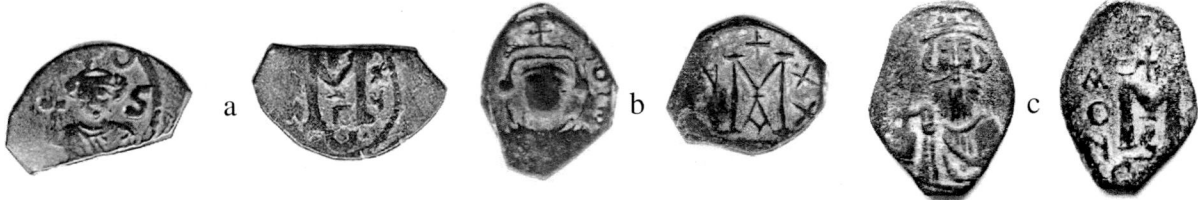

Figure 24   (a) Class III.1c   A star ✱ *and crescent* ⌣ *and S on the obverse*
6.30g   6.30h;   (b) and (c)   Class III.2   The Year 20 Mint   (b) 2.70g   9.00h [96]
(c)   2.86g   12.00h   Scale: 1:1

Figure 24a represents a group of coins with the symbols ✱, ⌣ and S in the obverse field. These have been the subject of a recent die-study by Tony Goodwin [97] and it is abundantly clear that they represent the output of a single mint. All the obverse dies except two depict a facing bust, sometimes bearded. The other two obverses have two facing busts and these are known with four reverses. It is suggested that this 'mint' should be called The Star and Crescent Workshop.

It is now very clear that the obverse types of Pottier *et al* Classes I to III are all actually interrelated via reverse die-links.

Byzantine-Arab Phase 1; Class IV   {Goodwin Types E and F}

The obverses of Class IV have a single standing figure which is obviously derived from the early coinage of Constans II produced at Constantinople. The reverses have either an M or an m, the latter being much more common. In fact the 'single standing figure' with reverse m is the most common type of Phase 1 coin to be found in the numismatic market today. There must have been several hundred dies and, therefore, a large number of 'workshops'. Many of them probably consisted of only one pair of dies and this explains the fact that apart from eleven significant production sites, known as The Year 20 Workshop, The LITOIE Workshop, The Pahlavi Workshop, The Years 7 and 9 Workshop, The Ugly Square Workshop, The CON Workshop, The Star and Crescent Workshop, The Lazy S Workshop, the Lazy BZ Workshop, The Alpha Workshop, and The OHO Workshop (see appendix 1 below), examples of die-linking are almost unknown, or, at least, unpublished. Full references to the original publications of all these workshops are given at the end of this paper.

The coinage of Pottier *et al* Class IV is illustrated in figures 25-27. Figure 25 illustrates examples of Pottier *et al* Class IV.1a, with an M reverse; figure 26 illustrates Class IV.1b with an m reverse. Style is variable and the standing figure is occasionally bearded.

---

[94] S J Mansfield, A Byzantine Irregular Issue of Year 20, **Numismatic Circular** C (3) (April 1992) 81-2.
[95] W A Oddy and S J Mansfield, The 'Year 20 Mint' Revised, **Journal of the Oriental Numismatic Society** 214 (Winter 2013) 4 - 11.
[96] Mansfield collection.
[97] T Goodwin, An enigmatic early Arab-Byzantine coin type, in J-M Doyen and C Morrisson (eds.), **Mélanges de numismatique et d'archéologie de Byzance offerts à Henri Pottier**, Cercle d'études numismatiques, Bruxelles, 2019, pp. 137-150.

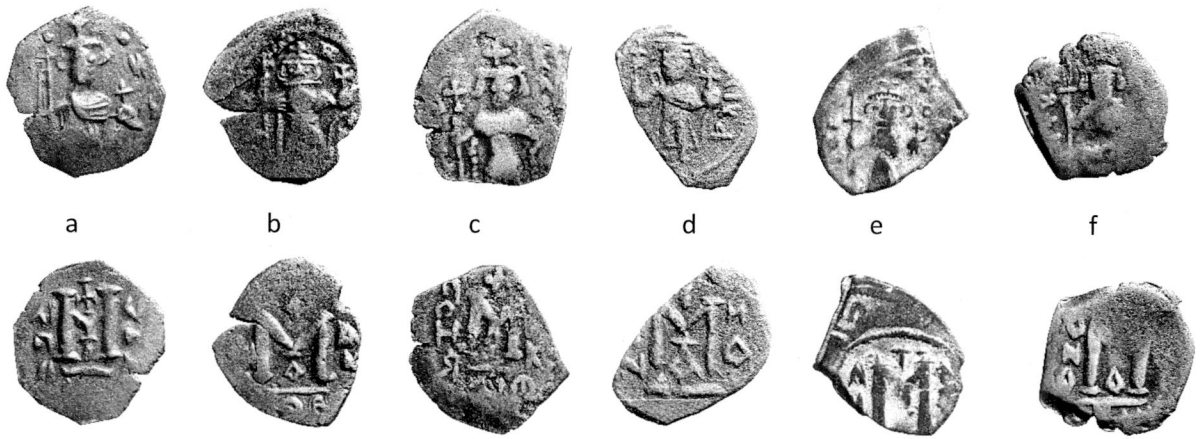

Figure 25. Class IV.1a with a single standing figure and an **M** *reverse*
(a)   3.59g   12.00h   (b)   3.26g   6.00h   (c)   3.72g   6.00h
(d)   2.52g   5.00h   (e)   4.14g   1.00h   (f)   3.02g   6.30h   Scale: 1:1

Figure 26. Class IV.1b with a single standing figure and an **m** *reverse*
(a)   4.71g   5.00h   (b)   4.09g   7.30h   (c)   2.94g   12.00h
(d)   3.70g   7.00h   (e)   3.23g   8.30h   (f)   2.34g   4.30h   Scale: 1:1

The **LITOIΕ (or ΛITOIΕ)** Workshop.

The coins of Class IV.1c are known as The **LITOIΕ** Workshop and have been tentatively ascribed to Emesa/Ḥimṣ on the basis of stylistic similarities of the reverse with the Phase 2 'facing bust' coinage of Ḥimṣ.[98] The same ground was reworked some years later by Karukstis who identified more and longer die chains,[99] seven altogether. The longest has five obverse dies and seven reverse dies. The number of **LITOIΕ** coins coming regularly onto the market in recent years suggests that a much more complex set of die relationships is awaiting to be discovered. Three coins of The **LITOIΕ** Workshop are illustrated in figures 27a, 27b and 27c.

The Lazy S Workshop

The coins of Class IV.1d are known as The Lazy **S** Workshop. It was first identified in 1995.[100] Seven coins were listed, but there was only one pair of die identities and no die-linking. The Lazy **S**

---

[98] A Oddy, The Christian Coinage of Early Muslim Syria, *ARAM* **15** (2003) 185-192.
[99] C Karukstis, Was Pseudo-Byzantine Coinage Primarily of Municipal Origin? *The Proceedings of the XIVth International Numismatic Congress Glasgow 2009*, (Glasgow, 2011), ed. Nicholas Holmes, volume 2, pp. 1477-91.
[100] A Oddy, Imitations of Constans II Folles of Class 1 or 4 Struck in Syria, *Numismatic Circular* **CIII** (4) (May 1995) 142-3.

coins are derived from the Class I coinage of Constans minted in Constantinople in AD 641-3. The Lazy S Workshop is described in detail elsewhere in this volume.

The Lazy BZ Workshop

The coins of Class IV.1e were published by Tony Goodwin in 1995 who illustrated six coins with a recumbent B (ie ⌒) above the m on the reverse.[101] Die-links were not indicated, but Goodwin suggested that there are "about 10 obverse and reverse dies". These coins have become known as the Lazy B Workshop. However, a survey of private collections and internet databases has revealed a number of stylistically related coins with the symbol S above the m and a coin has now been discovered (figure 27e) that die-links the Lazy S coins (figure 27f) and the Lazy ⌒ coins. (figure 27d). A paper is in preparation describing and illustrating the Lazy BZ Workshop.

Figure 27. Class IV.1c (a)-(c) and Class IV.1e (d)-(f)   (a)   3.97g   6.30h
(b)   2.67g   7.30h   (c)   3.09g   10.30h   (d)   2.35g   1.00h
(e)   3.77g   6.30h   (f)   2.04g   11.30h   Scale: 1:1

Discussion of Class IV

In the past 25 years several researchers have shown that the Class IV coins with a 'single standing figure' are die-linked to coins of Class III ('facing bust') and Class II ('two standing figures') and Class I ('three standing figures').

In 1995 Goodwin published a 'single standing figure' obverse combined with an M reverse and an m reverse (see appendix 1),[102] and in the same paper he linked a 'single standing figure' obverse to a 'two standing figures' obverse via the same m reverse (see appendix 1).[103] In 1997 Phillips and Goodwin linked two different m reverse dies to the same 'single standing figure' obverse (see appendix 4).[104] Three years later Goodwin illustrated three coins struck from two obverse dies ('single standing figure' and 'facing bust') and from two reverse dies (M and m). This chain has been extended by Pottier *et al* to include another 'facing bust' and 'two standing figures' (see appendix 1).[105]

---

[101] T Goodwin, 7th Century Arab Imitations of Byzantine Folles, **Numismatic Circular CIII** (9) (November 1995) 336-7.
[102] Goodwin (1995) *op. cit.* coin nos. 10 and 11.
[103] Goodwin (1995) *op. cit.* coin nos. 7 and 8.
[104] M Phillips and T Goodwin, A Seventh–Century Syrian Hoard of Byzantine and Imitative Copper Coins, **Numismatic Chronicle 157** (1997) 61-87, coin nos. C.12 and C.23.
[105] Pottier *et al* (2008) *op. cit.* pl. X.

'Single standing figure' obverses have also been die-linked in the same chain to both a 'two standing figures' obverse and to an unusual 'facing bust' which is derived from the coinage of Constantine IV.[106] As these coins have a legend in Pahlavi their status is ambiguous and, as with the coins inscribed *Muhammad/ba'd*, discussed briefly above, they could be either Phase 1 or Phase 2. 'Single standing figure' coins have also been die-linked to 'three standing figures' and 'facing bust' obverses.[107]

Byzantine-Arab Phase 1; Class V

Figure 29. Class V. (a) No wt.[108] (b) 3.40g [109] (c) No wt.[110] (d) 3.98g 1.00h [111] (e) No wt. [112]   Scale: 1:1

Finally, Class V, which has two busts on the obverse is only known from two obverse dies[113] and four reverse dies.

This class was first published by Tony Goodwin in 2006 [114] from a single specimen said to have been found in the Lebanon (figure 29d). Now a number of other 'two facing busts' coins have been discovered and Goodwin has shown that they are die-linked to coins of Class III.2b with a star and crescent on the obverse.[115] Hence they belong to The Star and Crescent Workshop. It is, therefore, a moot point whether the 'two facing busts' coins can be considered as a separate class.

Summary and Conclusions

The purpose of this paper is to review how the Phase 1 Arab-Byzantine coinage has been treated in publications during the past 30 years. To that end, it first looks at pioneering attempts, mostly by Tony Goodwin, to classify the Phase 1 coinage starting with overall appearance in 1993. Then, in

---

[106] A Oddy, Constantine IV as a Prototype for Early Islamic Coins, in A Oddy (ed.), *Coinage and History in the Seventh Century Near East 2*, London, 2010, pp. 95-109.
[107] T Goodwin, A Mint Striking Early Dated (?) Arab-Byzantine Coins, *Numismatic Circular* CXIX (1) (March 2011) 8-11.
[108] Goodwin (2019) *op. cit.* no. 61.
[109] Album 22 (14th May 2015) lot 92; Goodwin (2019) *op. cit.* no. 58.
[110] C Morrison, Un Lot de Monnaies Byzantines et Arabo-Byzantines du Cabinet des Médailles provenant de Syrie, *Bulletin de la Société française de numismatique*, 64 (5) (2009) 90-95, no. 336; Goodwin 2019, *op. cit.* no. 60.
[111] T Goodwin, A New Type of Seventh Century Syrian Pseudo-Byzantine Coin, *Journal of the Oriental Numismatic Society* 187 (Spring 2006) 46-47; Goodwin (2019) *op. cit.* no 59
[112] Private collection UK
[113] T Goodwin, An Enigmatic early Arab-Byzantine Coin Type, in J-M Doyen and C Morrisson (eds.) *Mélanges de numismatique et d'archéologie de Byzance offerts à Henri Pottier*, Cercle d'études numismatiques, Bruxelles, 2019, pp. 137-150.
[114] T Goodwin, A New Type of Seventh Century Syrian Pseudo-Byzantine Coin, *Journal of the Oriental Numismatic Society* 187 (Spring 2006) 46-47; Goodwin (2019) *op. cit.* no 59
[115] Goodwin (2019) *op. cit.* pp. 137-150

1994, the approach was changed to use the apparent prototype Byzantine coins as a basis to define groups within a hoard consisting mainly of 'three standing figures' types but with some examples of 'single standing figure', 'two standing figures' and 'facing bust' types. This resulted in five 'groups'. In 2002 the groups were extended based on the imagery on the obverse of the Phase 1 coinage as a whole and this now gave rise to nine 'groups'. This classification was again modified in 2004 when referring only to coins struck on oval flans. Nine groups were described, but they did not exactly match the nine groups of the 2002 publication. In 2015, Goodwin and Gyselen returned to an extended 2002 classification. Meanwhile, in 2008, Pottier *et al* suggested a scheme based on four classes corresponding to the four obverse types: 'three standing figures', 'two standing figures', 'facing bust' and 'one standing figure'. The publication of the 'two facing busts' type adds a fifth class. This was the outline used by Clive Foss for his arrangement of the Arab-Byzantine coinage in the Dumbarton Oaks catalogue.

Where all these schemes break down is when die-links are found between coins in different classes. This can be demonstrated on the following diagram:

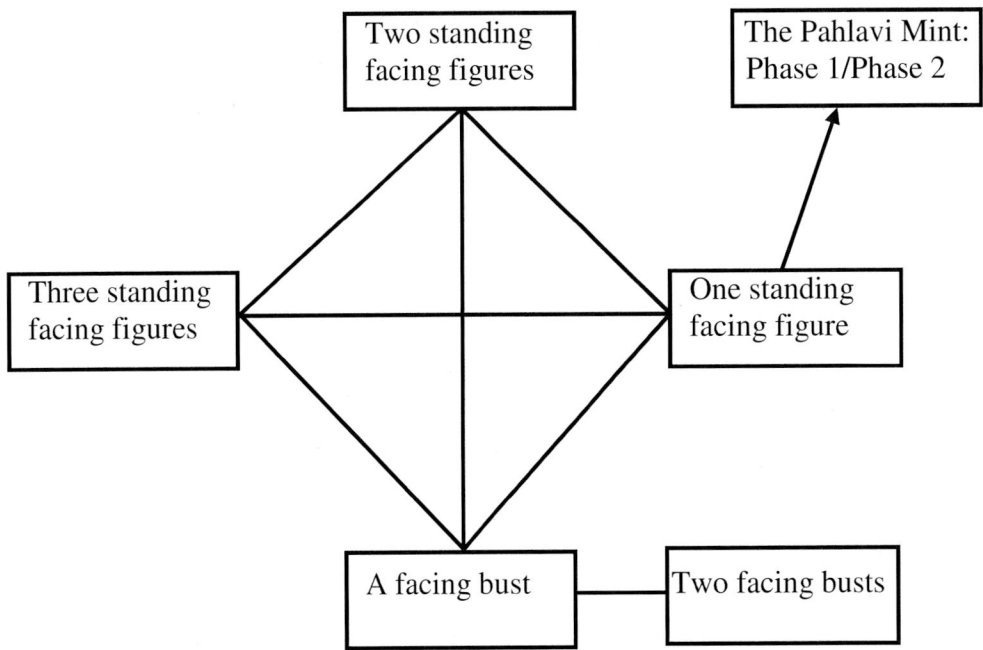

Perceptively, Clive Foss had anticipated this problem as early as 2003 in a review of the Ashmolean Syllogue where he wrote "[grouping] the whole series into nine classes according to their type [is] a rather old-fashioned method reminiscent of Walker's classification by prototype."[116]

What has now happened in the study of Phase 1 Arab- Byzantine Coinage is that numismatists have begun to concentrate on groups of stylistically, and physically, similar coins and started to use die-links to identify workshop assemblages.[117] These have shown that the classification systems used during the foundation period of serious study of Phase 1 no longer serve a purpose. What is required now are two things:
- The publication of an atlas - or atlases - of large numbers of Phase 1 coins to make them available to the scholarly community. This was suggested 20 years ago by Professor John Haldon in the discussion period at one of the early Seventh Century Syria Numismatic Round Tables but nobody has yet accepted the challenge.
- The publication of detailed die chains which must represent the product of one workshop.

---

[116] C Foss, The Coinage of the First Century of Islam, ***Journal of Roman Archaeology*** 16 (2003) 748-60.
[117] This was again predicted by Clive Foss who noted that "Goodwin and Oddy have also identified other coherent groups of these dateless mintless coins that can probably be identified as emanating from one mint."

Along the way this review has also raised a number of questions that, at the very least, need to be considered even if they are eventually discarded:
- Were the earliest imitations of Heraclius' Cyprus coins of years 17 to 19 that were struck on approximately round flans produced by the army on campaign in what is now Syria and Lebanon? If so they should not be included in the Phase 1 Arab-Byzantine coinage and should be reclassified as Military coins and analogous to those struck in Seleucia and in Isaura a few years previously.
- Was the palm branch on a group of roughly square coins an indication/proclamation of victory by the followers Islam in *Bilād al-Shām*?
- Does the Crozier held in the hands of some standing figures indicate minting activity under the authority of the local bishop?

APPENDICES

These summarise single die-links and short die chains published in the last 30 years. Major articles concentrating on one die chain are not included, but are listed at the end.

Appendix 1: T Goodwin, *Imitations of the Folles of Constans II*, Occasional Paper no. 28, Oriental Numismatic Society, April 1993; T Goodwin, 7th Century Arab Imitations of Byzantine Folles, *Numismatic Circular* **CIII** (9) (November 1995) 336-7; T Goodwin, Pseudo-Byzantine Coinage from Seventh Century Syria, *The Celator* (September 2000) 18-27; H Pottier, I Schulze and W Schulze, Pseudo-Byzantine Coinage in Syria under Arab Rule (638-c.670): Classification and Dating, *Revue Belge de Numismatique*, **CLIV** (2008) 87-155, plate X.

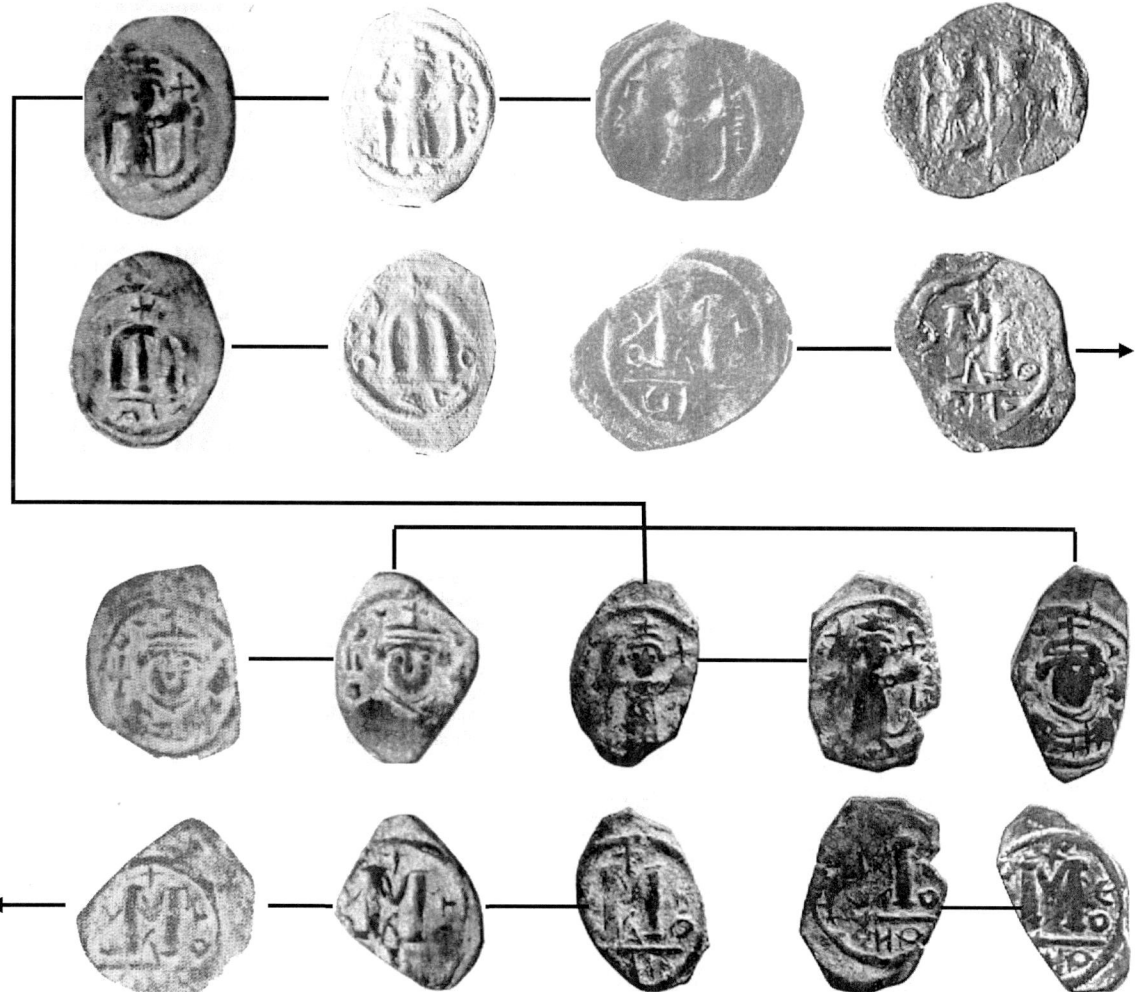

It is suggested that this 'mint' be known as **The OHO Workshop** after the legend in the reverse exergue on many of the coins.

Appendix 2: T Goodwin, *Imitations of the Folles of Constans II*, Occasional Paper no. 28, Oriental Numismatic Society, April 1993; T Goodwin, 7th Century Arab Imitations of Byzantine Folles, ***Numismatic Circular* CIII** (9) (November 1995) 336-7.

Appendix 3: T Goodwin, A Hoard of Imitative Byzantine Folles, ***Numismatic Circular* CII** (8) (October 1994) 357-9; T Goodwin, The dating of a Series of early Arab-Byzantine Coins, *Oriental Numismatic Society Newsletter* **181** (Autumn 2004) 5-9; H Pottier, I Schulze and W Schulze, Pseudo-Byzantine Coinage in Syria under Arab Rule (638-c.670): Classification and Dating, ***Revue Belge de Numismatique***, **CLIV** (2008) 87-155, plates IV and V.

The coins A and B, at the bottom of the previous page, were first published by George Bates in 1970.[118] He attributed them to non-imperial minting in Antioch at the time of the 'Persian' occupation but in 1977 Hahn (who knew of seven specimens from the same dies) thought that there was some sort of Byzantine control of the Antioch mint in the years 618-626.[119] Henri Pottier did not include these coins in his catalogue of minting in Syria during the 'Persian' occupation.[120] Several specimens have been seen on the market in recent years and Mansfield illustrates three of them and catalogues them as Phase 1.[121] The date has generally been read as year X/IIII, but examination with a lens indicates the possibility that it is X/ЧII, which is more likely for a Phase 1 'three standing figures' obverse which was derived from the Cypriot coinage of Heraclius in years 17, 18 and 19. Nevertheless, the coins do look 'odd' and seem to be part of a group with very similar obverses which require more thought.

Appendix 4: M Phillips and T Goodwin, A Seventh-Century Syrian Hoard of Byzantine and Imitative Copper Coins, *Numismatic Chronicle* **157** (1997) 61-87.

Appendix 5: H Pottier, I Schulze and W Schulze, Pseudo-Byzantine Coinage in Syria under Arab Rule (638-c.670): Classification and Dating, *Revue Belge de Numismatique*, **CLIV** (2008) 87-155, plate VI.

3.78g 5.00h

This group of coins was first recognised by Henri Pottier in 2004 [122] and a number of further specimens have been noted in the trade since then. The implication from Pottier's book is that he thought that the coins represented a minor mint active during the latter part of the Sasanian occupation. However, Pottier *et al* [123] assume that they are Arab-Byzantine Phase 1. Examination of

---

[118] G E Bates, Five Byzantine Notes, *Museum Notes* [of the American Numismatic Society] 16 (1970) 69-85, esp. pp. 80-82.
[119] W Hahn, Minting Activity in the Diocese of Oriens under Heraclius, *Numismatic Circular,* **LXXXV** (July-August 1977) 307-8.
[120] H Pottier, *Le Monnayage de la Syrie Sous L'Occupation Perse (610-630)*, Cahiers Ernest-Babelon 9, Paris, 2004
[121] [S Mansfield], *Early Byzantine Copper Coins: Catalogue of an English Collection*, Manchester, 2016, p. 311, nos. 23.25-27.
[122] Pottier, 2004, *op. cit*. pp. 139 and 161.
[123] H Pottier, I Schulze and W Schulze, Pseudo-Byzantine Coinage in Syria under Arab Rule (638-c.670): Classification and Dating, *Revue Belge de Numismatique*, **CLIV** (2008) 87-155, plate VI.

the coins shows that they do differ from the average Phase 1 coin by being larger and heavier and the suggestion here is that they are more likely to belong to the Sasanian (Persian) occupation.

--oOo--

In addition to the miscellaneous die-links collected together above, there are the following publications of single mints within the Phase 1 series which have been referred to in the course of this paper:

- **The Year 20 Workshop**: S J Mansfield, A Byzantine Irregular Issue of Year 20, *Numismatic Circular* C (3) (April 1992) 81-2; W A Oddy and S J Mansfield, The 'Year 20 Mint 'Revised, *Journal of the Oriental Numismatic Society* 214 (Winter 2013) 4 – 11.
- **The LITOIЄ Workshop**: A Oddy, the Christian coinage of early Muslim Syria, *ARAM* 15 (2003) 185-192; C Karukstis, Was Pseudo-Byzantine Coinage Primarily of Municipal Origin, *The Proceedings of the XIVth International Numismatic Congress Glasgow 2009*, (Glasgow, 2011), ed. Nicholas Holmes, volume 2, pp. 1477-91.
- **The Pahlavi Workshop**: A Oddy, Constantine IV as a Prototype for Early Islamic Coins, in A Oddy (ed.), *Coinage and History in the Seventh Century Near East 2*, London, 2010, pp. 95-109.
- **The Years 7 and 9 Workshop**: T Goodwin, A Mint Striking Early Dated (?) Arab-Byzantine Coins, *Numismatic Circular* CXIX (1) (March 2011) 8 -11.
- **The Ugly Square Workshop:** I Schulze, Ugly Square Flan Coins: Another Consistent Group within the Byzantine-Arab Transitional Coinage, in T Goodwin (ed.), *Arab-Byzantine Coins and History*, London, 2012, pp. 81-87
- **The CON Workshop**: A Oddy, A Die-Chain in the Phase 1 Arab-Byzantine Coinage of Greater Syria, in J-M Doyen and C Morrisson (eds.) *Mélanges de numismatique et d'archéologie de Byzance offerts à Henri Pottier*, Cercle d'études numismatiques, Bruxelles, 2019, pp. 277-292
- **The Star and Crescent Workshop**: T Goodwin, An Enigmatic early Arab-Byzantine Coin Type, in J-M Doyen and C Morrisson (eds.) *Mélanges de numismatique et d'archéologie de Byzance offerts à Henri Pottier*, Cercle d'études numismatiques, Bruxelles, 2019, pp. 137-150.
- **The Lazy S Workshop**: A Oddy, The Lazy S Workshop: Coin Production in Early Arab Syria, this volume.
- **The Lazy BZ Workshop**: T Goodwin, 7th Century Arab Imitations of Byzantine Folles, *Numismatic Circular* CIII (9) (November 1995) 336-7; and Oddy in preparation.
- **The Alpha Workshop**: see above in this paper.
- **The OHO Workshop**: T Goodwin, 7th Century Arab Imitations of Byzantine Folles, *Numismatic Circular* CIII (9) (November 1995) 336-7; T Goodwin, Pseudo-Byzantine Coinage from Seventh Century Syria, *The Celator* (September 2000) 18-27; H Pottier, I Schulze and W Schulze, Pseudo-Byzantine Coinage in Syria under Arab Rule (638-c.670): Classification and Dating, *Revue Belge de Numismatique*, CLIV (2008) 87-155, plate X.

Acknowledgements

As usual I am very grateful to many friends and colleagues for access to coins in their care and for discussion about the coinage of greater Syria in the Umayyad period. In particular I should mention Peter Donald, Gary Donald, Tony Goodwin, Nayef Goussous, Steve Mansfield, Marcus Phillips, Ingrid and Wolfgang Schulze, and Susan Tyler-Smith.

The Lazy S Workshop:
Coin Production in Early Arab Syria

Andrew Oddy [1]

Introduction

Elsewhere in this volume is presented an overview of the Phase 1 Byzantine-Arab coinage in which the coinage of several putative workshops [2] is described. One of these, originally called the Lazy S Mint, merits fuller discussion as it has recently been shown to be significantly more extensive than previously thought.

The Lazy S workshop

The Lazy S workshop was first identified in 1995.[3] Seven coins were listed, but there was only one pair of die identities and no die linking. The Lazy S coins are derived from the Class 1 coinage of Constans II minted in Constantinople in AD 641-3 (see Figure 1.1). The reverse of these reads ANA to the left of the m and NEOS to the right, with the *officina* and year of issue below. These regular coins of Constans II were extensively copied in Greater Syria after the Arab conquest and in some of them the S of NEOS has become horizontal (see Figure 1.2). Coins like this must have been the inspiration for the so-called Lazy S workshop. In the (presumably) first issue of the Lazy S workshop, the year and officina are omitted from the reverse legend which reads ANA to the left, NE to the right, and ∽O below the m (1:2.1, 5:2.2, 6:2.3, 8:2.4, 9:2.5, 10:2.6, 14:3.2, 17:3.3, 18:3.4).[4]

There are two other variations of the Lazy S reverse legends: one, known from only one die, has O ∽ below the m (22: 4.1) and the other has O ∽ O (13:3.1, 20:3.5, 21:3.6, 23:4.2, through to 58b:7.4). There is a die link between these two reverses (22:4.1 and 23:4.2).

Then in 2000, Charlie Karukstis showed that the Lazy S types with ∽O below the m are die linked to coins with ONL and ИKE below the m and stylistically linked to others with OKE or ••••• in the exergue on the reverse [5] (see figures 62:8.2 through to 94:10.3) and more recently Ingrid Schulze has published an obverse die link between a Lazy S reverse and one with H ⋔ in the exergue (7:7.5 and 24:7.6).[6]

---

[1] Andrew Oddy is an independent scholar waoddy@googlemail.com
[2] The production site of coins is usually called a mint. For most coinages throughout history, coins were produced under the auspices of a ruler or government. In discussion with Luke Treadwell, however, he pointed out that the Phase 1 coins were not produced by the government of the time in any formal sense. Because it is assumed that the Phase 1 coins were produced by local officials – magistrates, bishops, prominent citizens - to alleviate a shortage of small change, the use of the term 'mint' for the place of production is inappropriate. The use of the term 'workshops' avoids any implied supervision or control by the ruling Arabs.
[3] A Oddy, Imitations of Constans II Folles of Class`1 or 4 Struck in Syria, *Numismatic Circular* **103** (4) (1995) 142-3.
[4] Coins are indicated by their number in the table and by their number in the figures if they are illustrated. Thus 5:2.2 is coin 5 illustrated in figure 2.2.
[5] C P Karukstis, A Note on the Localization of Pseudo-Byzantine Coinage in Syria, *Numismatic Circular* **CVIII** (4) (August 2000) 158.
[6] I Schulze, The *al-wafā lillāh* Coinage: A Study of Style, in A Oddy (ed), *Coinage and History in the Seventh century Near East 2*, London, 2010, pp. 111-121, esp.p.118, Fig 12 nos. 4 and 5.

Karukstis listed fifteen of these ONL, ИКЄ, OKЄ and ••••• coins, some of which had (apparent) find-spots in Syria, Israel and Jordan, and he took this as an indication that the coins circulated widely away from their minting place. However, Karukstis' 'provenances' may only represent the location of the relevant dealer and cannot be taken as a reliable guide to area of circulation. Nevertheless, an OKЄ coin (81 in the list) has been excavated at Déhès in northern Syria,[7] which is about 420Km north of the putative Lazy S workshop-site at Ajloun (see below), and two other related coins (nos. 110, with TЄS below the m, and 118, with ИЄS below) have been excavated at Jerusalem, about 75 Km south of Ajloun.

The so-called 'Irbid Hoard' contained seven relevant coins: {nos. 14:3.2 (⌒ O), 32 and 40:5.6 (both O ⌒ O), 65 (ONL), 73 (OKЄ), 125:13.3 and 126:13.4 (••••)}. Irbid has become accepted [8] as the provenance of this very large hoard on the basis of evidence from the late Israeli dealer Shraga Qedar. However, he lived in Israel and there is a distinct possibility that 'Irbid' was a convenient invention of whoever sold the hoard to Qedar. For what it is worth, Irbid is 30 Km north of Ajloun.

The Israeli Antiquities Authority holds four Lazy S coins from excavations: 19a from Nabratein, 17a and 58b:7.4 from Bet She'an, and 58a from the Rehov hoard.[9] These provenances (see map at end) do provide evidence that Phase 1 coins did sometimes circulate well away from their place of manufacture although most of them were found within 75 Km of Ajloun.

An extensive search of private collections, museums, and dealers' lists and sale catalogues has revealed 64 Lazy S coins which are listed below. A selection to illustrate all the die varieties and die-links is illustrated in the figures. Additionally, a search for coins which are related in style to the ONL, NKЄ, and ИКЄ reverses has produced 82 coins which are also listed below.

The die links are illustrated schematically following the figures.

The coins which actually have a Lazy S on the reverse have been found to have 20 different obverse dies and 28 different reverse dies. With one exception, the obverse dies depict a standing facing figure with a cross on top of the head, a long cross in the right hand and a *globus cruciger* in the left hand. From the *globus cruciger*, a dotted line curves down to the bottom edge of the robe. This dotted line is derived from the edge of the cloak on the coins of Constans II (see figure 1.1), but is here meaningless. Letters sometimes appear to the left and right of the standing figure. On one die, no. O16, the long cross become a trident with a cross bar (46:6.4, 46a, 47, 48:6.5).

The interesting 'exception' to the main type of Lazy S obverse die is die number O1 on which the facing figure has a long cross to the right and a *globus cruciger* on a staff to the left. This is paired with only one Lazy S reverse die (2:8.1) but with three different reverse dies with letters in the exergue (62:8.2 to 70:8.6). Die O1 is stylistically very close to the obverse dies of a number of coins which have letters in the exergues on the reverse (dies O30 to O33).

The reverse dies with a lazy S in the exergue all have an m with a cross above and occasionally there are dots in the arches of the m, viz. ṁ. The legends usually consist of A/N/A or A/И/A in the left field and N/Є or A/N/Є in the right-field, where the N is sometimes written И or H. Other variations can be studied in figures 1.3 to 7.5.

---

[7] C Morrisson, Les Monnaies, pp.267-287, in J P Sodini et al. Déhès (Syrie du Nord) Campagnes 1976-1978, **Syria 57** (1980) 1-310, no.55.
[8] T Goodwin and R Gyselen, ***Arab Byzantine Coins from the Irbid Hoard,*** Royal Numismatic Society Special Publication no. 53, London, 2015.
[9] Excavated by Fanny Vitto and in process of publication by Nitzan Amitai-Preiss, to whom I am grateful for permission to include this coin here.

At some stage in the evolution of the workshop the ꙅO below the m was replaced by O ꙅO (5:2.2, 13:3.1, 20:3.5, 21:3.6, and 22:4.1 through to 58b:7.4). Logically, the ꙅO coins would be expected to come first and be followed by the O ꙅ O coins, but the die linking between 2:8.1 and 62:8.2 to 70:8.6 indicates that the ꙅO coins are directly linked with ONL, NKЄ, and ИKЄ coins. Hence, the actual chronology of the Lazy S workshop is unknown. Hopefully, more die links will solve this issue in the future.

One solution might be that there were two 'officinae' working at the same time, one producing the ꙅO coins and the other producing the O ꙅO coins. This does seem, however, to be a case of special pleading to solve a problem!

Examination of the die link diagrams (following the figures below) shows several groups of die linked coins and a number of pairs of dies that do not link to any others. Inevitably then, it must be asked whether this really is the product of one mint. It can be said that the fabric of all the coins is very similar and the shape of flans varies from an approximate circle to a quadrilateral with convex edges. The obverses are also sufficiently similar - except for die O1 - for a single mint to be postulated.

The coins without a Lazy S reverse, but which are either die-linked to them via die O1, or are somewhat similar in style, have a number of variations on the obverse and it must be said immediately that examination of the die link diagrams indicates that there are 16 die pairs which do not link to any others. They are O33/R39 (93:10.2), O34/R40 (94:10.3), O35/R41 (95:10.4), O36/R42 (96:10.5), O39/R44 (101:11.2), O40/R45 (102:11.3), O41/R46 (103:11.4), O42/R47 (104:11.5), O43/R48 (105:11.6), O44/R49 (106:12.1), O45/R50 (107:12.2), O49/R55 (127:13.5), O50/R56 (128:13.6), O51/R57 (130:14.1), O?/R58 (131:14.2), and O53/R59 (132:14.3). Whether all of these do belong to the Lazy S workshop is a matter for conjecture, and it is distinctly possible that some of these may not. For the present they are included in the hope that the discovery of more die links in the future will add to the picture.

Figure 12.2 to 13.2 illustrates coins (107-123) which must be related to the OKЄ, HKЄ, etc, coins but which have not yet been connected to them by a die link. On these coins, the *globus cruciger* which is normally held in the right hand of the standing facing figure has been replaced by what appears to be a bishop's crozier. This may indicate that these coins were struck by a local bishop rather than a magistrate or eminent citizen/landowner and Mark Whittow has suggested that officials, such as these, were the *de facto* local government:

> Yet the situation in the 630s was of course rather different. Nearly two decades of Persian rule had accustomed the provincial population of the East to the absence of Roman authority. In fact a generation had grown up without ever knowing Roman rule. Imperial control was still slowly being reconstructed when the Muslim invasions began, and much of Palestine, Syria and Transjordan was effectively self-governing under their bishops and local notables.[10]

Metrology
Diagrams 1 and 2 show that the weights of the majority of the Lazy S and related coins lie between 3 and 4.5g. The Lazy S and related coins belong to Class IV Group b in the paper by Pottier, Schulze and Schulze [11] where it is shown on graph 6 (p.106) that weights for this very large group peak between about 2.5 and 4.0g. The weights of the lazy S workshop, which peak at a slightly higher range of figures, suggest that when the Pottier *et al* Class IV Group b is sub-divided stylistically by

---

[10] M Whittow, *The Making of Orthodox Byzantium, 600 – 1025,* Basingstoke, 1996, p.88.
[11] H Pottier, I Schulze and W Schulze, Pseudo-Byzantine Coinage in Syria under Arab Rule (638-c.670): Classification and dating, **Revue Belge de Numismatique, CLIV** (2008) 87-155.

'workshop', the mean and median weights of the coins may well differ slightly from workshop to workshop. This is hardly surprising when it is believed that the Phase 1 workshops are local and not subject to central control. Until more workshops have been identified and the weight data analysed this remains conjecture. One obvious issue to test this hypothesis will be an analysis of the weights of the so-called LITOIE workshop [12] for which a large number of coins has been identified.

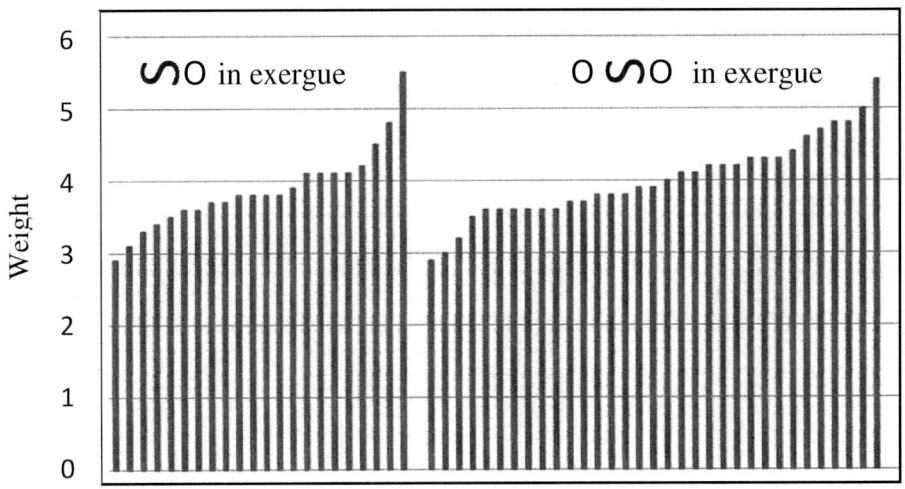

Diagram 1   Coin weights for the Lazy S types

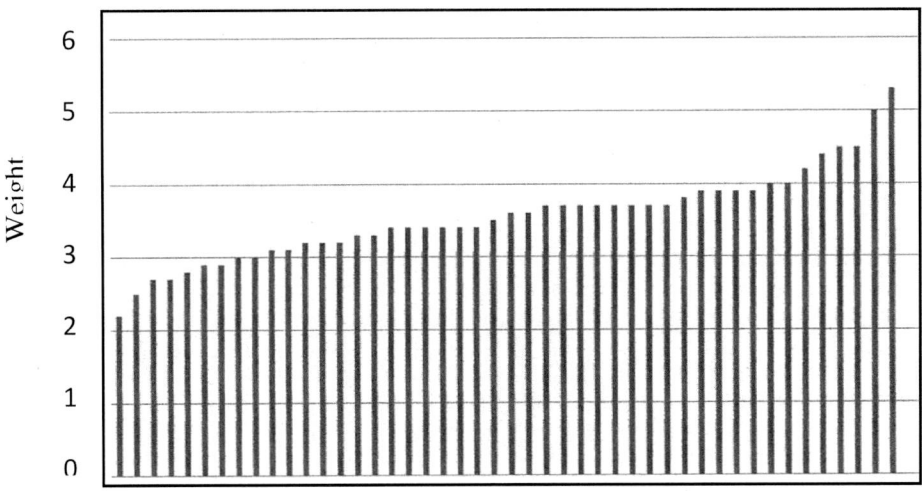

Diagram 2   Coin weights for coins with ONL, ИKϾ, OKϾ, ••••• in the exergue

Die axes
Examination of diagram 3 shows that there is, perhaps, very slight evidence for grouping at 3, 6, 11 and 12 hours. However the data is not sufficient to indicate that the dies were matched with a collar or similar alignment device. The best that can be said is that there is no compelling evidence that one particular alignment was regarded as preferable.

There is one comparable die axis study from a Phase 1 workshop which shows that, in this case, there was a definite alignment of the dies at 6 hours or 12 hours. The numbers at the two positions are

---

[12] A Oddy, The Christian Coinage of Early Muslim Syria, *ARAM* **15** (2003) 185-196.

similar with 26 at 6h and 22 at 12h.[13] A quick survey of 65 early imperial coins of Constans II has indicated that the preferred die axis was 7.00h. The range was between 5.00h and 8.00h, although 4 coins had a die axis of about 1.00h.

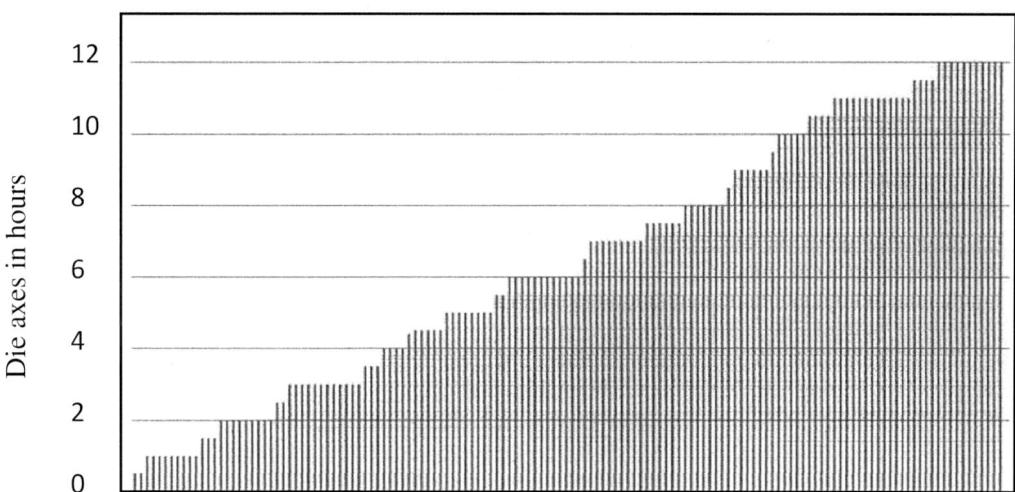

Diagram 3   Die Axes of the Lazy S and related coins

The Place of the Lazy S Workshop in the Phase 1 Byzantine-Arab Coinage
In conclusion it can be said that the Lazy S coins themselves undeniably fit within the body of the Phase1 Arab-Byzantine coinage being derived from the early coin types of Constans II. However, the form of the A, ie Λ, used on 5:2.2, 6:2.3, 7:7.5, 24:4.3, 61:7.6, 62:8.2 and 63:8.3 may indicate a relationship with the *al-wafā lillāh* coinage as suggested by Ingrid Schulze.[14]

Other points of similarity with the *al-wafā lillāh* coinage that were pointed out by Ingrid Schulze are a diagonal line on the robe of the standing figure, clearly seen on 1:2.1 and 49:6.6, dots within the m on the reverse, ie ṁ, as seen on 37:5.3, 43:6.2, 44:6.3 and 52:7.1, and a trefoil at the top of the staff held by the standing figure as seen on 46:6.4 and 48:6.5. These similarities are, however, scattered rather than systematic, so it might mean the same die cutters were involved rather than the same workshop.

Proof of a connection between the *al-wafā lillāh* coinage and the Lazy S workshop must await the discovery of an actual die link.

Finally there is the question of where the Lazy S workshop was located. In 2003, a small group of 'single standing figure' Phase 1 coins were obtained [15] in Ajloun [16] and five of them were Lazy S types: 21:3.6, 29:4.5, 33, 35, 42:6.1. This must be a strong indication that the Lazy S workshop was either at Ajloun or in the vicinity. This is indirectly supported by the presence of five Lazy S coins in the Goussous collection at the Jordan Ahli Bank Numismatic Museum in Amman when it was examined in 2003.[17] However, a dealer on VCoins, whose material is known to come from Jordan,

---

[13] T Goodwin, An Enigmatic Early Arab-Byzantine Coin Type, in **Mélanges de Numismatique et d' Archéologie de Byzance offerts à Henri Pottier** (eds. JM Doyen and C Morrisson), Bruxelles, 2019, 137-150.
[14] I Schulze, The *al-wafā lillāh* Coinage: A Study of Style, in A Oddy (ed), **Coinage and History in the Seventh century Near East 2**, London, 2010, pp. 111-121, esp.p.117-119.
[15] By the author.
[16] Ajloun is a hill town in the north of Jordan, located 76 kilometers (around 47 miles) north west of Amman. It is noted for its impressive ruins of the 12th-century Ajloun Castle.
[17] The Goussous Collection is derived from Jordanian dealers.

has (according to the archive of 'sold' photographs on his website) only handled two Lazy S coins in the past 10 years (or possibly more).[18]

Figure 1 (1) Regular Constans II follis of officina B and year one (= 641/2),   3.69g,   6.30h;
(2) Arab-Byzantine Phase 1 follis with pseudo officina A of 'year 1'   4.63g,   11.00h;
(3) Arab-Byzantine phase 1 follis of the 'lazy S' workshop. Dies O5/R9,   3.62g,   10.00h.

Figure 2[19] (1) 1, O1/R1, 3.65g, 3.00h; (2) 5, O2/R2, 5.48g, 10.00h; (3) 6, O3/R3, 3.81g, 3.00h
(4) 8, O3/R4, 4.05g, 3.30h; (5) 9, O4/R3, 3.73g, 9.30h; (6) 10, O4/R5, 4.12g, 2.00h.

---

[18] See the 'sold' archive of Hussam Zurqieh on his website on VCoins.
[19] The key to the figure captions is:, first the number in the figure, second the number in the corpus in the table below, third the die numbers, for the weight and fifth the die axis.

Figure 3 (1) 13, O5/R6, 3.35g, 7.00h; (2) 14, O5/R7, 4.09g, 2.30h; (3) 17, O5/R8, 2.90g, 11.00h; (4) 18, O5/R9, 3.64g, 10.00h; (5) 20, O6/R10, 4.76g, 5.00h; (6) 21, O6/R11, 3.30g, 11.30h.

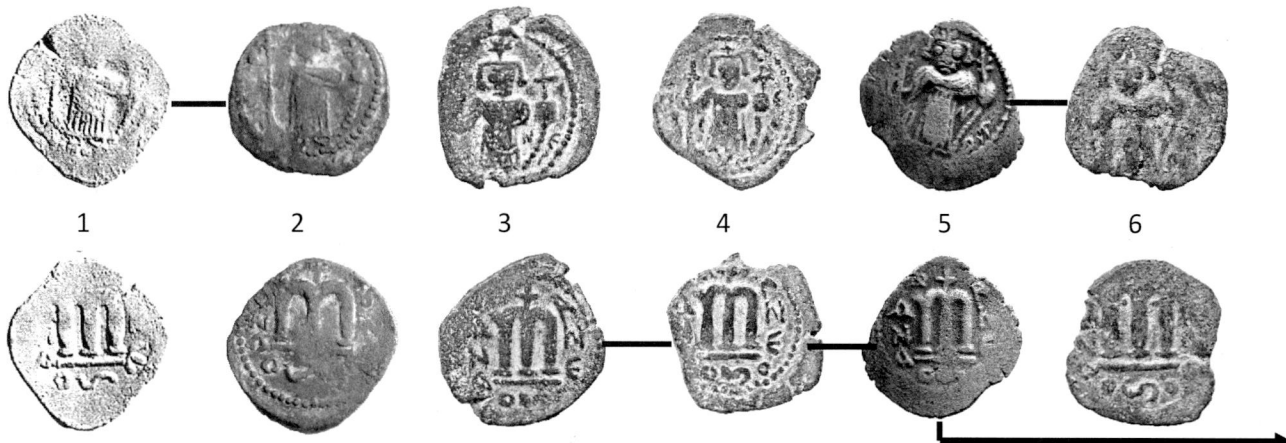

Figure 4 (1) 2, O7/R12, 3.80g, 12.00h; (2) 23, O7/R13, 3.64g, 1.00h; (3) 24, O8/R14, 4.84g, 4.30h; (4) 27, O9/R14, 3.65g, 11.30h; (5) 29, O10/R14, 3.65g, 11.30h; (6) 30, O10/R16, 3.60g, 7.00h.

Figure 5 (1) 31, O11/R14, 4.66g, 10.00h; (2) 34, O11/R15, 12.00h; (3) 37, O12/R16; 12.00h; (4) 38, O13/R17, 3.63g, 2.00h;n (5) 39, O14/R18, 3.68g, 4.00h; (6) 40, O15/R19; 4.12g, 6.00h.

Figure 6 (1) 42, O15/R21, 3.64g, 8.00h; (2) 43, O15/R21, 3.46g, 2.00h; (3) 44, O15/R22, 4.10g, 2.00h; (4) 46, O16/R22, 2.96g, 4.00h; (5) 48, O16/R23, 3.88g, 1.00h; (6) 49, O17/R24, 4.25g, 1.30h.

Figure 7 (1) 52, O17/R25, 5.03g, 7.00h; (2) 53, O18/R26, 3.98g, 9.00h; (3) 57, O19/R27, 3.59g, 12.00h; (4) 58b, O20/R28, 3.89g, 1.00h; (5) 7, O3/R3, 3.83g, 3.00h; (6) 61, O3/R30, 3.55g, 2.00h.

Figure 8 (1) 2, O1/R1, 3.80g, 4.30h; (2) 62, O1/R31, 3.00g, 4.30h; (3) 63, O1/R31, 3.72g, 3.00h; (4) 68, O1/R32, 3.87g, 7.00h; (5) 69, O1/R33, 3.73g, 11.00h; (6) 70, O1/R33, 2.81g, 12.00h.

Figure 9 (1) 72, O30/R34, 3.71g, 3.00h; (2) 75, O31/R34, 3.40g, 2.00h; (3) 78, O32/R35, 3.34g, 4.30h; (4) 79, O32/R35, 3.42g, 9.00h; (5) 83, O32/R36, 2.88g, 6.00h; (6) 89, O32/R37, 3.18g, 1.00h.

Figure 10 (1) 90, O32/R38, 4.52g, 11.00h; (2) 93, O33/R39, 5.28g, 11.00h; (3) 94, O34/R40, 3.30g, 2.00h; (4) 95, O35/R41, 11.00h; (5) 96, O36/R42, 2.70g, 12.30; (6) 97, O37/R43, 3.40g, 1.00h.

Figure 11 (1) 98, O38/R43, 3.23g, 3.30h; (2) 101, O39/R44, 3.60g, 7.30h; (3) 102, O40/R45, 2.70g, 10.30h; (4) 103, O41/R46, 3.04g, 3.30h; (5) 104, O42/R47, 6.00h; (6) 105, O43/R48, 2.86g; 5.30h.

Figure 12   (1)   106,   O44/R49,   2.47g,   8.00h;   (2)   107,   O45/R50,   2.20g,   3.00h; (3)   108,   O46/R51,   3.90g,   1.00h;   (4)   114,   O46/R51,   2.99g,   11.30h;   (5)   116,   O46/R52, 3.19g,   12.00h;   (6)   117,   O46/R52,   3.53g,   2.00h.

Figure 13   (1)   121,   O46/R53,   2.76g,   6.00h;   (2)   123,   O47/R53,   2.80g,   7.30h; (3)   125,   O47?/R54,   4.41g,   6.00h;   (4)   126,   O48/R54,   4.00g,   12.00h;   (5)   127,   O49/R55, 3.82g,   8.00h;   (6)   128,   O50/R56,   3.55g,   3.00h.

Figure 14   (1)   130,   O51/R57,   3.40g,   6.00h;   (2)   131,   O?/R58,   3.09g,   7.00h; (3)   132,   O53/R59,   4.05g,   10.00h;   (4)   134,   O54/R60,   3.14g,   10.30h;   (5)   135,   O54/R61, 2.97g,   3.00h;   (6)   136,   O54/R62,   4.54g,   3.00h.

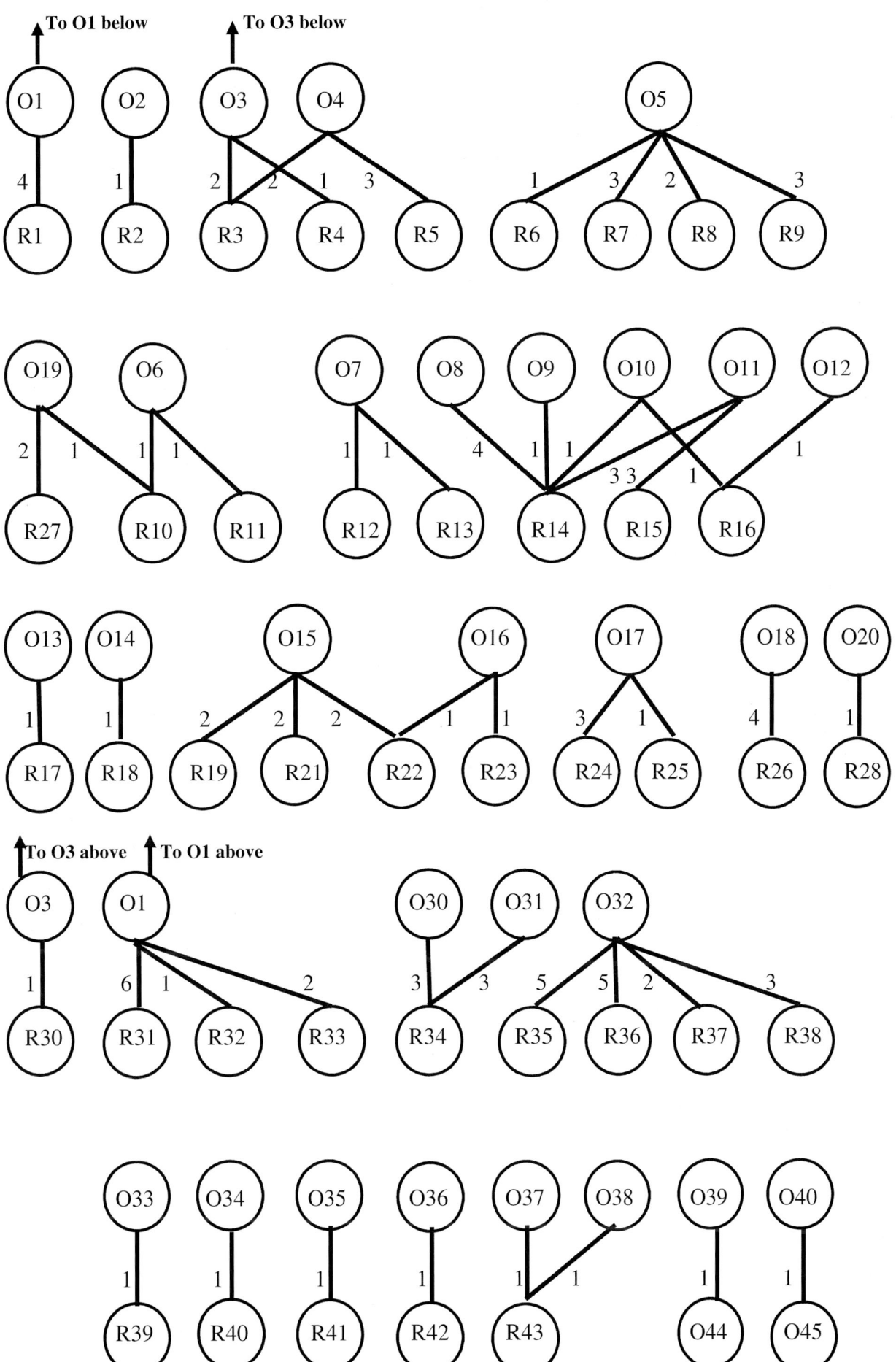

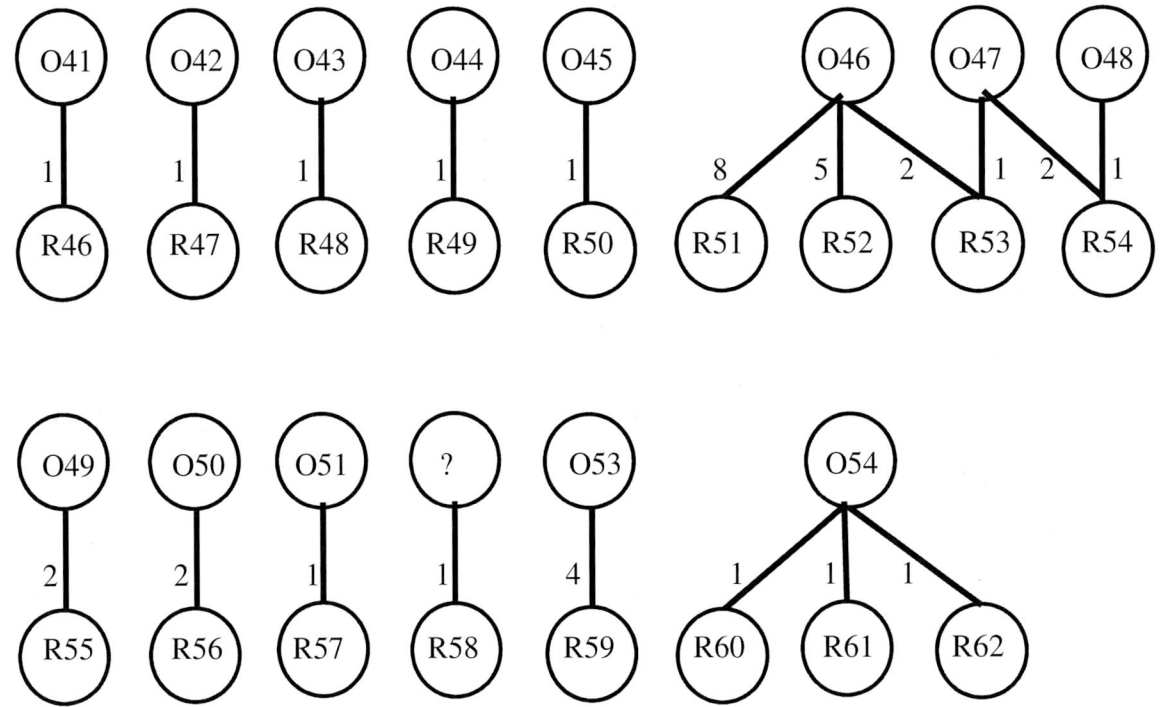

Details of all the Lazy S and related coins are given in the following list:

Coin no.	Fig. no.	Catalogue no.[20]	Ob. die	Rev. die	Weight	Die axis	Location
1	2.1	54	O1	R1	3.65g	3.00h	Goodwin collection
2	8.1	85	O1	R1	3.80g	4.30h	Goussous collection [21]
3		125	O1	R1	3.36g	4.30h	Goodwin collection [22]
4		117	O1	R1	3.50g	5.00h	Ex Karukstis coll [23]
5	2.2	48	O2	R2	5.48g	10.00h	Schulze collection
6	2.3	34	O3	R3	3.81g	3.00h	Schulze collection
7	7.5	128	O3	R3	3.83g	3.00h	ANS [24]
8	2.4	102	O3	R4	4.05g	3.30h	Mansfield collection[25]
9	2.5	12	O4	R3	3.73g	9.30h	Ex Karukstis coll.
9a		33	O4	R3	3.73g	3.00h	Schulze collection
10	2.6	52	O4	R5	4.12g	2.00h	Goodwin collection

---

[20] The 'catalogue number' relates to the number in the author's card file and is not relevant to this paper. It reflects the order which the coins became known and not the logical order presented here.
[21] N G Goussous, *Rare and Inedited Umayyad Copper Coins: the Goussous Collection in the Jordan National Bank Numismatic Museum,* Amman, 2004, p. 261 no. 116
[22] A Oddy, Imitations of Constans II Folles of Class 1 or 4 Struck in Syria, *Numismatic Circular* **103** (4) (1995) 142-3, no.1.
[23] C Karukstis, A Note on the Localization of Pseudo-Byzantine Coinage in Syria, *Numismatic Circular* **108** (4) (2000) p. 158 no. 1.
[24] A Oddy, Imitations of Constans II Folles of Class 1 or 4 Struck in Syria, *Numismatic Circular* **103** (4) (1995) 142-3, no.6.
[25] [S Mansfield], *Early Byzantine Copper Coins: Catalogue of an English Collection*, Manchester, 2016, p. 316 no. 23.72.

11		44	O4	R5	4.49g	4.00h	Schulze collection
12		39	O4	R5	4.07g	9.00h	Schulze collection
13	3.1	22	O5	R6	3.35g	7.00h	Schulze collection
14	3.2	93	O5	R7	4.09g	2.30h	Israel Museum 12768[26]
15		173	O5	R7	3.89g	2.30h	Zurqieh archive [27]
16		126	O5	R7	4.16g	1.00h	Trade in 1989 [28]
17	3.3	83	O5	R8	2.90g	11.00h	Eretz Israel Museum, Tel Aviv, 44643
17a		176	O5	R8	3.18g	4.00h	Israel Antiquities Authority 114142 [29]
18	3.4	147	O5	R9	3.64g	10.00h	Oddy collection
19		50	O5	R9	3.12g	4.00h	Goodwin collection
19a		179	O5	R9	3.69g	10.00h	Israel Antiquities Authority 80442 [30]
20	3.5	53	O6	R10	4.76g	5.00h	Goodwin collection
21	3.6	65	O6	R11	3.30g	11.30h	Oddy collection [31]
22	4.1	127	O7	R12	3.80g	12.00h	Trade in 1989 [32]
23	4.2	87	O7	R13	3.64g	1.00h	Goussous collection
24	4.3	47	O8	R14	4.84g	4.30h	Schulze collection [33]
25		100	O8	R14	4.84g	12.30h	Trade in Dec. 2011
26		66	O8	R14	3.59g	11.00h	Oddy collection
27	4.4	43	O9	R14	4.35g	8.00h	Schulze collection
28		167	O9	R14	4.20g	7.00h	Goussous collection [34]
29	4.5	170	O10	R14	3.65g	11.30h	Oddy collection [35]
30	4.6	27	O10	R16	3.60g	7.00h	Schulze collection [36]

---

[26] A Oddy, Imitations of Constans II Folles of Class I or 4 Struck in Syria, *Numismatic Circular* **103** (4) (1995) 142-3, no.4; R Milstein, A Hoard of Early Arab Figurative Coins, *Israel Numismatic Journal* **10** (1988-9) 3-26, no. 2; T Goodwin and R Gyselen, *Arab Byzantine Coins from the Irbid Hoard,* Royal Numismatic Society Special Publication no. 53, London, 2015, pp. 266-7, no. 2.

[27] See the archive of coins sold by Zurqieh on VCoins on the www.

[28] A Oddy, Imitations of Constans II Folles of Class 1 or 4 Struck in Syria, *Numismatic Circular* **103** (4) (1995) 142-3, no.3.

[29] EXCAVATED AT BET SHE'AN.

[30] EXCAVATED AT NABRATEIN..

[31] From Ajloun in Jordan

[32] A Oddy, Imitations of Constans II Folles of Class 1 or 4 Struck in Syria, *Numismatic Circular* **103** (4) (1995) 142-3, no.5.

[33] I Schulze, The *al-wafā lillāh* Coinage: a Study of Style, in A Oddy (ed) *Coinage and History in the Seventh Century Near East 2,* London, 2010, pp. 111-121, p. 118 no. 6.

[34] N G Goussous, *Rare and Inedited Umayyad Copper Coins: the Goussous Collection in the Jordan National Bank Numismatic Museum,* Amman, 2004, p. 262 no. 118.

[35] From Ajloun in Jordan.

[36] I Schulze, The *al-wafā lillāh* Coinage: a Study of Style, in A Oddy (ed) *Coinage and History in the Seventh Century near East 2,* London, 2010, pp. 111-121, p. 118 no. 7.

31	5.1	46	O11	R14	4.66g	10.00h	Schulze collection
32		109	O11	R14	3.77g	7.00h	Bibliothèque, Nationale, Paris [37]
33		64	O11	R14	3.24g	6.30h	Oddy collection [38]
34	5.2	94	O11	R15		12.00h	eBay 21.11.2016
35		62	O11	R15	2.94g	11.30h	Oddy collection [39]
36		84	O11	R15	3.79g	11.00h	Forschungsstelle für islamische Numismatik, Tübingen, 2007-1-2-5
37	5.3	97	O12	R16		12.00h	Shraga Qedar
38	5.4	29	O13	R17	3.63g	2.00h	Schulze collection
39	5.5	55	O14	R18	3.68g	4.00h	Goodwin collection
40	5.6	110	O15	R19	4.12g	6.00h	Bibliothèque, Nationale, Paris [40]
41		42	O15	R19	4.31g	7.00h	Schulze collection
42	6.1	67	O15	R21	3.64g	8.00h	Oddy collection [41]
43	6.2	130	O15	R21	3.46g	2.00h	Dumbarton Oaks collection [42]
44	6.3	49	O15	R22	4.10g	2.00h	Goodwin collection
45		86	O15	R22	3.80g	1.00h	Goussous collection [43]
46	6.4	131	O16	R22	2.96g	4.00h	Dumbarton Oaks collection [44]
46a		112	O16	?	4.21g	8.30h	Trade [45]
47		28	O16	?	3.60g	11.00h	Schulze collection
48	6.5	35	O16	R23	3.88g	1.00h	Schulze collection
49	6.6	40	O17	R24	4.25g	1.30h	Schulze collection
50		41	O17	R24	4.31g	1.30h	Schulze collection
51		98	O17	R24	5.40g	11.00h	Trade in June 2011
52	7.1	51	O17	R25	5.03g	7.00h	Goodwin collection [46]
53	7.2	99	O18	R26	3.98g	9.00h	Trade in 2015 [47]

---

[37] T Goodwin and R Gyselen, *Arab Byzantine Coins from the Irbid Hoard,* Royal Numismatic Society Special Publication no. 53, London, 2015, pp. 266-7, no. 11.
[38] From Ajloun in Jordan.
[39] From Ajloun in Jordan.
[40] T Goodwin and R Gyselen, *Arab Byzantine Coins from the Irbid Hoard,* Royal Numismatic Society Special Publication no. 53, London, 2015, no. 12.
[41] From Ajloun in Jordan.
[42] C Foss, *Arab-Byzantine Coins*, Dumbarton Oaks Byzantine Collection 12, Washington DC, 2008, p. 129 no. 28.
[43] N G Goussous, *Rare and Inedited Umayyad Copper Coins: the Goussous Collection in the Jordan National Bank Numismatic Museum,* Amman, 2004, p. 262 no. 117.
[44] C Foss, *Arab-Byzantine Coins*, Dumbarton Oaks Byzantine Collection 12, Washington DC, 2008, p. 129 no. 27; C Foss, Anomalous Arab-Byzantine Coins: Some Problems and Suggestions, *ONS Newsletter* no. 166 (winter 2001) no.5.
[45] Zurqieh on VCoins 22.6.2019.
[46] A Oddy, Imitations of Constans II Folles of Class 1 or 4 Struck in Syria, *Numismatic Circular* **103** (4) (1995) 142-3, no.7.
[47] See the archive of coins sold by Zurqieh on VCoins on the www.

54		71	O18	R26	4.56g	5.30h	Trade [48]
55		88	O18	R26		3.00h	Goussous collection
56		95	O18	R26	3.91g	9.00h	Trade in 2016 [49]
57	7.3	26	O19	R27	3.59g	12.00h	Schulze collection
58		175	O19	R27	4.19g	12.00h	Phillips collection
58a		146	O19	R10	3.71g	2.00h	Israel Antiquities Authority 10972 [50]
58b	7.4	177	O20	R28	3.89g	1.00h	Israel Antiquities Authority 114125 [51]
61	7.6	24	O3	R30	3.55g	2.00h	Schulze collection [52]
62	8.2	144	O1	R31	3.00g	4.30h	Goussous collection [53]
63	8.3	119	O1	R31	3.72g	3.00h	Ex Karukstis coll. [54]
64		153	O1	R31	3.39g	6.00h	Ex Karukstis coll. [55]
65		107	O1	R31	3.82g	6.00h	Bibliothèque, Nationale, Paris [56]
66		72	O1	R31	3.97g	12.00h	Oddy collection
67		140	O1	R31	4.41g	7.00h	Oddy collection
68	8.4	73	O1	R32	3.87g	7.00h	Oddy collection [57]
69	8.5	118	O1	R33	3.73g	11.00h	Ex Karukstis coll. [58]
70	8.6	15	O1	R33	2.81g	12.00h	Schulze collection
71		155	O1	?		7.30h	Unknown [59]
72	9.1	116	O30	R34	3.71g	3.00h	Ex Karukstis coll. [60]
73		111	O30	R34	4.99g	10.00h	Bibliothèque, Nationale, Paris [61]

---

[48] See the archive of coins sold by Zurqieh on VCoins on the www.
[49] See the archive of coins sold by Zurqieh on VCoins on the www.
[50] EXCAVATED AT REHOV by Fanny Vitto. To be published by Nitzan Amitai-Preiss.
[51] EXCAVATED AT BET SHE'AN.
[52] I Schulze, The *al-wafā lillāh* Coinage: a Study of Style, in A Oddy (ed) *Coinage and History in the Seventh Century Near East 2,* London, 2010, pp. 111-121, p. 118 no. 4.
[53] N G Goussous, H A Alzoud and A M Naghawy, *Inedited and Rare Islamic Coins*, Jordan Ahli Bank Numismatic Museum, Amman, 2014, p.2 no.4.
[54] C P Karukstis, A Note on the Localization of Pseudo-Byzantine Coinage in Syria, *Numismatic Circular* **CVIII** (4) (August 2000) 158, no. 3; S Album rare coins auction 19 (15 May 2014) lot 179.
[55] S Album rare coins auction 19 (15 May 2014) lot 183.
[56] T Goodwin and R Gyselen, *Arab Byzantine Coins from the Irbid Hoard,* Royal Numismatic Society Special Publication no. 53, London, 2015, no. 16.
[57] C Foss, *Arab-Byzantine Coins*, Dumbarton Oaks Byzantine Collection 12, Washington DC, 2008, p. 32 (this coin).
[58] C P Karukstis, A Note on the Localization of Pseudo-Byzantine Coinage in Syria, *Numismatic Circular* **CVIII** (4) (August 2000) 158, no. 2; S Album rare coins auction 19 (15 May 2014) lot 180.
[59] A S Kirkbride, Coins of the Byzantine-Arab Transition period, *Quarterly of the Department of Antiquities of Palestine* **13** (1947-8) 59-63 no.36.
[60] C P Karukstis, A Note on the Localization of Pseudo-Byzantine Coinage in Syria, *Numismatic Circular* **CVIII** (4) (August 2000) 158, no. 6.
[61] T Goodwin and R Gyselen, *Arab Byzantine Coins from the Irbid Hoard,* Royal Numismatic Society Special Publication no. 53, London, 2015, no. 15.

74		74	O30	R34	3.66g	12.00h	Oddy collection
75	9.2	122	O31	R34	3.40g	2.00h	Goussous collection [62]
76		23	O31	R34	3.51g	5.00h	Schulze collection
77		32	O31	R34	3.73g	1.00h	Schulze collection
78	9.3	80	O32	R35	3.34g	4.30h	Oddy collection
79	9.4	113	O32	R35	3.42g	9.00h	Ex Karukstis coll [63]
80		76	O32	R35	3.43g	8.00h	Oddy collection
81		154	O32	R35	3.87g	11.00h	Unknown [64]
82		78	O32	R35	3.36g	4.30h	Oddy collection
83	9.5	92	O32	R36	2.88g	6.00h	Oddy collection
84		37	O32	R36	3.95g	12.00h	Schulze collection
85		20	O32	R36	3.23g	2.00h	Schulze collection
86		56	O32	R36	3.90g	11.00h	Goodwin collection
87		60	O32	R36	3.67g	11.00h	Goodwin collection
88		81	O32	R37	4.49g	6.00h	Ex Slocum Collection
89	9.6	90	O32	R37	3.18g	1.00h	Trade [65]
90	10.1	61	O32	R38	4.52g	11.00h	Goodwin collection
91		115	O32	R38	3.16g	7.30h	Ex Karukstis coll [66]
92		152	O32	R38		10.30h	Goussous collection
93	10.2	151	O33	R39	5.28g	11.00h	Goussous collection
94	10.3	21	O34	R40	3.30g	2.00h	Schulze collection
95	10.4	145	O35	R41		11.00h	Goussous collection
96	10.5	165	O36	R42	2.70g	12.30h	Goussous collection [67]
97	10.6	159	O37	R43	3.40g	1.00h	Goussous collection [68]
98	11.1	168	O38	R43	3.23g	3.30h	Oddy collection
99		160	?	R43	4.20g	7.30h	Goussous collection [69]

---

[62] N G Goussous, *Rare and Inedited Umayyad Copper Coins: The Goussous Collection in the Jordan National Bank Numismatic Museum*, Amman, 2004, p. 260 no. 112.
[63] C Karukstis, A Note on the Localization of Pseudo-Byzantine Coinage in Syria, *Numismatic Circular* **CVIII** (4) (August 2000) 158, no.4; Album 19 (15 May 2014) lot 182.
[64] C Morrisson, Les Monnaies, pp.267-287, in J P Sodini et al. Déhès (Syrie du Nord) Campagnes 1976-1978, *Syria* 57 (1980) 1-310, no. 55, **EXCAVATED AT DÉHÈS IN NORTHERN SYRIA.**
[65] Heritage Auction 3032 (10th-12th April 2014) lot 24055.
[66] C Karukstis, A Note on the Localization of Pseudo-Byzantine Coinage in Syria, *Numismatic Circular* **CVIII** (4) (August 2000) 158, no.5; Album 19 (15 May 2014) lot 188.
[67] N G Goussous, *Rare and Inedited Umayyad Copper Coins: The Goussous Collection in the Jordan National Bank Numismatic Museum*, Amman, 2004, p. 260 no. 342.
[68] N G Goussous, *Rare and Inedited Umayyad Copper Coins: The Goussous Collection in the Jordan National Bank Numismatic Museum*, Amman, 2004, p. 260 no. 58.
[69] N G Goussous, *Rare and Inedited Umayyad Copper Coins: The Goussous Collection in the Jordan National Bank Numismatic Museum*, Amman, 2004, p. 260 no. 59.

100		30	?	R43	3.66g	5.00h	Schulze collection
100a		137		R43	3.07g	5.00h	Trade [70]
100b		68	?	R43	3.70g	5.00h	Trade [71]
101	11.2	161	O39	R44	3.60g	7.30h	Goussous collection [72]
102	11.3	121	O40	R45	2.70g	10.30h	Goussous collection [73]
103	11.4	169	O41	R46	3.04g	3.30h	Oddy collection
104	11.5	89	O42	R47		6.00h	Goussous collection
105	11.6	132	O43	R48	2.86g	5.30h	Oddy collection
106	12.1	13	O44	R49	2.47g	8.00h	Schulze collection
107	12.2	157	O45	R50	2.20g	3.00h	Goussous collection [74]
108	12.3	143	O46	R51	3.90g	1.00h	Goussous collection
109		91	O46	R51	3.09g	8.00h	Trade [75]
110		114	O46	R51	2.66g	7.30h	Israel Antiquities Authority [76]
111		124	O46	R51	3.52g	6.00h	British Museum [77]
112		136	O46	R51	3.02g	3.00h	Oddy collection
113		59	O46	R51	2.98g	5.00h	Goodwin collection
114	12.4	134	O46	R51	2.99g	11.30h	Trade [78]
115		135	O46	R51	3.01g	10.30h	Trade [79]
116	12.5	19	O46	R52	3.19g	12.00h	Schulze collection
117	12.6	101	O46	R52	3.53g	2.00h	Mansfield collection [80]
118		103	O46	R52	3.49g	6.00h	Israel Antiquities Authority [81]
119		17	O46	R52	2.99g	9.00h	Schulze collection
120		18	O46	R52	3.08g	3.00h	Schulze collection

---

[70] Zurqieh on VCoins on 22.6.2019.
[71] See the archive of coins sold by Zurqieh on VCoins on the www.
[72] N G Goussous, *Rare and Inedited Umayyad Copper Coins: The Goussous Collection in the Jordan National Bank Numismatic Museum*, Amman, 2004, p. 260 no. 60.
[73] N G Goussous, *Rare and Inedited Umayyad Copper Coins: The Goussous Collection in the Jordan National Bank Numismatic Museum*, Amman, 2004, p. 260 no. 62.
[74] N G Goussous, H A Alzoud nd A M Naghawy, *Inedited and Rare Islamic Coins*, Jordan Ahli bank Numismatic Museum, Amman, 2014, p.2 no.6.
[75] Zurqieh on VCoins February 2016; Vaughn on VCoins 17th January 2019.
[76] C Foss, Anomalous Arab-Byzantine Coins: Some Problems and Suggestions, *ONS Newsletter* **no.166** (Winter 2001) no. 8a; **EXCAVATED IN JERUSALEM.**
[77] J Walker, *A Catalogue of the Arab Byzantine and Post-Reform Umaiyad Coins*, British Museum, London, 1956, p.52 no.139 and pl.IX
[78] See the archive of coins sold by Zurqieh on VCoins on the www.
[79] See the archive of coins sold by Zurqieh on VCoins on the www.
[80] [S Mansfield] *Early Byzantine Copper Coins: Catalogue of an English Collection*, Manchester, 2016, p.320 no.24.1
[81] C Foss, *Arab-Byzantine Coins*, Dumbarton Oaks Byzantine collection 12, Washington DC, 2008, p.33; C Foss, Anomalous Arab-Byzantine Coins: Some Problems and Suggestions, *ONS Newsletter* **no.166** (Winter 2001) no. 8b; **EXCAVATED IN JERUSALEM.**

121	13.1	14	O46	R53	2.76g	6.00h	Schulze collection
122		38	O46	R53	3.97g	11.00h	Schulze collection
123	13.2	120	O47	R53	2.80g	7.30h	Goussous collection [82]
124		36	O47	R54	3.95g	9.00	Schulze collection
125	13.3	106	O47	R54	4.41g	6.00h	Bibliothèque, Nationale, Paris [83]
125a		148	O?	R54	3.50g	4.30h	Ramadan Collection [84]
126	13.4	108	O48	R54	4.00g	12.00h	Bibliothèque, Nationale, Paris [85]
127	13.5	150	O49	R55	3.82g	8.00h	Trade [86]
127a		104	O49	R55	3.15g	8.00h	Oddy collection
128	13.6	25	O50	R56	3.55g	3.00h	Schulze collection
129		31	O50?	R56	3.71g	5.00h	Schulze collection
130	14.1	139	O51	R57	3.40g	6.00h	Oddy collection
131	14.2	63	O?	R58	3.09g	7.00h	Trade [87]
132	14.3	105	O53	R59	4.05g	10.00h	Dumbarton Oaks collection [88]
132a		129	O53	R59		1.30h	Trade [89]
132b		11	O53	R59	3.52g	1.00h	Trade [90]
133		75	O53	R59	3.40g	6.00h	Oddy collection
134	14.4	138	O54	R60	3.14g	10.30h	Trade [91]
135	14.5	16	O54	R61	2.97g	3.00h	Schulze collection
136	14.6	45	O54	R62	4.54g	3.00h	Schulze collection

---

[82] N G Goussous, *Rare and Inedited Umayyad Copper Coins: The Goussous Collection in the Jordan National Bank Numismatic Museum*, Amman, 2004, p. 243 no. 61.
[83] T Goodwin and R Gyselen, *Arab Byzantine Coins from the Irbid Hoard,* Royal Numismatic Society Special Publication no. 53, London, 2015, no. 17.
[84] T Ramadan, An Arab-Byzantine Standing Imperial Figure Coin from Jund al-Urdun inscribed with the word "fils", *ONS Journal* no. 202 (Winter 2010) 46-47.
[85] T Goodwin and R Gyselen, *Arab Byzantine Coins from the Irbid Hoard,* Royal Numismatic Society Special Publication no. 53, London, 2015, no. 18. This reverse die (R54) has an Arabic word in the exergue which has been interpreted by Tareq Ramadan (An Arab-Byzantine Standing Imperial Figure Coin from Jund al-Urdun inscribed with the word "fils", *ONS Journal* no. 202 (Winter 2010) 46-47) to read *fils*. Goodwin and Gyselen, however, wonder whether the inscription may be a blundered reading of *dimashq* (ie the mint name of Damascus).
[86] Album 22 May 2015 lot 94
[87] See the archive of coins sold by Zurqieh on VCoins on the www.
[88] C Foss, *Arab-Byzantine coins*, Dumbarton Oaks Byzantine Collection 12, Washington DC, 2008, p.128, no.29; C Foss, Anomalous Arab-Byzantine Coins: Some Problems and Suggestions, *ONS Newsletter* no.166 (Winter 2001) no.7a.
[89] Vaughn on VCoins on 22.6.2019.
[90] Zurqieh on VCoins on 22.6.2019.
[91] See the archive of coins sold by Zurqieh on VCoins on the www.

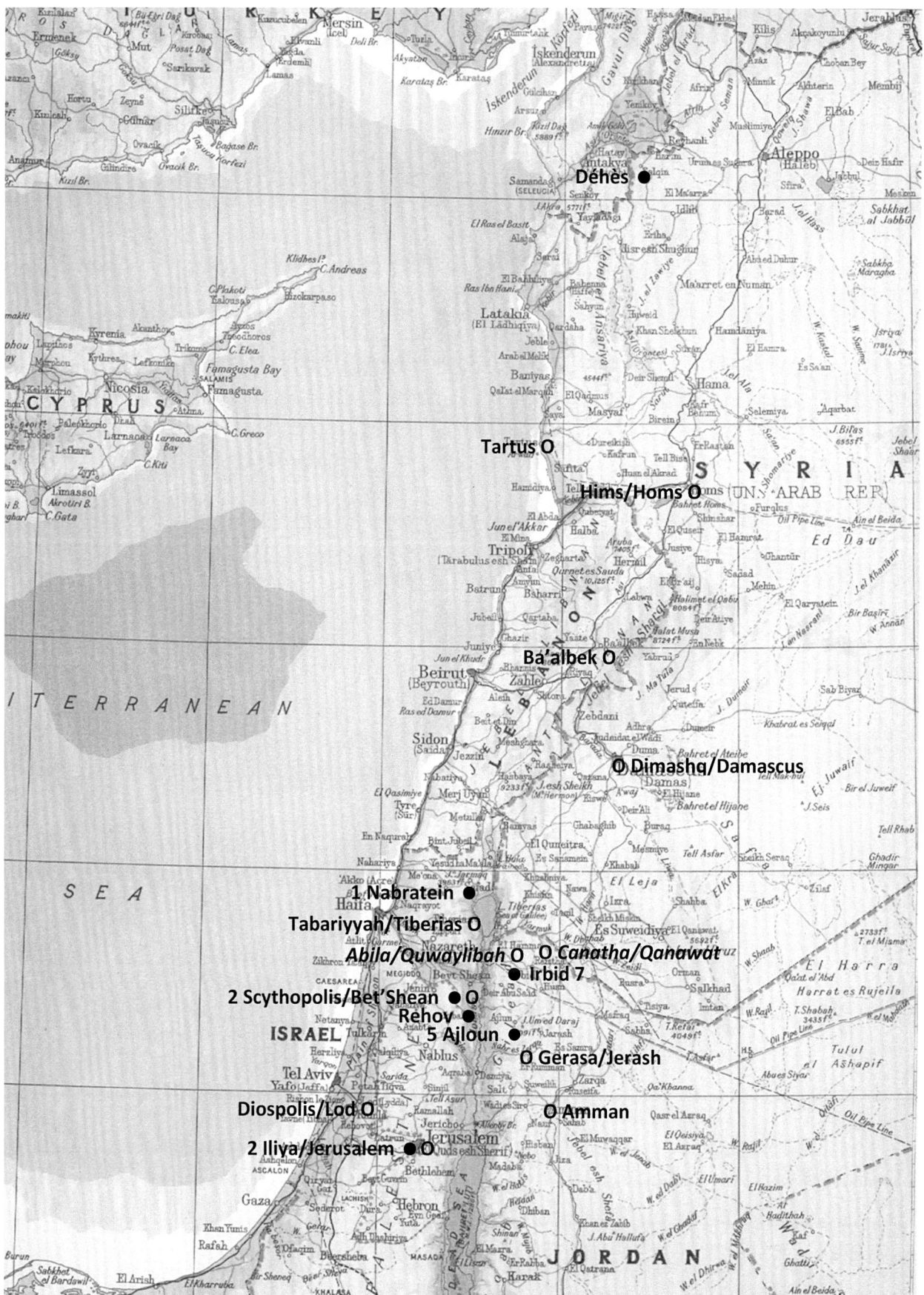

Key: ● indicates **find-spots of Lazy S coins**   O indicates main Phase 2 mints
The Phase 2 mints written in itallics (Abila and Canatha) have been identified from interpretations of the coin legends. Acceptance of these is not universal.

Acknowledgements

It is a great pleasure to thank numerous museum curators and colleagues from the Seventh Century Syria Numismatic Round Table who have provided photographs and discussed Arab Byzantine numismatics over a large number of years. Those to whom I am particularly indebted are Nitzan Amitai-Preiss, Tony Goodwin, Steve Mansfield, Marcus Phillips, Ingrid Schulze, Wolfgang Schulze, Luke Treadwell and Susan Tyler-Smith. Nayef Goussous has allowed me to record his collection during visits to Amman and I have benefited from the photographs of the comprehensive collection put together by Charlie Karukstis and subsequently sold by Steve Album (auction 19, 15th -17th May 2014). Coin no. 58a was excavated by Fanny Vitto, by whose kind permission, and that of Nizan Amitai-Preiss, it is listed here. The IAA coins were photographed by Clara Amit, to whom the author is especially grateful.

Postscript

When this paper had gone for editing, a reference was found to four more Lazy S coins from excavations.[92] Provenanced coins are so rare that it was important to include them. With the kind cooperation of the editor, this has been done without major disruption to the edited text.

---

[92] G Bijovsky, Arab-Byzantine Coins from Excavations in Israel – an Update, in A Oddy, I Schulze and W Schulze (eds.), *Coinage and History in the Seventh Century near East 4*, London, 2015, 95-114.

A very peculiar group of early Pseudo-Byzantine coins

Tony Goodwin[1]

This short tailpiece to Andrew Oddy's articles describes another die-linked group of Pseudo-Byzantine coins. This small group is unusual in a number of respects and it is probably fair to say that it is the strangest group that I have ever encountered in 30 years of studying the series. But before commencing the description it might be useful to correct a rather misleading impression that we as authors may have given in our articles about Pseudo-Byzantine coins. We have naturally concentrated on coins which have unusual images or a distinctive style or some other feature that marks them out as interesting. This has been particularly the case with publications of die-linked groups where distinctive features help greatly in picking out die-links among a mass of coins or coin images. We have therefore probably given many readers the impression that these unusual coins are representative of the series as a whole, but this is definitely not the case. At a rough guess around 80 - 90% of surviving Pseudo-Byzantine coins are nondescript copies of Constans II folles with a standing emperor on the obverse and a cursive m on the reverse (Type E). In the interests of balance what might be described as a 'typical' specimen is therefore shown in Fig. 1 below.

Figure 1. The most common type of Syrian Pseudo-Byzantine coin 3.12g 10h (1.5x actual size).

The die-linked group

Returning now to the main subject, I first came across an example of the group in a dealer's rummage tray over 25 years ago (Cat. 1) and was immediately struck by the crude, but imaginative rendering of the unusual standing figure on the obverse. The reverse also seemed to be rather unusual with an officina symbol – o – a letter that I had never previously seen used for this purpose. It was about 10 years before I found another die-linked example with a different reverse and another 5 years before I came across a third coin struck from different dies, but clearly in the same peculiar style. Since then I have located 6 more examples and so now the group comprises 9 coins struck from 3 different obverse and 4 reverse dies. All these are die-linked and all 7 known die combinations are illustrated in the catalogue at the end of this article.[2] The die-links are shown in Figure 2 below.

---

[1] Tony Goodwin is an independent scholar a.goodwin2@btopenworld.com
[2] The two other coins are die duplicates of Cat. 1 (5.16g 5h) and Cat. 2 (4.62g 7h), both in private collections.

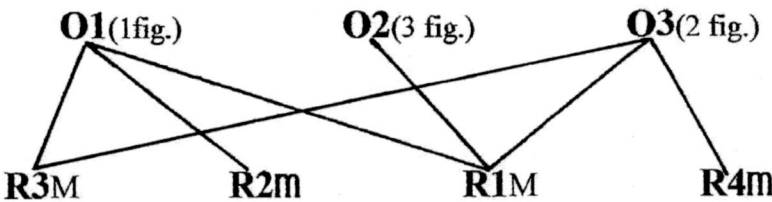

Figure 2. Die-links within the group

Judging by the small number of these coins that I managed to find in a 25 year period,[3] the output of the 'mint' was almost certainly small. Nevertheless it used three completely different types of obverse and three different types of reverse. Despite the crude die engraving the obverse images are quite imaginative and must have been engraved without any Byzantine prototype in front of the die engraver. However it is clear that all three derive from images of Heraclius, die O2 from Class 3 or 4 and O3 from Class 5. O1 shows a single standing figure, but the hand-on-hip and short flared tunic show that it must derive ultimately from the figure of Heraclius in military dress on his Class 5 folles. Two of the reverse dies have a capital **M** again probably deriving from folles of Heraclius, but one has a Constantinople mint mark (R1) and the other a blundered Cyprus mint mark (R3). The two other reverse dies (R2 and R4) with a cursive **m** both look like a confused recollection of more than one reverse type of Constans II. This variety of obverse and reverse types is highly unusual and, as far as I know, unprecedented for such a small mint.

The flan shapes are also distinctive, being roughly oval with some straight cut edges. This is typical of the common three-figure (Type B) Pseudo-Byzantine coins such as the example shown in Fig. 3. These coins often show traces of an undertype, usually a clipped follis of Phocas or Heraclius, but none of our die-linked group shows any such traces. This suggests that they were struck on new oval flans which had been clipped in order to appear similar to the Type B coins which were in general circulation at the time.

Figure 3. A typical Type B Pseudo-Byzantine coin 3.56g 6h (1.5x actual size).

With such a small sample there is little that can be reliably concluded about the metrology of the group, but the median weight of 4.715g is quite heavy for a Pseudo-Byzantine coin and close to the average of about 4.8g for the Type B coins.

---

[3] My experience in researching other distinctive groups of Arab-Byzantine coins is that, once one starts searching, numbers of new examples are found reasonably quickly.

Two remarkable obverse images

Figure 4: obverse dies O1 and O3 (Cats. 2 and 4)

The three obverse dies all look like the work of the same die engraver, who seems to have made up in imagination what he lacked in technical skill. O1 shows a standing figure wearing a flared tunic and perhaps a scabbard (see Cat. 1). One hand rests on his hip and the other holds a long cross. However, the strangest element of the design is the depiction of the head with the hair or headdress shown as two large diagonal elements with spikes on top. This weird arrangement cannot just have been the result of incompetence; it must have had some meaning for the die engraver, but I can make no sensible suggestion as to what that meaning was. Die O2 is relatively unremarkable and at first sight O3 looks like a typical Type B three-figure obverse, but closer examination reveals that, instead of standing facing, the left hand figure is walking towards the other two offering them a cross. He also appears to be wearing a chlamys which is decorated with spikes. Did the die engraver intend some specific Christian message here? Again I cannot suggest anything that would be more than wild speculation.

Where and when

There are clear similarities between our small group and the much larger group of Type B coins, both in terms of flan shape and average weight. Furthermore one die pair (Cat. 4) is by definition a Type B coin and die R3 (Cat. 3) is a typical Type B reverse. It therefore seems a reasonable provisional assumption that the group is roughly contemporary with the Type B coins, i.e. relatively early in the Pseudo-Byzantine series (late 640s /early 650s?), and from roughly the same area i.e. northern Syria.[4] None of the group has a known provenance but at least two have been offered by dealers alongside coins of Syrian/Lebanese origin, which provides some slight support for the Syrian origin.[5]

---

[4] For a discussion of the dating of Type B coins (their Class 1) see H. Pottier, I. Schulze and W. Schulze, 'Pseudo-Byzantine coinage in Syria (638–c.670). Classification and dating', ***Revue Belge de Numismatique*** 154, 2010, pp. 87-155. They record an average weight of 4.83g and demonstrate that later Pseudo-Byzantine coins were generally lighter.

[5] Acknowledgements: my thanks to Hugh Williams and Piotr Tomczyk for bringing three of these interesting coins to my attention.

Catalogue (all coins shown 1.5x actual size)

1. O1/R1. 4.23g 6h
Obv: Standing figure holding long cross, detatched gl. cr. to r.
Rev: M with cross above, ANNO - Ч (retrograde) + either side, o officina, CON in exergue.(Author's collection)

2. O1/R2. 6.28g
Obv: as last.
Rev: m with cross above, AИИO - XIIIO either side, KOC retrograde in exergue. (Leu Numismatik web auction 24.2.19 lot 1650)

3. O1/R3 4.65g 5h
Obv: as last, double struck.
Rev: M with cross above, AИИ. - III III either side, Γ officina, KVII in exergue. (Author's collection)

4. O2/R1 4.10g 12h
Obv: three standing figures holding crosses.
Rev: M with cross above, ANNO - Ч (retrograde) + either side, o officina, CON in exergue.(Author's collection)

5. O3/R1 weight unknown 12h
Obv: two standing figures holding long crosses.
Rev: as last. (Trade 2018)

6. O3/R4 4.78g 12h
Obv: as last.
Rev: m with ANNO – XIII either side, other details unclear.
(Williams collection)

7. O3/R3 4.81g 7h
Obv: as last.
Rev: as Cat. 3 above.
(Leu Numismatik forthcoming)

Greek Monograms and Countermarks in Seventh-Century Syria

David Woods[1]

The purpose of this paper is to re-examine the Greek countermarks stamped upon Byzantine and Arab-Byzantine copper coins circulating in the greater Syrian region during the period c.635-80, that is, during the period from immediately before the Islamic conquest of this region following the decisive Muslim victory at the battle of Gabatha (sometimes called the battle of Yarmuk also) in 638 until shortly after the beginning of the so-called Imperial Image phase of Arab-Byzantine coinage probably dateable to the 670s.[2] The Byzantine authorities used a number of different monograms as countermarks on the copper coins circulating in greater Syria during the initial stages of the Muslim invasion in the mid-630s, while local Syrian authorities used a number of different monograms, groups of Greek letters, or insect or animal forms even, to countermark the Byzantine and Arab-Byzantine coins circulating in their districts probably during the period c.660-80.[3] This paper will proceed in chronological order, dealing with the countermarks used by the Byzantine authorities during the mid-630s before proceeding next to examine those used by local Syrian authorities during the period c.660-80. However, in order to understand the significance of the monograms that Byzantine authorities used to countermark Byzantine coins circulating in the greater Syrian region during the mid-630s, one must first re-examine the more general use of monograms by the emperor Heraclius (610-41) upon his coinage.

The Evolution of the Imperial Monogram under the Emperor Heraclius

The imperial monogram was not a standard feature of any denomination coin by the time that Heraclius came to the throne in 610, but it had made sporadic appearances upon various denomination copper coins since the time of the emperor Theodosius II (408-50).[4] Heraclius began depicting his monogram upon the coinage when he introduced a new type of follis in his regnal year 15 (624/25). This type, which was last struck in his regnal year 19 (628/29), depicted his monogram to the left of the denomination M on the reverse of the follis. In fact, three different forms of the imperial monogram were actually used. The most common form used by the mints at both

---

[1] David Woods is the Head of the Department of Classics, University College Cork, Ireland: d.woods@ucc.ie.
[2] On the date and location of the battle of Gabatha, see D. Woods, 'Jews, Rats, and the Battle of Yarmuk', in A.S. Lewin and P. Pellegrini (eds.), *The Late Roman Army in the Near East from Diocletian to the Arab Conquest*, BAR International Series 1717 (Oxford, 2007), pp. 367-76.
[3] The standard treatment of the Byzantine countermarks from before the Muslim invasion remains W. Schulze, 'Countermarks from before the Arab Conquest', in W. Schulze and T. Goodwin, *Countermarking in Seventh Century Syria*, Supplement to ONS Newsletter 183 (2005), pp. 23-40. The standard treatment of the Greek countermarks used in the same region subsequently remains T. Goodwin, 'Countermarks from after the Arab Conquest', pp. 41-56, in the same volume.
[4] For a detailed discussion of the monograms forming the main device on the reverse of the copper coinage of the 5th century, see D. Woods, 'A Misunderstood Monogram: Ricimer or Severus?', *Hermathena* 172 (2002), pp. 5-21. For a broader survey of the use of imperial and royal monograms, see I. Garipzanov, 'Monograms as Graphic Signs of Authority on Early Medieval Coins (from the mid-Fifth to Seventh Centuries', in I. Garipzanov, C. Goodson, and H. Maguire (eds.), *Graphic Signs of Identity, Faith, and Power in Late Antiquity and the Early Middle Ages*, Cursor Mundi 27 (Turnhout, 2017), pp. 325-49.

Constantinople (*MIB* 162) and Nicomedia (*MIB* 177), as well as on a parallel type from Cyprus (*MIB* 198), was a bar monogram that has usually been interpreted as containing just two letters, the lower-case Latin h and the capital Latin R in abbreviation of the Latin name Heraclius (Fig. 1a).[5] A second form of monogram used by the mints at both Constantinople and Cyzicus (*MIB* 186), where it appears to have been the only form of monogram used, is very similar to the first except that it replaces the apparent capital Latin R with a letter P, either a Latin P or a Greek rho, and intrudes a letter K between the P and the letter h beneath it (Fig. 1b).[6] Since neither the Latin letter P nor the Latin letter K occur in the Latin name Heraclius, it is clear that this monogram must abbreviate the Greek form of his name, Ἡράκλειος (ΗΡΑΚΛΕΙΟΣ). To be clear, this means that the monogram contains a lower-case Greek letter eta rather than a lower-case Latin h, a Greek rho rather than a Latin P, and a Greek kappa. This suggests in turn that the first monogram probably also abbreviates Heraclius' name in Greek rather than in Latin. In fact, it contains the exact same three Greek letters – rho, kappa, and eta – with the difference that the kappa is better concealed within the Greek rho. To be more precise, the vertical or back of the rho also serves as the back of the kappa, while the lower part of the curve of the rho also conceals the upper frontal bar of the letter kappa as it kicks upwards. The only part of the kappa not concealed within the rho is the lower frontal bar as it kicks downwards. Finally, the third form of the monogram, which saw sporadic use at Constantinople alone, was rather different in that it was actually a cross monogram rather than a bar monogram (Fig. 1c).[7] A horizontal bar bisects the main vertical so that the monogram resembles the shape of a cross, and a letter C is added at the right-hand end of this bar. Strictly speaking, this could be either the Latin letter C or a Greek lunate sigma. However, given that the evidence of the second form of monogram in particular proves that the letter h is actually a Greek eta and the letter P a Greek rho, it is clear that the letter C here is best interpreted as a Greek form also, so as a Greek lunate sigma.

(a)   (b)   (c)

Fig. 1: (a) follis of Heraclius (MIB 162), Constantinople (25mm, 6.02g). Ex ebay April 2018; (b) follis of Heraclius (MIB 186), Cyzicus (20mm, 4.72g). Ex CNG, Auction 88, lot 1632 (14 September 2011); (c) follis of Heraclius (MIB 162), Constantinople (25mm, 7.09g). Ex Savoca Coins (ebay January 2018).

---

[5] The type from Cyprus depicts the monogram above the denomination M. The table at the back of *MIB* III depicts *MIB* 198 with the wrong form of monogram, that with unadorned cross-bar standard only after c.632.

[6] There are several slight stylistic variants in how the letter K is represented, to do with the relative angles and lengths of the bars projecting forward, but it is clearly the same letter always. The table at the back of *MIB* III is misleading in that it gives the impression that this form of monogram was unique to Cyzicus. For examples of this form of monogram on coins from Constantinople, see Grierson, *DOC* 100c; Mansfield, *EBCC* 17.86, 17.128-29. It can be difficult to distinguish between this form of monogram and the third form of monogram in some cases. The key distinguishing factor lies in the absence or presence of a bar extending to the left of the main vertical so that the monogram contains a full cross.

[7] There does not seem to have been any proper study yet of what workshops at Constantinople used this form of monogram and when exactly they did so. Grierson, *DOC* 2.1, p. 110, does not include it in his table of imperial monograms. For more examples, see Mansfield, *EBCC* 17.93, 17.96.

Fig 2:
(a) follis of Heraclius (MIB 164b), Constantinople (35mm, 9.26g). Ex CNG, E-Auction 288 (10 October 2012), lot 549.
(b) follis of Heraclius (MIB 164c), Constantinople (23mm, 7.06g). Ex Savoca Coins (ebay July 2018).
(c) follis of Heraclius (MIB 164e), Constantinople (23mm 4.59g). Ex Savoca Coins (ebay June 2018).
(d) half-follis of Justin II & Sophia (MIBEC 70d), Thessalonica (23mm, 5.65g). Ex VAuctions, Auction 323 (17 Mar 2017), lot 714.
(e) half-follis of Justin II & Sophia (MIBEC 70c), Thessalonica (22mm, 4.80g). Ex ebay July 2018.
(f) half-follis of Justin II & Sophia (MIBEC 70e), Thessalonica (23mm, 5.23g). Ex ebay May 2018.
(g) half-follis of Justin II & Sophia (MIBEC 70f), Thessalonica (22mm, 5.00g). Ex ebay January 2018.

In order to appreciate the significance of the addition of the horizontal bar and the lunate sigma to the same basic monogram formed from the Greek letters rho and eta as already described in the case of the first and second forms of monogram, one has to look forward to the variety of different marks used on the reverse of the next class of folles struck at Constantinople from regnal year 20 (629/30) to regnal year 27 (636/37) inclusive. There were five different marks all occurring in the same place on the reverse, immediately above the denomination M, although only two marks were normally used in the same year. These marks consisted of a small cross alone (*MIB* 164a), a small cross above a letter C (*MIB* 164b) (Fig. 2a), a staurogram ending in the letter omega (*MIB* 164c) (Fig. 2b), an imperial monogram formed from the Greek letters rho and eta once more with a horizontal bar between them (*MIB* 164d), and a small cross above a Greek letter theta (*MIB* 164e) (Fig. 2c).[8] The small cross was in fact the device that had traditionally appeared in that approximate position on the reverse of most folles since the emperor Anastasius (491-518) had reformed the coinage in 498. It was obviously a Christian symbol and the suspicion naturally arises that all, or most, of the other marks had a similar religious significance.[9] This is supported by the fact that the mark

---

[8] The tables at the back of *MIB* III give the mistaken impression that the mark on *MIB* 164e consists of a letter theta alone rather than a small cross above a theta.
[9] Grierson, *DOC* 2.1, p. 228, describes these marks as 'puzzling' and completely ignores their potential religious significance.

consisting of a small cross above a letter C is almost identical to a mark consisting of a small cross to the right of a letter C used on a half-follis of the emperor Justin II (565-74) struck at Thessalonica in regnal year 10 (574/75) (*MIBEC* 70d) (Fig. 2d). That this letter C abbreviates some religious or theological term is obvious from the fact that it occurs within a series of marks including the letters ΘKC, with macron above the last two letters, in abbreviation of θεοτόκος 'Mother of God' (*MIBEC* 70c) (Fig. 2e), ΘC in abbreviation of θεός 'God' or the associated adjective θεῖος 'divine' (*MIBEC* 70e) (Fig. 2f), and ΦC in abbreviation of φῶς 'light' (*MIBEC* 70f) (Fig. 2g), where a cross occurs in association with the last two abbreviations alone. In this context, therefore, it is clear that the lunate sigma alone with a cross probably abbreviates either the noun σωτήρ 'saviour' or the associated adjective σωτήριος 'saving' in reference to the fact that the crucified Christ was regarded as the saviour of the world.

The identification of the cross and lunate sigma used on the half-follis of Justin from Thessalonica with the cross and lunate sigma used on the follis of Heraclius from Constantinople suggests that the other marks used upon the same class of Heraclian follis should have a similar religious significance. Hence the theta of the cross above a theta probably abbreviates θεός 'God' or θεῖος 'divine' in the same manner as the theta and lunate sigma beneath a cross on another of the half-folles of Justin II from Thessalonica as already described. Furthermore, while the staurogram ending in the letter omega of the Heraclian series from Constantinople has no clear precedent in the series struck under Justin II in Thessalonica, it seems to contain three Greek letters – chi, rho, and omega – and, if this is correct, it probably abbreviates the name of Christ in the dative case, Χριστῷ 'to or for Christ'.[10]

One may now return to the interpretation of the third form of imperial monogram occasionally used on folles struck at Constantinople during regnal years 15-19 (624-29), that formed as a result of the addition of the horizontal bar with lunate sigma to the basic imperial monogram formed from the Greek letters eta and rho. This effectively combines the cross and lunate sigma, that is, the cross specifically identified as the saving cross of Christ, with the imperial monogram proper formed from the first two letters of the name of Heraclius in Greek. Hence it serves to emphasise the close bond between Heraclius and the cross of Christ, the message presumably being that he campaigns and conquers under the sign of the cross of Christ. Of course, the idea that the good Christian emperor conquers under the sign of the cross goes back as far as bishop Eusebius of Caesarea's account of how Constantine I (306-37) saw a cross of light in the sky sometime shortly before his defeat of his western rival Maxentius at the battle of the Milvian bridge in 312.[11]

---

[10] Grierson, *DOC* 2.1, p. 228, describes it 'as a mystery'.
[11] Eusebius, *Vita Constantini* 1.28. Similar visions of the cross were also claimed subsequently. See e.g. J.W. Drijvers, 'The Power of the Cross: Celestial Cross Appearances in the Fourth Century', in A. Cain and N. Lenski, **The Power of Religion in Late Antiquity** (Farnham, 2009), pp. 237-48.

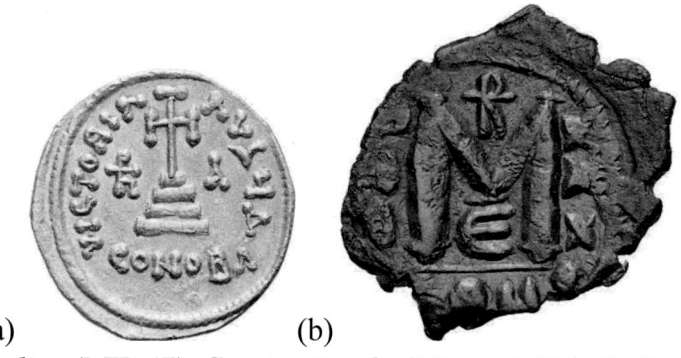

Fig 3: (a) solidus of Heraclius (MIB 47), Constantinople (19mm, 4.44g). Ex Roma Numismatics, E-Sale 56 (9 May 2019), lot 1239; (b) follis of Heraclius (MIB 167), Constantinople (26mm, 5.35g). Ex CNG, E-Auction 382 (7 September 2016), lot 478.

Finally, one should note here that the coinage of Heraclius displays one main form of imperial monogram from 632 onwards, a new form different to anything that had appeared on the coinage previously.[12] As far as the coinage is concerned, this monogram first appeared on the reverse of the new class of solidus seemingly introduced in 632 and lasting in production until 641 (*MIB* 39-53) (Fig. 3a). In this case, the monogram normally appears in the field to the left of the large cross on the reverse. It was also used as a mark above the denomination M on folles of Constantinople dated from regnal year 25 to 27 (634-37) inclusive (*MIB* 164d), as already noted, and continued as the sole mark used in the same place on the final class of folles struck at Constantinople during regnal years 30-31 (639-41) (*MIB* 166-67) (Fig. 3b). This form of imperial monogram was a simplification of the earlier form that had added a horizontal bar ending in a lunate sigma to the basic imperial monogram consisting of the letters eta and rho, the lunate sigma having been omitted. As to why the sigma was omitted, perhaps this was because it was realised that it was not strictly necessary. After all, everyone knew that the cross was the cross of the saviour Jesus Christ and that it would protect and save anyone who sought salvation through it. However, the fact that the sigma was dropped also meant that it became clear that the horizontal bar did not simply serve to include the sigma within the monogram, but was an important part of the monogram in and of itself. Hence the dropping of the sigma served to draw attention to the presence of a cross within the monogram. As to why this particular form of monogram emerged triumphant in the early 630s, one can hardly separate it from the fact that Heraclius developed a particularly strong association with the cross at this time because of his recovery of the remains of the True Cross from the Persians, who had seized them following the fall of Jerusalem in 614, and his final return of them to Jerusalem once more in the spring of 630.[13] One suspects, therefore, that he adopted this new form of monogram precisely in order to remind all that he had a very special relationship with the cross, as demonstrated by his recovery of the True Cross itself.

Byzantine Countermarks on Coins Circulating in Greater Syria

In his standard analysis of the countermarks used by Byzantine authorities in Syria before the Arab conquest, Schulze divides the countermarks into eight classes, not all of which are strictly relevant

---

[12] It is not entirely clear when the bar monogram consisting of the letters rho, kappa, and eta ceased being depicted next to the standing figure of Heraclius on the obverse of the folles struck at Constantinople during regnal years 20-27 (629-37) (*MIB* 164). Unfortunately, its inclusion there was inconsistent, but it was certainly still being depicted there as late as regnal year 22 (631/32). See e.g. Mansfield, *EBCC* 17.154-55.

[13] See C. Zuckerman, 'Heraclius and the Return of the Holy Cross', ***Travaux et Mémoires*** 17 (2013), pp. 197-218.

here either because the countermark in question was not in fact applied in Syria, or probably dates from much earlier than the 630s, or does not actually contain a monogram or similar groups of Greek letters.[14] I will focus here on those countermarks that were applied in greater Syria, or for primary use there at least, during the 630s onwards, and will do in the order that Schulze himself treats them.

Schulze's Class 1 consists of two different countermarks that he identifies as Type 1 and Type 2 where both are different forms of Heraclian monogram (Fig. 4). The difference between the types is that Type 1 includes a letter C as part of the monogram, normally at the left end of the central horizontal bar, while Type 2 does not. However, each type contains numerous subtypes, so that Schulze identifies 18 different subtypes to Type 1 (1a-1r) and five different subtypes to Type 2 (2a-e). He interprets Type 1 as containing three letters – Latin h, Latin R, and Latin C – in abbreviation of the name of Heraclius in Latin, and Type 2 as containing two letters – Latin h and Latin R in abbreviation of the same name once more.[15] In reality, however, some of the subtypes within Type 1 contain four Greek letters – eta, rho, kappa, sigma – where the kappa is largely concealed within the rho in the same way as in the main form of the imperial monogram used on the Heraclian folles struck at Constantinople during the period 624-29, while other subtypes within Type 1 contain only three letters – eta, rho, sigma. Hence the Type 1 monogram combines two or three letters from the Greek name of Heraclius with the letter sigma in reference to the saving power of the cross once more. Similarly, some of the subtypes within Type 2 contain three letters – eta, rho, kappa, while the other subtypes contain only two letters – eta and rho. Hence the Type 2 monogram contains two or three letters from the Greek name of Heraclius, but does not include a sigma in reference to the saving power of the cross, even though it does actually contain a cross.

Fig. 4: follis of Heraclius (MIB 164c), Constantinople (26mm, 5.37), with Class 1 Types 1 (below, with C) and 2 (above, without C) countermarks on obverse. Ex ebay February 2018.

---

[14] As Schulze, 'Countermarks from before the Arab Conquest' (see n. 3), pp. 30-37, himself argues, his Class 7 countermarks were probably applied in Cyprus during the 660s. Furthermore, he cannot date the use of his Class 8 countermark any more precisely than to the early 7th century, pp. 39-40, and it may have been applied in Egypt rather than Syria. In support of dating it to the rule of the Heraclii as consuls in 610, see D. Woods, 'The Byzantine Eagle Countermark: Creating a Pseudo-Consular Coinage under the Heraclii?', *Greek, Roman, and Byzantine Studies* 55 (2015), pp. 927-45.

[15] Schulze, 'Countermarks from before the Arab Conquest' (see n. 3), p. 24. C. Foss, *Arab-Byzantine Coins: An Introduction with a Catalogue of the Dumbarton Oaks Collection* (Washington, DC, 2008), p. 15, follows Schulze's interpretations. K.N. Economides, 'Byzantine Folles Countermarked with Heraclian Monograms Found in Cyprus', *Numismatic Chronicle* 163 (2003), pp. 193-204 argues similarly that the countermark described by Schulze as Class 1 Type 1 contains Latin letters, but he identifies them as h, R, C, and T and reads it as a combined monogram for both Heraclius and his eldest son Heraclius Constantine. He interprets the C suspended below the horizontal bar as the stem of a T taking the form Ⲧ, a standard epigraphic form on the coinage of this period. P. Lampinen, 'Countermarked Byzantine Folles and the Identification of a New Imperial Family Member', in K.G. Holum, A. Raban, and J. Patrich (eds.), *Caesarea Papers* 2 (Portsmouth, RI, 1999), pp. 399-404, even argues that this monogram refers to the *patricius* Theodore, commander of the Byzantine army in Palestine.

In addition to the Type 1 and Type 2 countermarks of Class 1, Schulze also identifies three very different countermarks that sometimes occur in association with Type 1 or Type 2 countermarks as Type 3 countermarks (Fig. 5). His Type 3a is clearly a small cross, and his Type 3c consists of two Greek letters, sigma and omega, standing next to each other, while his Type 3b seems to be identifiable as a lunate sigma combined with an omega in ligature form. Of 173 coins with Type 1 or Type 2 countermarks examined by Schulze, the Type 3a countermark only occurs once, in association with a Type 2 countermark, the Type 3b countermark occurs twice, in association with a Type 2 countermark in each case, and the Type 3c countermark only occurs once, in association with a Type 1 countermark.[16] While Schulze does not attempt to explain the significance of the Type 3b or Type 3c countermarks, two possibilities spring to mind given both the prominence of the cross in the associated imperial monograms of Types 1 and 2 and the importance of the cross more generally at this period. One possibility is that these countermarks abbreviate the Greek adjective σωτήριος 'saving' in reference to the saving power of the cross once more, while the other possibility is that they abbreviate the Greek term for cross in the dative case, σταυρῷ 'by the cross'. In either case, the countermarks proclaim the hope of being saved by the power of the cross.

Fig. 5: sketches of Class 1 countermarks, Types 3a-c, after Schulze, 'Countermarks from before the Arab Conquest' (see n. 3), p. 24.

As for the date of the Class 1 countermarks, the fact that the vast majority of host coins (118 of 173, so 68%) examined by Schulze were dated to regnal years 20-26 (629-36), and none later than this, fully supports his conclusion that they were most probably applied during the Arab invasion of Syria. However, while he dates the use of the countermarks to 633-36, it is important to note that they may actually have been applied to coins as late as 639 even. The key point here is that the mint at Constantinople seems to have struck far fewer folles in regnal year 27 (636/37) than it had done previously, and practically none in regnal years 28-29 (637-39), so that the supply of fresh coin from Constantinople to Syria must have effectively ceased during the period 636-39, and there would have been no coins of these dates available to act as host coins for the countermarks.[17] Indeed, the decision to countermark the existing supply of coins may be directly related to the fact the supply of fresh coin ceased during this period. On the basis of the numismatic evidence alone, therefore, one may tentatively prefer to date the use of these countermarks to sometime during the period 636-39 rather than to 633-36.

Schulze's Class 2 consists of a countermark in the form of a cross monogram (Fig. 6a) that very clearly spells the genitive form of the name of Heraclius in Greek, even if opinion has differed in the past as to which Heraclius this was. However, there is no good reason to doubt that the senior emperor Heraclius himself was indeed intended rather than his eldest son Heraclius Constantine or

---

[16] For full details of the analysis of these 173 coins, see W. Schulze, I. Schulze, & W. Leimenstoll, 'Heraclian Countermarks on Byzantine Copper Coins in Seventh-Century Syria', **Byzantine and Modern Greek Studies** 30 (2006), pp. 1-27.
[17] The table at the back of *MIB* III reveals that only one workshop struck folles at Constantinople in regnal year 27 (636/37), whereas four had been in operation previously. Furthermore, it suggests that no workshops at all produced folles during the next two years.

his younger son Heraclonas even.[18] The fact that Heraclius Constantine is always identified, when he is identified, simply by the letter kappa on the obverse of the folles struck during regnal years 20-27 (629-37) (*MIB* 164) supports this. Schulze follows earlier works in identifying two slightly different types within this class, which he calls Type a and Type b, but the very minor difference between them seems best dismissed as a slight error by an engraver rather any serious proof that two variants of the same monogram were genuinely intended.[19] Of the 6 Byzantine coins recorded by Schulze as hosting this countermark, 5 are folles of the period 629-37 (*MIB* 164), even if only 1 of these can be firmly dated (to regnal year 23 = 632/33), while the last is a half-follis of the same period. Add the example illustrated here dating to regnal year 20 (Fig. 6b), and the evidence suggests that countermarking occurred during the mid-630s.[20]

Fig. 6: (a) sketch of Class 2 countermark; (b) follis of Heraclius (29mm, 10.75g) with Class 2 countermark (MIB 164). Ex Savoca Coins (ebay December 2017).

Class 3 consists of another countermark in the form of a cross monogram (Fig. 7a-b), but the reading of this monogram is far more problematic than that of the Class 2 monogram. This monogram clearly contains four Greek letters – tau, omega, nu, kappa – but it is not clear what these abbreviate. It has traditionally been accepted that they abbreviate the Greek form of the name Constantine (Κωνσταντῖνος). However, Grierson is not sure whom is meant by this, Hahn prefers to interpret it in reference to the emperor now known as Constans II (641-68), the grandson of Heraclius, who was actually known as Constantine on his coinage, while Schulze hesitates once more between his short-reigned, sickly father Heraclius Constantine (641) or Heraclonas instead.[21] The problem here is that the latest dateable host coins date to Heraclius' regnal years 20-23 (629-

---

[18] Grierson, *DOC* 2.1, p. 56, claims that it is 'possible that it should be attributed to Heraclius Constantine or Heraclonas' simply on the basis that this monogram differs so greatly from earlier monograms of Heraclius upon the coinage, although also admitting that similar cross monograms do occur for Heraclius on silverware. For the latter, see Table II in E. Cruikshank Dodd, ***Byzantine Silver Stamps***, Dumbarton Oaks Studies 7 (Washington, DC, 1961).

[19] Schulze, 'Countermarks from before the Arab Conquest' (see n. 3), p. 24, distinguishes between a Type a, which may include an angular lunate sigma in ligature with the capital eta at the left end of the horizontal bar, and a Type b which depicts the capital eta alone. It is interesting to note that fragments of silk from the shrine of St Madelberta (d. 706) in Liège Cathedral preserve the same monogram as Class 2 Type b. See A. Muthesius, 'Memory and Meaning: Graphic Sign and Abstract Symbol in Byzantine Silk Weaving (from the Sixth to Tenth/Eleventh Centuries), in Garipzanov, Goodson, and Maguire, ***Graphic Signs of Identity*** (see n. 4), pp. 351-81, at 354-57.

[20] Schulze also records the occurrence of this countermark on a pseudo-Byzantine coin with three-figure obverse, as described by P. Pavlou, ***ONS Newsletter*** 127 (1991), p. 5. If the pseudo-Byzantine coin has not been overstruck on an earlier Byzantine coin hosting this countermark, then the most plausible explanation is that some pseudo-Byzantine coins were struck much earlier than has generally been thought, and that the obverse imitates the three-figure obverse of folles of the period 616-29 rather than that of the folles of the period 639-41.

[21] Grierson, *DOC* 2.1, p. 57; Hahn, *MIB* III, p. 141; Schulze, 'Countermarks from before the Arab Conquest' (see n. 3), p. 27.

33), so suggesting that the countermark was applied during the mid-630s once more.[22] This renders it highly unlikely that the monogram should have been intended in reference to any of Heraclius Constantine, Heraclonas or Constans II. At this point, therefore, one needs to question the assumption that this monogram must abbreviate a personal name rather something else instead. Attention has already been drawn to fact that the form of the imperial monogram used on the coinage from 632 onwards contained a cross as well as letters abbreviating the imperial name, and the possibility that this monogram may contain some reference to the cross deserves to be taken seriously. The most common slogan used in connection with the cross was the phrase that Constantine I allegedly saw in the sky next to his vision of a cross of light before the battle of the Milvian Bridge in 312. According to Eusebius, this phrase was τούτῳ νίκα 'Conquer by this!'. The popularity of this phrase at this approximate period can be judged in two ways. First, the same verb appears in the exergue of one of the two types of follis struck at Jerusalem in 614 as part of the legend XCNIKA abbreviating Χριστός νικᾷ 'Christ conquers!'.[23] Second, and more importantly, the legend ЄN TȢTO NIKA (ἐν τούτῳ νίκα) 'Conquer in this!', appears on the obverse of most of the different types of folles struck in the name of Constans II at Constantinople during the period 642-58. It should not surprise, therefore, that the monogram seems to conceal the phrase τούτῳ νίκα 'Conquer by this!'. To be specific, the vertical bar of the monogram reads T(OV)TW, while the horizontal bar reads N(I)K(A). Hence it is not really an imperial monogram at all. Finally, one should note the cleverness of this monogram in that the demonstrative pronoun T(OV)TW 'by this' refers to the cross within the monogram itself, so that the monogram is a perfectly self-contained unit.

Fig. 7: (a) sketch of Class 3 countermark; (b) half-follis of Heraclius (MIB 169) dated regnal year 2 (611/12) with Class 3 countermark (24mm, 5.07g). Ex ebay January 2018.

It should be noted here also that Schulze's Class 4 countermark does not actually consist of a specific countermark but rather a combination of a Class 2 countermark and a Class 3 countermark (Fig. 8). Schulze records far fewer specimens bearing a Class 2 or a Class 3 countermark than a Class 1 countermark, and it is clear that their use was far more restricted. To be more precise, he records 7 coins bearing a Class 2 countermark alone, 16 coins bearing a Class 3 countermark alone, and 10 coins bearing both a Class 2 countermark and a Class 3 countermark. These small numbers of specimens render the analysis of any patterns of use extremely difficult. Schulze seems to assume a basically sequential use of the Class 2 and Class 3 countermarks across two cities or pockets of

---

[22] The editor has drawn my attention to an unpublished example of what seems to be a pseudo-Byzantine coin with three-figure obverse hosting a Class 3 countermark. It is probably to be explained in the same way as the similar pseudo-Byzantine coin hosting a Class 2 countermark described above (see n. 19).
[23] *MIB* X28. In general, see S. Mansfield, 'Heraclean Folles of Jerusalem', in A. Oddy (ed.), ***Coinage and History in the Seventh Century Near East 2*** (London, 2010), pp. 49-55.

Byzantine territory during the last stages of the Arab conquest, that one countermark was applied in one city until it was captured by the Arabs, while the second countermark was applied in another city until that too was captured by the Arabs, even tentatively identifying these cities as Jerusalem and Caesarea. The Class 4 coins, those bearing both Class 2 and Class 3 countermarks, are then identifiable as coins that have moved from one city to another with the flow of refugees. However, nothing really excludes the sequential use of these countermarks within the same city or district. This city or district may have begun by applying the Class 2 countermark to its copper coinage, but have changed subsequently to the use of the Class 3 countermark instead, so moving from a political countermark naming the emperor to a religious countermark stressing the power of the cross as the military situation deteriorated even further.

Fig. 8: follis of Heraclius with both Class 2 and Class 3 countermarks (26mm, 10.59g). Ex Numismatik Lanz (ebay September 2018).

The relationship between Class 1 countermarks and Class 2 and Class 3 countermarks is as problematic as the relationship between Class 2 and Class 3 countermarks themselves. It is surely significant that no Class 2 or Class 3 countermark has been found in association with a Class 1 countermark on the same coin despite the fact that all the countermarks were focussed upon the same class of host coins, Heraclian copper coins from regnal year 20 onwards. This suggests that Class 1 countermarks were imposed within one large district, while Class 2 and Class 3 countermarks were imposed within another much smaller district. Indeed, the relationship between Class 1 Type 1 and Class 1 Type 2 countermarks parallels that between Class 2 and Class 3 countermarks to suggest that they may also have been used sequentially within the same district.

Finally, one cannot conclude any discussion of the Byzantine countermarks struck on coins circulating in greater Syria without remarking upon the relevance of Schulze's Class 3 countermark to the interpretation of his Class 7 countermark. The Class 7 countermark consist of a monogram containing three Greek letters – tau, kappa, and omega – where this occurs in two slightly different forms, Type a (Fig. 9a-b) and its retrograde form Type b (Fig. 9c-d). As Schulze states, however, Type b is 'obviously an error of the die cutter'.[24] Most of the coins with this countermark come from Cyprus, so it seems that this countermark was imposed there, although a few coins with this countermark have also been found in Syria. Furthermore, the host coins are almost exclusively folles and half-folles of Constans II, although Schulze also notes the existence of three coins of Constantine IV with this countermark, so that the countermarking is thought to have occurred during the period c.660-73.

---

[24] Schulze, 'Countermarks from before the Arab Conquest' (see n. 3), p. 30.

Fig. 9: (a) sketch of Class 7 countermark, Type a; (b) follis of Constans II (MIB 173), Constantinople (17mm, 2.46g), with Class 7 countermark, Type a, on the upper reverse. Ex CNG, E-Auction 305 (26 June 2013), lot 417; (c) sketch of Class 7 countermark, Type b; (d) pseudo-Byzantine follis with Class 7 countermark, Type b, on the lower reverse (25mm, 4.35g). Ex ebay December 2017.

It is important to note at this point that the monogram used in this countermark saw extensive use on the copper coinage also, but almost exclusively on the folles and half-folles struck under Constans II at Syracuse in Sicily. It was depicted above the denomination M on five of the six types of folles struck there during his reign (Fig. 10a), and was even the main device on the reverse of the half-folles struck there during the period c.648-52 (Fig. 10b).[25] It was also depicted above the denomination M on the final type of follis struck at Carthage under Constans II during the period 662-67, a factor that raises the suspicion that these coins may have been struck at Syracuse rather than Carthage.[26] Whatever the case, it is not clear why the mint at Syracuse should have favoured this monogram when other mints continued to prefer to depict a small cross above the denomination M in the traditional manner, but its use of this monogram above the denomination M in replacement of the traditional cross for such an extended period of time encourages the belief that it somehow conveyed the same basic message, that is, that it also served in some way to promote the veneration of the cross.

---

[25] For the folles, see Constans II, *MIB* 205, 206, 207, 209, 210. The exception is *MIB* 208 (652/53) which depicts the traditional small cross above the denomination M. For the half-folles, see *MIB* 211, 212.

[26] *MIB* 194. Since Constans II was resident at Syracuse during the period 663-68, it is possible that it may have become more active in the supply of coinage to Africa at this time.

(a)   (b)

Fig. 10: (a) follis of Constans II (MIB 209), Syracuse (20mm, 3.41g). Ex CNG, E-Auction 258 (22 June 2011), lot 518; (b) half-follis of Constans II (MIB 212), Syracuse (25mm, 5.19g). Ex CNG, E-Auction 153 (29 November 2006), lot 257.

The Class 7 countermark bears a striking resemblance to the Class 3 countermark in that each monogram includes the same vertical element with a tau at the top and an omega at the bottom. If, as has been argued in the case of the Class 3 countermark, this abbreviates the demonstrative pronoun T(OV)TW 'by this', then one should consider the possibility that it performs the same function in the case of the Class 7 countermark also. That would leave the letter kappa alone to be explained.[27] It cannot form part of an abbreviation of the term NIKA as in the case of the Class 3 countermark because there is no accompanying letter nu here. The obvious alternative is that it abbreviates the name Constantine (Κωνσταντῖνος) instead, so that the monogram implies that Constans II (Constantine) does something 'by this'. Hence the monogram seems to represent an abbreviation of some such statement as K(WNCTANTINOS) T(OV)TW (NIKA) 'Constantine conquers by this', where the viewer is expected to be able to identify the object referred to as 'this' either as a result of general familiarity with the use of this phrase of the cross or because Constans is depicted holding some form of cross (long cross or cross-on-globe) on the obverse of the coin.[28] In support of this interpretation, one notes that none of the folles from Syracuse depicting this monogram on the reverse bear the legend EN TUTW NIKA 'Conquer by this!' on the obverse. Hence there is no reduplication of the message concerning the conquering power of the cross. Furthermore, it may be precisely because this monogram abbreviates a declaration that 'Constantine conquers by this' that none of the folles from Constantinople bearing the legend EN TUTW NIKA 'Conquer by this!' on the obverse include this monogram on the reverse. Hence it seems that the folles from both mints emphasize that Constans II conquers by means of the cross, but they do so in very different ways, those from Constantinople by means of an explicit legend in full on the obverse, those from Syracuse by means of a severely abbreviated monogram on the reverse.

If this interpretation of the monogram is correct, then the imposition of this countermark upon the coins circulating in Cyprus, most of which were Constantinopolitan issues, and many of which already bore the legend EN TUTW NIKA on the obverse, represented a reduplication of a message already there. However, it is noteworthy that the countermark was normally placed on the reverse of

---

[27] Grierson, *DOC* 2.1, p. 58, suggests that 'the conspicuous K', taken as the first letter of the name Constantine, may have doubled as a mark of value, so that the countermarking was intended to revalue the folles so stamped as half-folles. This idea continues to receive support. See e.g. L. Zavagno, "Betwixt the Greeks and the Saracens': Coins and Coinage in Cyprus in the Seventh and the Eighth Century', **Byzantion** 81 (2011), pp. 448-483, at 469. Yet this is nonsense that takes no account of the fact that the exact same monogram, with a similarly 'conspicuous K', occurs on the reverse of most folles struck in Sicily during the reign of Constans, as already described. Whatever its precise significance, therefore, the kappa does not serve to revalue folles as half-folles.

[28] Alternatively, the kappa may serve a dual function, abbreviating both the name Constantine and some form of the verb κρατέω 'I rule, conquer' used as a synonym for νικάω.

the coins, that is, on the side that did not already bear the legend ЄN TȢTѠ NIKA.[29] It is arguable, therefore, that those imposing the countermark deliberately placed it on the reverse in order to avoid reduplication of a message already present on the obverse. As to the purpose of this countermarking, Schulze argues that it was economic, that it was intended 'to regulate the copper circulation and to revalue Byzantine copper coins – and, as an additional effect, to keep them on the island'.[30] Yet it is hard to disregard the fact that the stamping of a monogram normally associated with the coinage of Sicily upon the coins circulating in Cyprus occurred during the same approximate period that Constans II was resident in Sicily rather than at Constantinople. Another possibility, therefore, is that this countermarking was intended to signify some new administrative arrangement subjecting Cyprus to increased control by the court of Constans II in Sicily, that is, that two of the largest islands within the empire were being brought closer together in some way by an emperor who was re-inventing the Byzantine navy, even if it was Constantinople that continued to supply most of its copper coinage to Cyprus.[31]

Arab-Byzantine Countermarks on Coins Circulating in Syria.

Goodwin identified 40 different countermarks apparently imposed by local Syrian authorities on Byzantine and Arab-Byzantine coins circulating within their districts sometime after the Arab conquest.[32] He divided these into three groups, a Class A where the countermarks consist of Byzantine-style monograms and geometric designs, Class B where the countermarks consist of Arabic words, and Class C where the countermarks appear to consist of various images. The focus here will be upon the Class A countermarks. I will discuss these in the order that he lists them, but only those where some further comments about their interpretation seems necessary.

(a)   (b)

Fig. 11: (a) sketch of countermark A1; (b) follis of Constans II (24mm, 6.20g) dated regnal year 3 (643/44) (MIB 164) with A1 countermark on upper reverse. Ex ebay October 2018.

---

[29] Schulze, 'Countermarks from before the Arab Conquest' (see n. 3), p. 35, notes that the countermark was placed on the reverse in just over 80% of cases, but that this figure increases to about 90% if one disregards host coins of type *MIB* 175 where the occurrence of three standing figures on the reverse probably made it difficult for many to distinguish between obverse and reverse. In the present context, one should note that *MIB* 175 did not bear the legend ЄN TȢTѠ NIKA on either side, so if the intention had been to avoid duplicating this, it did not matter upon which side the countermark was imposed.
[30] Schulze, 'Countermarks from before the Arab Conquest' (see n. 3), p. 38.
[31] On the reforming activities of Constans II while in Sicily, particularly his creation of a navy, see C. Zuckerman, 'Learning from the Enemy and More: Studies in 'Dark Centuries' Byzantium', **Millenium** 2 (2005), pp. 79-136.
[32] For what follows, see Goodwin, 'Countermarks from after the Arab Conquest' (see n. 3), pp. 41-46.

Goodwin records 19 specimens bearing his countermark A1 (Fig. 11a-b), 3 Byzantine coins (2 of Heraclius, 1 of Constans II), 15 Pseudo-Byzantine coins, and 1 Imperial Image coin from Emesa. The countermark is a monogram that certainly contains the Greek letters alpha, nu, and tau, but may also include a lambda or an iota. He favours interpreting this monogram as ANT in abbreviation of the name of Antarados (Ἀντάραδος), offering two reasons in support of this interpretation. The first is that Antarados did in fact strike coins during the Imperial Image phase of coinage.[33] The second is that the fact that this countermark was used on a coin of Emesa suggests that the authority responsible for it was situated somewhere relatively near Emesa, as Antarados was. One may now add a third reason in further support of this interpretation, the existence of a specimen that displays the countermark A3 on the obverse in addition to the countermark A1 on the reverse (Fig. 12a). This is important because of the 17 specimens bearing countermark A3 reported by Goodwin, 10 are Imperial Image coins from Emesa, and only 1 an Imperial Image coin from Damascus. In other words, the countermark A3 was clearly being applied by some authority at or near Emesa, so that the authority applying the A1 countermark must also have been located at or near Emesa, which supports the location of this authority at Antaradus once more. Finally, the application of this countermark to a Byzantine follis dated to regnal year 12 (652/53) of Constans II provides a new *terminus post quem* for its continued use (Fig. 12b).

Fig. 12: (a) pseudo-Byzantine follis (26mm, 3.99g) with three countermarks, an A3 countermark on the obverse (to left of standing figure), an A1 countermark on the reverse (bottom), and a 2nd unclear countermark on the reverse (top). Ex ebay May 2018; (b) follis of Constans II (21mm, 4.60g) dated regnal year 12 (652/53) (MIB 170) with A1 countermark on lower reverse. Ex ebay September 2018.

The countermark A3 consists of three Greek letters grouped together, an omega above a kappa and a nu (Fig. 12a). Goodwin suggests that these should be read as KωN in abbreviation of KAΛωN 'fine' as found on the obverse of the Imperial Image coins of Antarados, although he is also open to the possibility that they could abbreviate the personal name of an official called Constantine (Κωνσταντῖνος) or something similar. However, if anyone had wanted to abbreviate the term KAΛωN, they would probably have abbreviated it as KAΛ rather than KωN, preferring to retain the

---

[33] See W. Schulze, 'The Byzantine-Arab Transitional Coinage of Ṭarṭūs', ***Numismatic Chronicle*** 173 (2013), pp. 245-59.

full stem of the adjective rather than the case-ending, as this would have made the meaning of the abbreviation much clearer. It is more likely, therefore, that these letters abbreviate some term beginning with either KωN or KNω. While it is not impossible that these could abbreviate a personal name, given that countermark A1 probably abbreviates the name of a town, one should probably start any investigation of this matter with due consideration of that possibility. As it happens, very few ancient towns had names beginning with KNω. In contrast, however, Constantine I and his sons renamed numerous towns throughout the empire after themselves, so several towns in the eastern half of the empire did have names beginning with KωN.[34] Of most relevance here, Constantius II (337-61) seems to have renamed Antarados as Constantia (Κωνστάντια) after himself in 346, but usage was inconsistent and later sources could use either or both names.[35] This raises the possibility that countermarks A1 and A3 refer to the same town, Antarados/Constantia, but that A1 refers to it by its original name, Antarados, while A3 refers to it by its new name after 346, Constantia. As it happens, it is arguable that the same authority based somewhere near Emesa did change its countermark over time because the fact that 15 of the 19 recorded host coins for countermark A1 were pseudo-Byzantine coins while 11 of the 17 recorded host coins for countermark A3 were Imperial Image coins does suggest a temporal difference, that is, that countermark A1 ceased being used when the vast majority of the coins in circulation were still pseudo-Byzantine, while countermark A3 was in use while the majority of coins in circulation were Imperial Image coins. However, if one assumes that the authority based in Antarados/Constantia that was responsible for the countermarking of the coinage was also responsible for the subsequent striking of Imperial Image coins there, then this reconstruction becomes problematic for the reason that the Imperial Image coins all bear the mint-name Antarados rather than Constantia, so that this reconstruction would require that the same authority first identified itself by the name Antarados (A1 countermark), decided next to use the name Constantia instead (A3 countermark), then returned finally to the use of the name Antarados (Imperial Image coins). This reconstruction would become much less problematic if one could explain the KωN or KNω of the A3 countermark in such a way that it did not require that the relevant authority changed its preferred title for its location so often. Interestingly, very few words in Greek actually begin with either KωN or KNω but one of these is the term κωνσίλιον 'council'.[36] It is possible, therefore, that a council based in Antarados, presumably the town-council, initially used a countermark abbreviating the name of its location (A1), replaced this with a countermark abbreviating the term 'council' instead (A3), and resumed the use of the town-name once more when it began striking Imperial Image coins. Or, alternatively, some body called the 'the council' based near Antarados and Emesa began countermarking coins about the same time that another body based at Antarados ceased countermarking coins. Finally, one should also note that the application of countermark A3 to a Byzantine follis dated to regnal year 16 (656/57) of Constans II provides a new *terminus post quem* for its continued use (Fig. 13).

---

[34] See N. Lenski, ***Constantine and the Cities: Imperial Authority and Civic Politics*** (Philadelphia, 2016), pp. 131-164.
[35] See R.W. Burgess, ***Studies in Eusebian and Post-Eusebian Chronography*** (Stuttgart, 1999), pp. 170-71, 272. There is some disagreement as to whether Antarados was renamed Constantina or Constantia, but the precise form of the new name does not matter here.
[36] For κωνσίλιον, see e.g. E.A. Sophocles, ***Greek Lexicon of the Roman and Byzantine Periods*** (Cambridge, MA, 1914), pp. 701-02; H.J. Mason, ***Greek Terms for Roman Institution: A Lexicon and Analysis*** (Toronto, 1974), p. 65.

Fig. 13: follis of Constans II (21mm, 3.62g) dated regnal year 16 (656/57) (MIB 173) with A3 countermark on obverse. Ex Savoca Coins (ebay June 2018).

Goodwin records 40 specimens bearing his countermark A4a resembling a six-limbed star (Fig. 14), 15 Byzantine coins and 25 Pseudo-Byzantine coins. However, he does not comment upon the potential significance of this apparent star. On the one hand, it could perhaps contain kappa and lambda in abbreviation of the Greek adjective ΚΑΛΟΝ 'fine' as found on the Imperial Image coins of Emesa, on some Imperial Image coins of the *jāza hādhā* type from the Pseudo-Damascus mint, and countermarked in Arabic translation (*ṭayyib*) on many Imperial Image coins from Gerasa.[37] One should note here also that countermark A5 seems to depict the letter kappa alone, although this letter could itself conceal a lambda also, while the simple monogram of countermark A10 may contain kappa, lambda, and omicron. On the other hand, the star may have some religious significance. A six-pointed star sometimes occurs above the denomination M on the Byzantine follis as an apparent alternative to the small cross or, far less frequently, the chi-rho symbol.[38] This six-pointed star may conceal the letters iota and chi in abbreviation of the name Jesus Christ in Greek (Ἰησοῦς Χριστός). Alternatively, the star may allude to the declaration of Christ at the end of the book of Revelation where he identifies himself with the morning star (*Rev.* 22.16): 'I, Jesus, have sent my angel to announce these things to you in the churches; I am descended from the family of David; I am the bright morning star (ὁ ἀστὴρ ὁ λαμπρὸς ὁ πρωϊνός)'.

Fig. 14: pseudo-Byzantine follis (2.43g) with A4a countermark on reverse. Ex Wilkes & Curtis, Auction 6 (15 June 2015), lot 36.

Goodwin records a mere 3 specimens bearing his countermark A7 (Fig. 15a) and another 3 bearing his countermark A8 (Fig. 15b). These countermarks resemble each other to such an extent, and are so different from any of the other countermarks, that it seems probable that the same authority was responsible for both. Both consist of simple monograms, containing two main letters each, theta and epsilon, with a smaller omicron above these, in the case of A7 and theta and beta alone in the case

---

[37] For its presence on the *jāza hādhā* type of the Pseudo-Damascus mint, see D. Woods, 'A Note on Arab-Byzantine Coins of the *Jāza Hādhā* Type', **Israel Numismatic Research** 14 (2019), forthcoming. A. Oddy, 'The Phase 2 Coinage of Gerasa under Muʿawiya and His Successors', in T. Goodwin, **Coinage and History of the Near East 5** (London, 2017), pp. 49-74, catalogues 86 coins of Gerasa, 45 of which bear the *ṭayyib* countermark

[38] See e.g. Constans II, *MIB* 162c, 167c, 170c, 172c, 173c.

of A8. Goodwin suggests that the monogram of A7 'could well be an abbreviation for the personal name Theodore', that is, that it may contain the first two letters of the name Theodore, but it could equally well abbreviate several similar popular names such as Theodosius, Theodotus, Theodulus, and so on. He then speculates that the theta of A8 abbreviates the same name but that the beta abbreviates this man's title or family name. The weakness of this approach is that it applies two different methods of interpretation to two very similar monograms. If one considers the sort of monograms that appear on a comparable body of material during the same approximate period, lead seals, one notes that these monograms do not always represent personal names: they sometimes represent various types of prayer also. Probably the most common of these prayers calls upon the Mother of God: Θεοτόκε, βοήθει 'Mother of God, help!' (Fig. 15c). Since the monogram of A8 would perfectly abbreviate this common prayer, although in a much simpler fashion than normal upon the seals, it or something similar deserves serious consideration as the preferred interpretation. This interpretation is then confirmed by the fact that the monogram of A7 seems to abbreviate a similar invocation, probably ὁ θεός, ἐλέησόν 'God, have mercy!' taken from a famous biblical verse, Psalm 56.2: Ἐλέησόν με, ὁ θεός, ἐλέησόν με, ὅτι ἐπὶ σοὶ πέποιθεν ἡ ψυχή μου καὶ ἐν τῇ σκιᾷ τῶν πτερύγων σου ἐλπιῶ, ἕως οὗ παρέλθῃ ἡ ἀνομία 'Have mercy on me, O God, have mercy on me, for in you my soul takes refuge and I will take refuge in the shadow of your wings until the disaster has passed'. Hence the authority responsible for countermark A7 implicitly alludes to some disaster from which it seeks rescue, presumably the continued Muslim occupation.

Fig. 15: (a) sketch of countermark A7; (b) sketch of countermark A8; (c) Byzantine lead seal (27mm, 21.27g) of c.AD600 with standard monogram spelling Θεοτόκε, βοήθει 'Mother of God, help!' above eagle. Ex CNG, Auction 99 (13 May 2015), lot 789.

Goodwin discusses countermarks A9 (Fig. 16a-b) and A11 (Fig. 16c-d) together because they resemble each other so much, to such an extent that if their monograms do not represent variations of the same combinations of name and office, then they ought to refer to persons holding the same office at least. They are complex cross monograms, far more complex than any other monograms within the Class A group of countermarks, so that it seems likely that they combine two elements, a personal name and some title or office, like many other such complex monograms found, for example, on lead seals.[39] However, they are very difficult to resolve since, despite their similarities,

---

[39] For a catalogue of 415 different monograms from the 6th and 7th centuries, chiefly from lead seals, see J.R. Martindale, ***The Prosopography of the Later Roman Empire, III: AD527-641*** (Cambridge, 1992), pp. 1556-73.

they present very different problems in each case. In the case of countermark A9, the chief problem lies in the fact that the monogram does not appear to contain a letter upsilon. Most monograms preserve a personal name in the genitive case, and since most male personal names decline like nouns of the second declension with genitive single ending in –OV, most monograms contain these letters, usually in their ligatured form, ȣ. This occurs exactly where it should normally occur in the case of the A11 monogram, but is noticeably absent in the case of the A9 monogram. A small minority of monograms preserve a personal name in the nominative case, and since most male personal names have a nominative single ending in –OC, such monograms should contain a letter sigma, but the A9 monogram does not contain this either. It is possible that the head of the rho may conceal an omicron and rather less so that the projecting bars of the kappa below the rho may conceal an upsilon (on its side), so that one could recover a genitive ending in this way, but this would be far from ideal. As for the monogram of countermark A11, the chief difficulty it presents is in understanding how to interpret the two apparent letter omicrons hovering unattached in the upper angles of the cross. If they are letters, then they should be unnecessary to resolve the monogram proper because it already contains an omicron at the top of its main vertical bar. On the other hand, they seem too obtrusive to serve some sort of decorative or ornamental purpose.

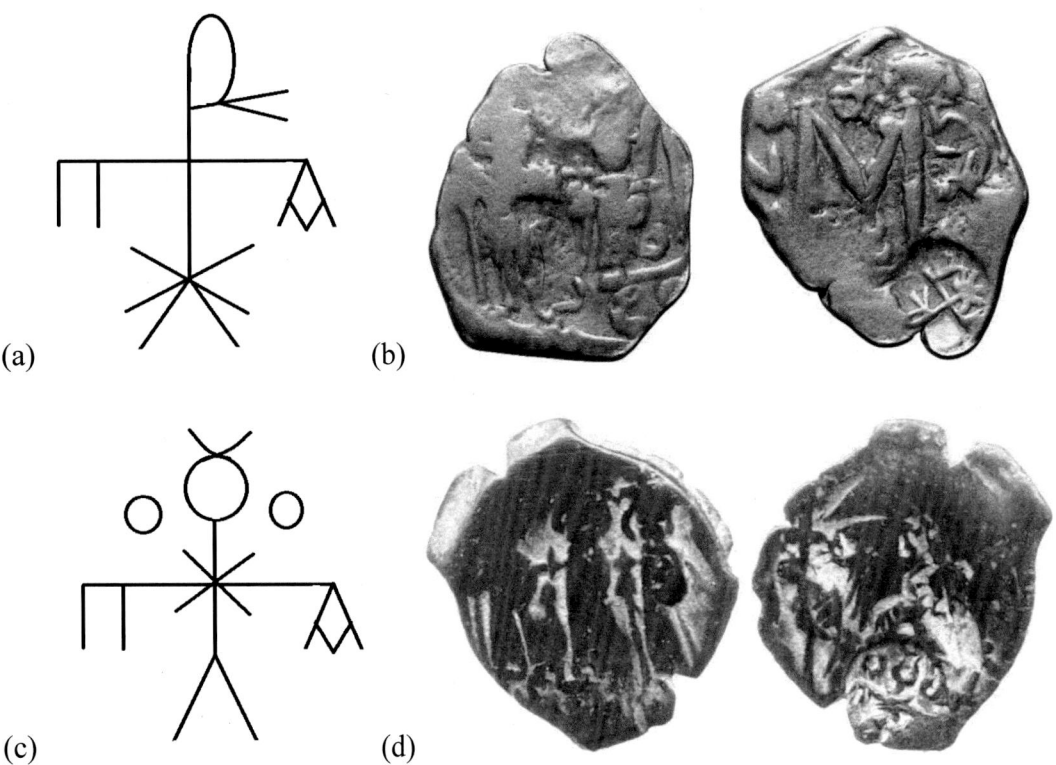

Fig. 16. (a) sketch of countermark A9; (b) follis of Heraclius (27mm, 5.84g) with countermark A9. Ex ebay May 2018; (c) sketch of countermark A11; (d) follis of Constans II (3.59g) with countermark A11 (MIB 175). Ex Wilkes & Curtis, Auction 6 (15 June 2015), lot 43.

Goodwin suggests that the A9 monogram could possibly be resolved as ΠΑΤΡΙΚΙΟC ΧΑΡΤΟΥΛΑΡΙΟC in reference to a man named Patrikios holding the office of *chartoularios* (to transliterate the Greek) and that the A11 monogram could possibly be resolved as ΠΑΥΛΟΥ ΧΑΡΤΟΥΛΑΡΙΟΥ in reference to a certain Paul holding the same office. In reality, of course, many other names are also possible, even accepting the presence of the exact same letters, although these the letters ΛЄO to the right.[8] It should have a reverse similar to the regular Imperial Image coin shown in Fig. 5c., with a reverse M and the Arabic legend around *ḍarb dimashq jā'iz* (current issue (of) Damascus), but instead it has a reverse m with a heavily blundered legend around, typical of a Type E Pseudo-Byzantine coin. I have been unable to find a die match for the reverse of 5b, but the Pseudo-Byzantine coin shown as Fig. 5a is reasonably close in style.

I am at present unable to offer a satisfactory explanation for this unusual hybrid. It could conceivably be the result of a stolen Damascus die being used by a Pseudo-Byzantine mint or even by a forger. Or it could possibly be a forgery by a die engraver who had previously worked at the Damascus mint, but in that case one might expect him to have produced a reasonable imitation of a Damascus reverse.

An interesting parallel to this example was found in the Irbid hoard and is shown in Fig. 6. This is not a mule of two different phases, but of two different mints. Again the obverse is the Damascus type with the star and crescent symbol, but, despite corrosion damage, it is clear that it was struck from a different die to that used for Fig. 5b.[9] Again I cannot offer a plausible explanation for this mule, but it seems very likely that its origin is connected in some way to that of our third example.

Figure 6: A second mule with the same obverse type as Example 3.
Obv: standing emperor with star and crescent above T and ΛЄO to the right.
Rev: m with cross above and long crosses either side, Arabic legend 'al-wafā' lillāh' in the exergue
(3.11g 9h, Irbid Hoard, Goodwin and Gyselen 2015 pp.264-265 cat. no. 490).

Examples 4 and 5

My next two examples are both mules mixing Damascus Imperial Image and Standing Caliph dies. Fig. 7b shows the first of these, which has a standing emperor obverse coupled with a symbol-on-steps reverse.[10] For comparison Fig. 7a is a late Damascus Imperial Image coin which is essentially the same as the Damascus coin in Fig. 5c, but this one is of rather different style with slightly blundered legends, particularly the word *jā'iz* on the left.[11] Fig. 7c is a normal Damascus Standing

---

[8] See Goodwin and Gyselen 2015 pp. 226 and 227, cat. nos 50 and 51 for further examples of Damascus coins with this symbol. Although not rare, the star and crescent symbol is less common than the bird or palm branch symbols.
[9] I have so far been unable to match either of these obverse dies with known Damascus coins, but the style of both appears to be absolutely 'correct'.
[10] So far as I know the type was first published by Tareq Ramadan in 2010, although it had been noted by Marcus Phillips at an informal meeting of the Round Table in about 2000. I know of four examples all struck from the same die pair: Fig. 7b, Ramadan 2010, Phillips collection and Goodwin 2018 Cat. 138.
[11] The reverse of this coin is also found with a two-figure reverse and it seems very likely that this two-figure type was the last to be struck by the Damascus mint before the change was made to the Standing Caliph type. Hence my description of Fig. 7a as a 'late' coin.

Imperial Image coinage (Fig. 4c), which we would expect to be later.[7] For comparison Fig. 4a shows a fairly typical Pseudo-Byzantine copy of Heraclius or Constans II with a heavily blundered reverse based distantly on a Byzantine prototype. The Damascus coin has a reverse with a capital **M** with a monogram above, officina ⊃, **ANO** – **XTII** either side and **ΔAM** in the exergue. The resemblance between the reverses of coins b and c is striking, the only difference being the substitution of **CON** for **ΔAM** on coin b. There only appear to be two explanations for this anomalous reverse:

1. That this is a relatively late Pseudo-Byzantine coin from a mint where an unusually competent die engraver developed this distinctive style of reverse, which was then adopted by the Damascus mint, which also perhaps took on the die engraver himself.

2. Or that this Pseudo Byzantine mint was producing coins after the Imperial Image series had started at Damascus and copied the Damascus reverse style along with the carefully made round flan. Again this would make our coin rather late in the Pseudo-Byzantine series and would be additional evidence of an overlap between phases.

In the absence of further evidence it is difficult to judge which of these two explanations is the most likely.

Example 3

Figure 5: Damascus Imperial Image coin with Pseudo-Byzantine reverse.
Coin a – Type E Pseudo-Byzantine (3.97g 3h, author's collection).
Coin b – mule with Damascus obv. and Pseudo-Byzantine rev. (3.08g 6h, author's collection).
Coin c - Damascus standing emperor type, Arabic rev. (4.38g 6h, CNG auction 424 lot 591).

This example (Fig.5b) is something of a puzzle – it has a Damascus standing emperor obverse, of perfectly normal style, with a symbol to the lower left comprising a star and crescent above a **T** and

---

[7] This coin is part of a die-linked group which also includes coins with a facing bust obverse, see Oddy 2019.

My first example (Fig. 3b) has a standing emperor on the obverse with a blundered version of the ENTϑTO – NIKA legend found on the Byzantine prototype. It is therefore a typical Pseudo-Byzantine obverse, similar in style to Fig. 3a, but instead of the expected cursive m reverse of Fig. 3a it has a capital M reverse from an Imperial Image coin of Hims (Emesa) with the mint name ЄMH – CIC and the Arabic word *ṭayyib* (good) in the exergue. For comparison Fig. 3c is an official Hims coin with the same reverse, but with the obverse legend KAΛON (good).

The obverse of this 'transitional' coin is quite good for a Pseudo-Byzantine coin, but the reverse is rather roughly engraved. In fact some apparently official Hims coins do have rather rough reverses and the reverse on the central coin might just about pass as official, but I am more inclined to think that this is the product of another mint striking Pseudo-Byzantine coins, probably outside Hims, which decided to produce a few Hims imitations for circulation in that city. They used one of their existing standing emperor obverse dies, either because they did not realise that the new Hims obverse was significantly different or because they thought that no one would notice that the legends were wrong. This coin is, so far as I know, unique, so presumably they quickly moved on to produce a better obverse, or perhaps they were instructed to stop imitating Hims. So this coin was probably not struck in the official Hims mint. But, rather than an outright forgery, it may have been an illicit issue from an otherwise legitimate Pseudo-Byzantine mint perhaps operating in Jund Qinnasrīn.

Example 2

Figure 4: Pseudo-Byzantine coin with Damascus-style reverse.
Coin a – Type C Pseudo-Byzantine with 'typical' reverse (4.55g 6h, author's collection).
Coin b – Type C Pseudo-Byzantine with 'Damascus reverse' (3.15g 6h, author's collection).
Coin c – Damascus standing emperor type, Greek rev. (4.13g 6h, CNG auction 298 lot 430).

My second example (Fig. 4b) is strictly a Pseudo-Byzantine coin with an obverse copying a Class 5 follis of Heraclius and a reverse with a pseudo-mint name of Constantinople along with a pseudo-date 17. But this reverse is very unusual because it closely matches the reverse on the Damascus

This looks very much like the reverse of an earlier Imperial Image coin, although it does not qualify as a 'transitional' coin because the earlier Amman coins had completely different reverse legends.

*Fig.2. ʿAmmān Standing Caliph types. Coin a – normal type (3.36g 10h, author's collection). Coin b – mintless type with **M** reverse, 3.88g (S. Album auction 22 lot 120).*

Fig. 2a shows a normal Amman coin and 2b the variety with the reverse **M**.[4] Why did the Amman mint strike this unusual variety? Possibly it was their first attempt to produce the new Standing Caliph type, and perhaps it did not meet with state approval, so the reverse had to be rapidly changed to a design that lined up with that at other mints. Whatever the correct interpretation, this variety is useful for our present purpose because, in contrast to the 'solidus', it is almost certainly an official issue and the result of a deliberate decision made by the mint.

Example 1

*Figure 3: Pseudo-Byzantine obverse and Ḥimṣ Imperial Image reverse.
Coin a – Pseudo-Byzantine Type E (6.34g 6h, S. Album auction 23 lot 70).[5]
Coin b – mule with Pseudo-Byzantine obverse and Ḥimṣ reverse (3.63g 7h, author's collection).[6]
Coin c – Ḥimṣ standing emperor type (4.19g 1h, CNG auction 333 lot 421).*

---

[4] Although this coin is mintless we can be certain that it was struck by the Amman mint because of the very close stylistic similarities between the obverses of the two varieties and the identical types of flan used for both varieties.
[5] Although the obverse is very similar in style to that of coin b, I should emphasise that this is an exceptionally fine example of a Type E Pseudo-Byzantine coin; for a more typical example see Fig. 1 of my other article in this volume.
[6] First published in Goodwin 1995 Cat. 14.

2. Or a forger could have obtained a stolen official die and paired it with whatever false die he had conveniently to hand.

3. An old die might have been re-used for a short period under emergency conditions, for example when the only available die broke. This could occur at either an official or unofficial mint, although it seems inherently unlikely at a large well managed official mint.

4. If the coin is official, it could be the first stage of a change of type, so for example the obverse was changed first and then the reverse shortly after. This would be a genuine transitional coin.

5. Finally, at the other end of the spectrum, an official mint might make a deliberate decision to produce a hybrid – perhaps a special coin aimed at Christians or for use in another town or jund with different preferences.

To assist in the assessment of our the six examples, let us first consider two contemporary cases, which are not 'transitional' coins within the definition of this article, but where we can be certain which of the above circumstances applied to the minting.

Fig. 1. A counterfeit Phocas/Heraclius hybrid 'solidus'.
Coin a – regular solidus of Phocas (4.50g 7h, CNG auction 102 lot 1141).
Coin b – fourée 'solidus' with Heraclius obv. and Phocas rev. (2.85g 12h, author's collection).
Coin c – regular solidus of Heraclius (4.44g 6h, CNG auction 412 lot 726).

Fig. 1b shows a copper-cored gold plated 'solidus', found in Jordan and almost certainly dating from the first half of the seventh century. Whilst the obverse copies a solidus of Heraclius (610-641) minted in the 620s (Fig. 1c), the reverse copies a solidus of Phocas (602-610) minted before 610 (Fig. 1a). Clearly this hybrid coin must be a forgery and yet the coin is well struck and the die engraving is competent, indeed it is well up to the normal standard of unquestionably official Arab-Byzantine coins. There is therefore an important conclusion to be drawn from this coin, namely that a coin of good style minted in seventh century Syria is not necessarily the product of an official mint.

The second case concerns the Standing Caliph coinage of Amman which includes an unusual variety with the symbol-on-steps on the reverse replaced by a capital **M** with the *shahāda* around.

What can we learn from 'Transitional' coins?

Tony Goodwin[1]

As most readers of this volume will know the Arab-Byzantine copper coinage of Greater Syria can conveniently be divided into three phases:

1. Pseudo-Byzantine coins which loosely copy (sometimes very loosely) official Byzantine prototypes, but have meaningless Greek or Latin legends, sometimes garbled versions of the prototype and sometimes just a jumble of meaningless letters (from 640s).

2. Imperial Image coins – still with Byzantine-style images, but which have meaningful legends, and usually mint names, in Greek or Arabic (c. 670 to early 690s).

3. Standing Caliph coins which have a completely new Islamic imagery and all Arabic legends (early 690s to c. 697).

(dates in brackets are approximate and there was some overlap between phases)

This classification has proved to be extremely robust and almost all Arab-Byzantine coins can be assigned to one particular phase without difficulty.[2] However, a very small number of coins exist which combine the obverse of one phase with the reverse of another. In 1995 I described these as 'transitional' coins on the basis that they might represent the point of transition from one phase to the next.[3] This article considers six examples of these rare coins and discusses what we can learn from them and in particular whether any of them truly represent an actual point of transition for a specific mint. All coins are illustrated at approximately 1.5x actual size.

Some preliminary considerations

Before examining actual examples, it will be useful to consider what circumstances might give rise to a hybrid or mule mixing a new obverse with an apparently obsolete reverse or vice versa:

1. At one end of the spectrum the coin could be the product of an illegal mint forging various types of coin and the dies were somehow mixed up.

---

[1] Tony Goodwin is an independent scholar a.goodwin2@btopenworld.com
[2] A potential problem is presented by imitations of Imperial Image or Standing Caliph coins where the legends are heavily blundered, but this problem is solved by assigning such coins to the phase that they imitate. So the numerous products of the Pseudo-Damascus mint are classified as 'Imperial Image' despite often having more or less meaningless legends. A more serious problem (in fact the only outstanding problem which I know of) is presented by the Constantine IV imitations with possible Pahlavi legends. These are at present classified as Pseudo-Byzantine Type I, but if the Pahlavi legend is meaningful there is a case for re-classifying them as 'Imperial Image'. However, there is considerable disagreement as to the reading of the legend and, in his comprehensive study of the series Oddy showed that they die-linked with Type E Pseudo-Byzantine coins of quite normal appearance (Oddy 2010), so there is also a case for retaining the present classification.
[3] Goodwin 1995. I do not regard the term 'transitional' as particularly satisfactory in this context, but a more precise name such as 'inter-phase hybrid' would I think be impossibly clumsy.

variety than earlier Byzantine countermarks within the same region, and their precise reading and significance must remain a mystery in many cases. Nevertheless, some do seem to have possessed religious significance.

were certainly two common names, particularly if one accepts that the office was described as *chartoularikos* rather than *chartoularios*, so obviating the need for the personal name in monogram A9 to contain a kappa. However, it is on the identity of the office concealed within the monograms that I wish to focus here. They may well conceal a reference to a *chartoularios/chartoularikos*, but they could also conceal a reference to a *charaktēs*, meaning 'stamper, coiner', in the genitive case at least (*-ou* ending once more). Since that is a much closer description of what the relevant person was actually doing, stamping his seal on coins, one should perhaps prefer to identify him as a *charaktēs* rather than a *chartoularios/chartoularikos*.

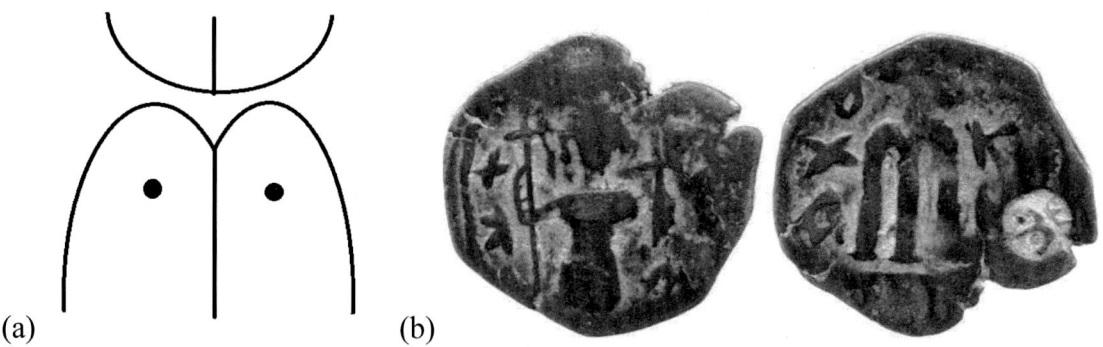

Fig. 17: (a) sketch of countermark A13; (b) pseudo-Byzantine follis (25mm, 4.18g) with countermark A13 on reverse. Ex Wilkes & Curtis, Auction 6 (15 June 2015), lot 52.

Finally, Goodwin says very little about his countermark A13 (Fig. 17a-b) except to note that the fact that dots occur between the arches of the apparent cursive m means that it resembles the reverses of some coins of the *al-wafā lillāh* type and so perhaps originate from the same locality. True, but his countermark A6 also includes decorative dots within the four angles of a cross, so A13 is not unique in possessing this sort of decoration. It is surely more important that the countermark seems to consist of two letters, a cursive mu and an epsilon. It could perhaps abbreviate the name of some town or village, whether Emesa (Ἔμεσα), Emmaus (Ἐμμαούς), or of some smaller settlement with name beginning Em- or Me-. However, with no good evidence for the provenance of the 4 specimens recorded by Goodwin, or for the others that have appeared in the trade since, no progress seems possible on this front. Alternatively, the monogram could perhaps abbreviate a personal name, whether Menelaus (Μενέλαος), Mercurius (Μερκούριος), or something similar. Unfortunately, there are simply far too many possibilities: two letters do not take one very far, particularly if one cannot determine their order or whether they abbreviate one word or two.

Conclusion

The main finding emerging from the present review of the countermarks used by Byzantine authorities during the 630s and by local Syrian authorities during the period c.660-80 is that modern commentators have consistently neglected the potential religious significance of many of the monograms used in these countermarks. Furthermore, they have tended to focus on the potential occurrence of personal names or titles to the exclusion of other possibilities, not least the occurrence of pious slogans or prayers. As far as the Byzantine countermarks are concerned, there is a strong – and quite unsurprising – emphasis on the power of the cross. They do not so much celebrate the name of the emperor, but his association with the saving power of the cross, if they refer to the emperor at all. As for the countermarks used by local Syrian authorities, they display a far greater they present very different problems in each case. In the case of countermark A9, the chief problem lies in the fact that the monogram does not appear to contain a letter upsilon. Most monograms preserve a personal name in the genitive case, and since most male personal names decline like nouns of the second declension with genitive single ending in –OV, most monograms contain these letters, usually in their ligatured form, ȣ. This occurs exactly where it should normally occur in the case of the A11 monogram, but is noticeably absent in the case of the A9 monogram. A small minority of monograms preserve a personal name in the nominative case, and since most male personal names have a nominative single ending in –OC, such monograms should contain a letter sigma, but the A9 monogram does not contain this either. It is possible that the head of the rho may conceal an omicron and rather less so that the projecting bars of the kappa below the rho may conceal an upsilon (on its side), so that one could recover a genitive ending in this way, but this would be far from ideal. As for the monogram of countermark A11, the chief difficulty it presents is in understanding how to interpret the two apparent letter omicrons hovering unattached in the upper angles of the cross. If they are letters, then they should be unnecessary to resolve the monogram proper because it already contains an omicron at the top of its main vertical bar. On the other hand, they seem too obtrusive to serve some sort of decorative or ornamental purpose.

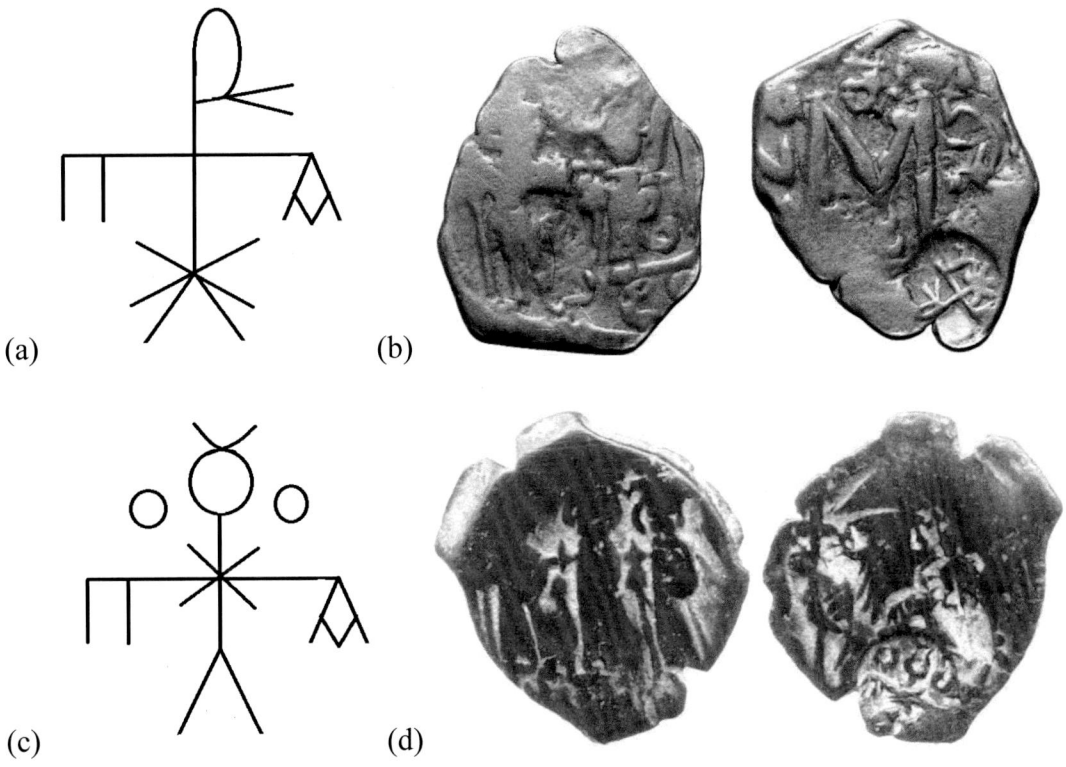

Fig. 16. (a) sketch of countermark A9; (b) follis of Heraclius (27mm, 5.84g) with countermark A9. Ex ebay May 2018; (c) sketch of countermark A11; (d) follis of Constans II (3.59g) with countermark A11 (MIB 175). Ex Wilkes & Curtis, Auction 6 (15 June 2015), lot 43.

Goodwin suggests that the A9 monogram could possibly be resolved as ΠΑΤΡΙΚΙΟC ΧΑΡΤΟVΛΑΡΙΟC in reference to a man named Patrikios holding the office of *chartoularios* (to transliterate the Greek) and that the A11 monogram could possibly be resolved as ΠΑVΛΟV ΧΑΡΤΟVΛΑΡΙΟV in reference to a certain Paul holding the same office. In reality, of course, many other names are also possible, even accepting the presence of the exact same letters, although these of A8. Goodwin suggests that the monogram of A7 'could well be an abbreviation for the personal name Theodore', that is, that it may contain the first two letters of the name Theodore, but it could equally well abbreviate several similar popular names such as Theodosius, Theodotus, Theodulus, and so on. He then speculates that the theta of A8 abbreviates the same name but that the beta abbreviates this man's title or family name. The weakness of this approach is that it applies two different methods of interpretation to two very similar monograms. If one considers the sort of monograms that appear on a comparable body of material during the same approximate period, lead seals, one notes that these monograms do not always represent personal names: they sometimes represent various types of prayer also. Probably the most common of these prayers calls upon the Mother of God: Θεοτόκε, βοήθει 'Mother of God, help!' (Fig. 15c). Since the monogram of A8 would perfectly abbreviate this common prayer, although in a much simpler fashion than normal upon the seals, it or something similar deserves serious consideration as the preferred interpretation. This interpretation is then confirmed by the fact that the monogram of A7 seems to abbreviate a similar invocation, probably ὁ θεός, ἐλέησόν 'God, have mercy!' taken from a famous biblical verse, Psalm 56.2: Ἐλέησόν με, ὁ θεός, ἐλέησόν με, ὅτι ἐπὶ σοὶ πέποιθεν ἡ ψυχή μου καὶ ἐν τῇ σκιᾷ τῶν πτερύγων σου ἐλπιῶ, ἕως οὗ παρέλθῃ ἡ ἀνομία 'Have mercy on me, O God, have mercy on me, for in you my soul takes refuge and I will take refuge in the shadow of your wings until the disaster has passed'. Hence the authority responsible for countermark A7 implicitly alludes to some disaster from which it seeks rescue, presumably the continued Muslim occupation.

Fig. 15: (a) sketch of countermark A7; (b) sketch of countermark A8; (c) Byzantine lead seal (27mm, 21.27g) of c.AD600 with standard monogram spelling Θεοτόκε, βοήθει 'Mother of God, help!' above eagle. Ex CNG, Auction 99 (13 May 2015), lot 789.

Goodwin discusses countermarks A9 (Fig. 16a-b) and A11 (Fig. 16c-d) together because they resemble each other so much, to such an extent that if their monograms do not represent variations of the same combinations of name and office, then they ought to refer to persons holding the same office at least. They are complex cross monograms, far more complex than any other monograms within the Class A group of countermarks, so that it seems likely that they combine two elements, a personal name and some title or office, like many other such complex monograms found, for example, on lead seals.[39] However, they are very difficult to resolve since, despite their similarities,

---

[39] For a catalogue of 415 different monograms from the 6th and 7th centuries, chiefly from lead seals, see J.R. Martindale, ***The Prosopography of the Later Roman Empire, III: AD527-641*** (Cambridge, 1992), pp. 1556-73.

Fig. 13: follis of Constans II (21mm, 3.62g) dated regnal year 16 (656/57) (MIB 173) with A3 countermark on obverse. Ex Savoca Coins (ebay June 2018).

Goodwin records 40 specimens bearing his countermark A4a resembling a six-limbed star (Fig. 14), 15 Byzantine coins and 25 Pseudo-Byzantine coins. However, he does not comment upon the potential significance of this apparent star. On the one hand, it could perhaps contain kappa and lambda in abbreviation of the Greek adjective ΚΑΛΟΝ 'fine' as found on the Imperial Image coins of Emesa, on some Imperial Image coins of the *jāza hādhā* type from the Pseudo-Damascus mint, and countermarked in Arabic translation (*ṭayyib*) on many Imperial Image coins from Gerasa.[37] One should note here also that countermark A5 seems to depict the letter kappa alone, although this letter could itself conceal a lambda also, while the simple monogram of countermark A10 may contain kappa, lambda, and omicron. On the other hand, the star may have some religious significance. A six-pointed star sometimes occurs above the denomination M on the Byzantine follis as an apparent alternative to the small cross or, far less frequently, the chi-rho symbol.[38] This six-pointed star may conceal the letters iota and chi in abbreviation of the name Jesus Christ in Greek (Ἰησοῦς Χριστός). Alternatively, the star may allude to the declaration of Christ at the end of the book of Revelation where he identifies himself with the morning star (*Rev.* 22.16): 'I, Jesus, have sent my angel to announce these things to you in the churches; I am descended from the family of David; I am the bright morning star (ὁ ἀστὴρ ὁ λαμπρὸς ὁ πρωϊνός)'.

Fig. 14: pseudo-Byzantine follis (2.43g) with A4a countermark on reverse. Ex Wilkes & Curtis, Auction 6 (15 June 2015), lot 36.

Goodwin records a mere 3 specimens bearing his countermark A7 (Fig. 15a) and another 3 bearing his countermark A8 (Fig. 15b). These countermarks resemble each other to such an extent, and are so different from any of the other countermarks, that it seems probable that the same authority was responsible for both. Both consist of simple monograms, containing two main letters each, theta and epsilon, with a smaller omicron above these, in the case of A7 and theta and beta alone in the case

---

[37] For its presence on the *jāza hādhā* type of the Pseudo-Damascus mint, see D. Woods, 'A Note on Arab-Byzantine Coins of the *Jāza Hādhā* Type', **Israel Numismatic Research** 14 (2019), forthcoming. A. Oddy, 'The Phase 2 Coinage of Gerasa under Muʿawiya and His Successors', in T. Goodwin, **Coinage and History of the Near East 5** (London, 2017), pp. 49-74, catalogues 86 coins of Gerasa, 45 of which bear the *ṭayyib* countermark

[38] See e.g. Constans II, *MIB* 162c, 167c, 170c, 172c, 173c.

full stem of the adjective rather than the case-ending, as this would have made the meaning of the abbreviation much clearer. It is more likely, therefore, that these letters abbreviate some term beginning with either KωN or KNω. While it is not impossible that these could abbreviate a personal name, given that countermark A1 probably abbreviates the name of a town, one should probably start any investigation of this matter with due consideration of that possibility. As it happens, very few ancient towns had names beginning with KNω. In contrast, however, Constantine I and his sons renamed numerous towns throughout the empire after themselves, so several towns in the eastern half of the empire did have names beginning with KωN.[34] Of most relevance here, Constantius II (337-61) seems to have renamed Antarados as Constantia (Κωνστάντια) after himself in 346, but usage was inconsistent and later sources could use either or both names.[35] This raises the possibility that countermarks A1 and A3 refer to the same town, Antarados/Constantia, but that A1 refers to it by its original name, Antarados, while A3 refers to it by its new name after 346, Constantia. As it happens, it is arguable that the same authority based somewhere near Emesa did change its countermark over time because the fact that 15 of the 19 recorded host coins for countermark A1 were pseudo-Byzantine coins while 11 of the 17 recorded host coins for countermark A3 were Imperial Image coins does suggest a temporal difference, that is, that countermark A1 ceased being used when the vast majority of the coins in circulation were still pseudo-Byzantine, while countermark A3 was in use while the majority of coins in circulation were Imperial Image coins. However, if one assumes that the authority based in Antarados/Constantia that was responsible for the countermarking of the coinage was also responsible for the subsequent striking of Imperial Image coins there, then this reconstruction becomes problematic for the reason that the Imperial Image coins all bear the mint-name Antarados rather than Constantia, so that this reconstruction would require that the same authority first identified itself by the name Antarados (A1 countermark), decided next to use the name Constantia instead (A3 countermark), then returned finally to the use of the name Antarados (Imperial Image coins). This reconstruction would become much less problematic if one could explain the KωN or KNω of the A3 countermark in such a way that it did not require that the relevant authority changed its preferred title for its location so often. Interestingly, very few words in Greek actually begin with either KωN or KNω but one of these is the term κωνσίλιον 'council'.[36] It is possible, therefore, that a council based in Antarados, presumably the town-council, initially used a countermark abbreviating the name of its location (A1), replaced this with a countermark abbreviating the term 'council' instead (A3), and resumed the use of the town-name once more when it began striking Imperial Image coins. Or, alternatively, some body called the 'the council' based near Antarados and Emesa began countermarking coins about the same time that another body based at Antarados ceased countermarking coins. Finally, one should also note that the application of countermark A3 to a Byzantine follis dated to regnal year 16 (656/57) of Constans II provides a new *terminus post quem* for its continued use (Fig. 13).

---

[34] See N. Lenski, ***Constantine and the Cities: Imperial Authority and Civic Politics*** (Philadelphia, 2016), pp. 131-164.

[35] See R.W. Burgess, ***Studies in Eusebian and Post-Eusebian Chronography*** (Stuttgart, 1999), pp. 170-71, 272. There is some disagreement as to whether Antarados was renamed Constantina or Constantia, but the precise form of the new name does not matter here.

[36] For κωνσίλιον, see e.g. E.A. Sophocles, ***Greek Lexicon of the Roman and Byzantine Periods*** (Cambridge, MA, 1914), pp. 701-02; H.J. Mason, ***Greek Terms for Roman Institution: A Lexicon and Analysis*** (Toronto, 1974), p. 65.

Goodwin records 19 specimens bearing his countermark A1 (Fig. 11a-b), 3 Byzantine coins (2 of Heraclius, 1 of Constans II), 15 Pseudo-Byzantine coins, and 1 Imperial Image coin from Emesa. The countermark is a monogram that certainly contains the Greek letters alpha, nu, and tau, but may also include a lambda or an iota. He favours interpreting this monogram as ANT in abbreviation of the name of Antarados (Ἀντάραδος), offering two reasons in support of this interpretation. The first is that Antarados did in fact strike coins during the Imperial Image phase of coinage.[33] The second is that the fact that this countermark was used on a coin of Emesa suggests that the authority responsible for it was situated somewhere relatively near Emesa, as Antarados was. One may now add a third reason in further support of this interpretation, the existence of a specimen that displays the countermark A3 on the obverse in addition to the countermark A1 on the reverse (Fig. 12a). This is important because of the 17 specimens bearing countermark A3 reported by Goodwin, 10 are Imperial Image coins from Emesa, and only 1 an Imperial Image coin from Damascus. In other words, the countermark A3 was clearly being applied by some authority at or near Emesa, so that the authority applying the A1 countermark must also have been located at or near Emesa, which supports the location of this authority at Antaradus once more. Finally, the application of this countermark to a Byzantine follis dated to regnal year 12 (652/53) of Constans II provides a new *terminus post quem* for its continued use (Fig. 12b).

(a)

(b)

Fig. 12: (a) pseudo-Byzantine follis (26mm, 3.99g) with three countermarks, an A3 countermark on the obverse (to left of standing figure), an A1 countermark on the reverse (bottom), and a 2nd unclear countermark on the reverse (top). Ex ebay May 2018; (b) follis of Constans II (21mm, 4.60g) dated regnal year 12 (652/53) (MIB 170) with A1 countermark on lower reverse. Ex ebay September 2018.

The countermark A3 consists of three Greek letters grouped together, an omega above a kappa and a nu (Fig. 12a). Goodwin suggests that these should be read as KωN in abbreviation of KAΛωN 'fine' as found on the obverse of the Imperial Image coins of Antarados, although he is also open to the possibility that they could abbreviate the personal name of an official called Constantine (Κωνσταντῖνος) or something similar. However, if anyone had wanted to abbreviate the term KAΛωN, they would probably have abbreviated it as KAΛ rather than KωN, preferring to retain the

---

[33] See W. Schulze, 'The Byzantine-Arab Transitional Coinage of Ṭarṭūs', *Numismatic Chronicle* 173 (2013), pp. 245-59.

the coins, that is, on the side that did not already bear the legend ЄN TȢTѠ NIKA.²⁹ It is arguable, therefore, that those imposing the countermark deliberately placed it on the reverse in order to avoid reduplication of a message already present on the obverse. As to the purpose of this countermarking, Schulze argues that it was economic, that it was intended 'to regulate the copper circulation and to revalue Byzantine copper coins – and, as an additional effect, to keep them on the island'.³⁰ Yet it is hard to disregard the fact that the stamping of a monogram normally associated with the coinage of Sicily upon the coins circulating in Cyprus occurred during the same approximate period that Constans II was resident in Sicily rather than at Constantinople. Another possibility, therefore, is that this countermarking was intended to signify some new administrative arrangement subjecting Cyprus to increased control by the court of Constans II in Sicily, that is, that two of the largest islands within the empire were being brought closer together in some way by an emperor who was re-inventing the Byzantine navy, even if it was Constantinople that continued to supply most of its copper coinage to Cyprus.³¹

Arab-Byzantine Countermarks on Coins Circulating in Syria.

Goodwin identified 40 different countermarks apparently imposed by local Syrian authorities on Byzantine and Arab-Byzantine coins circulating within their districts sometime after the Arab conquest.³² He divided these into three groups, a Class A where the countermarks consist of Byzantine-style monograms and geometric designs, Class B where the countermarks consist of Arabic words, and Class C where the countermarks appear to consist of various images. The focus here will be upon the Class A countermarks. I will discuss these in the order that he lists them, but only those where some further comments about their interpretation seems necessary.

(a) (b)

Fig. 11: (a) sketch of countermark A1; (b) follis of Constans II (24mm, 6.20g) dated regnal year 3 (643/44) (MIB 164) with A1 countermark on upper reverse. Ex ebay October 2018.

---

²⁹ Schulze, 'Countermarks from before the Arab Conquest' (see n. 3), p. 35, notes that the countermark was placed on the reverse in just over 80% of cases, but that this figure increases to about 90% if one disregards host coins of type *MIB* 175 where the occurrence of three standing figures on the reverse probably made it difficult for many to distinguish between obverse and reverse. In the present context, one should note that *MIB* 175 did not bear the legend ЄN TȢTѠ NIKA on either side, so if the intention had been to avoid duplicating this, it did not matter upon which side the countermark was imposed.
³⁰ Schulze, 'Countermarks from before the Arab Conquest' (see n. 3), p. 38.
³¹ On the reforming activities of Constans II while in Sicily, particularly his creation of a navy, see C. Zuckerman, 'Learning from the Enemy and More: Studies in 'Dark Centuries' Byzantium', ***Millenium*** 2 (2005), pp. 79-136.
³² For what follows, see Goodwin, 'Countermarks from after the Arab Conquest' (see n. 3), pp. 41-46.

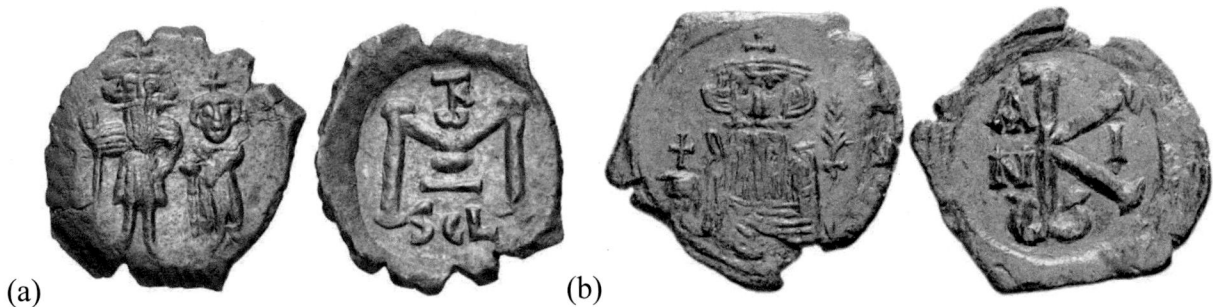

(a) (b)

Fig. 10: (a) follis of Constans II (MIB 209), Syracuse (20mm, 3.41g). Ex CNG, E-Auction 258 (22 June 2011), lot 518; (b) half-follis of Constans II (MIB 212), Syracuse (25mm, 5.19g). Ex CNG, E-Auction 153 (29 November 2006), lot 257.

The Class 7 countermark bears a striking resemblance to the Class 3 countermark in that each monogram includes the same vertical element with a tau at the top and an omega at the bottom. If, as has been argued in the case of the Class 3 countermark, this abbreviates the demonstrative pronoun T(OV)TⲰ 'by this', then one should consider the possibility that it performs the same function in the case of the Class 7 countermark also. That would leave the letter kappa alone to be explained.[27] It cannot form part of an abbreviation of the term NIKA as in the case of the Class 3 countermark because there is no accompanying letter nu here. The obvious alternative is that it abbreviates the name Constantine (Κωνσταντῖνος) instead, so that the monogram implies that Constans II (Constantine) does something 'by this'. Hence the monogram seems to represent an abbreviation of some such statement as K(ⲰNCTANTINOS) T(OV)TⲰ (NIKA) 'Constantine conquers by this', where the viewer is expected to be able to identify the object referred to as 'this' either as a result of general familiarity with the use of this phrase of the cross or because Constans is depicted holding some form of cross (long cross or cross-on-globe) on the obverse of the coin.[28] In support of this interpretation, one notes that none of the folles from Syracuse depicting this monogram on the reverse bear the legend ЄN TꙊTⲰ NIKA 'Conquer by this!' on the obverse. Hence there is no reduplication of the message concerning the conquering power of the cross. Furthermore, it may be precisely because this monogram abbreviates a declaration that 'Constantine conquers by this' that none of the folles from Constantinople bearing the legend ЄN TꙊTⲰ NIKA 'Conquer by this!' on the obverse include this monogram on the reverse. Hence it seems that the folles from both mints emphasize that Constans II conquers by means of the cross, but they do so in very different ways, those from Constantinople by means of an explicit legend in full on the obverse, those from Syracuse by means of a severely abbreviated monogram on the reverse.

If this interpretation of the monogram is correct, then the imposition of this countermark upon the coins circulating in Cyprus, most of which were Constantinopolitan issues, and many of which already bore the legend ЄN TꙊTⲰ NIKA on the obverse, represented a reduplication of a message already there. However, it is noteworthy that the countermark was normally placed on the reverse of

---

[27] Grierson, *DOC* 2.1, p. 58, suggests that 'the conspicuous K', taken as the first letter of the name Constantine, may have doubled as a mark of value, so that the countermarking was intended to revalue the folles so stamped as half-folles. This idea continues to receive support. See e.g. L. Zavagno, "Betwixt the Greeks and the Saracens': Coins and Coinage in Cyprus in the Seventh and the Eighth Century', ***Byzantion*** 81 (2011), pp. 448-483, at 469. Yet this is nonsense that takes no account of the fact that the exact same monogram, with a similarly 'conspicuous K', occurs on the reverse of most folles struck in Sicily during the reign of Constans, as already described. Whatever its precise significance, therefore, the kappa does not serve to revalue folles as half-folles.

[28] Alternatively, the kappa may serve a dual function, abbreviating both the name Constantine and some form of the verb κρατέω 'I rule, conquer' used as a synonym for νικάω.

Fig. 9: (a) sketch of Class 7 countermark, Type a; (b) follis of Constans II (MIB 173), Constantinople (17mm, 2.46g), with Class 7 countermark, Type a, on the upper reverse. Ex CNG, E-Auction 305 (26 June 2013), lot 417; (c) sketch of Class 7 countermark, Type b; (d) pseudo-Byzantine follis with Class 7 countermark, Type b, on the lower reverse (25mm, 4.35g). Ex ebay December 2017.

It is important to note at this point that the monogram used in this countermark saw extensive use on the copper coinage also, but almost exclusively on the folles and half-folles struck under Constans II at Syracuse in Sicily. It was depicted above the denomination M on five of the six types of folles struck there during his reign (Fig. 10a), and was even the main device on the reverse of the half-folles struck there during the period c.648-52 (Fig. 10b).[25] It was also depicted above the denomination M on the final type of follis struck at Carthage under Constans II during the period 662-67, a factor that raises the suspicion that these coins may have been struck at Syracuse rather than Carthage.[26] Whatever the case, it is not clear why the mint at Syracuse should have favoured this monogram when other mints continued to prefer to depict a small cross above the denomination M in the traditional manner, but its use of this monogram above the denomination M in replacement of the traditional cross for such an extended period of time encourages the belief that it somehow conveyed the same basic message, that is, that it also served in some way to promote the veneration of the cross.

---

[25] For the folles, see Constans II, *MIB* 205, 206, 207, 209, 210. The exception is *MIB* 208 (652/53) which depicts the traditional small cross above the denomination M. For the half-folles, see *MIB* 211, 212.

[26] *MIB* 194. Since Constans II was resident at Syracuse during the period 663-68, it is possible that it may have become more active in the supply of coinage to Africa at this time.

Byzantine territory during the last stages of the Arab conquest, that one countermark was applied in one city until it was captured by the Arabs, while the second countermark was applied in another city until that too was captured by the Arabs, even tentatively identifying these cities as Jerusalem and Caesarea. The Class 4 coins, those bearing both Class 2 and Class 3 countermarks, are then identifiable as coins that have moved from one city to another with the flow of refugees. However, nothing really excludes the sequential use of these countermarks within the same city or district. This city or district may have begun by applying the Class 2 countermark to its copper coinage, but have changed subsequently to the use of the Class 3 countermark instead, so moving from a political countermark naming the emperor to a religious countermark stressing the power of the cross as the military situation deteriorated even further.

Fig. 8: follis of Heraclius with both Class 2 and Class 3 countermarks (26mm, 10.59g). Ex Numismatik Lanz (ebay September 2018).

The relationship between Class 1 countermarks and Class 2 and Class 3 countermarks is as problematic as the relationship between Class 2 and Class 3 countermarks themselves. It is surely significant that no Class 2 or Class 3 countermark has been found in association with a Class 1 countermark on the same coin despite the fact that all the countermarks were focussed upon the same class of host coins, Heraclian copper coins from regnal year 20 onwards. This suggests that Class 1 countermarks were imposed within one large district, while Class 2 and Class 3 countermarks were imposed within another much smaller district. Indeed, the relationship between Class 1 Type 1 and Class 1 Type 2 countermarks parallels that between Class 2 and Class 3 countermarks to suggest that they may also have been used sequentially within the same district.

Finally, one cannot conclude any discussion of the Byzantine countermarks struck on coins circulating in greater Syria without remarking upon the relevance of Schulze's Class 3 countermark to the interpretation of his Class 7 countermark. The Class 7 countermark consist of a monogram containing three Greek letters – tau, kappa, and omega – where this occurs in two slightly different forms, Type a (Fig. 9a-b) and its retrograde form Type b (Fig. 9c-d). As Schulze states, however, Type b is 'obviously an error of the die cutter'.[24] Most of the coins with this countermark come from Cyprus, so it seems that this countermark was imposed there, although a few coins with this countermark have also been found in Syria. Furthermore, the host coins are almost exclusively folles and half-folles of Constans II, although Schulze also notes the existence of three coins of Constantine IV with this countermark, so that the countermarking is thought to have occurred during the period c.660-73.

---

[24] Schulze, 'Countermarks from before the Arab Conquest' (see n. 3), p. 30.

33), so suggesting that the countermark was applied during the mid-630s once more.[22] This renders it highly unlikely that the monogram should have been intended in reference to any of Heraclius Constantine, Heraclonas or Constans II. At this point, therefore, one needs to question the assumption that this monogram must abbreviate a personal name rather something else instead. Attention has already been drawn to fact that the form of the imperial monogram used on the coinage from 632 onwards contained a cross as well as letters abbreviating the imperial name, and the possibility that this monogram may contain some reference to the cross deserves to be taken seriously. The most common slogan used in connection with the cross was the phrase that Constantine I allegedly saw in the sky next to his vision of a cross of light before the battle of the Milvian Bridge in 312. According to Eusebius, this phrase was τούτῳ νίκα 'Conquer by this!'. The popularity of this phrase at this approximate period can be judged in two ways. First, the same verb appears in the exergue of one of the two types of follis struck at Jerusalem in 614 as part of the legend XCNIKA abbreviating Χριστός νικᾷ 'Christ conquers!'.[23] Second, and more importantly, the legend ƐN TȣTO NIKA (ἐν τούτῳ νίκα) 'Conquer in this!', appears on the obverse of most of the different types of folles struck in the name of Constans II at Constantinople during the period 642-58. It should not surprise, therefore, that the monogram seems to conceal the phrase τούτῳ νίκα 'Conquer by this!'. To be specific, the vertical bar of the monogram reads T(OV)TѠ, while the horizontal bar reads N(I)K(A). Hence it is not really an imperial monogram at all. Finally, one should note the cleverness of this monogram in that the demonstrative pronoun T(OV)TѠ 'by this' refers to the cross within the monogram itself, so that the monogram is a perfectly self-contained unit.

Fig. 7: (a) sketch of Class 3 countermark; (b) half-follis of Heraclius (MIB 169) dated regnal year 2 (611/12) with Class 3 countermark (24mm, 5.07g). Ex ebay January 2018.

It should be noted here also that Schulze's Class 4 countermark does not actually consist of a specific countermark but rather a combination of a Class 2 countermark and a Class 3 countermark (Fig. 8). Schulze records far fewer specimens bearing a Class 2 or a Class 3 countermark than a Class 1 countermark, and it is clear that their use was far more restricted. To be more precise, he records 7 coins bearing a Class 2 countermark alone, 16 coins bearing a Class 3 countermark alone, and 10 coins bearing both a Class 2 countermark and a Class 3 countermark. These small numbers of specimens render the analysis of any patterns of use extremely difficult. Schulze seems to assume a basically sequential use of the Class 2 and Class 3 countermarks across two cities or pockets of

---

[22] The editor has drawn my attention to an unpublished example of what seems to be a pseudo-Byzantine coin with three-figure obverse hosting a Class 3 countermark. It is probably to be explained in the same way as the similar pseudo-Byzantine coin hosting a Class 2 countermark described above (see n. 19).
[23] *MIB* X28. In general, see S. Mansfield, 'Heraclean Folles of Jerusalem', in A. Oddy (ed.), ***Coinage and History in the Seventh Century Near East 2*** (London, 2010), pp. 49-55.

his younger son Heraclonas even.[18] The fact that Heraclius Constantine is always identified, when he is identified, simply by the letter kappa on the obverse of the folles struck during regnal years 20-27 (629-37) (*MIB* 164) supports this. Schulze follows earlier works in identifying two slightly different types within this class, which he calls Type a and Type b, but the very minor difference between them seems best dismissed as a slight error by an engraver rather any serious proof that two variants of the same monogram were genuinely intended.[19] Of the 6 Byzantine coins recorded by Schulze as hosting this countermark, 5 are folles of the period 629-37 (*MIB* 164), even if only 1 of these can be firmly dated (to regnal year 23 = 632/33), while the last is a half-follis of the same period. Add the example illustrated here dating to regnal year 20 (Fig. 6b), and the evidence suggests that countermarking occurred during the mid-630s.[20]

Fig. 6: (a) sketch of Class 2 countermark; (b) follis of Heraclius (29mm, 10.75g) with Class 2 countermark (MIB 164). Ex Savoca Coins (ebay December 2017).

Class 3 consists of another countermark in the form of a cross monogram (Fig. 7a-b), but the reading of this monogram is far more problematic than that of the Class 2 monogram. This monogram clearly contains four Greek letters – tau, omega, nu, kappa – but it is not clear what these abbreviate. It has traditionally been accepted that they abbreviate the Greek form of the name Constantine (Κωνσταντῖνος). However, Grierson is not sure whom is meant by this, Hahn prefers to interpret it in reference to the emperor now known as Constans II (641-68), the grandson of Heraclius, who was actually known as Constantine on his coinage, while Schulze hesitates once more between his short-reigned, sickly father Heraclius Constantine (641) or Heraclonas instead.[21] The problem here is that the latest dateable host coins date to Heraclius' regnal years 20-23 (629-

---

[18] Grierson, *DOC* 2.1, p. 56, claims that it is 'possible that it should be attributed to Heraclius Constantine or Heraclonas' simply on the basis that this monogram differs so greatly from earlier monograms of Heraclius upon the coinage, although also admitting that similar cross monograms do occur for Heraclius on silverware. For the latter, see Table II in E. Cruikshank Dodd, ***Byzantine Silver Stamps***, Dumbarton Oaks Studies 7 (Washington, DC, 1961).

[19] Schulze, 'Countermarks from before the Arab Conquest' (see n. 3), p. 24, distinguishes between a Type a, which may include an angular lunate sigma in ligature with the capital eta at the left end of the horizontal bar, and a Type b which depicts the capital eta alone. It is interesting to note that fragments of silk from the shrine of St Madelberta (d. 706) in Liège Cathedral preserve the same monogram as Class 2 Type b. See A. Muthesius, 'Memory and Meaning: Graphic Sign and Abstract Symbol in Byzantine Silk Weaving (from the Sixth to Tenth/Eleventh Centuries), in Garipzanov, Goodson, and Maguire, ***Graphic Signs of Identity*** (see n. 4), pp. 351-81, at 354-57.

[20] Schulze also records the occurrence of this countermark on a pseudo-Byzantine coin with three-figure obverse, as described by P. Pavlou, *ONS Newsletter* 127 (1991), p. 5. If the pseudo-Byzantine coin has not been overstruck on an earlier Byzantine coin hosting this countermark, then the most plausible explanation is that some pseudo-Byzantine coins were struck much earlier than has generally been thought, and that the obverse imitates the three-figure obverse of folles of the period 616-29 rather than that of the folles of the period 639-41.

[21] Grierson, *DOC* 2.1, p. 57; Hahn, *MIB* III, p. 141; Schulze, 'Countermarks from before the Arab Conquest' (see n. 3), p. 27.

In addition to the Type 1 and Type 2 countermarks of Class 1, Schulze also identifies three very different countermarks that sometimes occur in association with Type 1 or Type 2 countermarks as Type 3 countermarks (Fig. 5). His Type 3a is clearly a small cross, and his Type 3c consists of two Greek letters, sigma and omega, standing next to each other, while his Type 3b seems to be identifiable as a lunate sigma combined with an omega in ligature form. Of 173 coins with Type 1 or Type 2 countermarks examined by Schulze, the Type 3a countermark only occurs once, in association with a Type 2 countermark, the Type 3b countermark occurs twice, in association with a Type 2 countermark in each case, and the Type 3c countermark only occurs once, in association with a Type 1 countermark.[16] While Schulze does not attempt to explain the significance of the Type 3b or Type 3c countermarks, two possibilities spring to mind given both the prominence of the cross in the associated imperial monograms of Types 1 and 2 and the importance of the cross more generally at this period. One possibility is that these countermarks abbreviate the Greek adjective σωτήριος 'saving' in reference to the saving power of the cross once more, while the other possibility is that they abbreviate the Greek term for cross in the dative case, σταυρῷ 'by the cross'. In either case, the countermarks proclaim the hope of being saved by the power of the cross.

Fig. 5: sketches of Class 1 countermarks, Types 3a-c, after Schulze, 'Countermarks from before the Arab Conquest' (see n. 3), p. 24.

As for the date of the Class 1 countermarks, the fact that the vast majority of host coins (118 of 173, so 68%) examined by Schulze were dated to regnal years 20-26 (629-36), and none later than this, fully supports his conclusion that they were most probably applied during the Arab invasion of Syria. However, while he dates the use of the countermarks to 633-36, it is important to note that they may actually have been applied to coins as late as 639 even. The key point here is that the mint at Constantinople seems to have struck far fewer folles in regnal year 27 (636/37) than it had done previously, and practically none in regnal years 28-29 (637-39), so that the supply of fresh coin from Constantinople to Syria must have effectively ceased during the period 636-39, and there would have been no coins of these dates available to act as host coins for the countermarks.[17] Indeed, the decision to countermark the existing supply of coins may be directly related to the fact the supply of fresh coin ceased during this period. On the basis of the numismatic evidence alone, therefore, one may tentatively prefer to date the use of these countermarks to sometime during the period 636-39 rather than to 633-36.

Schulze's Class 2 consists of a countermark in the form of a cross monogram (Fig. 6a) that very clearly spells the genitive form of the name of Heraclius in Greek, even if opinion has differed in the past as to which Heraclius this was. However, there is no good reason to doubt that the senior emperor Heraclius himself was indeed intended rather than his eldest son Heraclius Constantine or

---

[16] For full details of the analysis of these 173 coins, see W. Schulze, I. Schulze, & W. Leimenstoll, 'Heraclian Countermarks on Byzantine Copper Coins in Seventh-Century Syria', **Byzantine and Modern Greek Studies** 30 (2006), pp. 1-27.
[17] The table at the back of *MIB* III reveals that only one workshop struck folles at Constantinople in regnal year 27 (636/37), whereas four had been in operation previously. Furthermore, it suggests that no workshops at all produced folles during the next two years.

Caliph coin also with typically blundered legends.[12] Both these Damascus mints appear to have produced coins with other mint names,[13] so their status is a little uncertain, but I think that they are probably actually a single mint which went straight from minting Imperial Image to Standing Caliph coins. Our potential 'transitional' coin has a reverse which is also blundered, but the style is rather different. The reverse symbol-on-steps is elliptical rather than round and the die-engraving, with thick deeply engraved lines, is different from the usual rather delicate Damascus style. The obverse is quite crude and has the same thick, deep die engraving. Although it is a standing emperor, it is not in the Damascus style, it has no legends and I have been unable to find any close parallels.

Figure 7: Damascus mule with Imperial Image obverse and Standing Caliph reverse.
Coin a – Damascus standing emperor type, Arabic rev. (2.96g 12h, author's collection).
Coin b – Mule with standing emperor obv. and symbol-on-steps rev., mint name 'mashq' downwards to right (ebay pharaoh's crypt 11.2018).
Coin c – Small module Standing Caliph coin of Damascus (2.48g 12h, Goodwin 2018 Cat. 102).

Example 5 is the opposite type of hybrid with a Standing Caliph obverse and an Imperial Image reverse. Only two rather poorly preserved specimens of this hybrid are known (Figs. 8b and 8c), but interestingly they are struck from two different die pairs, suggesting that this may have originally been a more extensive issue than example 4. Whilst all four dies could well be the work of the same individual, it is clear that they are not by the same hand as example 4 and indeed they may be the products of a different mint. In this example both the caliph images and the rather delicate die engraving are quite similar to many normal Damascus Standing Caliph coins (Fig. 8d). Also there

---

[12] There were undoubtedly two distinct Damascus Standing Caliph mints. 7c is a product of the most prolific of these which struck small module coins with blundered legends, quite similar in both module and style to the last of the Imperial Image coins such as 7a. The other mint produced larger coins with caliph figures quite similar to those found on the gold dinars and legends, more or less correctly written, which include the caliph's name (see Goodwin 2017 p. 59).
[13] See I. Schulze 2010 and 2015.

appears to be a reverse die-link between 8b and a rather unusual Damascus Imperial Image coin shown in Fig. 8a. Because both coins are worn and corroded it is not possible to be absolutely certain of this, but the two dies are certainly very similar and undoubtedly by the same die engraver. Although 8a is essentially the same type as Figs. 7a and 5c, the reverse legend is slightly more blundered than that of 7a and the standing figure has a three stranded whip hanging to his left, very similar to that found on the normal Damascus Standing Caliph coins hanging to the caliph's right.

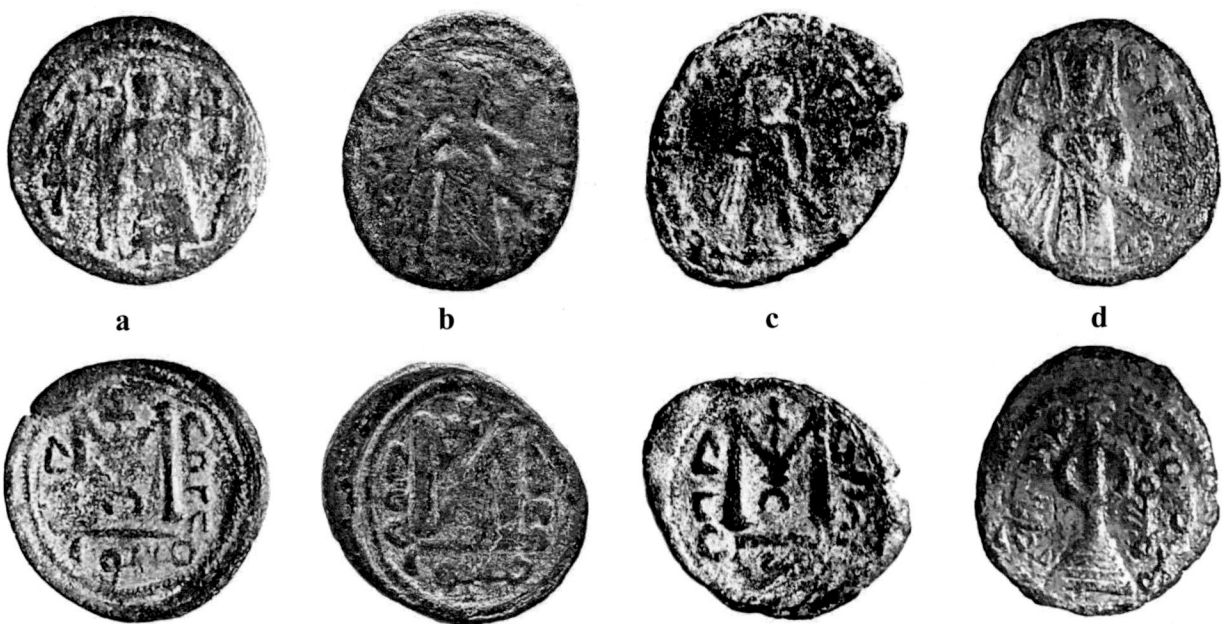

Figure 8: Damascus mules with Standing Caliph obverse and Imperial Image reverse.
Coin a – Damascus standing emperor type, Arabic rev. (2.76g 2h, author's collection).
Coin b – Mule with standing emperor obverse and Arabic reverse as coin 7a (EIM)[14]
Coin c – as coin b, but different dies (3.20g 6h, Foundation collection).
Coin d – Small module Standing Caliph coin of Damascus (2.48g 12h, Goodwin 2018 Cat. 102).

So it seems very likely that we have here an actual transition between the Imperial Image type in Fig. 8a and the Standing Caliph type in 8d via 8b and c. It is also quite possible that 8a is a product of the same mint that produced coins like 7a along with the late Damascus two-figure type. I would therefore tentatively suggest that coins 7b and c may represent the first short-lived Standing Caliph issue of this particular Damascus mint which used a conservative Imperial Image style reverse. As mentioned above the status of this mint (or two mints) is uncertain. The die engravers were undoubtedly less skilled than those who worked on earlier (and undoubtedly official) Imperial Image coins such as those shown in Figs. 2c and 3c. This may well be a result of all skilled craftsmen being transferred to the production of the new precious metal coinage, but it is uncertain whether the management of the mint remained the same or whether minting of the copper coinage was effectively 'contracted out'.

---

[14] Eretz Israel Museum 44679, image thanks to Ingrid Schulze.

Example 6

Figure 9. Yubnā

Coin a – Obv. Standing emperor, no legends. Rev. Retrograde m *with yubnā - filasṭīn either side. (2.33g 12h, ABC p.119. No.1, Nasser D. Khalili Collection of Islamic Art).*
Coin b – Obv. Standing Caliph, 'muḥammad ra – sūl allāh' either side. Rev. Same die as Coin a. (2.72g 6h, ABC p.142. No.154, Nasser D. Khalili Collection of Islamic Art).
Coin c – As Coin b, but different dies (4.07g 3h, ABC p. 120. No.4, Nasser D. Khalili Collection of Islamic Art).[15]

My final example is from is from the mint of Yubnā and is known from two specimens both struck from the same pair of dies. But before discussing these it may be helpful to give a little background on this unusual mint. Although essentially a Standing Caliph mint, it seems likely that it started production with two obverse dies, a Standing Emperor (Fig. 9a) in the style of Damascus and a Standing Caliph in the style of Īliyā (Fig. 9b), both paired with the same reverse die. The Standing Emperor was quickly abandoned and the mint then went on to produce a variety of Standing Caliph images and arrangements of the reverse legend as shown in Figs. 10 and 11 below.

Figure 10. Yubnā Standing Caliph images.

---

[15] These images and the two subsequent figures are adapted from Goodwin 2005 = ABC.

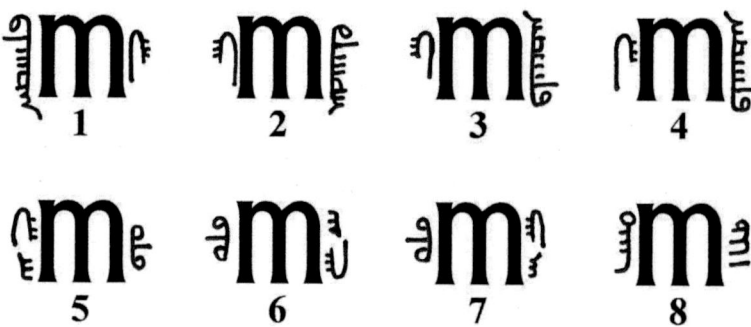

Figure 11. Different arrangements of Yubnā reverse legends.

This great variety, unparalleled at any other Standing Caliph mint, along with the poor production standards leads to the conclusion that the Yubna mint operated under difficult circumstances. It might have moved around, probably minted intermittently and certainly suffered changes in personnel.

Figure 12. Example 6 - Yubnā Standing Caliph coins with Pseudo-Byzantine reverse.
Coin a – Obv. Standing Caliph with 'muḥ(ammad)' downwards to right and '(s)ūl allāh' upwards to right. Rev. m blundered Greek legend either side (2.65g 5h, Goodwin 2018 Cat. 73).
Coin b. Same obverse die as a, but with a different blundered Greek reverse die (2.78g 10h, Goodwin 2018 Cat. 71).
Coin c. Same obverse die, but with Arabic reverse, blundered 'filasṭīn' upwards to right of m (2.62g 10h, Goodwin 2018 Cat. 70).

The potential 'transitional' coins are shown in Fig. 12a and b. They are both struck from the same normal Yubnā obverse die, but from two different Pseudo-Byzantine reverse dies, both with blundered Greek legends. The two reverse dies are so similar that they must be the work of the same illiterate die engraver. In this case we do have an obverse die-link to a reverse die with Arabic legends (Fig. 12c). The Arabic is blundered, but no more so than on many Yubnā coins which are apparently official issues of the mint. Unsurprisingly I was unable to find a reverse die-link, but the dies appears typical of Palestinian Pseudo-Byzantine coins, which are generally cruder than their northern counterparts and are often struck on irregularly shaped flans.[16] Two typical examples are shown in Fig. 13 below and it is interesting to note that 13a has a similar elongated flan to Fig. 12b above.

Figure 13. Two typical crude Palestinian Pseudo-Byzantine coins: a – 3.53g 10h, b – 2.60g 6h (author's collection).

It is just possible that example 6 is a contemporary forgery, but I think it much more likely that it is an official product of the Yubnā mint produced by poorly skilled operatives who had previously produced crude Pseudo-Byzantine coins. The only available Arabic reverse die had just broken and two old dies were hastily brought into service whilst a new proper die is cut. Alternatively new reverse dies were hastily cut and this was the best that could be managed. In practice most users probably did not even notice the missing Arabic.

Some general conclusions

Can we draw any general conclusions from these 6 examples?

Firstly Example 5 is probably the only one that might possibly represent a genuine transition, although the status of the mint concerned is not entirely clear. Otherwise none of them are genuinely 'transitional' in the sense of a short-lived intermediate stage between two phases.

Secondly some examples could be outright forgeries, but most of them are probably not.

And thirdly, I think that some of these examples suggest a rather lax control of minting, probably involving what we would call 'contracting out'. These mints were still officially sanctioned, but not subject to close official supervision. Perhaps this was at least partly the result of skilled mint personnel being diverted onto the new programme of post-reform precious metal coinage.

---

[16] Compare the Palestianian coins illustrated in Fig. 13 with the Syrian example shown in Fig. 1 of my other article in this volume.

Postscript

Finally it is worth noting that odd hybrids continue to occur in Syrian Umayyad and early Abbasid post-reform coinage. Fig.14 shows two examples: coin a mixes the reverse of an early mintless type with a later reverse from Manbij and coin b has a Hims obverse coupled with a Damascus reverse..

Fig. 14. Post-reform hybrids.
Coin a – mintless reverse coupled with later Manbij reverse (3.93g, Album auction 33 lot 366).
Coin b – Ḥimṣ Dimashq mule, obv. jerboa, rev. 'ḍarb dimashq', (1.35g, author's collection).

Bibliography

Goodwin, T., 1995, '7th Century Arab Imitations of Byzantine Folles', ***Numismatic Circular*** CIII, pp. 336-337.

Goodwin, T., 2005, ***Arab-Byzantine Coinage***, London

Goodwin, T., 2018, ***The Standing Caliph coinage***, London.

Goodwin, T. and Gyselen, R., 2015, ***Arab Byzantine Coins from the Irbid Hoard***, London.

Oddy, A., 2010, 'Constantine IV as a Prototype for Early Islamic Coins' in ***Coinage and History in the Seventh Century Near East*** 2 (A. Oddy, ed.) pp. 95-110.

Oddy, A., 2019, 'A Die-Chain in the Phase 1 Arab-Byzantine coinage of Greater Syria' in ***Mélanges de numismatique et d'archéologie offerts â Henri Pottier*** (J-M. Doyen and C. Morrisson eds.), Brussels.

Ramadan, T., 2010, 'A rare Arab-Byzantine hybrid coin of Damascus', ***Journal of the Oriental Numismatic Society*** 203, pp. 43-44.

Schulze, I., 2010, 'The Standing Caliph coins of Damascus, new die links – new questions', ***Journal of the Oriental Numismatic Society*** 204, pp. 3 – 6.

Schulze, I., 2015, 'Can we believe what is written on the coins? Enigmatic die links and other puzzles' in ***Coinage and History in the Seventh Century Near East*** 4 (A. Oddy, ed.) pp. 115 – 135.[17]

---

[17] Acknowledgements: my thanks to Ingrid Schulze and Marcus Phillips with whom I have had productive discussions on some of these coins.

Yet again on Justinian II's gold coinage, 'Abd al-Malik's monetary reform, and the 'War of images'

Federico Montinaro[1]

In an article recently published in the *Numismatic Chronicle* Michael Humphreys attempted to offer a solution to a vexed question in Dark-centuries Byzantine and Islamic numismatics.[2] Famously, rare extant dinars struck under 'Abd al-Malik between 693 and 697 (AH 74 to 77) display, on the obverse, the image of a standing caliph holding a sword in the sheath with, inscribed circularly, the identification of the ruler or the shahada and, on the reverse, the dating. These pieces are commonly taken to represent the earliest, if short-lived, 'independent' Islamic gold coinage, superseding, that is, earlier issues from earlier decades of Islamic rule in the Near East, which imitated closely, if to various degrees, contemporary or recent Byzantine models (fig. 1).[3] However, 'Abd al-Malik's dinars still bear a marked resemblance to the loosely contemporary Byzantine solidi issued by the emperor Justinian II, whose first reign lasted from 685 to 695. Justinian II, now famously mutilated in his nose, regained the throne in 705, following a bloody civil war, and occupied it until he was killed in 711. The Byzantine coins in question, belonging to one of several designs minted under Justinian II (see below), are unprecedented in that they present, on the obverse, the bust of Christ, defined in the surrounding inscription as *rex regnantium*, and, on the reverse, the emperor, standing and wearing the festal garment known as *loros*, a strip of which loops over the emperor's left arm and hangs to the side (fig. 2a).

Figure 1: 'Abd al-Malik's Standing Caliph gold coinage (ANS)

References in both Christian and Muslim ninth-century literary sources to 'Abd al-Malik's monetary reforms, concomitant with the caliph's pushing the Islamisation of the administration in the former Byzantine territories and the breaking of a Byzantine-Arab treaty, has lead twentieth-century scholars of the Near East to speculate on the nature of the obvious similarity between the Byzantine and the Muslim coinages, with either being regarded alternatively as the model for the other in a 'War of images' between the two powers.[4] Humphreys' main contention is that a series of dated Byzantine lead seals can be useful in dating Justinian II's relevant issue more precisely than

---

[1] Federico Montinaro is Research Associate at the Department of Ancient History, Eberhard Karls Universität Tübingen. Email: federico.montinaro@uni-tuebingen.de.
[2] Humphreys, 'War of images'.
[3] See Goodwin, 'The Standing Caliph coinage'.
[4] The term was first employed by Grabar, 'Iconoclasme', also referring to it as "guerre froide". See also Treadwell, 'Byzantium and Islam'.

has so far been done and thus prove Byzantine precedence incontestably. Building upon my earlier study of the seals in question, I hope to demonstrate that they do not represent a secure tool for refining the accepted approximate chronology of the Byzantine coins. This is the starting point for re-evaluating the question of 'precedence' through the analysis of the cultural and social context in which both the Byzantine and the Muslim coinages were meant to circulate.

Justinian II's gold issues

In 1959, Justinian's gold coinage was the subject of a study by James Breckenbridge, whose classification into four issues and fundamental chronology are today universally accepted.[5] Breckenbridge's greatest merit consists perhaps in having identified, on stylistic grounds a short-lived issue minted at the beginning of the second reign, but before the accession of Justinian's son Tiberius (see below). Now the short-lived issue (Type 3) bears, in the same way as an earlier one attributed to Justinian's first reign already did (Type 2), the unprecedented bust of Christ and had formerly been attributed to the first reign as well. The main difference between the two Christ types is that the earlier one (Type 2) bears on the reverse the standing emperor with *loros* regarded as the parallel to the standing caliph of 'Abd al-Malik's gold coinage, whereas the second Christ type (Type 3) has a simple bust, with the emperor holding a patriarchal cross in the right hand and a globe with cross in the left one, with the inscription *pax*. Finally, the last issue (Type 4) must be dated to the accession of Justinian's son, Tiberius, who is represented on the reverse together with his father and of whom we know from an eighth-century Greek chronicle that he waited, possibly for several months, for Justinian to regain the throne before joining him in Constantinople from the family's exile on the Black Sea (figs 2b and 2c).

Figure 2a: Justinian II's gold coinage, Type 2 (MIB 3, pl. 38, no. 8a)

Figure 2b: Justinian II's gold coinage, Type 3 (MIB 3, pl. 46, no. 1)

---

[5] Breckenbridge, 'Numismatic iconography'.

Figure 2c: Justinian II's gold coinage, Type 4 (MIB 3, pl. 46, no. 2a)

Type 2 has itself customarily been linked to one major event of Justinian's first reign: the summoning so-called Quinisext Council – or Council *In trullo*, from the name of the venue at the Palace –with the aim of completing the works of the Third Council of Constantinople, or Sixth Ecumenical, which had taken place under Justinian II's predecessor. Now the most reliable chronological indication for the date of the council is found in Canon 3 produced by the same assembly of bishops and prescribing the deposition of those clergymen "who entered into a second marriage, enslaved to sin, and still had not chosen to mend their ways by the fifteenth of January last, of the past fourth indiction, of the Year Six Thousand One Hundred and Ninety-Nine".[6] The text implies that the canons were written down in the fifth indiction, yet, in my understanding, before January, thus between 1st September and 31st December 691, and that the council must have taken place before that date, certainly over several months and starting in all probability exactly at the date set as the deadline for the repentance of twice-married clergymen, in January 691. As for the connection between the council and the minting of Justinian II's Type 2, this is often believed, since Breckenbridge, to be borne out by Canon 82 instead:

> "In some depictions of the venerable images, the Forerunner is portrayed pointing with his finger to a lamb, and this has been accepted as representation of grace, prefiguring for us through the law the true Lamb, Christ our God. Venerating then these ancient representations and foreshadowings as symbols and prefigurations of truth handed down by the Church, nevertheless, we prefer grace and truth, which we have received as fulfilment of the law. Therefore, in order that what is perfect, even in paintings, may be portrayed before the eyes of all, we decree that henceforth the figure of the Lamb of God who takes away the sins of the world, Christ our God, should be set forth in images in human form, instead of the ancient lamb; for in this way we apprehend the depth of the humility of the World of God, and are led to the remembrance of his life in the flesh, his passion and his saving death, and of the redemption which thereby came to the world".[7]

Dating Justinian II's earliest Christ type

There are good reasons to separate the two Christ types with one emperor on the reverse, the first being Breckenbridge's contention that the second one (Type 3) displays the signs of the evolution in design and script under the two emperors who ruled in the interval between Justinian II's two reigns, Leontios and Tiberius III. Thus, the Christ figure on this issue bears patent resemblance to the one seen in the last of Justinian II's issues, which, as we have seen, displays two emperors on the reverse. Furthermore, the first Christ type (Type 2), does not seem either to have been minted or to have circulated in the West. This circumstance was explained by Breckenbridge as a result of the papal opposition to Justinian's ecclesiastical policy and more precisely to the disciplinary rulings

---

[6] Nedungatt and Featherstone (eds and trans.), 'The Council In Trullo', p. 71.
[7] Nedungatt and Featherstone (eds and trans.), 'The Council In Trullo', pp. 162-4.

issued by the council *In trullo*, as attested by the Roman *Liber pontificalis*. Michael Humphreys has now argued that the first Christ type – and the Quinisext Council for that matter, although without a thorough discussion of the chronological indications in the acts, such as the one I provided above – should be dated more precisely to 691, rather than 692. He has done so on the authority of a so far overlooked source: the so-called seals of the *kommerkiarioi*.

The *kommerkiarioi* were undoubtedly among the top officials in seventh- and eighth-century Byzantium.[8] As with many other middle Byzantine officeholders, they are almost entirely documented by the lead seals they or their personnel employed in the exercise of official tasks. Thus the seals show that they held the highest consular and patrician titles and name the region or regions (a city, a province, a landmark) of which a single *kommerkiarios* was in charge. However, the seals issued under the authority of *kommerkiarioi* display an extraordinary feature: the presence of an imperial portrait basically identical with that found on contemporary coins. They are also explicitly dated according to the indiction. There is much debate today as to the exact duties performed by the *kommerkiarioi*, on which the literary sources are silent. Hypotheses go from responsibilities in running the state controlled production and marketing of silk, to the administration of customs, to the involvement in the provisioning of armies and the collection of taxes in kind.

The chronology of the corpus of seals of *kommerkiarioi*, which includes today hundreds of specimens, was put on solid ground in the 1970s by George Zacos, who painstakingly compared the iconography of the pieces in his own collection with contemporary coinage.[9] As Humphreys has now pointed out, there exist seals stemming from the *kommerkiarioi* George the Patrician and Theophylact dating from a fourth-to-sixth indiction and bearing the image of a standing emperor with *loros* (fig. 3).[10] Now, seals issued under Justinian II in the preceding indictions indeed display a standing emperor with chlamys, the imperial dress found on the gold coinage of Type 1.[11] The fourth indiction in connection with the *loros* was therefore identified by Zacos with the year 690/691 and Humphreys regards the two pieces which bear this date as unimpeachable evidence for dating the issue of Type 2 to the same year. George and Theophylact disappear from the record between 695 and 705 but are commonly thought to have reappeared during Justinian's second reign, as illustrated by seals dating from a seventh indiction, or 708/709, already bearing the joint portrait of Justinian II and his son Tiberius[12]. There is, however, as I have attempted to show elsewhere, a major flaw in this reconstruction. Dozens of dated seals certainly issued, under the authority of other *kommerkiarioi*, in the years 690/1 to 695/6 continue to show the standing emperor with chlamys. This led me, in my earlier study of the *kommerkiarioi*, to postdate George and Theophylact's seals 'with *loros*' by an indictional cycle, with the result of obliterating the attestations of such type on dated seals of Justinian II's first reign, which form the basis of Humphrey's argument for a more precise dating of the coinage.[13]

---

[8] See, on what follows, Montinaro, 'Commerciaires'; Montinaro, 'Killing Empire'.
[9] Zacos and Veglery, 'Byzantine lead seals'.
[10] Montinaro, 'Commerciaires', catalogue, nos 109-17.
[11] Montinaro, 'Commerciaires', catalogue, nos 34-51.
[12] Montinaro, 'Commerciaires', catalogue, nos 118-20.
[13] Montinaro, 'Commerciaires', catalogue, nos 52-85, with the discussion, pp. 424-6. Zacos and Veglery, 'Byzantine lead seals', no. 167, a related seal with *loros* of George and Theophylact as ἄρχοντες τοῦ βλαττίου, is dated by the editors to the fourth indiction, but the reading seems too optimistic.

Figure 3: Seal of the kommerkiarioi *George the Patrician and Theophylact (Montinaro, 'Commerciaires', no. 115)*

I am far from claiming to have disentangled the complex chronological problems posed by both coins and seals for good. In particular, I am unable to explain the discrepancy between the iconographies of the two mediums in the years 690-5, although this discrepancy seems to me less alarming than the one affecting the seals alone in Zacos' reconstruction. Humphreys may still be right in dating Justinian II's Type 2 to 691, that is to what I regard as the date of the Council *In trullo*. If I nonetheless allow myself to pull the carpet from under my opponent's feet, it is with the aim of once and for all freeing the debate around the 'war of images' of contentious points of form and of beginning to turn to meaning. For why, after all, were an emperor and a caliph even bothering with attempting to appropriate internationally a special imagery for which both had, if needed, sufficient precedents at home?[14]

Emperor and Christ

In a paper recently read to the Leeds Medieval Conference, Maria Vrij argued that the juxtaposition of the bust of Christ and the standing emperor on Justinian II's gold coins may have served the purpose of emphasizing the separation between secular and sacred power encapsulated in the Gospels' "render unto Caesar" (Mk 12:17), in reference to taxes, on the very medium, the *solidus*, by which (most) taxes were paid in the Early and Middle Byzantine periods. I am quoting this example not to single out a colleague, but rather to illustrate a general trend in modern interpretations of the iconography of Justinian II's gold coinage towards detaching as much as possible the two entities found together on the coin. Thus, whether linking Justinian II's early Christ type to the Quinisext Council or not, other scholars have traditionally stressed the relation of subordination between Christ and the emperor implied by the positioning of the former, rather than latter, on the obverse of the coins, as exemplified in Constance Head's statement that "here the message is basically one of the emperor as Christ's deputy and as the upholder of orthodoxy".[15]

Yet, I would argue, there was for Byzantine authorities no other acceptable way of putting Christ and the emperor on the same piece than having the former 'reigning', quite literally, over the latter, out of learned fear of God. In fact, a ninth-century Byzantine observer, who claimed to be writing in 836 to the emperor Theophilos in the name of the Melkite patriarchates on the question of icon veneration, took a slightly different approach from modern scholars while interpreting imagined coins of Constantine I, otherwise praised for his role in summoning the Council of Nicaea, which

---

[14] Eighth-century BC Syrian basalt stelae depicted anthropomorphic bulls with sword, as pointed out by Schulze, 'Symbolism'. Rare copper coins of Heraclius with sword, vaguely similar in design to the Standing Caliph, minted in Constantinople and Thessalonica, and dating from a twentieth year, on which see Phillips, 'Arab state', pp. 59-60. In the early seventh century, the Lombard king Agilulf had himself represented on the famous Bargello crown as an enthroned Christ holding a sword on his lap. None of these pieces could of course have served as a direct model for 'Abd al-Malik gold coinage.

[15] Head, 'Justinian II', pp. 57-8.

happened to be identical with Justinian II's issues. The text, commonly known as the *Letter of the three patriarchs*, is best preserved in its Old Church Slavonic version. The author displayed some readiness to blur the boundaries between secular and sacred as he explained the iconography of the non-existent coins as a symbol of the emperor's "conciliation", literally the "peaceful treaty with the Lord" (показал ... ко господоу мирныѧ жертвы), rather than mere submission to God:

> "[Constantine] utterly destroyed the dark second Judas, repugnant of God, who was the same kind of traitor and son of the Devil and heir to Gehenna, with all his teachings – I mean Arius, who shares a name with wrath, who sent the Church into grievous uproar, who put forth lawless statements full of every kind of impiety [...]. This is why the council of three hundred eighteen holy fathers, which assembled in Nicaea by order of the holy emperor, deposed and anathematized Arius, and confessed the Son of God, our Lord Jesus Christ, to be one essence with the Father, and made the creed of the supernatural and eternal Holy Trinity, like a pillar of fire, shine out to all regions. And as a foremost and elect decoration, a sign of piety in Christ, our true God, he minted the heavenly sign of Christ the Savior on the royal gold coins, and together with his own likeness, portrayed upon in the venerated divine and human image, showing the power of the heavenly king, and conciliation with God, and the establishment of a deep peace, so that there would be 'one flock' (Jn 10:16) and one power over angels and men".[16]

Incidentally, the reference to the Christ type, unattested before Justinian II and popping up again thereafter precisely upon the reestablishment of icon veneration following Theophilos' death, in 843, on Michael III and Theodora's coinage, strongly suggests that the *Letter* was indeed written at least seven years after its purported date of composition, for it is hard to imagine that, one and a half centuries later, its author should have known Justinian II's coinage.[17]

However, what really must have struck the imagination of the theologically less advised and arguably less cautious contemporary user of Justinian II's currency is precisely the two figures' being on the same coin: Christ and the emperor were being identified. The Heraclians, of whom Justinian II was the last scion, had experimented with such imagery, which went well beyond the traditional imitation of Christ initiated by the first Christian emperors and could fall little short of trespassing the limits imposed by that same fear of God that would ultimately hold back Justinian's moneyers. As Mischa Meier has recently shown, George of Pisidia, Heraclius' court poet, established an unprecedented association between the emperor and Christ by addressing the former indirectly by the hapax κοσμορύστης, basically translating to "Saviour".[18] Heraclius' nephew and successor, Constans II, deployed subtler connections, by defining himself, famously, as "emperor and priest" and equating himself, on different mediums, to the Old Testament's Melchizedek, after whose order Jesus had been made, in the New Testament's interpretation, a "high priest for ever" (Heb 6:20, after Ps 110).[19] These developments, I would argue further, had, from their origins in Heraclius' successful efforts to reconquer Palestine from the Persians, an ideal setting in disputed, holy land.

The centre of the world

In fact, the most astounding instance of what the simple audience must have seen as an identification between a Byzantine emperor and Christ is found in the seventh-century Western Mesopotamian Syriac *Apocalypse* falsely attributed to the fourth-century martyr Methodius of Olympus. The text, as Sebastian Brock has long ago shown and I have most recently reargued

---

[16] Afinogenov (ed. and trans.), 'The Slavonic Letter', pp. 56-9.
[17] For Michael III and Theodora's coins, see *DOC* 3, 1, pl. 28, nos 2-3.
[18] Meier, 'Herakles – Herakleios – Christus'.
[19] See, on this, my forthcoming monograph on Constans II.

against Stephen Shoemaker, was composed in the year 692 and soon enjoyed official endorsement at the court in Constantinople, with early translations appearing in Greek, Armenian, and Latin, and, later on, in Old Church Slavonic.[20] After narrating, in the future tense, the hoped-for Byzantine reconquest of the Near East from the Muslims, the text goes on to describe the last Christian emperor's entrance into the Holy City, Jerusalem:

> "Then, all of a sudden, the pangs of affliction will be awakened, like those of a woman giving birth, and the king of the Greeks shall go out against them in great wrath; he will be awakened against them like 'a man who has shaken off his wine' - someone who had been considered by them as though dead. He will go forth against them from the sea of the Kushites, and will cast desolation and destruction on the wilderness of Yathrib, and in the midst of their forefathers' dwelling place. And the sons of the kings of the Greeks will descend upon them from the countries of the west and finish off with the sword the remnant left over from them in the Promised Land. Fear shall fall upon them from all who are round about them. They, their wives, their children, their leaders, all their encampments, all the land of the wilderness which belonged to their forefathers shall be delivered into the hand of the kings of the Greeks; they shall be given over to the sword and devastation, to captivity and slaughter. The yoke of their servitude shall be seven times more oppressive than their own yoke, and they shall be in harsh affliction, from hunger and from exhaustion; they shall be slaves, together with their wives and children, and they shall serve in slavery those who were (previously) serving them. Their slavery shall be a hundred times more bitter than the one they imposed"[21].

The text goes on:

> "The moment the Son of Perdition appears, the king of the Greeks shall go up and stand on Golgotha and the holy Cross shall be placed on that spot where it had been fixed when it bore Christ. The king of the Greeks shall place his crown on the top of the holy Cross, stretch out his two hands towards heaven, and hand over the kingdom to God the Father. And the holy Cross upon which Christ was crucified will be raised up to heaven, together with the royal crown"[22].

But entering Jerusalem was not the prerogative of Byzantine emperors, real or imagined. Abū Bakr is said to have visited the city upon the conquest and the first Umayyad caliph, Muʿāwiya, certainly did so, accepting there royal oath from the Arab tribes before moving the seat of his power from Medina to Damascus, as attested by the contemporary Syriac *Maronite chronicle*.[23] As the Byzantine emperor of Pseudo-Methodius' *Apocalypse*, Muʿāwiya ascended to Golgotha, the site of the Church of the Holy Sepulchre:

> "In AG 971, Constans' eighteenth ear, many Arabs gathered at Jerusalem and made Muʿāwiya king and he went up and sat down on Golgotha; he prayed there, and went to Gethsemane and went down to the tomb of the blessed Mary to pray in it. In those days, when the Arabs were assembled there with Muʿāwiya, there was an earthquake and a violent tremor and the greater part of Jericho fell, including all its churches, and of the House of Lord John at the site of our Saviour's baptism in the Jordan every stone above the ground was overthrown, together with the entire monastery. The monastery of Abba Euthymius, as

---

[20] On the text and its context, see, within a vast literature, Möhring, 'Der Weltkaiser', pp. 54-104, already suggesting a link between Justinian II's Christ coins and the *Apocalypse*, and further Montinaro, 'Reconstructions imaginaires', pp. 269-71, esp. on the date. See also the insightful comments by Stoyanov, 'Apocalypticizing warfare', pp. 405-17.
[21] Palmer (ed. and trans.), 'West-Syrian chronicles', pp. 237-8.
[22] Palmer (ed. and trans.), 'West-Syrian chronicles', p. 240.
[23] On Muʿāwiya's accession, see Marsham, 'The architecture of allegiance'.

well as many convents of monks and solitaries and many other places also collapsed in this (earthquake). In July of the same year the emirs and many Arabs gathered and proffered their right hand to Muʿāwiya. Then an order went out that he should be proclaimed king in all the villages and cities of his dominion and that they should make acclamations and invocations to him. [...] Furthermore, Muʿāwiya did not wear a crown like other kings in the world. He placed his throne in Damascus and refused to go to Muḥammad's throne"[24].

Jerusalem was becoming the 'Holy House', *Bayt al-Maqdis*, revered by Jews, Christians, and Muslims alike[25].

Conclusions

It is precisely in connection with the Standing Caliph coins that Jack Tannous has recently warned us against the excesses of positivism:

> "In discussions of the evolution of Islam in the seventh century, the coin reforms of ʿAbd al-Malik and the building of the Dome of the Rock have commonly been pointed to as marking a new phase in the development and articulation of the religious movement initiated by Muḥammad. But changing numismatic iconography, the use of Qurʾānic slogans on coins, the use of certain formulae in papyri documents, or the erection of certain monumental buildings actually tells very little. [...] Indeed, if we think of the relationship between rulers and the religious systems they have used to legitimate their rule throughout history, it quickly becomes apparent that we cannot even be sure what something like the Dome of the Rock, the Standing Caliph coin, or an aniconic, post-Reform coin tells us about the actual personal beliefs of ʿAbd al-Malik, much less any of his successors or any group of Muslims under his authority".[26]

While the latter may be true and one would never claim to know the last words about any human heart, once all the pieces of the Standing-Caliph puzzle are brought together, the study of coins proves far from trivial for adjusting the focus of that same cultural and social history of the religious communities of the Early Medieval Near East which Tannous has so compellingly retold. Jerusalem, the *convidado de piedra* in that scholar's awe-inspiring study, is, I would lastly argue, the key to understanding the 'War of images'. There is no need here to rehearse the evidence for early Muslim coinage in the city, which appears to have been the first to mint the Standing Caliph type, on copper, perhaps as early as 691.[27] As far as the more conspicuous gold coinage is concerned, in fact, one need not assume further 'precedence' on either the Byzantine or the Muslim side. The emperor and the caliph would easily have got word of the imminent introduction of a radically new design by the other power. Whatever their respective links to internal developments in the Byzantine and the Muslim Empires, the Christ type and the Standing Caliph were in all probability strictly contemporary. They marked a concerted parting of ways as much as they represented conflicting attempts at appropriating, through a series of cross-references, the holiest place shared by the three great monotheisms of the Early Medieval Near East. The history of this appropriation, virtual or real, would have obvious ramifications down to Crusader times and beyond.

---

[24] Palmer (ed. and trans.), 'West-Syrian chronicles', pp. 31-2. Constans II' eighteenth year corresponds to 659/60.
[25] See, for example, Elad, 'Medieval Jerusalem'.
[26] Tannous, 'The making', p. 294.
[27] See Schulze, 'The Standing Caliph', with the remarks of Goodwin, 'Review'.

Bibliography

D. E. Afinogenov (ed. and trans.), *Mnogosložnyj svitok: the Slavonic letter of the three patriarchs to emperor Theophilos* (Paris, 2014).

J. D. Breckenbridge, *The Numismatic Iconography of Justinian II* (New York, 1959).

A. Elad, *Medieval Jerusalem and Islamic Worship* (Leiden, 1995).

T. Goodwin, Review of Schulze, 'The Standing Caliph Coins of Jerusalem', *NC* 176 (2016), pp. 486-7.

T. Goodwin, *The Standing Caliph coinage* (London, 2018).

A. Grabar, *L'iconoclasme byzantin* (Paris, 1957).

C. Head, *Justinian II of Byzantium* (Madison, WI, 1972).

M. Humphreys, 'The War of Images Revisited', *NC* 173 (2013), pp. 229-44.

A. Marsham, 'The Architecture of Allegiance in Early Islamic Late Antiquity: The Accession of Muʿāwiya in Jerusalem, ca. 661 CE', in A. Beihammer, S. Constantinou, and M. Parani (eds) *Court Ceremonies and Rituals of Power in Byzantium and the Medieval Mediterranean* (Leiden and Boston, 2013), pp. 87-114.

M. Meier, 'Herakles – Herakleios – Christus. Georgios Pisides und der kosmorhýstes', in H. Leppin (ed.), *Antike Mythologie in christlichen Kontexten der Spätantike* (Berlin and New York, 2014), pp. 167-92.

H. Möhring, *Der Weltkaiser der Endzeit* (Stuttgart, 2000).

F. Montinaro, 'Les premiers comerciaires byzantins', *Travaux et mémoires* 17 (2013), pp. 351-538.

F. Montinaro, 'Killing *empire*: Goldilocks and the three Byzantine *kommerkiarioi*', *Journal of European Economic History* 46, 2 (2017), pp. 165-72.

F. Montinaro, 'Reconstructions imaginaires: une note sur Byzance et l'Islam du VIIe au Xe siècle' *Semitica et Classica, Supplementa* 1 (2019), pp. 269-75.

G. Nedungatt and M. Featherstone (eds and trans.), *The Council In Trullo Revisited* (Rome, 1995).

A. Palmer (ed. and trans.), *The Seventh Century in the West-Syrian Chronicles* (Liverpool, 1993).

M. Phillips, 'Coinage and the Early Arab state', in A. Oddy, I. Schulze, and W. Schulze (ed.), *Coinage and History in the Seventh-Century Near East* 4 (London, 2015), pp. 53-71.

I. Schulze, *The Standing Caliph Coins of Jerusalem* (Munich, 2016).

W. Schulze, 'Symbolism on the Syrian standing caliph copper coins', in A. Oddy (ed.) *Coinage and History in the Seventh-Century Near East* 2 (London, 2010), pp. 11-21.

Y. Stoyanov, 'Apocalypticizing Warfare: From Political Theology to Imperial Eschatology in Seventh- to Early Eighth-Century Byzantium', in K. B. Bardakjian and S. La Porta (eds), ***The Armenian Apocalyptic Tradition*** (Leiden, 2014) pp. 379-433.

J. Tannous, ***The Making of the Medieval Middle East*** (Princeton, 2018).

L. Treadwell, 'Byzantium and Islam in the late 7th century AD' in T. Goodwin (ed.), ***Arab-Byzantine coins and history*** (London, 2012), pp. 145-5.

G. Zacos and A. Veglery, ***Byzantine lead seals*** 1 (Basle, 1972).

Die Chains and Die Links with the Mint Name Ḥalab

Ingrid Schulze [1]

Ten years ago Tony Goodwin presented the die link Fig. 1[2] between coins bearing the mint names of Ḥalab and Tanūkh as well as an uncertain mint name that might be the attempt of an unskilled die cutter to write Tanūkh. As there is no town named Tanūkh, but only a tribe with the name Banū Tanūkh, his suggestion that the large mint of Ḥalab struck coins for and in the name of the tribe is plausible.

Figure 1

Goodwin focussed attention on the possibility that different die cutters produced these dies. His article ends with the statement

> *"Further work needs to be done, most obviously the continuing search for die links, but also a stylistic analysis across mints to identify die engravers producing dies for more than one mint."*[3]

---

[1] Ingrid Schulze is an independent scholar: ingridschulze@wg-s.de
[2] Goodwin (2010a), p. 38 fig. 2.
[3] Goodwin (2010a), p. 40.

Although during recent years some more die links between 'mints' in jund Qinnasrīn were found[4], I followed Goodwin's suggestion and started to bring the die link Fig. 1 into a larger context by

- looking for more dies with the mint name Ḥalab and counting their numbers

- identifying the linkage of these dies to coins with other mint names

- making a stylistic analysis of these dies and their links and

- trying to attribute linked coins to a main, a secondary or a separate mint.

The examination starts with the first coin of the die link (obverse 1 with Tanūkh reverse). The initial pictures of the coin in Fig. 1 are replaced here by pictures of a duplicate with some more details[5].

Figure 2

---

[4] Cf. the compilation in Schulze W. (2017), p. 137 f.
[5] All pictures are enlarged at different scales to make details more visible. The average size of the coins is about 20mm.

As to be seen in Fig. 2, obverse 1 not only occurs with the Tanūkh reverse, but also with a Ḥalab reverse (a). When the obverse die was worn and damaged, it was combined with a reverse die showing a questionable mint name (b): at first glance it looks like Ḥalab, but it is written incorrectly and may be regarded again as the attempt of an unskilled die cutter, to write Ḥalab. This reverse was found with two other obverses in rough style (c and d) and finally the link leads to a proper Ḥalab reverse (e) which we will meet again later in another context (Fig. 8).

The examination continues with the second coin of the initial link Fig. 1:

Figure 3

Some duplicates were found and a new obverse, which looks quite curious with an unusual depiction of the legs and feet of the caliph. So far we have just examined the new connections of obverse 1.

The next step is the examination of obverse 2 (Fig. 4). In addition to the known reverses – questionable Tanūkh (a and b) and Ḥalab (c) – an interesting new Ḥalab reverse was found (enlarged picture and d) with the mint name written with a dot below the final *bā'*. Diacritical dots are very rare on Standing Caliph coins, but we know of one example from Sarmīn[6] and another Ḥalab reverse with a dot from Walker[7]. There are some more dies showing this detail and I will come back later to this phenomenon (Fig. 10). In Fig. 4 we can make an interesting observation concerning obverse 2. Until now we only knew this obverse with the protruding left shoulder of the caliph that looks somewhat misshapen. Obviously this was not the case when the die was fresh, as can be seen on the enlarged picture. Something must have happened to the die: the shoulder grows and the damage beside it increases. In this bad state the obverse was combined with the odd Tanūkh (a and b) and an awful Ḥalab reverse (c), maybe in a secondary mint where the less skilled engravers worked. This assumption is supported by checking the small series bearing also the reverse of coin c: neither the depiction of the caliph nor the mode of production looks professional. This obverse also occurs with the odd Tanūkh reverse (left), and in addition reverse c is combined with another obverse (right).

---

[6] Goodwin (2010b), p. 43.
[7] Walker (1956), no. 106.

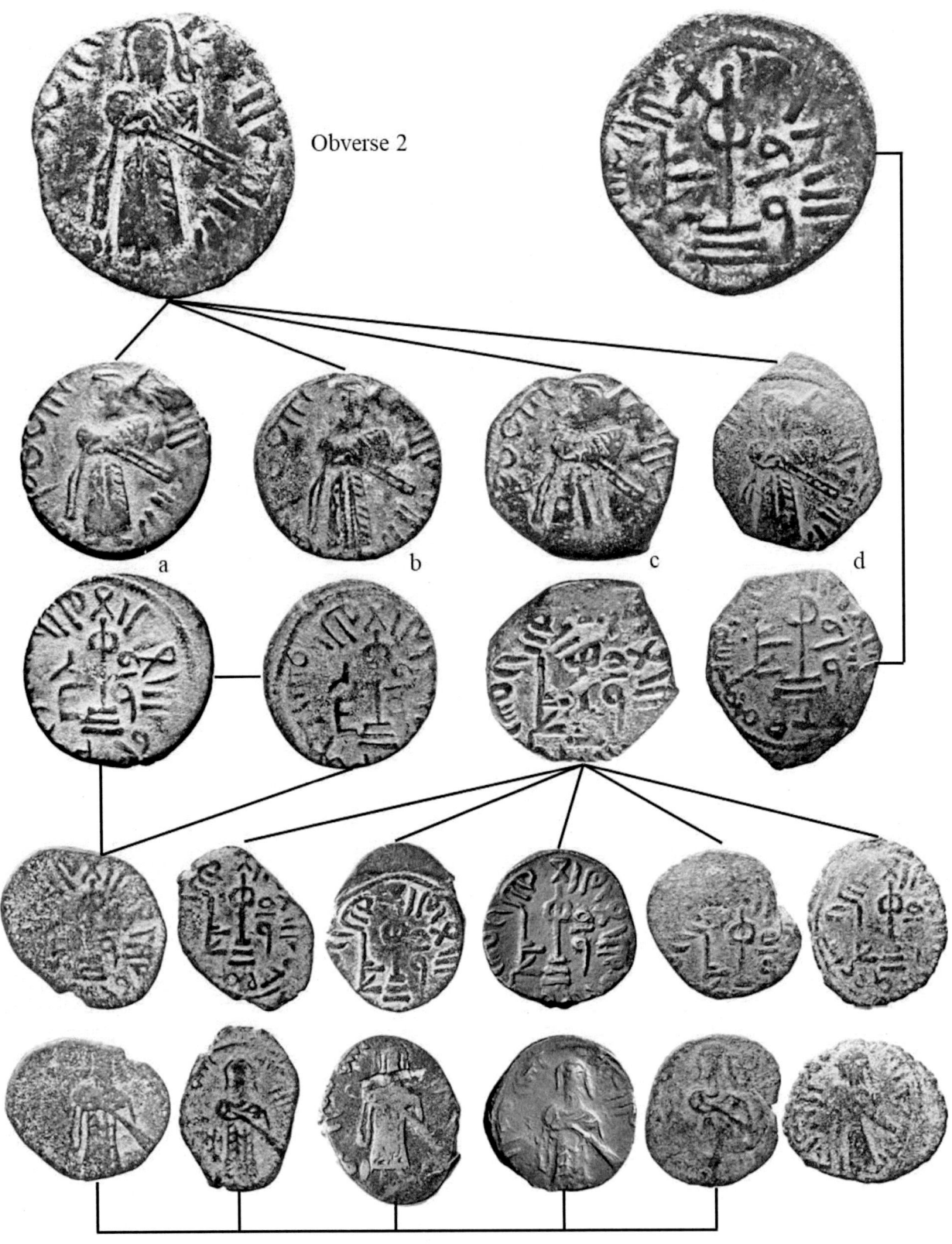

Figure 4

The new additions to the initial link are summarized in Fig. 5. The numbers indicate the specimens recorded so far.

The new reverse where the mint name Ḥalab is written with a dot beneath the final *bā'* is quite numerous and occurs with some other obverses, and thus the link can be continued. On Fig. 6 we start again with obverse die 2.

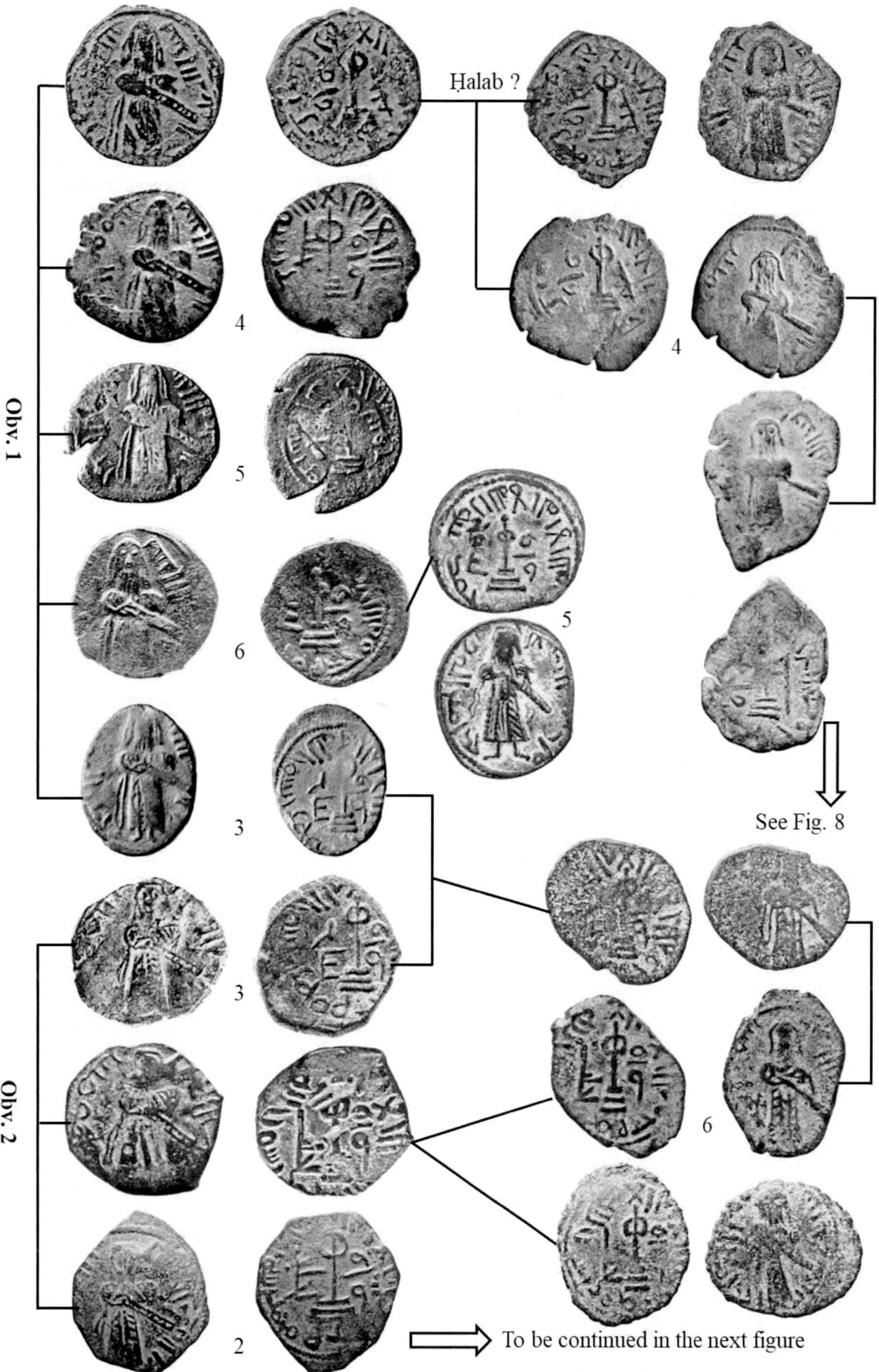

Figure 5

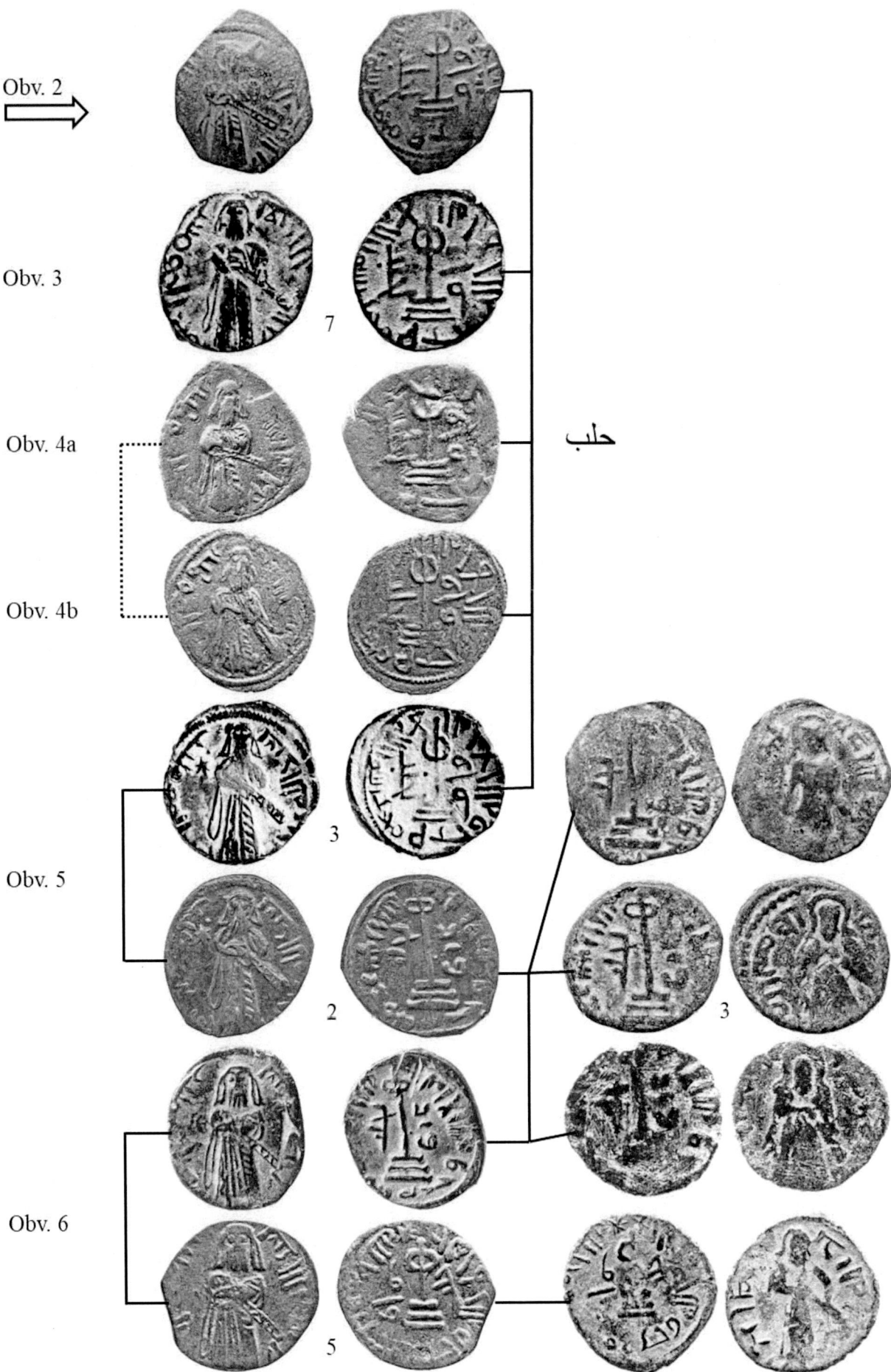

Figure 6

The continuation of the die chain on Fig. 6 shows some interesting obverses:
Obverses 3 and 6 are of good style, fitting well to obverses 1 and 2 (Fig. 5). Obverse 5 is somewhat extraordinary with a star and a dot beside the right shoulder of the caliph. Obverses 5 and 6 are combined with a clumsy reverse showing some engraving faults: the pole of the symbol on steps is not upright, the *wāfin* is not correct and the marginal legend is incomplete and poorly written. The mint name *bi-ḥalab* to the left <u>downwards</u> is a rare variant that I only know from one other die in the whole series of Ḥalab coins. This odd reverse leads to a small group of coins with obverses far away from the 'normal' style of this series – a new handwriting (in a secondary mint?) is obvious. The second reverse of obverse 6 is worthy of particular notice: there is a star at the end of the marginal legend. It was Nützel[8] who described this coin already in 1898, mentioning this star. This unusual detail was forgotten for more than 120 years and never referred to in the literature. This extraordinary reverse of obverse 6 is found now with a completely blundered obverse.

Most interesting are the obverses 4a and 4b. It seems to be clear that we are dealing with two different dies, regarding shape and direction of the sword. A tiny unusual detail caused me to have a closer look: a little crescent left of the caliph's head on both obverses.

Obverse 4a   Obverse 4b

Figure 7

Comparing the dies carefully it becomes clear that we are dealing with only one die, which was altered in the encircled section: the caliph got a right arm and a new sword. In Fig. 6 the obverses in both stages of appearance share the same reverse. Our die chain can be extended again:

In Fig. 8 we see our obverses 3, 4a and 4b with the already known 'dotted' Ḥalab reverse and another one with *ḥalab* in the right field. This die we already know from Fig. 5; there it is linked to a questionable Ḥalab reverse. In addition the altered die 4b has a third Ḥalab reverse with an extremely blundered marginal legend[9] (middle row right). The biggest surprise is in the last row of Fig. 8: Besides three Ḥalab reverses our altered die 4b is combined with two reverses, where the mint name is a questionable Anṭākiya. A part of the link was already published by W. Schulze[10] in 2016. The wrong spelling of the mint name with *qāf* instead of *kāf* caused him to regard these coins as products of an unofficial mint. Now we see that the small link is imbedded into a colossal die chain.

---

[8] Nützel (1898), no. 49.
[9] Zeno 175302, here qualified by a member of Santa Rosa as modern forgery.
[10] Schulze W. (2017), p. 134 fig. 11.

Figure 8

For completeness it should be mentioned that the artistic obverse 5 with star and dot is the largest in number of the die chain so far: it occurs with 6 different reverses in a high number of duplicates, see Fig. 9.

Obv. 5

Figure 9

When we summarize Figs 5, 6, 8 and 9 we state that the initial link of Fig. 1 developed into a fantastic die chain with 15 obverse dies and 16 reverse dies, and it is to be expected that even more die matches will appear. Although all the coins are linked they seem to come from different mints due to the differences in engraving, style and production.

Fig. 10 shows the six 'better' obverses which were in use in the main mint. Even here the style of engraving is not uniform, for instance shape and design of the robes differ, and it may well be that the additional decorations like crescent and star and dot in the left field are 'signatures' of the die cutters.

Figure 10

Fig. 11 makes the differences in style obvious: beside the two dies given to the secondary mint after damage or re-engraving (arrowed), we see the caliph in a very different shape. Only the third caliph in the upper row (the one with only a Tanūkh reverse – Figs 3 and 5) seems to imitate the style produced in the main mint.

Figure 11

As far as the reverses are concerned we see in Fig. 12 the 'better' ones from the main mint, and in Fig. 13 the less well cut dies with questionable mint names:

Figure 12

Figure 13

How do we have to imagine the production of the complete die chain?
In a well engraved chain of Ḥalab coins, two reverses of Tanūkh as well as a questionable Tanūkh, a questionable Ḥalab and two reverses of a misspelled Antākiya are integrated. This could mean that damaged or failed dies are given by the main mint to one or more secondary mints, where they are combined with other dies which do not fit in with the usual appearance of the Ḥalab coins. If we start from the idea that we are dealing with several production places for the die chain, they must have worked side by side but on different levels of quality.

The key reverse for the chain is the one with the dot under Ḥalab, which connects five of the six main obverses (Fig. 6).
As mentioned above, there are other reverses with a dot under Ḥalab:

Walker 106

Figure 14

We already know the first coin. The obverse of the Walker coin no. 106 also occurs with another reverse without dot, while the third obverse even has three more reverses without dot – all dies are of good style and production. The last obverse die has a different appearance and looks more like the product of a secondary mint. No die matches could be found so far.
How should we interpret the dot?

What is written on the coins is the most common *bi-ḥalab*, which in Arabic would need not one but two diacritical dots under each *bā'*. This is the argument for Goodwin to regard the single dot most probably as mere decoration[11]. Walker mentions the dot and even emphasises in other descriptions when there is no dot[12]. On all four dies the dot has the exact and correct position; so that one could speculate that the die cutter wanted to write the city's name correctly in contrast to the curious and questionable Tanūkh and the wrongly spelled Antākiya.

After this little detour to the dots I would like to come back to die links. When looking for die matches and duplicates for the impressive die chain that has been discussed in detail, I noticed three more links between Ḥalab and Tanūkh which I will present briefly because of their interesting style. They still need to be examined further for additional die matches.

The first pair (Fig. 15) shows a wonderfully engraved caliph with an impressive face. What is really strange is the pattern of the robe: the parallel lines to the right are not – as usual – straight diagonal but slightly curved and roughly horizontal.

Tanūkh Ḥalab

Figure 15

---

[11] Goodwin (2010b), p. 43 fn. 7.
[12] Walker (1956), nos 108, 110, 112, 114.

Fig. 16 shows a caliph with an unusual left shoulder which is depicted with only two rough lines. Here the diagonal lines are at the right side of the caliph's robe what can also be observed on other obverses.

Tanūkh   Ḥalab   Ḥalab

Figure 16

The third example (Fig. 17) shows the caliph far away from the usual style and in addition the production is careless.

Tanūkh   Ḥalab

Figure 17

As already mentioned these links need further research. Are they part of a die chain or products of small separate workshops?

The assumption that a large and important mint like the one of Ḥalab produced coins for and in the name of small towns seems to be reasonable. But why do we have die links between Ḥalab and Qinnasrīn, the second largest mint in the jund Qinnasrīn? One example is to be seen in Fig. 18:

Ḥalab   Ḥalab   Ḥalab   Qinnasrīn

Figure 18

The obverse die is of good style and could well be a part of our initial link (compare Fig. 6 obverse 3). Was the obverse die, when worn, given to the nearby mint of Qinnasrīn?

A completely different picture emerges in Fig. 19: the cutter of the obverse die was unskilled and incompetent. He tried to copy the image of the caliph – the result is clumsy – and he completely failed with the marginal legend – the result is nonsense. The Ḥalab reverse is also incorrect while the two Qinnasrīn reverses seem to be correct. Where might this workshop have been situated?

Ḥalab   Qinnasrīn   Qinnasrīn

Figure 19

Just for entertainment on Fig. 20 another link is shown which could be called 'network of incompetence' to demonstrate again the different quality of engraving. Four obverse dies (the last one below to the right excluded) and four reverse dies are connected with each other. None of the dies is correct. Apart from the clumsy and most unusual appearance of the caliph the obverse marginal legend on the first die is retrograde, the *wāfin* and the mint name Ḥalab are more and more blundered. All the dies seem to be products of at least four unskilled die cutters who tried to imitate known dies without real knowledge about what they are doing. The final surprise is to be seen in the last row – a link to a Ḥimṣ reverse. This link was published and discussed by Goodwin ten years ago[13]. Now we can see it in a larger context. In the meantime the same Ḥimṣ reverse appeared with a new peculiar blundered obverse (last coin below to the right – neither in Ḥalab nor in Ḥimṣ style). This die chain surely has nothing to do with the main mint of Ḥalab. I propose to call such coins products of a separate mint, which does not necessarily mean that they are irregular as Goodwin considers[14]. The problem here is that the appearance of this group, reaching over different junds, is in no way comparable with the official coins of the named mints. Thus the use of the term 'secondary mint' is doubtful. This does not conclusively prove that this mint is an irregular one in the sense that contemporary forgeries were struck there. For such a conclusion we do not have enough knowledge of the framework of 'main' and 'secondary' mints. However, in this special case with utmost caution I avoid the term 'secondary mint' and replace it by 'separate mint'.

---

[13] Goodwin (2010a), p. 39 fig. 3.
[14] Goodwin (2010a), p. 39.

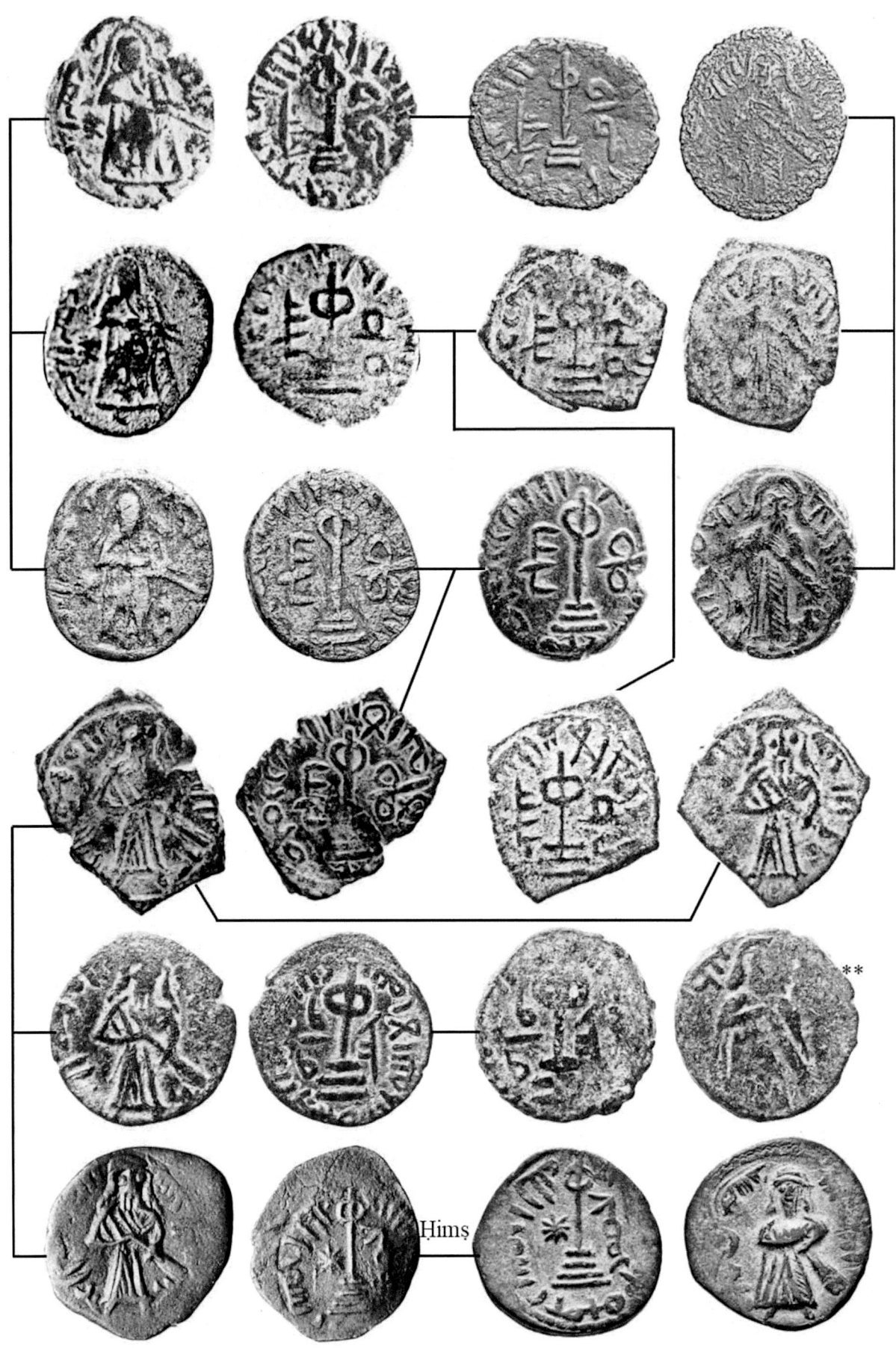

Figure 20

** This obverse occurs also with three other Ḥalab reverses

Strangely enough there is even another link between Ḥalab and Ḥimṣ and a third reverse where the mint name is not yet deciphered (Fig. 21). Here we meet a new element of decoration, something that looks like an epsilon, on the obverse as well as on the reverses together with a star, except on the Ḥalab reverse where we see the usual *wāfin*. The depiction of the caliph is curious, the marginal legends are faulty and the production of the coins careless. None of the coins are complete. Unfortunately the undeciphered mint name is often interpreted as Ḥimṣ[15] or Ḥalab[16] although it can easily be distinguished from Ḥimṣ by the position of the 'epsilon' in the left field. As for the link in Fig. 20 also here a new obverse for the Ḥimṣ reverse could be found, again not in Ḥimṣ style. As there are some more series of Ḥalab coins with this enigmatic 'epsilon' a careful analysis of the dies should be done.

Ḥalab   undeciphered mint name   Ḥimṣ

Figure 21

---

[15] Goodwin (2018), no. 188.
[16] Foundation collection.

A last example of a peculiar link can be seen on Fig. 22. For the depiction of the caliph the die cutter did his best, but he had no feeling for proportions. Thus the head is too big and the arms are too thin. The production is again careless.

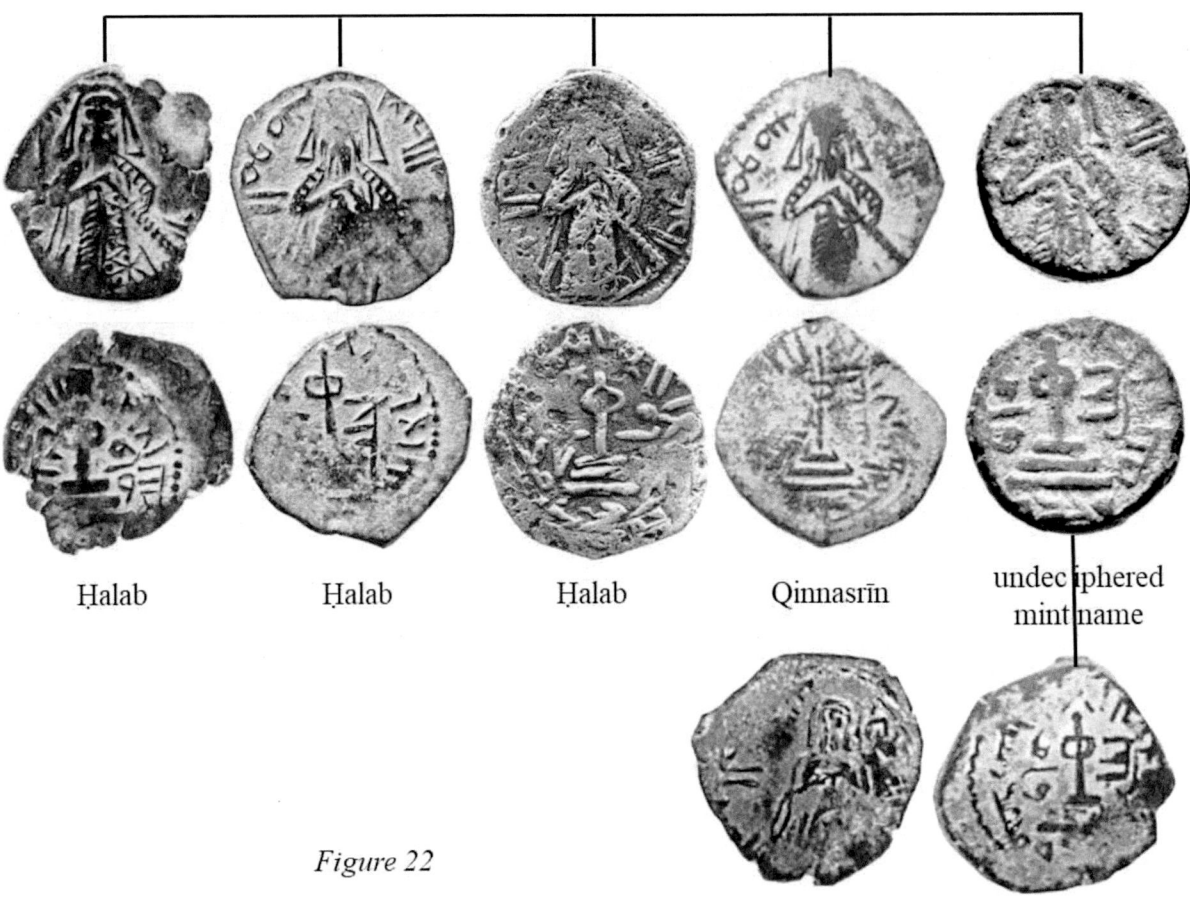

Figure 22

All the small links in Figs 15 to 22 need further research to find out, whether they are part of a larger emission like our first link or isolated emissions of small workshops that received the right to make coins.

Summary

In the course of this article I have demonstrated by a stylistic analysis, that there are coins with the mint name Ḥalab which are evidently struck by a 'main' mint and were linked to other coins with the same or other mint names in a blundered version. These mints, connected by links to the main mint were named 'secondary' mints. I proposed that dies, which were worn, damaged or otherwise redundant, were still used in these secondary mints. There often unskilled die cutters produced additional obverse dies and reverse dies with different mint names familiar to them.

In Fig. 23 the complete link of Figs 1 to 13 is summarized in a compressed way. The curved lines connect the dies of the main mint while the dotted squares connect the products of the secondary mints. The dashed line shows the movement of a reverse die from the main mint to a secondary mint.

For the mints of which the coins were not linked to the 'main' mint and instead produced blundered coins with different mint names I used the expression 'separate' mint. Examples of this are shown in Figs 19 to 22, but are not integrated into the general conspectus of Fig. 23.

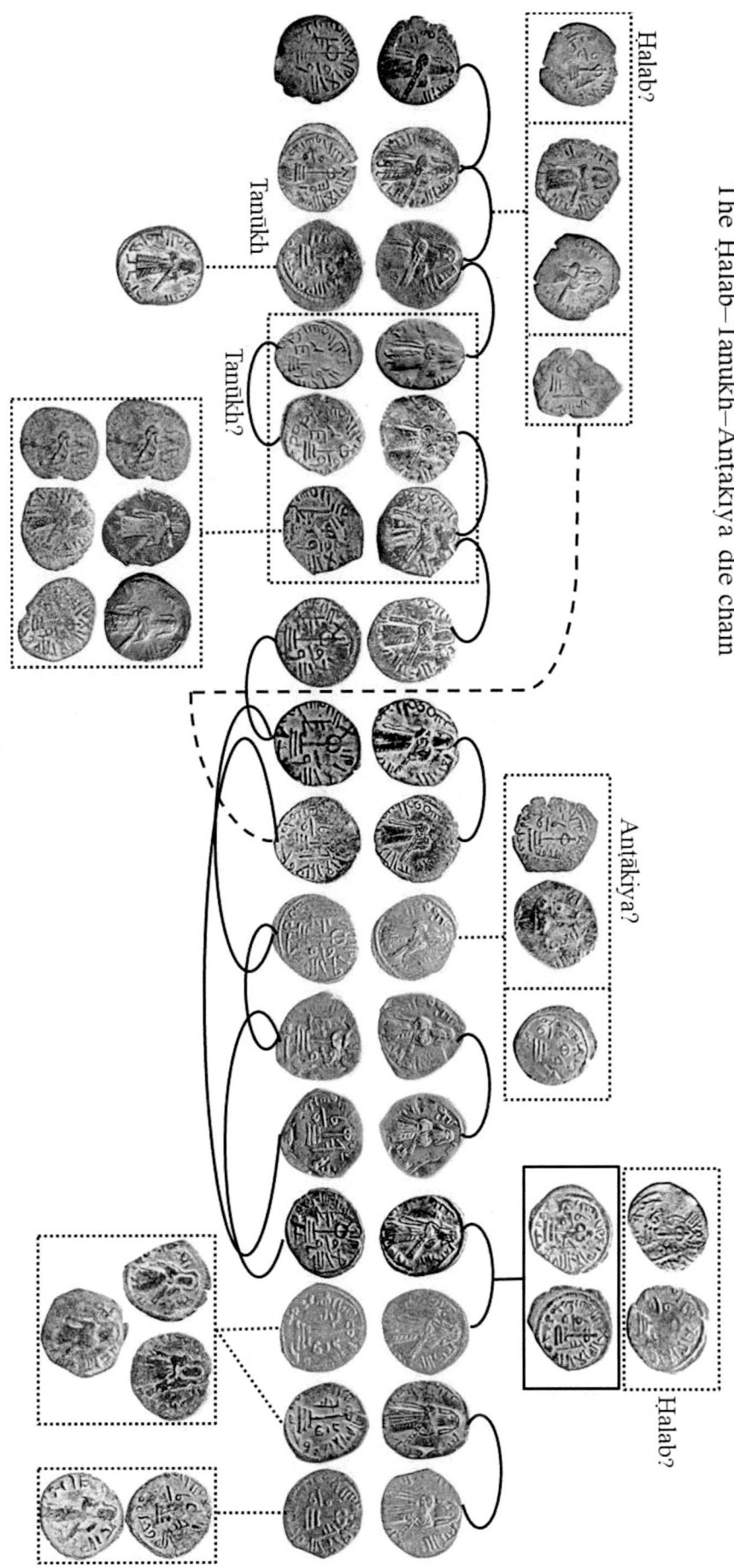

Figure 23

How can this classification and distinction be explained?

To answer this question we have to remember the basis of Islamic law concerning the money circulation in earlier times as Stefan Heidemann has described it:[17] The Islamic right only provides gold and silver coins as absolute equivalent. They only serve as standard of value, given by Allāh, to lighten the exchange of products and services. The value of gold and silver coins was tied to their substance and dealing with them for profit was forbidden. Copper coins had a special position because they were not tied to the substance. The leadership of the state and the long-distance traders were only interested in gold and silver coins. They were indifferent to the circulation of petty money. The solution to the problem of providing people with small change for daily use was usually transferred to local governors, emirs or even bishops. Occasionally mints were leased and the coins produced by private management. This means that these mints away from the main mints may not be called unofficial.

After all we can start from the idea that in jund Qinnasrīn like in other junds[18] the production of copper coins was organized locally. The products of secondary or separate mints were not unofficial or irregular, but part of the contemporary circulation. The output of new coins was demand-oriented.

Because secondary or separate mints were involved in this system of money production we cannot believe at the first glance the 'mint names' written on the coins. I published this insight a few years earlier[19]. For example, if we read Ḥalab as mint name, then the coin may well come from a smaller mint whose production place we do not (not yet) know. The same applies to other names of mints in jund Qinnasrīn. So, we definitely have to reject the idea that a Standing Caliph coin that indicates a particular mint, actually originates from the named place.

In this article I have not examined the weights of the coins. On the one hand, this seemed superfluous to me in view of the fact that up to the end of Umayyad rule the folles circulated side by side with old and worn Greek, Roman and Byzantine coins, mainly *minimi*, supplemented by foreign coins, clipped coins and even simple piece of metal. The exact weight or size of the coins was not significant; what mattered was the number of coins involved in any given transaction.[20] On the other hand a weight examination could be interesting to determine whether the separate or secondary mints worked with the same weight standard as the main mint(s). But before we can do that, we have to know which coin belongs to which subsidiary mint – an extremely difficult task.

In short, there is still a lot to do.

Supplement

'…and it is to be expected that even more die matches will appear.'
The nightmare came true when the article was ready for publication: a coin, offered in trade, questions the results found so far, or at least makes the situation even more complicated. The new coin has the altered obverse die 4b (Figs 6 and 7) which hitherto was found combined with two Ḥalab reverse dies from the main mint, one questionable Ḥalab and two questionable Anṭākiya reverse dies from a secondary mint. The new coin however has a reverse with the mint name Ḥimṣ, not just any but exactly the die that we already know from Fig. 20 (last row) – the link that was attributed to a separate mint. A short version of the new connection is shown in Fig. 24:

---

[17] Heidemann (2002), 353–63; similar Ilisch (2010), 27 and (2016), 252.
[18] Cf. e. g. for jund al-Urdunn Schulze and Schulze (2019, 257 f. and Schulze and Schulze forthcoming.
[19] Schulze I. (2015)
[20] Schulze and Schulze (2018), 197, 202 f.

Figure 24

This link, combining reverses attributed above to main, secondary and separate mints, is difficult to explain. At first glance there are two possibilities: either the odd link shown in Fig. 20 was produced in the same secondary mint as the smaller links beside the main link (dotted squares in Fig. 23), which for me is hard to imagine; or the altered obverse die was given away (sold?) to a separate workshop for further use.

Certainly there are other possibilities. For example we do not know anything of the sequence of the Standing Caliph coinage in jund Qinnasrīn. Did the main, secondary and separate mints work at the same time or successively? Were dies of the main mint re-used much later in secondary and/or separate mints? Did the mints work continuously over the years or in several shorter phases – possibly with different die cutters?

The door is wide open for speculation.

Acknowledgement

Many friends have generously provided images of their coins for this research, namely Elisabeth and Robert Darley-Doran, Tony Goodwin, Steve Mansfield, Andrew Oddy und Nikolaus Schindel. I thank you all as warmly as Lutz Ilisch who made the holdings of the University Tübingen accessible to me.

Bibliography

Goodwin (2010a)	T. Goodwin, 'Die Links between Standing Caliph Mints in Jund Qinnasrin', *Coinage and History in the Seventh Century Near East 2* (A. Oddy ed.) (London 2010), pp. 35–40.
Goodwin (2010b)	T. Goodwin, 'A Standing Caliph Fals Issued by 'Abd al-Rahmān at Sarmin', *Coinage and History in the Seventh Century Near East 2* (A. Oddy ed.) (London 2010), pp. 41–43.
Goodwin (2018)	T. Goodwin, *The Standing Caliph Coinage* (London 2018).
Heidemann (2002)	S. Heidemann, *Die Renaissance der Städte in Nordsyrien und Nordmesopotamien. Städtische Entwicklung und wirtschaftliche Bedingungen in ar-Raqqa und Harrān von der Zeit der beduinischen Vorherrschaft bis zu den Seldschuken* (Leiden, Boston and Köln 2002).
Ilisch (2010)	L. Ilisch, 'Abd al-Malik's Monetary Reform in Copper and the Failure of Centralization', *Money, Power and Politics in Early Islamic Syria – A review of current debates* (J. Haldon ed.) (Farnham 2010), pp. 125–146.
Ilisch (2016)	L. Ilisch, ,'Einordnung und Datierung der Fundmünze aus dem großen Hof', *Qasr al-Mschatta – Ein frühislamischer Palast in Jordanien und Berlin 1* (J. Cramer et al. eds) Berliner Beiträge zur Bauforschung und Denkmalpflege 16 (Petersberg 2016), pp. 249–261.
Nützel (1898)	H. Nützel, *Katalog der Orientalischen Münzen 1, Die Münzen der östlichen Chalifen* (Berlin 1898).
Schulze and Schulze (2018)	I. and W. Schulze, 'Working with coins in Jerash: Problems, solutions and preliminary results', *The Archaeology and History of Jerash – 110 Years of Excavations* (A. Lichtenberger and R. Raja eds) Jerash Papers 1. (Turnhout 2018), pp. 195–2015.
Schulze and Schulze (2019)	I. and W. Schulze, 'Umayyad Numismatics in Bilād al-Sham with Particular Reference to Jund al-Urdunn', *Byzantine and Umayyad Jerash Reconsidered – Transitions, Transformations,* Continuities (A. Lichtenberger and R. Raja eds) Jerash Papers 4. (Turnhout 2019), pp. 239–264.
Schulze and Schulze forthcoming	I. and W. Schulze 'The coins of the Danish-German Jerash Northwest Quarter Project 2012–2016 and the Umayyad Money Circulation in Jund al-Urdunn', forthcoming.
Schulze I. (2015)	I. Schulze, 'Can we believe what is written on the coins? – Enigmatic die links and other puzzles', *Coinage and History in the Seventh Century Near East 4* (A. Oddy, I. Schulze and W. Schulze (eds) (London 2015), pp. 115–135.
Schulze W. (2017)	W. Schulze, 'Anṭākiya – A new Standing Caliph mint and die links in the jund Qinnasrīn', *Coinage and History in the Seventh Century Near East 5* (T. Goodwin ed.) (London 2017), pp. 129–140.
Walker (1956)	J. Walker, *A Catalogue of the Muhammadan Coins in the British Museum vol. II, A Catalogue of the Arab-Byzantine and Post-Reform Umaiyad coins* (London 1956).

The Standing Caliph Coins with the Mint Name
Qūrus (قُورس)
A new Die and a new Die Link

Wolfgang Schulze [1]

In the Proceedings of the 15th Seventh Century Syrian Numismatic Round Table held 2016 in Oxford[2] I presented an overview of the Standing Caliph coins with the mint name Qūrus. I could show three obverse dies O1-O3 and two reverse dies R1 and R2 and a type O4/R3 – possibly of a secondary mint – not of interest here.

In the meantime I found a fourth obverse die, now designated O3a.

The reverse of O3a is already known as R2.

Figure. 1:
The four obverse and the two reverse dies of the Qūrus Phase 3 coins.

---

[1] Wolfgang Schulze is an independent scholar: schulze@wg-s.de
[2] W. Schulze, 'The Standing Caliph Coins with the mint name Qūrus', *Coinage and History in the Seventh Century Near East 5* (T. Goodwin ed.) (London 2017), pp. 141-51.

Three specimens with the obverse die O3a and two different reverses are known:

Figure 2: Three coins with obverse die O3a:
Album auction 30, January 2018, lot 181, 3.00g;
Baldwin's of St. James's auction 4, May 2017, lot 104, 3.46g;
Schulze collection ex Morton and Eden auction 89, October 2017, lot 139, 4.26g.

Die O3a is rather similar to die O2, but there are some clear differences.

Figure 3

For example the opening down the front of the Caliph's robe is striking on O3a and missing on O2. Furthermore the strings falling from the elbow are slightly different. There is no doubt that both dies are made by the same die cutter.

As became clear from Fig. 2 die O3a has as reverses R1 and R2 and now I can update the linkage within the Qūrus coins in this way:

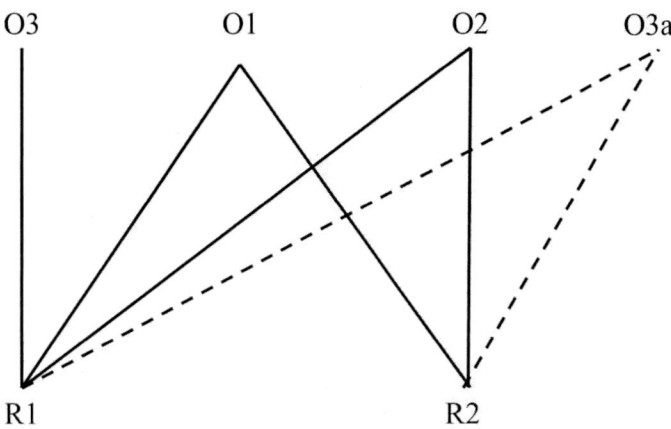

Figure 4: Linkage of the Qūrus dies.
The new connections are marked as dashed lines.

Also in the Proceedings of the 15th Seventh Century Syrian Numismatic Round Table held 2016 in Oxford[3] I identified Walker's P.12[4], listed by him as mintless, as a Standing Caliph coin of Ḥalab. And it is exactly this coin which is linked to the new die O3a of Qūrus.

And in addition there is in the Goodwin collection another coin with the same obverse, but now the mint name Ḥalab is written on the right side:

Qūrus O3a/R2	Ḥalab	Ḥalab
(Schulze coll.)	(Schulze coll.)	(Goodwin coll.)
	= Walker P.12	

Figure 5: New die link Qūrus – Ḥalab.

---

[3] W. Schulze, 'Anṭākiya – A new Standing Caliph mint and die links in the jund Qinnasrīn', **Coinage and History in the Seventh Century Near East 5** (T. Goodwin ed.) (London 2017), pp. 129-40.
[4] J. Walker, **A Catalogue of the Muhammadan Coins in the British Museum vol. II, A Catalogue of the Arab-Byzantine and Post-Reform Umaiyad coins** (London 1956).

While Qūrus O1 and O3 are linked to Qinnasrīn and Qūrus O2 is linked to Ḥalab, now we have another link of O3a to two Ḥalab coins.

As result the linkage of the Qūrus coins to other mints can be updated in this way:

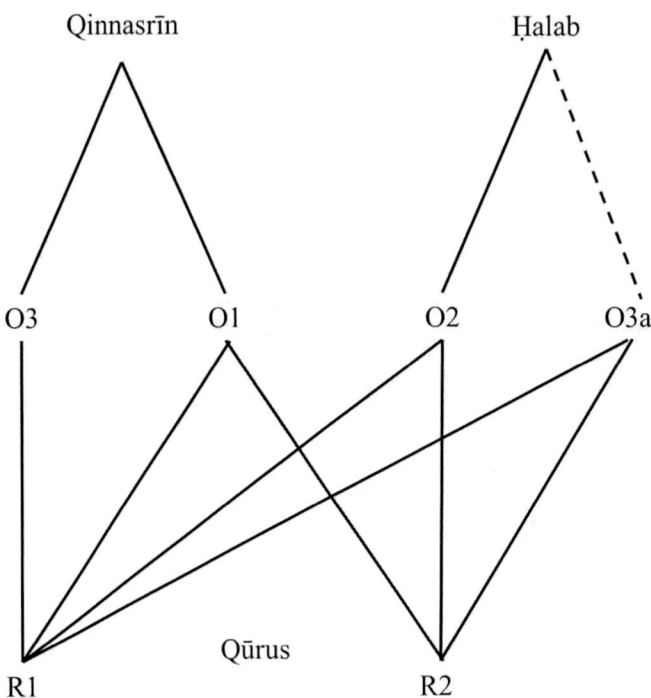

Figure 6: Die links between Qinnasrīn, Ḥalab and Qūrus.
Again the new die link is marked as dashed line.

This additional die link between Qūrus and Ḥalab strengthens the already several times suggested possibility that in jund Qinnasrīn the larger mints – namely Ḥalab and Qinnasrīn – minted coins for and in the name of other places.

From Scythopolis to Baysān: A Glimpse at the Coins of The Hebrew University's Excavations at Beth Shean

Nitzan Amitai-Preiss[1]

Introduction

Palestine was divided into three provinces in an edict of 409 CE: Palaestina Prima, Palaestina Secunda, and Palaestina Tertia. The city of Scythopolis was the capital of Palaestina Secunda as of 409 CE.[2] The Roman city was called Nysa-Scythopolis. It ceased minting coins in 240 or 241 CE in the later years of Gordian III (239-244 CE).[3] The city continued to be called by the latter part of its name, Scythopolis, throughout the Byzantine era[4] and into the Muslim period. This name is attested on bronze coins minted in that city from some time after the Muslim conquest (around 670 CE) until c. 692-3 CE.[5] These coins carry this name as their mint. They show two imperial figures on a double throne, both nimbate, holding in their hands cruciform sceptres and a cross between their heads; inscription: CKYΘO ΠOΛHC.[6]

The centre of the ancient city of Beth Shean was unearthed from 1980-81 and from 1986-2003 by two archaeological teams' excavations: first the Hebrew University's team headed by the late Prof. Yoram Tsafrir and by Prof. Gideon Foerster. The numismatist for the Arab-Byzantine coins and the Muslim coins was the current author.[7] The second team, from the Israeli Antiquities Authority (IAA), was headed Dr Gabi Mazor and by Dr Rachel Bar-Natan. (Their numismatist was Ariel Berman, who published the coins of one area of their excavation: the theatre pottery workshop).[8] This article will concentrate on the Hebrew University teams' archaeological excavations and finds.

---

[1] Dr Nitzan Amitai-Preiss is a lecturer on Islamic Archaeology at the Hebrew University of Jerusalem, (Israel); she is also a numismatist. E-mail: amitaipr@mscc.huji.ac.il
[2] Codex Theodosianus 7, 4, 30. On the soldiers who served in these three provinces, see B. Isaac, *The Limits of the Empire: the Roman Army in the East* (Oxford, 1990), p.208.
[3] R. Barkay, *The Coinage of Nysa-Scythopolis-Beth-Shean*, Corpus Nummorum Palaestinensium Vol. 5 (Jerusalem, 2003), pp.224-231, Nos.79-97.
[4] This is proved for instance by the Christian monk, and historian of monastic life in Palestine, Cyril, a native of Scythopolis who lived c.525-c.559 CE. See B. Baldwin and A.-M. Talbot, 'Cyril of Scythopolis', in A. Khazhdan (ed.), *The Oxford Dictionary of Byzantium* (Oxford, 1991), p.573.
[5] A. Oddy, 'The Phase 2 Coinage of Scythopolis under Mu'awiya and his Successors', in A. Oddy, I. Schulze and W. Schulze (eds.), *Coinage and History in the Seventh Century Near East*, 4, p.176.
[6] N. Amitai-Preiss, A. Berman and S. Qedar, 'The Coinage of Scythopolis-Baysān and Gerasa-Jerash', *Israel Numismatic Journal*, 13 (1999), pp.137, 141-144, group A.
[7] I want to thank my two team colleagues, Dr Benny Arubas and Shoshana Agadi, for the help they have provided me over the course of the thirty years I have been connected to this team. Two articles have been published so far about coins from the excavations: N. Amitai-Preiss, 'Umayyad Coin Hoards from Beth Shean Excavations of the Hebrew University', *Israel Numismatic Journal*, 14 (2002), pp.224-238. The second article which is about coins from the excavations, written about coins minted at Scythopolis, is mentioned in note 6. In a future publication of coins from the 'Street of the Monuments', the Islamic coins will be published by the current author, and the earlier coins will be published by Dr Yoav Farhi and by Dr Gabi Bijosky.
[8] A. Berman,.'The Coins', in R. Bar-Natan and W. Atrash (eds.), *Baysān: The Theater Pottery Workshop* (Jerusalem, 2011), pp. 87-151.

The City

In 635, after the beginning of the Muslim conquest (the process of conquest took place 635-641 CE), the city as well as the whole region entered a new political era. However the city of Beth Shean, enjoyed a peaceful shift of control to the new rulers, apparently maintaining its Byzantine framework and cultural heritage architecture until at least 659-660 CE. In that year the Byzantine city, in which there had been a long process of slow change, came to an abrupt end, apparently as a result of an earthquake. This year also marks the beginning of the rule of the Umayyad dynasty. All the major components of the civic centre were destroyed and were not rebuilt.

The archaeological evidence from the city centre shows that the inhabitants of the city now preferred to bring industrial facilities close to commercial zones that were still concentrated along the traditional main streets. In part of the eastern Roman-Byzantine bathhouse a production and/or textiles-dyeing facility was built. The former civic centre was now dominated by a continuous and crowded bazaar (*sūq*), mainly along major streets between industrial areas.[9] The city at some point started to be called Baysān, a return to a Semitic name, yet a new one, and not its original Biblical times name Bet Shean. Evidence for its two names can be seen on its Arab-Byzantine coins. On the Imperial Image coinage it was first called Scythopolis CKVΘO ΠΟΛHC (written in Greek), and then it started to be called *Baysān* بيسن, as seen on both M-value coins and on K-value coins minted by the city.[10] The first occurrence in a historical source is much later, during the Abbasid period, al-Balādhurī's, (d. 892) *Futūh al-Buldān* ('The Conquering of the Countries').[11]

The division of the 22,669 coins unearthed at the Beth Shean excavations (The Hebrew University's team):

Pre-Islamic:
- Hellenistic 65
- Roman 689
- Late Roman 8621
- Byzantine 3011
- Sasanian 3

Islamic:
- Arab-Byzantine 2684
- Umayyad post-reform 7150
- Abbasid 424
- Ayyubid 12
- Mamluk 80
- Ilkhanid 1
- A few Ottoman objects were unearthed, but not coins.

---

[9] The last two paragraphs are based on the introduction of Dr Benny Arubas, in Shulamit Hadad, *Islamic Glass Vessels from the Hebrew University Excavations at Bet Shean, Qedem Reports 8 - Excavations at Bet Shean* Volume 2 (Book 2), 2005.

[10] Amitai-Preiss et al., 'The Coinage of Scythopolis' - for the name Scythopolis on M value see pl.17 Nos. a1-A8b. On K value see Pl.19, No. B1. for Baysān on M value see pl.19, No.A18 on K value see pl.19No.B2-B3.; See also A. Oddy, 'The Phase 2 Coinage of Scythopolis' (found in note 6 above) for Scythopolis on M value p.157, Figure 6, a and for the k value see figure 3, a. For Baysān see Oddy for M value see p.167, Figure 15, and for k value p.168, Figure 16.

[11] Aḥmad ibn Yaḥyā al-Balādhurī, *Kitab Futūh al-Buldān* (Leiden, 1866), al-Urdun's cities, pp.158-160.

The current article deals with the 'Standing Caliph' coins unearthed at the Beth Shean excavation (see the table below). Such coins were not minted in the county of al-Urdunn, which Bet Shean belonged to.[12] Only 'Twin Standing Caliph' coins were minted at either Scythopolis or Jerash.[13]

A mere number of sixteen Arab-Byzantine bronze coins from the Bet Shean (Hebrew University) excavations are of the 'Standing Caliph' type. Five coins definitely have Dimashq as their mint, one has Ḥims,[14] one has Fistin Filastin. One is probably a mint in Qinnasrin according to its style,[15] a title and name or a mint? can be seen on it (see Fig 1 below). All the others may have Dimashq as their mint also.[16] For comparison a table of the number and mints of 'Standing Caliph' coins from excavations in the North of Israel (al-Urdunn) will be found at the end of this article. All the excavations in the North of Israel have yielded only a few Standing Caliph coins: one Fistin mint (from a Tiberias excavation) and three Dimashq (one from Bet Shean, two from a village - called today Neve Ur).

The table below reveals that four major groupings are formed:
Group 1: Locus 608, basket 8495 (a shop) – two 'Standing Caliph' coins
Group 2: Locus 809, basket 10655 – two 'Standing Caliph' coins-
Group 3: Locus 812, basket 542579 – three 'Standing Caliph' coins
Group 4: Locus 785, basket 13312 – five 'Standing Caliph' coins (three Ḥims, one Dimashq, one unclear mint)
The remaining seven coins are isolated finds in each of their loci.

All these four groups, as well as the eight remaining isolated finds were unearthed alongside other bronze coins earlier than the Islamic period (Late Roman or Byzantine), as well as other types of Arab-Byzantine bronze coins. The additional bronze coins are as follows:

Alongside Group 1: Three Late Roman coins (which could have been used as a small denomination below a fals),[17] one Umayyad Imperial Image, three Tabariya 3-figure type (one with shahada reverse).

Alongside Group 2: Three Byzantine coins: Justin I (minted 522-527 CE), Constans II (minted 642-643 CE and 652-658 CE); seven Umayyad Imperial Image coins.

Alongside Group 3: Byzantine: Mauricius Tiberius (588 CE), 1 Umayyad: anonymous post-reform fals and a bulla.

Alongside Group 4: Three Arab-Byzantine coins, all with a standing imperial figure (nothing else can be said about them).

Discussion

Nineteen mints struck 'Standing Caliph' coins, six of which had also minted Imperial Image coins (Ḥims, Dimashq, ʿAmmān, Baʿalbakk, Īliyā and Ludd). Thirteen other mints may have been

---

[12] T. Goodwin, *The Standing Caliph Coinage*, London, 2018, p.58
[13] ibid, p.58.
[14] ibid. pp.64-65
[15] I want to thank Tony Goodwin for this attribution.
[16] Ibid. pp.59-62.
[17] For an overstike of an anonymous Umayyad coin minted over a Late Roman coin of Constantius II (351-354 CE) N. Amitai-Preiss, 'Some Arab-Byzantine and Umayyad Coins from the Hebrew University Collection', *Israel Numismatic Journal,* 11, (1990-91), p.97, No.4.

established in order to mint 'Standing Caliph' coins, possibly for payments to the troops securing the frontiers to the north of Syria (eleven of those were situated in northern Syria).[18]

Since none of those nineteen mints were in the county of al-Urdunn, it seems that the sixteen 'Standing Caliph' coins found at Bet Shean in the Hebrew University excavations point to the economic situation, i.e. to the ties between the provinces. It shows that the county of al- Urdunn, and in particular Scythopolis-Baysān, had ties with Ḥimṣ and Dimashq and Fisṭin/Filasṭin. A further piece of evidence for ties with Ḥimṣ is a find from the Bet Shean excavation, of a rectangular shaped lead seal with the name of this city engraved on it.[19] Another connection of Baysān to another county, namely Filasṭīn, is a find of a partial bronze weight which carries the name of one of the latter's governors, Saʿīd ibn ʿAbd al-Malik, engraved on it.[20]

Thus the sixteen 'Standing Caliph' coins could have come by trade, or by troops, to the city of Baysān. Troops must have been part and parcel of a capital of a county, a title Scythopolis (Bet Shean) had since 409 CE and well into the seventh century. The notion that these Standing Caliph coins could have together come either by trade, or by troops, is also proven by the four sets of more than one Standing Caliph coin found during the excavations at Bet Shean, as was seen above.

Figure 1. Standing Caliph coin of an unknown mint in Qinnasrin (2054) county based on style (carrying a name of an official and title مدبر and محمد ؟ Muhammad ? mudabir[21] ? or an unknown mint name). Approximately 1.5x actual size.

Figure 2. Standing Caliph coin of Ḥimṣ (2056). Approximately 1.5x actual size.

---

[18] I. and W. Schulze, 'Umayyad Numismatics in Bilād al-Shām with Particular Reference to Jund al-Urdunn', in A. Lichtenberger and R. Raja, **Byzantine and Umayyad Jerash Reconsidered, Transitions, Transformations, Continuities,** Turnhout, 2019, p. 246.

[19] This object will be published by the author with two other similar objects.

[20] E. Khamis, 'A Bronze Weight of Saʿîd b. ʿAbd al-Malik from Bet Shean/Baysân', **Journal of the Royal Asiatic Society**, 12 (2), 2002, pp.143–154. This weight is related to this figure's career as governor of *jund* Filasṭīn between February 743 and April 744 C.E., after he previously was the governor of Mosul, see ibid., p.148.

[21] A title *mudabir kabir* of an administrative nature engraved on an Umayyad lead seal was found in Israel's trade markets see N. Amitai-Priess, **The Administration of Jund al-Urdunn and Jund Filasṭin during the Umayyad and Early ʿAbbbasid Periods according to Seals and Other Small Finds**. Ph.D. diss., Ben Gurion University of the Negev, Beer Sheva, 2007, p.140, No.59 and for the explanation see p.54. This title *mudabir* is based on the Syriac *medabberānā* , mentioned in A. Palmer, S. Brock, S., and R. Hoyland, **The Seventh Century in the West Syrian Chronicle**, Liverpool, 1993, p.202.

Table of the 'Standing Caliph' Coins from the Bet Shean Excavation

Cat. No.	Area	Locus	Locus Location	Basket	Coins Catalogue Notes
4563	E	608	Street of the Monuments, a shop	8495	Standing Caliph, Cut Dimashq ?
4564	E	608	Street of the Monuments, a shop	8495	Standing Caliph, Cut Dimashq ?
4758	E	611	Street of the Monuments, northeastern portico area	11536	Standing Caliph, Dimashq ?
4894	E	809	Street of the Monuments, the Nymphaeon	10655	Standing Caliph, Dimashq ?
4933	E	812	Valley Street, the Basilica area	542579	Standing Caliph, Mint ?
4934	E	812	Valley Street, the Basilica area	542579	Standing Caliph, Mint ?
4935	E	812	Valley Street, the Basilica area	542579	Standing Caliph, Cut Mint ?
5562	E	876	Palladius Street, northwestern portico	10460	Standing Caliph, Dimashq
5662	E	886	Palladius Street, carriage way	11044	Standing Caliph, Dimashq,
15953	E	64653	Street of the Monuments, northeastern portico area	646391	Standing Caliph, mint: Fistin[22] Filastin
29232	E	04510	Street of the Monuments, a section of the carriage way	045067	Standing Caliph, Dimashq
1761a	G	762	Silvanus Street, the eastern bath	7885	Standing Caliph, Dimashq
2054	G	785	Silvanus Street, the eastern bath	13312	Standing Caliph, mint from Qinnasrin county, maybe with name and title of official
2055	G	785	Silvanus Street, the eastern bath	13312	Standing Caliph, Dimashq ?
2056	G	785	Silvanus Street, the eastern bath	13312	Standing Caliph, Ḥimṣ
2057	G	785	Silvanus Street, the eastern bath	13312	Standing Caliph, Dimashq

---

[22] See Goodwin, *The Standing Caliph Coinage*, 2018, p.53, Fig.3, b.

Table of the 'Standing Caliph' Coins from Other Excavations in the North of Israel Sites that were in the al-Urdunn County

Bet Shean Israeli Antiquities Authority Excavation (Theater Umayyad Pottery Workshop)	Neve Ur	Tiberias Foerster Excavation (Berman,[23] Coins in Stacey 2004)	Hirschfeld Tiberias Excavations 1989-1994[24]	Hammat Gader[25]
One Dimashq coin (Berman, 'The Coins' 2011:115, No.433).	Two coins minted at Dimashq Berman and Bijovsky[26] 2004:179, Nos.10-11.	One with Fistin coin (Filastin ?)	None	None

---

[23] A. Berman, 'The Coins', in D. Stacey, *Excavations at Tiberias, 1973-1974*, (2004, No.43, IAA Reports 21, pp.221-245.
[24] D. Ariel and R. Milstein, 'The Muslim Coins', Hirschfeld Y., *Excavations at Tiberias 1989-1994*, 2004, Jerusalem.
[25] N. Amitai-Preiss and A. Berman, 'Muslim Coins', in Y. Hirschfeld, *The Roman Baths of Hammat Gader: final report*, Jerusalem, Israel Exploration Society, 1997, pp.301-318.
[26] A. Berman and G. Bijovsky, 'The Coins from Neve Ur', `*Atiqot*, 43, pp.177-184.

The Umayyad Coins excavated during the Danish-German Jerash Northwest Quarter Project 2012–2016

Summary [1]

Ingrid and Wolfgang Schulze [2]

The archaeological excavation in the Northwest quarter of Jerash during the years 2012-2016 was a Danish/German joint venture under the leadership of Prof. Achim Lichtenberger (University of Münster) and Prof. Rubina Raja (University of Aarhus). We were invited to work with the coins. At first we will give a summary of the 803 coins which were found during the excavation:

1	Hellenistic (2nd/1st century BC)	1
2	Judaean (1st century)	1
3	Nabataean (1st century)	1
4	Roman Imperial	2
5	Roman Provincial	14
	Late Roman (4th and 5th century)	
6	Larger coppers	45
7	Æ3	57
8	*minimi* (Æ4)	214
9	Late Roman *minimi* not closer attributed, possibly including some early Byzantine	241
	Byzantine up to Constans II	
10	Various denominations	45
11	*minimus*	1
12	Umayyad pre-reform (c. 639 – c. 697)	12
13	Umayyad post-reform (c. 697 – 749)	53
14	'Abbasid	–
15	Ayyubid (12th/13th century)	2
16	Mamluk	–
17	Not identified	103
18	No coin	11
		803

Table 1: Overview of the 803 coins found during the Danish-German Jerash Northwest Quarter Project

---

[1] For legal reasons, we must not reproduce the full text of our paper given in Worcester. Nevertheless, the summary given here contains some of its essential results mainly related to Umayyad pre-reform coins. More reading is possible in Schulze 2018, Schulze 2019 and Schulze and Schulze forthcoming.

[2] Ingrid and Wolfgang Schulze are independent scholars: ingridschulze@wg-s.de schulze@wg-s.de

We will not discuss this table in detail. It is comparable with many other excavation results from the jund al-Urdunn. However, the large number of Late Roman *minimi* with a diameter of 5-12mm and a weight of 1g or lower is conspicuous.

These *minimi* formed an important, even a major, part of the money circulation during the fifth and even into the early seventh century. 'To fulfil the constant need of small change money, quantities of small bronze coins – *minimi* – circulated alongside the official issues. These *minimi* included worn and illegible earlier coins which remained in circulation for long periods, poorly manufactured local imitative issues, clipped coins and pieces of metal that could hardly be classified as coins, and coins from foreign areas. They were all an integrated part of the monetary currency in circulation during the Byzantine period throughout the Empire, including Palestine.'[3] The official coins were supplemented by ancient coins or even pieces of metal. 'Virtually anything could circulate because the coins were struck not by weight or exact size, but by given quantities circulated in closed bags. Most important, though, was the continued use of old coins.'[4]

This *minimi* series with the mixture of other old coins was very interesting for us. To explain the reason we must come back to the history of Jerash:
On January 18 of the year 749 an earthquake shook large parts of Palestine and Western Transjordan. Gerasa suffered so strongly from the devastating earthquake, that civic life came to an abrupt halt and the city was largely abandoned for centuries. Still for the year 1225 the contemporary geographer Yāqūt describes Gerasa from hearsay as a 'total ruin'.

Umayyad coins were found in different trenches during the Danish-German Jerash Northwest Quarter Project. Most interesting for us were the four Umayyad houses, destroyed during the earthquake of 749 and never touched since then.
Here we had the unique chance to study the money circulation in Umayyad times for a fixed date.

The coin finds in the Umayyad houses can be summarized thus[5]:
One Judaean coin of the first century, one Roman Imperial coin, one Roman Provincial coin, 72 Late Roman coins, of which 57 are *minimi*, and 14 Byzantine coins, of which 9 are folles belonging to the reigns of Justinian I to Constans II, one half follis of Anastasius and 4 questionable smaller specimens.
Of the seven Umayyad pre-reform coins, four are of Phase 1 and three of Phase 2. Four of the 17 post-reform coins were minted in Ṭabarīya (Tiberias), one in Īliyā (Jerusalem) and two in Jerash (Gerasa). The others are mintless types or without legible mint name.

As already described, old Roman coins, Roman and Byzantine *minimi*, and foreign coppers formed an important part of the money circulation from the fifth to the early seventh century. This is exactly the mixture we found in the Umayyad houses which were destroyed in the year 749. Now we can state that this phenomenon lasted at least up to the end of Umayyad rule.

This is not something new. In almost all relevant excavations in the Near East we find Umayyad coins together with large numbers of older petty money. The problem previously lay in the specific dating, because we never had excavation coins found in clear and exclusive Umayyad layers. Now, with the excavation of coins in exclusively Umayyad buildings destroyed at a fixed date, we can prove the previous vague assumption.

---

[3] Bijovsky 2012, p. 3f.
[4] Foss 2015, p. 954.
[5] A small hoard with Byzantine and Umayyad coins found in one of the relevant houses (cf. Lichtenberger and Raja 2015) is not considered here.

A mixture of copper pieces – from various places and periods and of various sizes and weights – formed the money circulation in daily use during the Umayyad rule.

We compared the results of the Northwest Quarter excavation with the completely published coins from other excavations in Jerash (Spanish excavations in the Agora/Macellum, American-British-Australian excavations around the North Theatre and the 1928–34 American excavations in the South Tetrapylon and other places)[6] and found a similar picture with an overwhelming mass of Roman coins, but unfortunately without clear Umayyad level.

In the five excavation reports 38 specimens are listed of the large Scythopolis coins of the Justin II prototype and 10 of the Gerasa mint. With three further specimens found under the drain below the Cardo Maximus the total for Gerasa is 13.

	Northwest Quarter (Schulze)	North Theatre (Bowsher)	Macellum (Marot)	Agora (Goicoechea)	South Tetrapylon etc. (Bellinger)
Phase 1 (Pseudo-Byzantine)	7		2[7]		
Phase 2 (with mint names)					
Scythopolis (Justin II type)	2	2	4	4[8]	26[9]
Gerasa (Justin II type)			4	2	4
Gerasa (2 Standing Caliph type)	1				2[10]
Canatha (Justin II type)					2[11]
Tiberias	1				
Amman	1				
Baalbek				1	
Damascus			1		
Phase 3 (Standing Caliph)					
Damascus			1		1
Amman			1[12]		
uncertain			17	9	

Table 2: The 95 Umayyad pre-reform coins found in five excavations at Jerash

Why did we find more Scythopolis coins than Gerasa coins in Jerash itself?
The answer to this question may be found in the extraordinary money circulation in the administrative district of al-Urdunn. In contrast to the Umayyad gold and silver coins the

---

[6] Goicoechea 1986, pp. 41–56; Marot 1998; Bowsher 1986; Bellinger 1938 (an abstract of this book is given by Bellinger in Kraeling 1938, pp. 497–503).
[7] Marot 1998 no. 1442 was re-attributed from Gerasa into this group.
[8] Of the 6 specimens originally listed by Goicoechea 2 were re-attributed to Gerasa by Oddy 2017a, p. 53.
[9] Oddy 2017a, p. 52f. re-attributed 4 of the 32 Scythopolis coins listed by Bellinger to Gerasa.
[10] Two further specimens were found during the excavation of the congregational mosque and the Macellum. Many thanks to Alan Walmsley for this hint.
[11] Oddy 2017b, p. 76f. re-attributed 2 of the 32 Scythopolis coins listed by Bellinger to Canatha.
[12] This Phase 3 coin with M-reverse does not bear a mint name, but is usually attributed to Amman.

production of copper coins was in the hand of local governors, emirs or bishops. Sometimes the right of minting was leased to private entrepreneurs.[13] The output of coins was demand-oriented.

It is noteworthy that no Standing Caliph mint was situated in al-Urdunn. Instead there were used the large *fulūs* imitating the Justin II prototype. The reason for this phenomenon may be found in the exceptional economic structure of Scythopolis/Baysān, which was a specialized industrial zone that included a large pottery and other industries like textile dying and lime production. Evidently the usual admixture of old coins like Roman and Byzantine *minimi*, foreign currency, and *fulūs* was not sufficient for the local and supra-regional trade, and for this reason the local authorities introduced a heavier currency corresponding to the industrial demand. Presumably for the same reason this coin type also was adapted for Jerash, where active commercial settlements on a smaller scale were established.

Our next step was to compare the results of the five excavations in Jerash with those of eight other excavations in al-Urdunn, namely Pella[14], Hippos[15], Baysān (2)[16] and Tiberias (4)[17]. The results of this comparison are complex and cannot be explained in detail here.[18] The result for the Umayyad pre-reform coins shows this table:

Total of identified coins by type	4512	1107	656	1869	487	
	Jerash 5 excav.	**Pella**	**Hippos**	**Baysān** 2 excav.	**Tiberias** 4 excav.	**Total**
Phase 1 (Pseudo-Byzantine)	9	2[19]	13	44	4	72
Phase 2 (with mint names)						
Scythopolis (Justin II type)	38	1	2	6	1 (K)	48
Gerasa (Justin II type)	10					10
Gerasa (2 Standing Caliph type)	5[20]					5
Canatha (Justin II type)	2					2
Tiberias	1	1		13	4	19
al-wafā lillāh type				10	1	11
Amman	1					1
Baalbek	1				1	2
Damascus	1		1	11	1	14
Alexandria		1				1
Phase 3 (Standing Caliph)						
Damascus	2			2		4
Amman	1			1		2
[Jerusalem]					1[21]	1
Total	71	5	16	87	13	**192**

Table 3: General conspectus with the results for Umayyad pre-reform coins evaluated from 13 excavation reports

---

[13] Heidemann 2002, pp. 353–63; similar Ilisch 2010, p. 27 and 2016, p. 252.
[14] Walmsley 2001.
[15] Berman 2013.
[16] Berman 2011; Bijovsky and Berman 2014.
[17] Berman 2004; Bijovsky 2004; Milstein and Ariel 2004; Bijovsky and Berman 2008.
[18] A comprehensive study will be available in Schulze and Schulze forthcoming.
[19] Walmsley 2001, nos 014 and 015 were re-attributed to this group.
[20] Here are included two unpublished specimens found during the excavations of the congregational mosque and the Macellum, cf. Table 2 and footnote.
[21] The attribution of this coin is questionable, cf. Schulze 2016, p. 36f.

Like Jerash, Baysān and Tiberias, Pella and Hippos were severely destroyed during the earthquake of 749. The find evidence of Umayyad pre-reform coins is quite sparse (5 for Pella, 16 for Hippos). Remarkable is a comparatively high proportion of Phase 1 coins at Hippos (13 specimens).

Of the Phase 2 Scythopolis Justin II type *fulūs* one was found at Pella and two at Hippos. This shows that both cities participated in the special money circulation in jund al-Urdunn. No Phase 3 coins were found at either Pella or Hippos. Considering the small find evidence it seems that during Umayyad rule both cities were economically less important and less settled populous than for example Baysān or Jerash. The same goes for the post-reform coins, which are – as usual – more numerous but comparably sparse. Nevertheless their widespread catchment area points out that trade and industry had flourished since the reign of 'Abd al-Malik.

Bibliography

Bellinger 1938	A. R. Bellinger, *Coins from Jerash, 1928–1934*, ANS Numismatic Notes and Monographs 81 (New York 1938)
Berman 2004	A. Berman, 'The Coins', *Excavations at Tiberias, 1973–1974: The Early Islamic Periods* (D. Stacey ed.) IAA Reports 21, pp. 221–245.
Berman 2011	A. Berman, 'The Coins', *Bet She'an II – Baysān – The Theater Pottery Workshop* (R. Bar-Nathan and W. Atrash eds) IAA Reports 48, pp. 87–151.
Berman 2013	A. Berman, 'General Conspectus of Coins Chronology and Mints found at Hippum-Sussita' *Hippos-Sussita of the Decapolis – The First Twelve Seasons of Excavations 2000-2011 Volume I* (A. Segal et al. eds) (Haifa 2013), pp. 289–98.
Bijovsky 2004	G. Bijovsky, 'Coins', *Excavations at Tiberias, 1989–1994* (Y. Hirschfeld ed.) IAA Reports 22, pp. 169–75.
Bijovsky 2012	G. Bijovsky, *Gold Coin and Small Change: Monetary Circulation in Fifth – Seventh Century Byzantine Palestine* (Trieste 2012)
Bijovsky and Berman 2008	G. Bijovsky and A. Berman, 'The Coins', *Tiberias: Excavations in the House of the Bronzes, Final Report I* (Y. Hirschfeld and O. Gutfeld eds) QEDEM 48, pp. 63–100.
Bijovsky and Berman 2014	'The Coins from Bet She'an (Youth Hostel)', *Atiqot* 77, pp. 59–113.
Bowsher 1986	J. M. C. Bowsher, 'The Coins', *Jerash Archaeological Project 1981–1983 I* (F. Zayadine ed.) (Amman 1986), pp. 253–63.
Foss 2015	C. Foss, 'Coinage and circulation in Byzantine Palestine', *Journal of Roman Archaeology 28*, pp. 954–46.
Goicoechea 1986	E. Goicoechea, *Excavaciones en al Agora de Gerasa en 1983*, (Madrid 1986)
Heidemann 2002	S. Heidemann, *Die Renaissance der Städte in Nordsyrien und Nordmesopotamien. Städtische Entwicklung und wirtschaftliche Bedingungen in ar-Raqqa und Ḥarrān von der Zeit der beduinischen Vorherrschaft bis zu den Seldschuken* (Leiden–Boston–Köln 2002).
Ilisch 2010	L. Ilisch, 'Coinage and Economy of Syria-Palestine in the Seventh and Eights Centuries CE', *Money, Power and Politics in Early Islamic Syria – A review of current debates* (J. Haldon ed.) (Farnham 2010), pp. 21–44.

Ilisch 2016	L. Ilisch, 'Einordnung und Datierung der Münze aus dem großen Hof', ***Qasr al-Mschatta. Ein frühislamischer Palast in Jordanien und Berlin 1*** (Johannes Cramer et al eds) Berliner Beiträge zur Bauforschung und Denkmalpflege 16 (Petersberg 2016), pp. 249–261.
Kraeling 1938	C.H. Kraeling (ed.), ***Gerasa – City of the Decapolis*** (New Haven 1938).
Lichtenberger and Raja 2015	A. Lichtenberger and R. Raja, 'A Hoard of Byzantine and Arab-Byzantine Coins from the Excavations at Jerash', ***The Numismatic Chronicle 175***, pp. 299–308.
Marot 1998	T. Marot, ***Las Monedas del Macellum de Gerasa*** (Madrid 1998).
Milstein and Ariel 2004	R. Milstein and D. T. Ariel, 'Coins', ***Excavations at Tiberias, 1989–1994*** (Y. Hirschfeld ed.) IAA Reports 22, pp. 57–8.
Oddy 2017a	A. Oddy, 'The Phase 2 Coinage of Gerasa under Mu'awiya and his Successors', ***Coinage and History in the Seventh Century Near East 5*** (T. Goodwin ed.) (London 2017), pp. 49–74.
Oddy 2017b	A. Oddy, 'A new Byzantine-Arab mint: Canatha of the Decapolis', ***Coinage and History in the Seventh Century Near East 5*** (T. Goodwin ed.) (London 2017), pp. 75–83.
Schulze 2016	I. Schulze, ***The Standing Caliph Coins of Jerusalem*** (München 2016)
Schulze and Schulze 2018	I. Schulze and W. Schulze, 'Working with Coins in Jerash: Problems, Solutions, and Preliminary Results', ***The Archaeology and History of Jerash. 110 Years of Excavations*** (A. Lichtenberger and R. Raja eds) Jerash Papers 1 (Turnhout 2018), pp. 195–205.
Schulze and Schulze 2019	I. Schulze and W. Schulze, 'Umayyad Numismatics in Bilād al-Shām with particular Reference to Jund al-Urdunn', ***Byzantine and Umayyad Jerash Reconsidered. Transitions, Transformations, Continuities*** (A. Lichtenberger and R. Raja eds) Jerash Papers 4 (Turnhout 2019), pp. 239–64.
Schulze and Schulze forthcoming	I. Schulze and W. Schulze, 'The coins of the Danish-German Jerash Northwest Quarter Project 2012–2016 and the Umayyad Money Circulation in Jund al-Urdunn', forthcoming.
Walmsley 2001	A. Walmsley, 'Catalogue Section 6: Islamic Series', ***Pella in Jordan 1979–1990 – The Coins*** (K. Sheedy et al. eds) (Sidney 2001), pp. 147–53.

Coins and Papyri in 6th/7th Century Egypt

Tasha Vorderstrasse[1]

Introduction

In 2010, in a brief overview of coins in Egypt, I noted the following:

> It is hoped that this brief survey of some of the evidence from this period demonstrates that the study of Egyptian coin circulation still remains problematic. Its study is hampered by the lack of publication or full publication of some sites, but interesting trends are beginning to emerge as the publications continue to appear. Despite the shortcomings of the evidence, it nonetheless gives us important information for understanding the Byzantine and Early Islamic administration and economy in Egypt.[2]

Recently published archaeological evidence has now added to our understanding of Late Antique Egypt. Further, there has been more discussion of the coin types from Egypt in this period by Goodwin in two 2015 articles.[3] The small amount of archaeological evidence found in Egypt remains a challenge, but recent publications from Antinoe, the Naqlun and White Monasteries, and an unpublished hoard from Naga ed-Deir, mean that we can start to combine the archaeological with the textual evidence to come to a conclusion about the economy of Upper Egypt in this period. This paper will look at the evidence (or lack thereof) from the cities of Antinoe and Akhmim, along with the town of Medinet Habu and the monasteries of Wadi Sarga, Bala'izah, Naga ed-Deir, and the White Monastery. This will be combined with the papyrological information from this period in order to start to come to a more complete picture about coin use in this transitional period.

Recent Work

The most significant of the recent numismatic publications has been that of the coins from Antinoe. While Antinoe has been excavated intensively, the initial excavations were primarily concerned with the textiles that came from the well-preserved graves at the site. Therefore, coins were not a focus of interest and largely remained unpublished except for the work of Milne.[4] Recently, however, the Italian excavations that have taken place there since the 1930s have been published in a book and several articles by Castrizio.[5] This is part of a general trend in publishing studies of the older excavations at the site, including not only the work by the Italians which started in the 1930s, but also the earlier work of Gayet[6] and de Monins Johnson.[7]

---

[1] Oriental Institute, University of Chicago. Email: tkvorder@uchicago.edu
[2] Vorderstrasse, 'New Evidence', p. 60.
[3] Goodwin, 'The Egyptian Arab-Byzantine Coinage'; Goodwin, 'Some Aspects'.
[4] Milne, 'Report on the Coins'.
[5] Castrizio, 'Le monete "bizantine"'; Castrizio, 'Il tesoretto aureo'; Castrizio, *La monete*; Castrizio,'Ritrovamenti di monete'.
[6] Calament, *La revelation d'Antinoe*.
[7] E. O'Connell, 'John de Monins Johnson'.

Milne's publication in 1947 remained for a long time the only publication of coins from Antinoe.[8] This article focused on the coins found in John de Monins Johnson's 1913-1914 excavation at the site and included both a bronze hoard as well as single excavation finds. The bronze hoard of 1914 consisted of 110 coins, all but one from the Alexandria mint dating from the reigns of Justinian I (32 coins) to Heraclius (8 coins) and including a number of imitations.[9] Milne described the hoard as "rather uninteresting"[10] and only of use because it helped provide some information about the sequence of the coins from Egypt. He argued that it was a currency hoard based on the differential wear patterns and should therefore be taken as indicative of what was in circulation at the time.[11] The single excavation coins were not very numerous,[12] but this is likely due to the fact that the excavations were concentrating on the graves where they would find textiles rather than on the settled areas.

The Italian excavations, now that they are published, demonstrate that in addition to bronze coins being used at Antinoe, there was also gold coinage in circulation. A hoard from the church of St. Colluthus at Antinoe found in 1974, contained a mixture of Late Roman and early Byzantine solidi and one tremisses. The majority of the hoard consists of Late Roman coins from the reigns of Constantius II through Zeno, and then a small number of coins of Justinian. The coins all come from mints outside Egypt, mostly from Antioch and Nicomedia, but also from western Roman empire mints as well.[13] This hoard is similar to the Alexandria Chatby Hoard which contained both Late Roman and early Byzantine coins, although the number of early Byzantine coins was greater than the late Roman ones and there were no western Roman Empire coins.[14] The Abu Mina hoard also contained a mix of Late Roman and Early Byzantine coins with a majority of Early Byzantine to Late Roman but the coins are primarily from the mint of Constantinople.[15] The Tod hoard, which comes from just south of Luxor is a much smaller hoard but contains primarily gold coins of Valens I and Valentinian and one coin of Justinian which was evidently outside the interest of the author, as it was not fully published.[16] Similarly, the Morgan pectoral[17], which may or may not come from Antinoe (Akhmim has also been suggested as a possible place of origin)[18], contains a mixture of Late Roman and early Byzantine gold coins.

This mixture of Late Roman and early Byzantine gold coins together in hoards has not only been observed in Egypt, but also by Bijovsky for Palestine.[19] In her publication of a similar hoard from the site of Ashkelon in Israel, she notes that there are similar hoards found in both Palestine and Egypt.[20] This was also discussed by Noeske[21], but as Bijovsky points out, he did not address the question of what mints were represented in the different hoards. Bijovsky argued that Egyptian hoards were deposited in the late 7th century, rather unlike the Palestine hoards which she believes were deposited

---

[8] For the coins' current location see E. O'Connell, 'John de Monins Johnson', pp. 421, 454, 459, no. 1 (which notes that the coins that were sent to the Manchester Museum of the University of Manchester cannot now be located), 461-462).
[9] Milne, 'Report on the Coins', pp. 109-113.
[10] Milne, 'Report on the Coins', pp. 111.
[11] Milne, 'Report on the Coins', pp. 111-112.
[12] Milne, 'Report on the Coins', pp. 113-114.
[13] Castrizio, 'Il tesoretto aureo'.
[14] Dutilh, 'Une trouvaille'.
[15] Noeske, *Münzfunde aus Ägypten*, pp. 15-16.
[16] Schwartz, 'Inscriptions et objets', pp. 96-98.
[17] Dennison, *A Gold Treasure*, pp. 109-116.
[18] For a recent discussion of the provenance of the hoard see Williams, "'Into the hands'".
[19] Bijovsky, et al., 'A Byzantine Hoard'.
[20] Bijovsky, et al., 'A Byzantine Hoard', Table 2, p. 203.
[21] Noeske, *Münzfunde aus Ägypten*, pp. 77-81.

in the 6th century. Bijovsky found the pattern strange but it seems to reflect the high value coins that were in circulation at the time rather than what one might expect of a saving hoard.[22] Castrizio, in his discussion of the St. Colluthus hoard, notes the similarities with some hoards from Egypt and Palestine,[23] but unlike Bijovsky and Noeske does not attempt to provide a complete list of the Palestinian material or discuss it in detail since it is not the focus of his work.

None of these authors compare these mixed late Roman/early Byzantine gold hoards to gold hoards from Egypt containing only late Roman or only early Byzantine gold coins, but doing so is nonetheless instructive. The fourth century hoards from Clysma[24] and Karanis[25] as well as the Upper Egyptian town of Qau el-Kebir (Antaeopolis)[26], all contained a majority of Antioch coins, and the Karanis, Qau, and Karnak gold hoards[27] also contained coins from Nicomedia and coins from the western Roman empire. They therefore appear to be similar in their composition to the mixed Antinoe St. Colluthus hoard, the Tod hoard, and the Morgan pectoral. This could suggest that high value western Roman imperial coins came into the eastern Roman empire in the 4th century together with the bronze issues that are found at sites such as Antioch and stayed in circulation until the 6th and 7th centuries AD.

In addition to the gold hoard, Castrizio also documented a Byzantine bronze hoard from St. Colluthus church.[28] This hoard contained one Ostrogothic coin minted in Pavia, in addition to coins from Justinian through Heraclius which were minted in Alexandria, as well as imitation Alexandria coins of the DOC 106 type that are usually dated to Phocas,[29] which were minted in the same type of coin mold found at the White Monastery (see below). This argues for the local production of these types of coins in upper Egypt.[30]

Further, Castrizio[31] also published the coins from the Italian excavations at Antinoe from 1937-2007, specifically from the excavation years of 1937-1938, 1978-1993, 2000, and 2005-2007. Castrizio published the coins by year rather than giving an actual overview, which makes it difficult to reconstruct the total for circulation purposes. Despite this issue, Castrizio does publish photographs of every coin, wherever possible, which makes it extremely useful for comparative purposes. The mints of the coins of the 6th and 7th centuries are primarily from Alexandria, with coins from Carthage during the reign of Justinian being the most notable outlier, which would seem to contradict Meadow's assertion that the currency of Egypt was operated as a closed system.[32] In addition, there are coins of the imitation DOC 16 type, as well as 61 ΠAN coins and 37 post-reform Umayyad coins.

It is the so-called ΠAN coins which are of particular interest here. Most scholars have argued that these coins were minted in Panopolis (Akhmim) and this is why they have this particular abbreviation on

---

[22] Bijovsky, et al., 'A Byzantine Hoard', pp. 203-205 and no. 9.
[23] Castrizio, 'Il tesoretto aureo', p. 3.
[24] Bruyère, *Fouilles de Clysma-Qolzoum*, p. 91.
[25] Arce, 'A Solidus Hoard'.
[26] Brunton, *Qau and Badari*, pp. 29-30.
[27] Noeske, *Münzfunde aus Ägypten*, pp. 388-389. The Karnak hoard, which is not published elsewhere, apparently contained around 500 solidi.
[28] Castrizio, *La monete*, pp. 26-28, Tav. 1, 75-126.
[29] As Goodwin, 'Some Aspects', pp. 27-28, notes, there has been the assumption that these coins date to the reign of Phocas because the mint in Alexandria seems to have ceased producing coins. Goodwin has suggested that at least some of these coins should be regarded as 6th rather than 7th century and indeed, that many of these coins may in fact have an earlier date. See Castrizio, *La monete*, p. 10, who also alludes to this problem.
[30] Goodwin, 'Some Aspects', p. 28.
[31] Castrizio, *La monete*.
[32] Meadows, 'Bronze Coins from Alexandria', pp. 233-234.

them. The precise date of the minting of these coins (pre or post-Islamic conquest) remains unclear. There have, however, been other proposals for where these coins are minted. Noeske thinks the coins were a private issue of the Coptic Patriarch Benjamin I when he was staying in the Panopolis region in 629-631 and were probably minted in the White Monastery. He claims that the patriarch was trying to address issues of coin circulation for the population at the time and improve their economic circumstances.[33] There is, however, no evidence for the patriarch minting coins although the coins have very definite Christian influences (see below). Bates and Domaszewicz wanted to suggest that the ΠAN or ΠON was a misspelling for ROM[34], but this has largely not met with any acceptance. Castrizio, however, had a different suggestion based on the archaeological finds. He notes that the coins are rare elsewhere, but they are almost one-quarter of the coins found by the Italian excavation in the northern necropolis. Further, chemical analysis shows that they are not the same as coins minted in Alexandria, leading him to suggest that the coins were minted somewhere nearby in Antinopolis. The difficulty with this suggestion is how to reconcile the abbreviation ΠAN with Antinopolis. Castrizio suggests that it is an abbreviation for Polis Antinou, but this does not seem altogether likely.[35] It is true that there is mention of the "standard of Antinoe" in the papyri[36] in addition to the "Alexandria standard" that is also specified in the papyri as well. References to this standard seem to start in the 6th century and continue after the Islamic conquest before disappearing in the 9th century. Local standards are also attested into the 8th century AD.[37] The papyrological evidence could therefore argue for Castrizio's idea of a local mint, but it is not altogether clear that is has to be Antinoe since multiple local standards are attested.[38] Further, the presence of a large number of ΠAN coins in a Naga ed-Deir bronze hoard excavated by Reisner was unknown to Castrizio.[39] But the presence of these coins at Naga ed-Deir near Panopolis argues against the assumption the coins might not have been minted at Antinoe.

In addition to issues behind where the ΠAN coins were minted, the appearance of the coins is also unusual. While the obverse of the coins imitates Heraclius' issues at Alexandria, showing the joint bust of Heraclius and Heraclius Constantine, the reverse is very unusual and has definite Christian overtones to it, showing an alpha and an omega on either side of a cross. Indeed, Woods has recently argued on the basis of the Christian imagery that the ΠAN is not a mint mark at all but rather an abbreviation of the Greek word "Almighty" or παντοκράτωρ.[40] The alpha and omega is a very popular motif in Christian art of Egypt in this period and appears frequently on funerary stelae, wall paintings, and textiles.[41] Goodwin has suggested that it might have been a "Christian token" given its very religious imagery.[42] These suggestions will be investigated more thoroughly in the forthcoming article on the Naga ed-Deir hoard.

---

[33] Noeske, 'Finds of Coins', pp. 218-219. This conclusion is not accepted by Goodwin, 'The Egyptian Arab-Byzantine Coinage', p. 211, no. 29. He agrees that the coins were issued by a bishop or monastery but that the coins date to after the Islamic conquest.
[34] Domaszewicz and M. L. Bates, 'Copper Coinage', pp. 103, 107, no. 54. See Goodwin, 'Review', p. 419 (who states that the "conclusion [of Domaszewicz and Bates] is hard to accept"; Castrizio, 'Le monete "bizantine"', pp. 6-7; Castrizio, *La monete*, p. 11; Noeske, 'Finds of Coins', p. 218, no. 112 (who states that he does not agree with the viewpoint of Domaszewicz and Bates); Goodwin, 'The Egyptian Arab-Byzantine Coinage', pp. 211-212.
[35] Castrizio, 'Le monete "bizantine"', pp. 7-8; Castrizio, *La monete*, pp. 10-14.
[36] Papaconstantinou, 'A preliminary prosopography', p. 636.
[37] Bruning, *The Rise of a Capital*, pp. 69-73. See also discussion in Maresch, *Nomisma und Nomismatia*, pp. 98-114.
[38] Goodwin, 'The Egyptian Arab-Byzantine Coinage', p. 211, thinks that Panopolis is the more likely site of production but that evidence from the site needs to be published. Goodwin concludes that the mint is "somewhere in northern Upper Egypt."
[39] Forthcoming publication by Vorderstrasse.
[40] Woods, 'Deciphering', pp. 205-206. I would like to thank David Woods for sending me a copy of this article.
[41] Della Francia, 'Symbols in Coptic Art'.
[42] Goodwin, 'Review', p. 419.

Presence or Absence of Credit

While the excavations from Antinoe suggest more coins in circulation in upper Egypt than there has previously been evidence for, the amount of actual coins in circulation was apparently not that large. There was evidently an issue of liquidity and a need for actual coins to pay taxes, for example, as there is ample evidence for individuals loaning money in exchange for objects.[43] If the money was not repaid by a certain time, the lender was allowed to sell the objects, presumably to recover the value of the debt. There was also a heavy monetary penalty if the borrower tried to dispute the agreement.[44]

The site of Medinet Habu has been studied extensively for its Coptic language documents, including those that concerned a family of pawnbrokers in the late 7th/8th centuries.[45] Wilfong, who studied these documents, points out the dichotomy between the archaeological and textual evidence. The excavators only found a small number of coins even though the textual evidence suggests that both gold and bronze coins were in circulation. It was also evident that Hölscher was not interested in the coins. He notes that two "large" hoards, presumably of bronze coins, were found in the ruins of the Late Antique village. One was found in House 21 in a jar with coins dated to the 4th-6th centuries AD, as well as another that had evidently been contained in a bag that was no longer preserved.[46] The first hoard is only vaguely described and there is no information at all for the second hoard. In addition to the two hoards, Hölscher mentions a single gold coin of Heraclius found in House 77.[47] An examination of the excavation records has so far not revealed any detailed information about the coins.

While Papaconstintinou felt that the evidence indicated that people were poor in the region and this is why they had to pawn objects in exchange for money, it seems more likely that the issue is one of liquidity.[48] The individuals in Medinet Habu had access to material capital, indicated by their ability to pawn objects as well as parcels of land and houses, some of which were quite substantial. Further, this seems to be indicated by the fact that many of them were paying interest on their loans in kind rather than in coins.

Excavations at the White Monastery in Egypt have revealed a number of coin hoards, including possibly two gold hoards found in 1987 that contained 400 gold coins and a broken container. Noeske quoted Morrisson writing in 1990, noting that 820 gold coins of the 6th-7th centuries were found at the White Monastery contained in jars, one of which was unearthed on December 19, 1987. One hoard had 220 larger pieces and 180 smaller examples (total of 400). The second had 301 larger and 119 smaller examples (total of 420). According to Morrisson, the coins were said to date to reigns of Justinian, Phocas, and Heraclius and were minted in Constantinople but she was not able to examine the hoards and this information came from the Supreme Council of Antiquities.[49]

The hoard of 400 coins was published by Gabra in 2003. The coins had been divided into two lots when it went into the Coptic Museum. Noeske suggests that this was based on size and weight. The

---

[43] Papaconstantinou 2016b: 633-636.
[44] Papaconstantinou, 'A preliminary prosopography', p. 637.
[45] Wilfong, 'The Archive of Money-Lenders'; Wilfong, *Women of Jeme*; Papaconstantinou, 'A preliminary prosopography', p. 642; Papaconstantinou '"Choses de femme"'; Papaconstantinou 'Credit, debt', p. 623. For another money-lender see Cromwell, 'Managing'.
[46] Hölscher, *Post-Ramessid Remains*, pp. 37, 50.
[47] Hölscher, *Post-Ramessid Remains*, p. 50.
[48] Papaconstantinou 'Credit, debt', p. 623.
[49] Noeske, 'Finds of Coins', pp. 215-216.

first group, found on 17 December 1987, contained 220 solidi of Phocas and Heraclius from the mint of Constantinople. It is not clear how many of each coin type was found. The second group of 180 semisses of Constans II was found on 31 December 1987.[50] Noeske thought that these two groups were actually two separate hoards as he felt it was not clear when they were actually concealed. He suggests that they were deposited at two separate times, even though they were found in the same place and very close to the same time. He argues that the first group was a hoard deposited at the time of the Persian conquest of Egypt, while the second hoard was deposited at the time of the Islamic conquest, as was the second hoard of 420 coins which was not examined by Gabra.[51]

Gold coins have been found in other monasteries, such as in the Monastery of Apa Jeremias, and a single gold coin from 103 AH of Yazid II found in the monastery of St. John the Little in the Wadi Natrun.[52] Bronze coins from the same site have not been studied.[53] At the Naqlun monastery, quite a few Islamic period gold coins have been found. Two hoards of gold coins were discovered at the monastery, one of 80 gold dinars and fragments of dinars (18 intact coins and 62 cut pieces) of the 9th/early 10th century that included 11 Tulunid, 7 Aghlabid, and Abbasid coins,[54] another of 13 Fatimid gold dinars, mostly of the caliph al-Mu'izz (952-976).[55] An unknown number of dinars of the Fatimid caliph al-Hakim were found in the rubbish, although these are not specified as a hoard.[56] In addition, there were single finds of three gold coins from the site consisting of late 9th century examples.[57]

While it is therefore evident that monasteries had access in some cases to large amounts of capital, the papyrological evidence indicates that not many actually lent money in Late Antiquity. Some of the transactions seem to have been quite low level but other monasteries, however, seem to have had access to substantial amounts of capital, such as the otherwise unknown monastery of Apa Hierax in the Oxyrhynchite region that lent 130 solidi to a private individual.[58]

Monasteries evidently also supplemented their income through the production of coins in the 7th century and later, as evidenced by archaeological finds. Noeske's 2009 report states that there were 1,185 coins found in the White Monastery, although he does not publish them. What Noeske does note, however, is that the White Monastery also seems to have produced its own coins. This is attested by a doubled-sided pottery disk mold for producing a total of 21 coins on each side of an imitation dodecanummia of Phocas, which was found in the excavations at the White Monastery in 1992. While cast coins are well known in the 7th century, he notes that they are largely found in the north of Egypt. It is therefore interesting that a mold producing such coins would be found in the White Monastery.[59] At the time of publication, Noeske was unaware that coins such as this had been found in Antinoe by the Italian excavations. At the monastery of Naqlun, archaeologists discovered two bronze dies

---

[50] Gabra, 'Die Münzschätze'.
[51] Noeske, 'Finds of Coins', pp. 216-217.
[52] 'Umayyad Coin Discovered in Egypt', http://medievalnews.blogspot.com/2010/05/umayyad-coin-discovered-in-egypt.html (accessed November 11, 2019).
[53] D. Brooks Hedstrom, et al, 'New Archaeology at Ancient Scetis', p. 226.
[54] Godlewski, 'Naqlun (Nekloni) Excavations in 2008-2009'p. 203, Fig. 12; Godlewski, 'Naqlun, Egypt: Excavations in 2012' 199-200; Maślak, 'The Burning of the Monastery? pp. 170, 172.
[55] Godlewski, 'Naqlun (Nekloni). Preliminary Report, 2005', p. 199, Fig. 3; Maślak, 'The Burning of the Monastery?', p. 161, who also notes that this hoard was not found in a destruction layer.
[56] Godlewski, 'Naqlun (Nekloni) Excavations in 2008-2009', p. 209; Maślak, 'The Burning of the Monastery?', p. 175. Neither source mentions how many dinars were found.
[57] Morisot, 'Quelques monnaies', pp. 328-329; Maślak, 'The Burning of the Monastery?', pp. 157, 160.
[58] Markiewicz, 'The Church'; Papaconstantinou, 'A preliminary prosopography', pp. 634, 646-647; Papaconstantinou 'Credit, debt', pp. 617-618, 623-624.
[59] Noeske, 'Finds of Coins', pp. 213-214.

wrapped in straw that would have been used to mint "Abbasid" dinars of the 9th/10th century.[60] Godlewski stated that, "Such objects, associated with the production of coins, are extremely rare and their presence in a monastic complex is startling at the very least."[61]

Apart from the large numbers of gold coins found from the White Monastery, evidence for large amounts of coins seem to be limited in the region. At the site of Wadi Sarga in Antaeopolis, Robert Campbell Thompson's excavations only found a limited number of coins at the site. Byzantine coins minted in Alexandria (3 of Justinian, 1 of Tiberius, and 3 of Heraclius) and one post-reform Umayyad bronze coin.[62] In contrast, the situation at the nearby monastery of Bala'izah coins are largely unpublished, but four silver dirhems were found there, including an Umayyad silver dirhem of Umar II (719 AD), and three Abbasid dirhems.[63]

Conclusion

While the Egyptian archaeological evidence for coinage in the 6th-7th centuries remains behind that in some other parts of the eastern Mediterranean, evidence is gradually accumulating that helps to shed light on the situation in Upper Egypt. This includes the publication of excavations such as Antinoe and the forthcoming publication of the hoard of coins from Naga ed-Deir, but the coins from some sites remain unknown or largely unknown. The site of Medinet Habu (Jeme) which produced so many of the papyri that help us reconstruct life in Egypt in this period provides very little information about the coins found in excavations, while other sites such as Deir al-Bala'izah, remains largely unknown. The evidence that does exist, however, does not point to a highly monetized economy, a view backed up by the papyri which suggests that many money loans were made to pay taxes. As the coins of the region continue to become better known and the papyri studied in further detail, we can further study how the evidence of the coins and papyri interact and help complement each other to provide a better view of the economy of the region.

Bibliography

J. Arce, 'A Solidus Hoard from the Vicinity of Karanis', **Revue suisse de numismatique** 66 (1987), pp. 181-187.

G. Bijovsky, D. Sandhaus, and I. Milevski, 'A Byzantine Hoard of Gold Coins from Ashqelon, Barnea, B-C Neighborhood', *Israel Numismatic Research* 9 (2014), pp. 193-212.

J. Bruning, *The Rise of a Capital: Al-Fusṭāṭ and Its Hinterland, 18-132/639-750* (Leiden, 2018).

G. Brunton, *Qau and Badari III*, British School of Archaeology in Egypt and Egyptian Research Account 50 (London, 1930).

---

[60] Godlewski, 'Naqlun (Nekloni). Preliminary Report, 2005', p. 199, Fig. 6; Godlewski, 'Naqlun (Nekloni) Excavations in 2008-2009', p. 200, Fig. 7; Maślak, 'The Burning of the Monastery?', p. 173.
[61] Godlewski, 'Naqlun (Nekloni). Preliminary Report, 2005', p. 199.
[62] Campbell Thompson, 'Introduction', p. 9. It is not clear if all the coins went to the British Museum or not, since Campbell Thompson only describes them generally. Specific identification of the coins is based on the British Museum website and were made by Amelia Dowler. I would like to thank Elisabeth O'Connell for the information about who identified the coins.
[63] Petrie, *Gizeh and Rifeh*, p. 30. See discussion in Edgerton, 'Review', p. 59.

B. Bruyère, *Fouilles de Clysma-Qolzoum (Suez) 1930-1932*, Fouilles de l'institut français d'archéologie orientale 27 (Cairo, 1966).

F. Calament, *La revelation d'Antinoe par Albert Gayet: Histoire, archéologie, museographie*, Bibliothèque d'études coptes 18 (Cairo, 2005).

R. Campbell Thompson, 'Introduction', in W. E. Crum and H. I. Bell (eds.), *Wadi Sarga: Coptic and Greek Texts from the Excavations Undertaken by the Byzantine Research Account* (Hauniae, 1922), pp. 1-28.

D. Castrizio, 'Le monete "bizantine" dalla Necropoli Nord di Antinoupolis (1979-2006) e la serie a leggenda PAN. Relazione preliminare', in R. Pintaudi (ed.), *Antinoupolis I*, Istituto Papirologico "G. Vitelli" – Scavi e materiali, Volume I (Florence, 2008), pp. 217-227
'Il tesoretto aureo dal complesso del santuario di San Colluto della Necropoli Nord di Antinoe', in R. Pintaudi (ed.), *Antinoupolis I*, Istituto Papirologico "G. Vitelli" – Scavi e materiali, Volume I (Florence, 2008), pp. 229-278.
La monete della necropoli nord di Antinoupolis (1937-2007), Istituto Papirologico "G. Vitelli" – Scavi e materiali, Volume 2 (Florence, 2010).
'Ritrovamenti di monete arabo-bizantine dagli scavi d'Antinopoli d'Egitto. Note preliminari', in B. Callegher and A. D'Ottone (eds.), *The 2nd Simone Assemani Symposium on Islamic coins* (Trieste, 2010), pp. 22-33.

J. Cromwell, 'Managing a Year's Taxes: Tax Demands and Tax Payments in 724 CE', *Archiv für Papyrusforschung und verwandte Gebiete* 60 (2014), pp. 229-239.

L. Della Francia, 'Symbols in Coptic Art: Alpha and Omega', in A. S. Atiya (ed.), *Claremont Coptic Encyclopedia* (New York, 1991), pp. 2160-2162.

W. Dennison, *A Gold Treasure of the Late Roman Period* (New York, 1918).

L. Domaszewicz and M. L. Bates, 'Copper Coinage of Egypt in the Seventh Century', in J. Bacharach (ed.), *Fustat Finds: Beads, Coins, Medical Instruments, Textiles, and Other Artifacts from the Awad Collection* (New York and Cairo, 210), pp. 88-111.

E.-D. J. Dutilh, 'Une trouvaille de 191 monnaies d'or byzantines et de 1 pièce en argent', *Revue belge de Numismatique* (1905), pp. 155-164.

W. F. Edgerton, 'Review of *Bala'izah: Coptic Texts from Deir el-Bala'izah in Upper Egypt* by Paul Kahle', *Journal of Near Eastern Studies* 15 (1956), pp. 58-64.

G. Gabra, 'Die Münzschätze aus dem Shenute-Kloster bei Sohag', in I. Blöbaum, J. Kahl, and S. D. Schweitzer (eds.), *Ägypten-Münster: Kulturwissenschaftliche Studien zu Ägypten, dem Vorderen Orient und verwandten Gebieten* (Wiesbaden, 2003), pp. 125-128.

W. Godlewksi, 'Naqlun (Nekloni). Preliminary Report, 2005', *Polish Archaeology in the Mediterranean* 17 (2007), pp. 195-205.
'Naqlun (Nekloni) Excavations in 2008-2009', *Polish Archaeology in the Mediterranean* 21 (2011), pp. 193-211.

'Naqlun, Egypt: Excavations in 2012', *Światot* 10 (2012), pp. 193-201.

T. Goodwin. 'Review of *Fustat Finds - Beads, Coins, Medical Instruments, Textiles and Other Artifacts from the Awad Collection* by Jere L. Bacharach', *Numismatic Chronicle* 163 (2003), pp. 417-420.

'The Egyptian Arab-Byzantine Coinage', in A. Oddy, I. Schulze, and W. Schulze (eds.), **Coinage and History in the Seventh Century Near East** 4 (London, 2015), pp. 205-216.

'Some Aspects of 7th C Egyptian Byzantine Coinage', in A. Oddy, I. Schulze, and W. Schulze (eds.), **Coinage and History in the Seventh Century Near East** 4 (London, 2015), pp. 27-36.

D. Brooks Hedstrom, Stephen J. Davis, T. Herbich, S. Ikram, D. McCormack, M.-D. Nenna, and G. Pyke, 'New Archaeology at Ancient Scetis: Surveys and Initial Excavations at the Monastery of St. John the Little in Wādī al-Naṭrūn (Yale Monastic Archaeology Project)', **Dumbarton Oaks Papers** 64, pp. 217-227.

U. Hölscher, **Post-Ramessid Remains: The Excavation of Medinet Habu Volume 5**, Oriental Institute Publications 55 (Chicago, 1954).

K. Maresch, *Nomisma und Nomismatia: Beiträge zur Geldgeschichte Ägyptens im 6. Jahrhundert n. Chr.* (Opladen, 1994).

T. Markiewicz, 'The Church, Clerics, Monks and Credit in the Papyri', in A. Boud'hors, J. Clackson, L. Louis, and P. Sijpesteijn, **Monastic Estates in Late Antique and Early Islamic Egypt** (Cincinnati, 2009), pp. 178-204.

S. Maślak, 'The Burning of the Monastery? Story Blazed on the Walls of Monastic Buildings at Nekloni (Naqlun)', in A. Łatjar, A. Obłuski, and I. Zych (eds.), **Aegyptus et Nubia Christiana. The Włodzimierz Godlewski Jubilee Volume on the Occasion of his 70th Birthday** (Warsaw, 2016), pp. 149-186.

A. Meadows, 'Bronze Coins from Alexandria. Reviewed Work: *Les monnaies des fouilles du Centre d'études alexandrines. Les monnayages de bronze à Alexandrie de la conquête d'Alexandre à l'Égypte moderne. Études Alexandrines 25* by O. Picard, C. Bresc, T. Faucher, G. Gorre, M.-C. Marcellesi, C. Morrisson', **The Bulletin of the American Society of Papyrologists** 51 (2014), pp. 229-239.

J. G. Milne, 'Report on the Coins found at Antinoe in 1914', **Numismatic Chronicle** 7 (1947), pp. 108-114.

C. Morisot, 'Quelques monnaies découvertes à Deir al-Malak', **Annales islamogiques** 34 (2000), pp. 327-333.

H. C. Noeske, *Münzfunde aus Ägypten. I, Die Münzfunde des ägyptischen Pilgerzentrums Abu Mina und die Vergleichsfunde aus den Diocesen Aegyptus und Oriens vom 4.-8. Jh. n. Chr. : Prolegomena zu einer Geschichte des spätrömischen Münzumlaufs in Ägypten und Syrien*, Studien zu Fundmünzen Band 12 (Berlin, 2000).

'Finds of Coins and other Related Objects from the Monastery of Apa Shenute at Suhag', **Dumbarton Oaks Papers** 63 (2009), pp. 210-219.

E. O'Connell, 'John de Monins Johnson 1913/1914 Egypt Exploration Fund Expedition to Antinoupolis (Antinoe), with an Appendix of Objects', in R. Pintaudi (ed.), *Antinoupolis II*, Istituto Papirologico "G. Vitelli" – Scavi e materiali, Volume 2, (Florence, 2014), pp. 415-466.

A. Papaconstantinou, 'A preliminary prosopography of moneylenders in early Islamic Egypt and South Palestine', *Mélanges Cécile Morrisson, Travaux et mémoires* 16 (2010): 631-48.
'"Choses de femme" et accès au crédit dans l'Égypte rurale sous les Ommeyades', in O. Delouis, S. Métivier, and P. Pagès (eds.), *Le saint, le moine et le paysan: mélanges d'histoire byzantine offerts à Michel Kaplan*, Byzantina Sorbonensia 29 (Paris, 2016), pp. 551-561.
'Credit, debt, and dependence in early Islamic Egypt and Southern Palestine', *Mélanges Jean Gascou: textes et études papyrologiques (P.Gascou), Travaux et Mémoires* 20 (2016), pp. 613-642.

W. M. F. Petrie, *Gizeh and Rifeh* (London, 1907).

J. Schwartz, 'Inscriptions et objets de l'époque romaine et byzantine, trouves à Tôd', *Bulletin de l'institut français d'archéologie orientale* 50 (1956), pp. 89-98.

T. Vorderstrasse, 'New Evidence for Coin Circulation in Byzantine and Early Islamic Egypt', in A. Oddy (ed.), *Coinage and History in the Seventh Century Near East 2* (London, 2010), pp. 57-60.

T. Wilfong, 'The Archive of Money-Lenders from Jême', *The Bulletin of the American Society of Papyrologists* 27 (1990), pp. 169-181.
Women of Jeme: Lives in a Coptic Town in Late Antique Egypt (Ann Arbor, 2002).

E. D. Williams, '"Into the hands of a well-known antiquary of Cairo": The Assiut Treasure and the Making of an Archaeological Hoard', *West 86th* 21 (2014), pp. 251-272.

D. Woods, 'Deciphering the Dodecanummia of Heraclius and Constans II', *Israel Numismatic Journal* 13 (2018), pp. 195-208.

The weight standard of copper coins as a means for understanding the Syrian tradition of the seventh century

Dietrich Schnädelbach[1]

Introduction

Weights may be confusing if the fact that they belong to different categories is overlooked. These categories are:
1. Principal weights, i.e. weights which can be standardised directly using the water content of a cube with the edge of one, one half or one third foot, thus leading to one, 1/8 or 1/27 talent.
2. Reference (basic) weights, i.e. fractions of principal weights or multiples thereof.
3. Ordinary (commercial) weights, i.e. enhanced or reduced reference weights.

The vast majority of surviving balance weights are ordinary weights. This is not surprising since these are adjusted to serve the needs of everyday business. These weights have caused some confusion because they were mistaken for reference weights. This is not surprising since little has been done so far to determine the exact mass of the principal weights. It was therefore not possible to establish whether a given weight is a reference weight, i.e. directly related to a principal weight or an ordinary weight, which is not directly related to a principal weight but to a reference weight.

In order to manufacture coins it is necessary to fix a standard weight, i.e. the average weight the coins shall have, and a tolerance, i.e. a limit for the deviation from the standard weight that the weight of a coin may have. This is how the weight of Syrian copper coins from the seventh century was fixed. Consequently, their standard weight is a reference weight and thus directly linked to the weight system used at the time in the region where the coins were manufactured or of the region where the coins circulated[2]. If the weight of individual coins is expressed in weight units of the time, a histogram should provide a symmetrical weight distribution and a distinct maximum indicating the standard weight.

In the case of gold or silver coins there is a nominal weight above the standard weight that defines the value at which the coins have to be taken. The difference between the nominal weight and the standard weight is the seigniorage which covers the costs of minting and in addition may offer a profit for those who are in charge of minting. Consequently, in the case of gold and silver coins the nominal value is the reference weight and the standard weight is a reduction thereof. Therefore, if a histogram is used to determine the relation of gold and silver coins to the weight system of the time, the situation is more difficult than in the case of copper coins. Since the nominal weight is usually identical with the upper limit of the weights of individual coins (i.e. standard weight plus tolerance) the histogram may be used to determine the upper limit of the weight distribution. This can be difficult since overweight coins may obscure the position of the upper limit. Nevertheless, there

---
[1] Dietrich Schnädelbach is an independent scholar   schnaedelbachs@arcor.de
[2] It goes without saying that a uniform sample of coins is needed, i.e. the coins should be of the same emission and not be clipped or otherwise adulterated

should be a simple and rational relation between the nominal weight and the standard weight. Thus it is possible to use a histogram for the determination of the nominal weight of gold and silver coins[3].

Research based on the coins of class 1 of Tartus

Wolfgang Schulze published an article on the Byzantine-Arab transitional coinage of Tartus[4]. These coins were struck to weight standards which do not seem to fit into the weight systems of the time. Consequently, a major research program was necessary in order to clarify the situation.

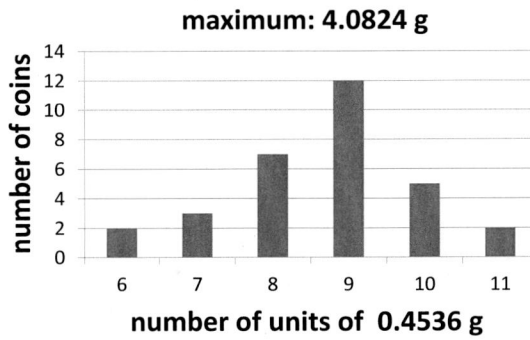

Figure 1: Tartus class 1

Figure 2: Histogram of 31 coins of Tartus class 1

Tartus class 1 (figure 1) provides 31 coins with known weights. Figure 2 presents the histogram of these coins using an interval of 0.4536 g. It shows a clear maximum at 4.0824 g and an almost symmetrical weight distribution. The standard weight of 4.0824 g is in the magnitude of a *mithqāl*. In Syria the *mithqāl* was usually 1/100 of a *ratl*[5]. Consequently, the relevant *ratl* should weigh 408.24 g. The *ratl* of 408.24 g is attested by a *wuqiyya*[6] of Abū Ja'far Ashinās weighing 34.02 g [7]. Thus it appears to be an Abbasid *ratl*. This raises the question whether we can really expect a *ratl*, which later became known as an Abbasid *ratl*, to be used in Syria at the beginning of Umayyad rule. The Abbasid *ratl* was divided into 90 *mithqāls* but the division of an Abbasid *ratl* into 100

---

[3] Examples see below. Böckh's attempt to determine the weight of the Roman pound using the weights of gold coins[3] shows how difficult this may be if the reference weight is not known beforehand but is to be determined from the coins. Böckh should have got 326.592 g, the weight of the Roman gold pound. However, he got 327.45 g. This may be due to the fact that he was not aware that the nominal weight of some emissions of Roman gold coins was not at the upper limit of the weight distribution but between the upper limit and the standard weight. For instance in order to pay his troops Caesars minted an enormous amount of aurei (Bahrfeldt no. 19) using the booty from Gallia. In order to facilitate the production, the tolerance was doubled thus shifting the nominal weight between the upper limit of the weight distibution and the standard weight. In addition, since Böckh did not know the weight system, he was not able to convert the weight of coins into weight units of the time and hence he was not able to determine the standard weight expressed in weight units of the time. It follows that he was unable to relate the upper limit with the standard weight and thus could not identify and exclude coins exceeding the upper limit.
August Böckh, *Metrologische Untersuchungen über Gewichte, Münzfüsse und Masse des Alterthums in ihrem Zusammenhang,* Berlin 1838, Reprint Karlsruhe 1978, pp.13-15
M. v. Bahrfeldt, *Die Römische Goldmünzenprägung während der Republik und unter Augustus*, Halle 1923

[4] Wolfgang Schulze, 'The Byzantine-Arab Transitional Coinage of Tartus', *The Numismatic Chronicle* 173 (2013), pp 245-259

[5] Paul Balog, Umayyad, Abbasid and Tulunid Glass Weights and Vessel Stamps', *ANS Numismatic Studies* no 13. New York 1976. Balog pp. 13f presents four *ratls* weighing between 431.87 g and 441.00 g and thus representing 100 Umayyad *mithqāls* of 4.320 g to 4.410 g.

[6] The *wuqiyya* (ounce) is 1/12 of the *ratl*. The ratl is a weight of the magnitude of the British pound troy and the British imperial pound.

[7] Balog as footnote 5, p. 16 refers to BMC 27 g.

mithqāls is not reported. In order to see whether there are sound reasons to believe that the *ratl* of 408.24 g could have been used in Syria in Umayyad times, an extensive research on the definition of basic weights by the weight of certain volumes of water was performed. It was found that in addition to the talent of 25.92 kg, which is defined by the water content of a cube with an edge of the Roman foot, a second talent of 32.6592 kg exists which is defined by the water content of a cube with an edge of the Assyrian foot. If a cube with the edge of half an Assyrian foot is used, we get 4082.4 g which represents 10 of the above *ratls*. Thus the *ratl* of 408.24 g is 1/80 talent[8] and resembles the Roman pound of 324.0 g, which is 1/80 of the talent of 25.92 kg.

According to Sawelski, the Babylonian is the oldest known weight system. The Babylonian talent is divided into 60 minae (544.32 g) which in turn are divided into 60 shekels (9.072 g). In total Sawelski mentions three different minae, used for different purposes: A mina of 545.7 g (544.32 g) for weighing silver, a mina of 409.3 g (408.24 g = 1/80 talent) for weighing gold and a mina of 491.2 g (489.888 g = 10/9 of 544.32 g) for "weighing ordinary substances"[9]. Thus according to Sawelski, the talent of 32.6592 kg is the Babylonian talent. This is confirmed by Herodotus (see below).

One may wonder whether a weight of 32.6592 kg could really be used by the people of the time. However, for them this weight was simply one talent and could be divided into several minae. These weights, their fraction and multiples, would be represented by balance weights and not by figures in grams. Therefore the question as to which precision these weight units were defined has to be treated separately[10]. Nevertheless, for mathematical reasons 32.6592 kg should be rounded to four figures resulting in 32.66 kg. Though, throughout this paper calculated weights are not rounded but the calculated results are given as such. Similar weights might otherwise be mistaken as identical and the reader would be unable to trace the given weight back to its basis.

According to Arianna d'Ottone Rambach there are two weights from Yazīd b. 'Abd al-Malik and 'Abd Allāh b. Yazīd III[11]. The weight of the piece of Yazīd b. 'Abd al-Malik is given as 340 g. It represents a weight standard of 340.2 g which is 12.5 ounces of the *ratl* of 326.592 g (otherwise known as the Roman/Byzantine gold-pound), which is 1/100 of the talent of 32.6592 kg. The piece of 'Abd Allāh b. Yazīd III is given as 337.55 g. It represents a weight standard of 337.5 g which is 12.5 ounces of 324.0 g (otherwise known as the Roman/Byzantine pound), which is 1/80 of the talent of 25.92 kg. These weights demonstrate that both weight systems were used by the Umayyads[12].

---

[8] Thus it is not at all surprising that this *ratl* was still used in Mecca in the 17th century. Walther Hinz, ***Islamische Masse und Gewichte umgerechnet ins metrische System***, Leiden/Köln 1970, p. 28.

[9] F.S. Sawelski, ***Die Masse und ihre Messung***, Moskau/Leipzig 1977, pp.39-40
The difference between the weights given by Sawelski and the weights related to the correct Babylonian talent (32,592 kg) can be explained as follows: Since Böckh used Roman gold coins to establish the weight of the Roman pound of 327.45 g he actually found a heavy version of the Roman gold-pound. If this pound is taken, the Babylonian talent is 32.745 kg. This is obviously the background of Sawelski's calculations. The Russian pound of 409.5 g Sawelski mentions (p. 41) is 325/324 of 408.24 g and thus related to the Babylonian weight system.

[10] For more information see Dietrich Schnädelbach, article 'The Origin of Measures and Weights' on www.academia.edu

[11] Arianna d'Ottone Rambach, 'Arabic Glass (coin weights, jetons and vessel stamps) from Umayyad Syria', in Tony Goodwin (ed.) ***Coinage and History in the Seventh Century Near East Vol. 5***, London 2016, pp. 175-195

[12] Weights of 12.5 ounces are usually seen as silver pounds. Below it will become clear that the weight of 340.2 g is indeed a silver pound consisting of 80 units of 4.2525 g.

If we compare the talent of 32.592 kg, the hundredweight of the Roman pound (32.40 kg) and the talent of 25.92 kg we see that the relations between these weights are very simple: 126 to 125 to 100. This demonstrates that it was no problem at all to use both weight systems in parallel, as it was done since the Bronze Age. Further, the examination of balance weights shows that right from the beginning minae which were divided into 100 or 90 units existed. In addition, light minae of 9/10 of the minae of 100 units were common. In other words there is no question that the *ratl* of 408.24 g was used in Syria in the 7th century and it was divided into 90 and 100 *mithqāls*.

This raises a very serious question: how is it possible that two talents, which are standardised using two totally different measures of length, provide such a simple relation to each other? This question requires a detailed and complex description of the developments and procedures leading to this situation[13]. However, in order to cut a long story short: the background is the fact that the Assyrian and the Roman foot both originated from a basic measure of length which is the diameter of the reflection of the sun as it would, for instance, be observed on the surface of water.

One important but unusual feature of the talent of 32.6592 kg is that it can be divided by seven. Thus it can be divided into 70 *ratls* of 466.56 g. Since the mina of 466.56 g is well attested among the balance weights excavated at Olympia[14], it is very likely that it was this talent Herodotus had in mind when he reports that the Babylonian talent consisted of 70 Euboic minae[15]. Consequently, Mommsen is wrong when he states that the report of Herodotus cannot be correct[16]. This demonstrates once more that it is of greatest importance to keep in mind that terms such as "mina" were used as generic terms and did not indicate a distinct weight out of the large number of weights which were used in parallel.

It goes without saying that most fractions of the talent of 32.6592 kg can also be divided by seven. Thus 1/8 talent of 4082.4 g represents not only 10 *ratls* of 408.24 g but also 7 *ratls* of 582.3 g which is equal to 5/4 of 466.56 g. If 1/27 talent is divided by seven, we get 172.8 g which represents 40 drachmae of 4.320 g or 2/5 of the Attic mina of 432.0 g. Almost all *mithqāls* of this weight system can also be divided by seven. This has created great confusion since the *dirhams* of two third of the *mithqāls* belonging to the weight systems based on the talent of 32.6592 kg can be seen as 7/10 of the *mithqāls* belonging to the weight systems based on the talent of 25.92 kg. However, the latter *mithqāls* are also related to *dirhams* of two thirds. Table 1 gives some examples.

Table 1:   The principal talents

Talent of 32.6592 kg		Talent of 25.92 kg	
Mithqāl 1	2/3 of *mithqāl* 1 = 7/10 of *mithqāl* 2	mithqāl 2	2/3 of *mithqāl* 2
4.536 g	3.024 g	4.320 g	2.880 g
4.2525 g	2.835 g	4.050 g	2.700 g
4.0824 g	2.7216 g	3.888 g	2.592 g

---

[13] For more information see Dietrich Schnädelbach, article "The Origin of Measures and Weights" on www.academia.edu
[14] Konrad Hitzl, *Die Gewichte griechischer Zeit aus Olympia*, Berlin/New York 1996
Half minae: Nos. 229, 241, 271; quarter minae: No. 377; eighth minae: Nos. 416, 421, 426, 431.
[15] A. Horneffer (translator), **Herodot Historien**, Stuttgart 1963 p. 222
[16] Theodor Mommsen: *Geschichte des römischen Münzwesens*. Berlin 1880, Nachdruck Graz 1956, p 24

Islamic authors mentioned a *dirham* which is 7/10 of a *mithqāl*[17]. However, since the weight systems of the talent of 32.6592 kg and the talent of 25.92 kg were used in parallel, it is obvious that the authors of the time needed to focus on the difficult calculation procedures needed to relate given weights of one system to the weights of the other system[18]. This does not indicate that the weight of the *dirham* was not two third of the *mithqāl* once the weights of the same weight system were concerned. In order to see whether Umayyad *dirham* weights can generally be seen as two thirds of a *mithqāl* 194 metal weights ranging from 50 to one *dirham* were examined. The form of the selected weights suggests that they are probably from Umayyad times.

The 194 *dirham* weights were taken from the following sources
Lionel Holland, **Islamic Bronze Weights from Caesarea Maritima**. ANS MN 31 (1986), pp.171-201 (Together 85 weights: Polyhedra 39, Spheroids 3, Barrels 43[19]).
Henri Pottier, **Nouvelle Approche de la Livre Byzantine**. Revue Belge de Numismatique CL – 2004, pp. 131-132 (Together 59 weights: Polygonaux 35, bi-tronconiques 24)
Münz Zentrum, **Gewichte aus drei Jahrtausenden, Teil I bis IV**, Auctions XXXII (1978), XXXVII (1979), XLV (1981), XLIX (1983) (Together 20 weights: shapes of weights like Holland)
Collection of the author (Together 31 weights: Shapes of weights like Holland)

All *dirhams* examined can be described as two thirds of a *mithqāl* or 1/150 of a *ratl* (table 2). However, it turned out that only a minority of 35 weights represent the reference weight, whereas 159 pieces represent ordinary (commercial) weights. Of these 25 represent enhanced reference weights, whereas the vast majority of 134 weights (69 per cent) represent reduced reference weights.

The weights are mainly related to the *ratls* of 453.6 g (43), 437.4 g (49) and 432.0 g (30). In addition the *ratls* of 450.0 g (23) and 440.8992 g (19) are of some importance. In the case of the *ratl* of 440.8992 g this is surprising since it is 9/10 of 489.888 g (= 24/25 of 510.3 g) and other *ratls* of 9/10 such as 459.27 g (9/10 of 510.3 g = 1/8 of 4082.4 g), 408. 24 g (9/10 of 453.6 g), 405.0 g (9/10 of 450.0 g), 388.8 (9/10 of 432.0 g) are obviously of minor importance, though *dirhams* related to these *ratls* exist.

The *dirham* of two thirds of the *mithqāl* probably existed since the Bronze Age. In Troy Schliemann discovered several treasures. One included six silver ingots weighing 190 to 171 grams. According

---

[17] Walther Hinz, as footnote 8, p. 31: The *ratl* of Baghdād is reported to consist of 128 4/7 *dirhams*. This relation is true if the *ratl* of 408.24 g is divided by 3.1752 g which is the *dirham* of 7/10 of 4.536 g. However, this *ratl* consists of 135 *dirham* of 3.024 g which is 2/3 of 4.536 g.

[18] Ulrich Rebstock, **Rechnen im islamischen Orient**, Darmstadt 1992

[19] The Islamic barrel weights resemble the shape of the spherical Byzantine commercial weights. Simon Bendall (**Byzantine weights**, London 1996) publishes a weight of this type which, according to its inscription, was issued by Justinian I. Thus the barrel weights continue the traditional Byzantine shape and therefore probably represent the earliest Islamic commercial weights. Some polyherda weights bear inscriptions showing that they were issued by Fatimid authorities. (Tony Goodwin, 'Medieval Islamic Copper-Alloy Money Weights from Bilad al-Sham', **Israel Numismatic Research** 7/2012, p. 173). The spheroid weights were probably issued between the barrels and the polyhedral weights. However, it should be noted that they all are based on the same reference weights. Some authors present *dirham* weights such as "a little over 2.9 g" (Holland, see Goodwin p. 170) and 2.98 g (Pottier, see Goodwin p. 171) which are based on the average calculated from a major number of weights. The reference weights of the central group of weights in table 2 span from 3.024 g to 2.880 g with a mean of 2.952 g. The weights presented by Holland and Pottier are close to 2.952 g. Nevertheless, it is questionable to calculate an average of weights which may not belong to the same weight standard.

to Schliemann these weights are silver talents[20]. The weight of two of these ingots is given as 173 g. Since 172.8 is 1/7 of the principal weight of 1/27 talent (1209.6 g), it makes sense to assume that this weight is meant. On the other hand 172.8 g is 1/150 of the talent of 25.92 kg. If we divide both by 60, we get the mina/*ratl* of 432.0 g and the *dirham* of 2.880 g which is 1/150 of the mina and hence two thirds of the *mithqāl* of 4.320 g. Thus, it appears that the *dirham* of two thirds of the *mithqāl* is part of a very long lasting tradition.

Table 2: Early *dirham* weights

ratl (g)	*dirham* (g)	number of reference weights	number of enhanced w.	number of reduced w.	total number
486.0	3.240	-	-	1	1
466.56	3.1104	-	-	3	3
459.27	3.0618	-	-	7	7
453.6	3.024	-	-	43	**43**
450.0	3.000	1	-	22	23
441.0	2.940	3	-	3	6
440.8992	2.939328	7	-	12	19
437.4	2.916	15	4	30	**49**
432.0	2.880	4	17	9	**30**
425.25	2.835	1	3	-	4
419.904	2.79936	3	-	1	4
414.72	2.7648 g	-	-	1	1
408.24	2.7216	-	1	-	1
405.0	2.700	-	-	1	1
388.8	2.592	1	-	1	2
total		35	25	134	194

The *ratl* of 408.24 g as a silver weight

It was mentioned above that the *ratl* of 408.24 g was divided into 90 or 100 *mithqāls*. Like some other *ratls* it may also be divided into 96 *mithqāls* or 144 *dirhams* (table 3)[21]. Thus it appears that the Egyptian *ratl* of 144 *dirhams* mentioned by Hinz[22] is a generally appearing phenomenon. Finally, the *mithqāls* of 1/96 *ratl* may otherwise be also seen as 1/100 of other *ratls*.

Table 3: *Ratls* divided into 96 *mithqāls* or 144 *dirhams*

Ratl (g)	*mithqāl* of 1/96 *ratl* (g)	*dirham* of 1/144 *ratl* (g)
408.24	4.2525	2.835
414.72	4.320	2.880
419.904	4.374	2.916
432.0	4.500	3.000

---

[20] Heinrich Schliemann, ***Bericht über die Ausgrabungen in Troja in den Jahren 1871 bis 1873***, new edition Düsseldorf/Zürich 1990, p. 218

[21] Already in ancient times it was common to use in parallel weight units composed of 100 or 96 smaller units: August Oxé, 'Kor und Kab. Antike Hohlmaße und Gewichte in neuer Beleuchtung', ***Bonner Jahrbücher*** 147 (1942) p. 94

[22] Walther Hinz, as footnote 8, p. 29

The *mithqāl* of 4.2525 g plays an important role in the Islamic weight system. On the one hand Maqrīzī refers to a silver *mithqāl* which is identical to the weight of the Sasanian drachm[23] which is 4.2525 g (see below). On the other hand 4.2525 g was later the standard weight of the Umayyad post reform dinar[24]. In the latter case 4.2525 g was not a reference weight but a reduction (63/64) of the reference weight of 4.320 g.

The nominal weight of the Sasanian drachm of Yazdagard III (figure 3) was 4.2525 g. The histogram of 48 drachms of Yazdagard III shows a maximum at 4.1391 g which is 73/75 of 4.2525 g (figure 4). Apart from one overweight coin, the weight distribution ends at 4.2525 g which demonstrates that this is the upper limit defined by the standard weight plus tolerance. Since the nominal weight is identical with the upper limit, the seigniorage in this case is identical with the tolerance. That the drachm of 4.2525 g was a Sasanian silver weight is further confirmed by the total weight of the Sasanian silver hoard from Orumiyeh which is 5120.04 g. This corresponds to 301 tetradrachms[25],[26] of 17.01 g (4 x 4.2525 g) yielding 5120.01 g[27]. Therefore, it is likely that 4.2525 g is the Sasanian weight unit Maqrizi had in mind. That the drachm of 4.2525 g was used as a silver weight in Umayyad times is confirmed by the fact that 4.2525 is 1/80 of the silver pound of 340.2 g mentioned above.

Figure 3: Drachm of Yazdagard III[28] *Figure 4: Drachms of Yazdagard III*

The weight of the Arab-Sasanian drachms was lighter than the weight of their Sasanian predecessors. The nominal weight of the Arab-Sasanian drachms was 4.0824 g. This is confirmed by 40 coins of Salm b. Ziyād and 'Abd Allāh b. Khāzim from the years 63-71 H[29] (figure 4). Figure 6 shows a distinct maximum indicating the standard weight of 3.99168 g, which is 44/45 of 4.0824 g. This standard weight is confirmed by a coin weight of 'Abd al-Malik weighing 3.99 g[30]. The nominal weight is once more identical with the upper limit of the weight distribution. This is

---

[23] Adel Allouche (translator), ***Mamluk Economics, a Study and Translation of al-Maqrīzī's Ighāthah***, University of Utah Press 1994, pp. 56-57

[24] Harald Witthöft, ***Münzfuß, Kleingewichte, pondus Caroli und die Grundlagen des nordeuropäischen Maß- und Gewichtswesens in fränkischer Zeit***, Ostfildern 1984, p. 46

[25] According to Robert Göbl the tetradrachm was a Sasanian weight unit. Robert Göbl, '***Sasanian Numismatics***', Braunschweig 1971, p. VII

[26] According to Susan Tyler-Smith the treasure of Khusru II contained "two hundred thousand purses of silver coinage, containing eight hundred million mithqāls". Thus one purse represents four thousand *mithqāls* or one thousand tetradrachms. Susan Tyler-Smith, ***The Coinage Reforms (600-603) of Khusru II and the Revolt of Vistāhm***, London 2017, p. 3

[27] It is a typical feature of hoards that they contain a round number of units which is slightly enhanced.

[28] Robert Göbl, as footnote 25, no. 232

[29] Stephen Album, 'An Arab-Sasanian Dirham Hoard from the Year 72 Hijri', ***Studia Iranica*** Tome 21 – 1992 fascicule 2, pp. 161-195

[30] Ariana d'Ottone Rambach, as footnote 11, p. 189, no. 6

slightly obscured by two overweight coins. However, since the weight distribution is symmetrical it is clear that the relevant figure is the one which is symmetrical to the lower end of the weight distribution.

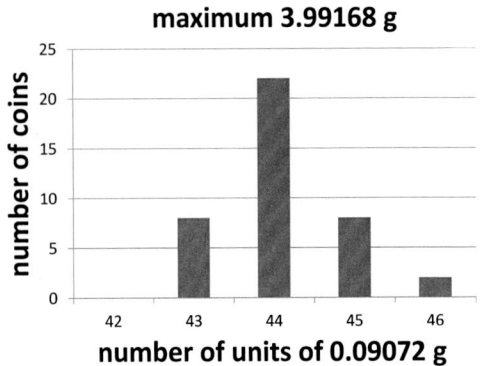

Figure 5: Drachm of 'Abd Allah b. Khāzim[31]

Figure 6: 40 drachms

However, this is just one example. Other coin weights from Umayyad times show that there were several different standard weights relating to the nominal weight of 4.0824 g[32]. Nevertheless, it is clear that the 4.0824 g, standard weight of the copper coins of Tartus class 1, is identical to the nominal weight of the Arab-Sasanian drachms. Thus no matter what the exchange rate of copper to silver was, it would have been easy to exchange copper coins of Tartus class 1 and Arab-Sasanian drachms.

Research based on the coins of classes 2 and 3 of Tartus

The coins of Tartus classes 2 and 3 (figure 6) seem to be of the same weight standard. Consequently, they were here taken together. The histogram shows a clear maximum at 4.6656 g (figure 8). (The secondary maximum may be neglected since it is probably caused by the accumulation of heavy coins.) The standard weight of the coins Tartus classes 2 and 3 is 1/100 of the *ratl* of 466.56 g which in turn is 1/70 of the talent of 32.6592 kg (see above). The standard weight of 4.6656 g is surprising, since it is well above the range of the usual Islamic *mithqāls* which ends at 4.536 g. However, if we assume that the *ratl* of 408.24 g was divided into 90 *mithqāls* of 4.536 g right from the beginning, we may assume that other *ratls* were divided into 90 *mithqāls* as well. Table 3 shows that other well established *ratls*, once they are divided by 90, provide as well heavy *mithqāls*, which appear as standard weights of copper coins from the Byzantine-Islamic transitional period.

Table 4: ***Ratls* divided into 90 *mithqāls***

Ratl (g)	*mithqāl* of 1/90 *ratl* (g)	comment
408.24	4.536	sextula of the gold-pound of 326.592 g
414.72	4.608	-
419.904	4.6656	Tartus classes 2 and 3
425.25	4.725	Pseudo Byzantine folles with pseudo mint marks

---

[31] Stephen Album, as footnote 29, no. 135
[32] For instance two other weights presented by Arianna d'Ottone Rambach, as footnote 11, no. 1: 3.95 g from 'Abd al-Malik represents 3.954825 g = 31/32 of 4.0824 g; no. 22: 3.94 g from Zāmil b. 'Amr represents 3.9366 g = 27/28 of 4.0824 g.

		KYΠP and CON[33]
453.6	5.040	*fulūs* Gerasa type 1 (see below)

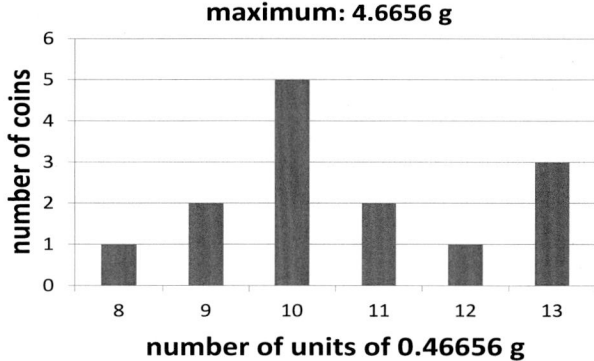

Figure 7: Tartus classes 2 and 3 *Figure 8: Tartus classes 2 and 3*

At the meeting in Oxford 2016, Andrew Oddy presented the Phase 2 Coinage of Gerasa [34]. The coins of Gerasa group 1 (figure 9) and Gerasa group 2 (figure 11) provide examples of heavy copper coins exceeding by far the weight of two ordinary *mithqāls* (figures 10 and 12).

Figure 9: Gerasa group 1 *Figure 10: Gerasa group 1*

Table 5 demonstrates that the standard weights of the coins of Gerasa group 1 and Gerasa group 2 correspond to Egyptian *qedets* (see table 9). Thus it may well be that weight units which were common in the Bronze Age were still used in Islamic times. The copper coins from Seventh Century Syria include a major number of heavy *mithqāls*, which can be seen as half Egyptian *qedets*.

Table 5: Standard weights of the *fulūs* of Gerasa groups 1 and 2

Group	Standard weight	= two *mithqāls* of	= *qedet* of
1	10.08 g	5.040 g	10.08 g
2	9.450 g	4.725 g	9.450 g

---

[33] Dietrich Schnädelbach,. 'The Roman/Byzantine and Islamic Weight Systems – Two sides of the same coin' in Tony Goodwin (ed.) ***Coinage and History in the Seventh Century Near East Vol. 5***, London 2016, pp. 166-167.

[34] Andrew Oddy, 'The Phase 2 Coinage of Gerasa under Mu'awiya and his Successors', in Tony Goodwin (ed.) ***Coinage and History in the Seventh Century Near East Vol. 5***, London 2016, pp. 49-74

  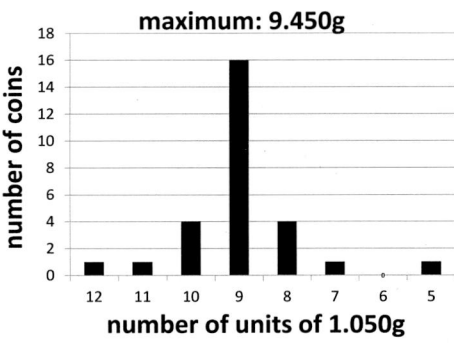

Figure 11: Gerasa group 2   *Figure 12: Gerasa group 2*

Balog published a weight of 3 *dahmās* (figure 13). Its inscription is "weight of three [dahmās] / full weight" and its present weight is 28.18 g but "two small chips are missing". Thus it probably represents 28.35 g and is equal to 3 units of 9.450 g, the standard weight of the coins of Gerasa group 2 (Figure 11). This weight demonstrates that there may be a major number of traditional weight units which are overlooked since they are usually not represented by official weights and not mentioned by Islamic authors. Accordingly the standard weights of copper coins may provide insights into the traditional weight systems which are otherwise not available (table 6).

Figure 13: Balog no. 802

Table 6:   Heavy *mithqāls* represented by heavy Syrian *fulūs*

Heavy *mithqāl*	*fals*	reference
4.6656 g	9.3312 g	Tartus classes 2 and 3
4.725 g	9.450 g	Gerasa group 2, pseudo mint marks CON, KYΠP[35]
5.040 g	10.08 g	Gerasa group 1

Fals **glass weights**

Balog[36] and Miles[37] published a major number of glass weights all providing the inscription *fals* of xx *qīrāt/kharrūbah*. In addition they usually name the official responsible for their emission. This series starts in Umayyad times and was continued by subsequent dynasties. If the weight of the pieces and the number of *qīrāt/kharrūbah* given in the inscription are used to calculate the *mithqāl* of 25 *qīrāt/kharrūbah*[38], the resulting *mithqāls* are in the range of 4.608 g until 5.040 g which is

---

[35] Dietrich Schnädelbach as footnote 33
[36] Paul Balog as footnote 5
[37] George C. Miles, 'Contributions to Arabic Metrology I', *ANS NNM* no. 141, New York 1958 and 'Contributions to Arabic Metrology II', *ANS NNM* no. 150, New York 1963
[38] In a few cases a *mithqāl* of 24 *qīrāt/kharrūbah* is the basis of a *fals* weight. This situation is also reflected by the weights themselves since the majority of weights representing *mithqāls* are inscribed "*fals* of 25 *qīrāt/kharrūbah*".

above the range of the usual *mithqāls* ending at 4.536 g. Apart from the two lightest units, this range is represented by the Egyptian *qedets* listed below.

The *mithqāls* at the basis of the *fals* glass weights represent the same range of weights as some heavy copper coins from Seventh Century Syria. However, whereas the standard weights of the copper coins are reference weights, the *fals*-weights are usually representing ordinary (common) weights. This suggests that these weights were used for commercial transactions. Since the weight of the pieces is usually given to two decimal figures only, it is often not possible to select in a given case from several *mithqāls* which may be the relevant reference weight the true one. Nevertheless, it is clear that *fals* weights are mainly reduced reference weights.

Fals qabīr and *ratl qabīr*

A few weights carry the inscription "*fals kabīr*". In several cases pieces having the same weight provide inscriptions with and without the addition *kabīr*. The database of the British Museum provides two examples issued by the Umayyads demonstrating this situation (table 7).

Table 7: Fals weights of 30 *qīrāt/kharrūbah* with and without the inscription "*kabīr*"

Catalogue no.	weight (g)	*qīrāt/kharrūbah*	further inscription
oa + 4321	5.83	30	*kabīr*
oa + 4172	5.83	30	-

In this case it is fortunately very clear that the correct weight of these pieces is 5.832 g which consists of 30 *qīrāt/kharrūbah* of 0.1944 g which are 1/25 of the *mithqāl* of 4.860 g. So far both pieces seem to be identical. Why then is it necessary to explain that one piece is "*kabīr*" (heavy)? 5.832 g can also be seen as 81/80 of 5.760 g which is 30 *qīrāt/kharrūbah* of 0.192 g which is 1/24 of the *mithqāl* of 4.608 g. Since the weight is always given in *qīrāt/kharrūbah* and since the *fals* weights are usually reduced reference weights, it makes sense to assume that "*kabīr*" indicates that this is an enhanced weight. Balog publishes a few *ratl* weights which according to their inscriptions are "*kabīr*". It makes sense to assume that the reason is the same as in the case of the *fals kabīr*.

Table 8: *Ratl* weights with and without the inscription "*kabīr*"

Balog no	weight (g)	inscription (as given by Balog)
572	493.63	Ordered the amīr Ibrāhim b. Sālih / Ratl kabīr full weight
791	237.02	One-quarter ratl, full weight. Ordered by Yahyā.[39]

For example, the weight of 493.63 g (table 8) may represent 493.5168 g which is 51/50 of 483.84 g or 493.92 g which is 49/48 of 483.84 g (see below *qedet* of 9.6768 g). In both cases "*kabīr*" refers to an enhanced reference weight. The weight of 237.02 g (table 8) represents 237.0816 g which is half of 474.1632 g or 49/50 of 483.84 g. Thus it appears that also in the case of the *ratl kabīr* the term "*kabīr*" indicates an enhanced weight. Consequently, the weights in the range of the *ratl kabīr* as defined by Balog are just *ratls* of 100 heavy *mithqāls*. It is very likely that the range of the heavy *mithqāls* is here the same as in the case of the *fals* weights.

---

[39] Yahyā was a 'Abbāsid official. Nevertheless the weight is relevant in this context since it is the only piece representing a heavy ratl that lacks the inscription "*kabīr*". Balog (p. 285) comments: "Notwithstanding the denomination, this is a one-half ratl kabīr."

483.84 g is a *ratl* consisting of 160 *dirhams* of 3.024 g (2/3 of 4.536 g). According to Hinz[40] the *ratl kabīr* of 160 *dirhams* was used in Egypt in the 17th century. The examples above show that this *ratl* was used at least from the 'Ābbasid time but probably also from the Umayyad time onward. Two other Egyptian *ratls* demonstrate that the *ratl kabīr* was a fundamental unit. The *ratl jarwī* of 312 *dirhams* represents 39/40 of two *ratl kabīr* and a *ratl* of Damiete of 330 *dirhams* represents 33/32 of two *ratl kabīr*. Since the *ratl* of 483.84 g can also be seen as a weight of 50 Egyptian *qedets* of 9.6768 g (see table 9 below) it suggests like the *ratl* of 408.24 g (see above) which can be seen as a weight of 50 Egyptian darics of 8.1648 g that basic weight units were used at least from the Bronze Age onwards.

Qedets of two *mithqāls* represented by Egyptian weights

Petrie[41] published more than 2800 stone weights from ancient Egypt. The biggest group within this corpus, more than 800 pieces, is represented by the *qedet* weights. Among these are 89 reference weights (table 9) representing several different *qedet* standards, fractions or multiples thereof. The vast majority represent ordinary (commercial) weights (i.e. enhanced or reduced reference weights).

Table 9 Egyptian *qedets* representing two heavy *mithqāls* of Islamic times

Qedet (g)	number	*mithqāl* (g)	Relations
9.000	4	4.500	1/72 of 324.0 g; 3/320 of 960.0 g
9.072 [42]	7	4.536	1/72 of 326.592 g; 1/90 of 408.24 g
9.216	13	4.608	96/100 of 4.800 g; 3/625 of 960.0 g
9.3312	13	4.6656	96/100 of 4.860 g; 2/175 of 408.24 g
9.4058496	9	4.7029248	96/100 of 4.89888 g; 9/625 of 326.592 g
9.450	11	4.725	5/432 of 408.24 g
9.600	5	4.800	1/200 of 960.0 g
9.6768	4	4.8384	96/100 of 5.040 g; 4/135 of 326.592 g
9.720	10	4.860	1/84 of 408.24 g; 3/200 of 324.0
9.79776	8	4.89888	3/100 of 326.592 g; 3/250 of 408.24
10.08	5	5.040	1/81 of 408.24 g
Together	89		

Summary

- Islamic weight systems are based on the talents of 25.92 kg and 32.6592 kg which are part of a tradition persisting at least since the Bronze Age.
- The *ratl* may be divided into 100 *mithqāls* and 150 *dirhams*
  or into 90 heavy *mithqāls* and 135 heavy *dirhams*.
- In addition some *ratls* may be divided into 96 *mithqāls* and 144 *dirhams*.
- Finally there were heavy *ratls* of 100 heavy *mithqāls* or 160 *dirhams*.

---

[40] Walther Hinz as footnote 8, p. 29
[41] Sir W.M. Flinders Petrie, ***Ancient Weights and Measures***, The British School of Archaeology in Egypt 1926, reprint Warminster (Wiltshire, England) and Encino (California, USA)
[42] The *qedet* of 9.072 g has the same weight as the shekel of 1/60 of the Babylonian mina of 544.32 g (see above). According to Sawelski (as footnote 11, p. 40) this mina was well known to the Egyptians since the weight of 60 *qedet* is rather often mentioned in Egyptian documents.

From Ancient to Medieval: The Significance of Fixed Die Axes

Marcus Phillips[1]

Introduction

'Die Axis' is the term numismatists use to describe the orientation of the design on one side of a coin in relation to the other. At present British and Euro coins have the obverse and reverse designs pointing the same way. American coins are struck with one side inverted in relation to the other.

A few years ago I showed some solidi of Heraclius and Constans II to some students and asked them for their reaction. I thought the main thing they would notice would be the long grotesque beards. What caught their attention was that they were 'upside down'. I forgot to ask them if they had ever been to America.

This anecdote illustrates two points. First, it is unwise to try and second guess how people (ancient or modern) did or will, react to changes in coin design. Second, die axis is something that people sometimes notice if they are asked to look at coins. People in the ancient world looked at coins more carefully than we do.

The terms and symbols used by numismatists to describe die axes vary. Clock times, arrows and degree numbers are the usual methods. The die axis of a modern British coin could be represented as 12 o'clock (or 12h), ↑↑ (or just ↑) or 0° or 360°; a US coin as 6 o'clock (or 6h), ↑↓ or 180°.

Modern methods of coin production require a fixed die orientation but there seems to be no particular significance in the choice. English milled coins were originally struck on a 180° axis but 0° became more usual after the recoinage of 1816. A fixed standard was only introduced with the Jubilee coinage of 1887 and this seems to have been for purely technical reasons.[2]

The majority of coins of Late Antiquity were struck on a fixed die axis. In the case of late Roman and Byzantine coins this was 180°. Axumite coins, especially the gold, are normally a very precise 0°. It is generally thought that medieval coins, at least in the West, were struck on a random die axis – indeed the editors of *Medieval European Coinage* have been, informally, criticised for bothering to record them at all. The attitude of individual numismatists also varies. Some take the view that unless the coin is struck on a precise vertical axis then the axis is irregular. Others take a more relaxed view: was the moneyer trying to coin on regular axis or did he not care? If the former is the case then a small deviation can be allowed depending on the type of die used.

---

[1] Marcus Phillips is co-editor of the Numismatic Chronicle. senmerv@hotmail.com. I am grateful to Tony Goodwin for supplying data on coins from his own collection and Susan Tyler-Smith for much time consuming checking of figures. I am of course solely responsible for any errors in these.

[2] 'The reason for the change in 1887 is not well documented but looks to be technical in origin, arising from difficulties with the new Jubilee effigy. It is important, if coins are to be fully and properly struck, for the obverse and reverse designs to balance each other, with areas of high relief on one side avoiding areas of high relief on the other. In the case of the Jubilee coinage this consideration dictated an upright die axis, our Deputy Master explaining to his opposite number at the Sydney Mint that 'the exigencies of the Head make it necessary that the coins should in future be struck with the obverse and reverse designs both pointing the same way…'. Thereafter this practice became the rule,' email 16 May 2019 from Abigail Kenvyn to whom I most grateful.

In the discussion at the meeting Hugh Williams made an important observation. He had noticed on late Roman coins that very often the axis was off the vertical by approximately 20° (the smallest amount measurable) but the deviation was always one way: either 20° or 200° never 340° or 160°. This can be explained as follows: as the striker raised his right arm there was a natural tendency for the torso to twist and pull the left hand, which was holding the upper die, to the right. Even if the die was marked and the striker was aiming at a vertical axis there was still a tendency to move the die round. This would certainly be the case with round dies; it might be less of a tendency with square dies. It would also vary according to the skill of the people involved.

Random die axis

A fixed die axis will be obvious when it is successfully achieved. What is less clear is when the mint was aiming at a fixed axis but, for whatever reason, failed to achieve it. It is all too easy to then assume that no serious attempt was being made to maintain a fixed die axis. It is therefore worth looking at the results where a random die axis was clearly operating. This was the case with the French gros tournois introduced by Louis IX in 1266. The analysis by Mario Schlapke of the 3,142 gros tournois in the Erfurt (Michaelisstraße) hoard gave the following picture (*Fig. 1*).[3]

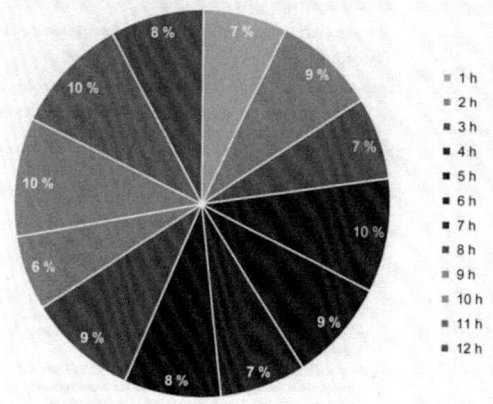

Fig. 1. Die axes of French gros tournois in the Erfurt hoard.

Provided the sample is big enough random die axes will be random. When they are not, and one particular axis or axes seems to predominate, this should be taken as a sign that a fixed die axis was at least being aimed at and more examples need to be checked before drawing conclusions.

Another problem with recording die axes is how one defines 'obverse' and 'reverse'. This is discussed in Appendix 1.

In his British Museum *Catalogue* John Walker noted that while the early (AH 77–9) post reform gold and the imitative North African gold was struck on a regular 180° axis it later became haphazard. Both the silver and copper throughout were irregular. For this reason he omitted to record the die axes.[4] This set an unfortunate precedent. Until now the tendency has been to ignore the die axis even on the many rare 'experimental' silver types that have emerged since Walker's catalogue. As a general hypothesis, I would argue that the reason whole series of coins have been regarded as being struck on a random die axis is that no one has checked.[5] In the case of western

---

[3] Schlapke, 'Münzen und Barren des Efurter Schatzfundes', p. 41, fig. 33.
[4] Walker, ***BMC Arab Byzantine***, p. v.
[5] By contrast students of ancient numismatics have discussed the subject at some length, indeed the earliest study was in 1906, Macdonald, 'Fixed and loose dies'. For Greek coins see de Callataÿ, ***Monnaies grecques et l'orientation des axes***, for Roman see Burnett, 'Die axis in Italy and Rome', with an up to date bibliography.

medieval coins there seem to be a number of attempts to strike on a regular die axis, one example being the London portrait pennies of Alfred the Great.[6]

In practice large numbers of the so-called Pseudo-Byzantine (Phase 1) coins are struck on a vertical, usually 180°, die axis. Coins of phase 2 and 3 sometimes have a regular die axis as will be examined below. The simplest explanation for this is that the producers of these coins began by simply carrying on a tradition but without attaching too much importance to it. They may also have been concerned that regular die axes would facilitate the coins' acceptance by the public. They were after all in competition with official Byzantine coins. This vertical die axis continued in an attenuated form with the Umayyad Imperial Image and Standing Caliph issues (Phases 2 and 3) but as the coins get more 'Islamic' the mints ceased to bother. The sum total of this line of argument is that the subject is of interest only to collectors and tells us nothing of importance.

In this article I argue that it is worth exploring an alternative approach. The (partial or total) abandonment of attempts at a fixed die axis is one way of separating the coinages of the ancient world from those that emerged from the end of Antiquity in both east and west. This could be related to changes in technology or reflect a more casual attitude to coinage in general. On the other hand more fundamental cultural attitudes could have been involved. The following discussion is far removed from seventh-century Syria but this is necessary given the nature of the sources.

The survival of the classical tradition

Why bother to have a regular die axis? If you decide to have one why chose one axis rather than another? Late Roman and Byzantine coins are on a 180° die axis. This means that if you contemplate the emperor's portrait and then turn it over in the simplest way, with the fingers of one hand, you see the reverse image the right way up. This reverse design, on late Roman coins at least, conveys a political message. After the reforms of Anastasius the reverses of Byzantine copper coins merely conveyed information about the value etc. of the coin, but under Constans II there was more of an attempt at a political message on the reverse despite the squalid appearance of the coins.

If you have a 0° die axis it is more awkward. Either you have to twist the coin with your wrist or else you use two hands. This does not necessarily stop people using it, Axumite coinage has already been mentioned, but a 0° die axis is generally less common in late antiquity. On the other hand with large coins, and particularly medals, where it is easier to use two hands to turn them, a 0° axis is preferable. It is sometimes referred to as the 'medallic axis' because it is normal for Renaissance medals. For one series an axis of 180° was chosen, apparently because the patron concerned was a keen student of ancient Roman coins.[7]

One of the very few medievalists to discuss die axis was Philip Grierson when he published the die of a ducat of the Venetian doge Alviso III Mocenigo (1763–78). This, of course was for use in a mechanical press and had visible holes for the pegs used to orientate it.[8] Grierson pointed out that a number of medieval mints outside the Byzantine empire occasionally struck coins on a regular die axis. He singled out the coins of the Normans of Sicily after the reforms of Roger II in 1143, Venice after the introduction of the grosso and the ducat, the independent coinages of Bulgaria and Serbia and the early copper coins of the crusader princes of Antioch. These are all coinages which, in one way or another, were influenced by Byzantine practice. In all these instances Grierson surmised that they must have involved some kind of mechanical device consisting of a system of pegs and sockets.

---

[6] I am grateful to William Mackay for pointing this out to me.
[7] See Smołucha-Sładkowska, 'First early-Renaissance medals with inverted reverses', for details and a general discussion the subject.
[8] Grierson, 'Pegged Venetian coin dies'.

The case of Southern Italy

The Normans, who gradually conquered South Italy and Sicily in the eleventh century, struck a varied and heterogeneous coinage that initially reflected local customs and usage.[9] In 1140 Roger II (1105–54) carried out a reform of the coinage which involved the introduction of a dated silver ducalis (*MEC* 212) and its third (*MEC* 214). Both were carefully struck on a vertical die axis, usually 180°. Grierson attributed this to the influence of Byzantine workmen who organized the minting for Roger.[10] This idea was not taken up in *MEC*. Other Norman issues copied the fixed die axis, even the little copper coins of William II (1166–89) (*MEC* 433–437). There were exceptions. On many of the coins the die axis cannot be ascertained but on the small gold tari they seem to be irregular.

In 1191 South Italy and Sicily came under Hohenstaufen control and fixed die axes were abandoned. They were revived again in 1231 by Frederick II (1197–1250) who introduced the gold augustalis and its half (*MEC* 515–517). The conscious classical (or proto-Renaissance) style of the piece was enhanced by a carefully controlled 180° die axis. The same applied to the real of Charles of Anjou (1266–85) although this was a less successful combination of classical and Gothic. As a patron of the arts Charles can hardly have been satisfied with this reverse design with its oversized and clumsy shield.

Frederick augustale
CNG auction 65, lot 1184

Charles of Anjou real
Ars Classica 89, lot 669

In 1278 Charles, carried out a reform of the coinage finally ending the coinage of gold taris. He set up a new mint in the Bay of Naples but he was in Rome and he asked for some proofs of the new coins to be sent to him. His observations on the trial pieces he received are a remarkable and very unusual recorded case of a medieval ruler taking a personal interest in the precise design of his coins.[11]

As usual with such documents the text is repetitive. Charles complained that the lettering was too small and crowded, and the impression not sharp enough; but his main concern, at least it is mentioned first and he stresses the importance of it, is that the coin is 'upside down'! The head of the angel and the Virgin should correspond with the top of the shield and their feet with the pointed end of the shield. In other words it should have a 0° die axis.

We do not know whether Charles was unique in taking such an interest in his coins or whether some other medieval rulers did the same. It most likely varied with different individuals and cultures. What may be significant is that Charles introduced a Gothic style coin with a religious scene

---

[9] Grierson and Travaini, **MEC South Italy**, pp. 76–193 is the most convenient and detailed source for the events and coins mentioned.
[10] Grierson was fond of the idea mint of workers and officials from Constantinople being drafted to organise other mints, but he struggled to explain the fixed die axis on Venetian grossi.
[11] The relevant part of the original is reproduced in Appendix 2.

thereby deliberately reversing the classical ethos of the previous issues and in doing so changed the die axis. Was this just a matter of personal taste or a conscious rejection of the classical tradition? We do not know but the key point is he wanted his coins to impress and he thought this die axis was an important part of this.

Charles I gold carlino (saluto) 4.37 grams   *Charles II silver carlino (saluto) 3.22 grams*
CNG Triton 7, lot 1178   *CNG Auction 66, lot 1927*

The new gold issue was accompanied by a silver coin of identical design and the same prescriptions applied. Lucia Travaini was able to examine a 38 such coins of both Charles I and Charles II (1285–1309) from the Oschiri hoard and found that a fairly high proportion varied between 340° and 20°, but never more than that. A few were around 180°.[12] So an attempt was made by the mint to carry out Charles' orders but the dies must have been round and aligned by eye. The practice ceased in 1303 when the striking of gold was abandoned and the silver gigliato introduced. Grierson wondered whether this was because of the adoption of the more conventional floreate cross design on the reverse. The gigliati seem to have been struck on a far greater scale and it may have been just a matter of practicality and logistics.

Fixed die links on the coins of Nur al-Din

The idea that there was a direct link between a fixed die axis and the old Roman tradition may seem far fetched. There is, however, corroborative evidence from the other end of the Mediterranean. In the late tenth and early eleventh centuries the Byzantines temporarily regained much of the territory in Syria and Anatolia which they had lost in the seventh century and, as in the seventh century, large numbers of official Byzantine coppers are found outside the frontiers of the reconquered Byzantine territory.

Byzantine coins of this period were widely imitated.[13] By far the commonest signed imitations are those of the Zengid atabeg Nur al-Din Mahmud (1146–74) which copy the folles of Constantine X (1059–67). They have no mint but are usually attributed to Aleppo. They were issued nearly 100 years after the prototype which makes them almost contemporary with the coins of Roger of Sicily. These are almost invariably on a 180° axis, with only one recorded with the axis at 0°. The consistency is such that Spengler and Sayles echo Grierson in suggesting the possibility of pegged dies.[14] The coins vary enormously in style but even the crudest pieces (which may be unofficial) are consistently on a 180° axis.

---

[12] Travaini, 'Ripostiglio di Oschiri', pp. 58–60.
[13] Phillips, 'Eastern copies of tenth and eleventh century Byzantine coins'.
[14] Spengler and Sayles, **Turkoman Figural Bronze Coins**, p. 59.

Good style Nur al-Din, 4.21 grams   *Crude Nur al-Din, 2.59 grams*

Nur al-Din also struck an extensive issue of fulus at Damascus and the die axis here is always irregular. Strange as it may seem there would seem to be a direct connection between a fix die axis on coins reflecting Roman and Byzantine imagery and its deliberate abandonment on Islamic style coins.

Die axes on Sasanian coins

Anyone familiar with Sasanian coins will know that they are certainly on a regular die axis but it is usually 90°, sometimes 270°. When the coin was turned over in the hand this put the reverse design on its side. This made it much easier to read the mint and date, but this cannot be the reason why it was originally adopted. The change was made under the founder of the dynasty Ardashir I (224–40) whose coins had no mint or date. The coins of the Parthians had been struck on a 0° axis. Ardashir seems to have adopted a 'sideways' i.e. 90° or 270° axis from the first and this remained the practice until the end of the dynasty. Why chose such a strange axis? One reason could be that Ardashir wanted to repudiate his predecessors but could hardly emulate the Romans so he chose a third way.

A large sample of coins of Khusrau II (590–628) analysed by Susan Tyler-Smith produced the following results.[15]

Total: 1940 coins
Regular die axis
90°   57%
270°   24%

Including coins with axis 10° off the vertical either way
80°–110°   66%
260°–280° 28%

The percentage of coins with an intended die axis of 270° seems surprising but the mints may have been under pressure to maximise output given the number of very worn dies used. We know from surviving examples that Sasanian dies at this period were round and a 10° variation either way is to be expected.

Sasanian dies

Two iron trussle dies from the time of Khusrau II are in the Berlin Münzkabinett. They were said to have been found in Mosul encased in lead which had preserved them.[16] They both show the reverse design with fire altar and attendants. Of course their existence does not prove that round dies were

---

[15] Tyler-Smith, 'Year 12 hoard'.
[16] Nützel, 'Sasanidische Münzstempel', Museum accession nos 1909/137–8; object nos 18201599 = YZ (Yazd) year 11; 18204574 = AW (Ahwaz) year 15. Both are illustrated on the Museum's website. The photo reproduced here was taken by S. Tyler-Smith.

always used or that the fire altar was always the reverse.[17] There are some quite obvious notches on one of the dies (YZ Yazd, year 11) one of which could indicate a positioning mark. That is, it showed the striker where to align the die. Unfortunately for this idea there are several other notches but assuming the biggest one was aligned against a mark at 0° or 180° on the lower die it would give an axis of 90° or 270°; but not a very precise one. There are no similar marks on the other die. For the moment it seems best to assume that the dies were marked in a temporary way, perhaps with chalk, though this would not have been very precise.

Reverse die for Sasanian drachm of Khusro II
Mint of Yazd, year 11

Die axes on Arab-Byzantine gold

The different issues of gold coins in Byzantine style are usually described in detail in sale catalogues but die axes are rarely given, as was also the case with the old museum catalogues. When George Miles compiled his catalogue he could only record the die axes of two coins.[18]

As already noted the die axis on the small North African gold coins is usually 180°. Curiously the die axis on coins of the Byzantine mint of Carthage tended to be rather irregular though Grierson thought they were aiming at 90°.[19] If so they were not very accurate to judge by the data given in *DOC*.

Pseudo-Byzantine gold

The early 'altered cross' types vary a good deal in style and design and are presumably the product of more than one 'mint' so one would not expect much consistency with die axis. The example published by Miles (using the arrow system to record the axis) was around 200° i.e. just off the vertical but one does not know by how much. This is the same as the axis, recorded by William

---

[17] Schindel, *SNS Israel*, p. 124, points to a double headed coin as possible evidence that the head side could sometime have been the upper die. The piece in question: *SNS* 3, pl. 140, no. N5, is a small, barely legible, copper coin found at Merv which seems unlikely to have been typical.
[18] Miles, 'Earliest Arab gold', nos 6, 15.
[19] Grierson, *Byzantine Coins*, p. 42.

Metcalf, of the imitative solidus in the Daphne hoard; the only recorded example of a gold imitation in a hoard.[20] Metcalf recorded the die axis of the other 65 coins in the hoard which were all gold and from Constantinople. These were either exactly 180° or 200°, again using the arrow method.

The results were:

Ruler	No. in hoard	Die axis 180°	Die axis 200°
Maurice	1	0	1
Focas	23	7	16
Heraclius	32	21	11
Constans II	7	5	2
Constantine IV	2	1	1
Total	65	34	31

Table 1. Die axes of Byzantine gold coins in the Daphne hoard

Nearly half the official gold coins had a die axis just off the vertical though all were obviously aiming at 180°. This confirms Hugh William's argument that the mints were aiming at 180° but occasionally the striker inadvertently moved the upper die off the vertical to the right in the manner described. Standards seem to have varied and a larger sample might give a different picture.

True 180° axes are recorded for two imitations sold by CNG who, exceptionally among auctioneers, always record the die axis.[21] The same applies to *SICA* no. 606. To judge by the shapes of other examples in sale catalogues a 180° axis was certainly quite common but one needs more data from proper examination of the coins.[22]

CNG Triton 20, lot 1137
4.42 grams

CNG Triton 22, lot 1226
4.33 grams

Shahada solidi and Standing Caliph dinars

Both these groups were apparently struck at one central mint and one would expect more uniformity. Once again not only are die axes usually not noted but, in the case of the *shahada* solidi, there is less irregularity in the flans which makes it difficult to even guess the axis. There is also some divergence of opinion regarding authenticity. One example, which fetched £160,000 and was said to die link with two other examples, is nonetheless denounced as false on the zeno web site![23]

---

[20] Metcalf, 'Three seventh century hoards', at pp. 91–6. The 'hoard' did not have a confirmed provenance.
[21] **Classical Numismatic Group** Triton sales 20 (9 January 2017) lot 1137 (three figure type); ibid., 22 (7 January 2019) lot 1226 (two bust type).
[22] For example **Stephen Album**, Auction 23 (10 September 2015) lot 68 (two bust type); **Baldwin's** Islamic Coin Auction 24: 'Horus collection' (9 May 2013) lot 3999 = **Numismatica Genevensis** 8 (24 November 2014), lot 226.
[23] **Baldwin's** ICA 24, 'Horus collection' (9 May 2013) lot 4000. The die axis appears to be irregular, that is approximately 130°. The obverse die = **Spink** (Zürich) Auction 18 (February 1986) lot 86, the reverse die = al-'Ush,

Baldwins ICA 24 (9 May 2013) lot 4000.
Die axis apparently close to 0°

With the even rarer standing caliph types one die axis is recorded as 180° (*SICA* 705) and piercings or flan damage on the Jena and British Museum specimens respectively clearly indicate a 180° axis.[24] Miles recorded the dies on the the ANS example as approximately 220°.[25]

Jena Standing Caliph AV coin   *British Museum Standing Caliph AV coin*

Die axes on 'experimental' silver

The same personnel who had produced the Sasanian coins continued to produce the Arab-Sasanian and these generally use the 90° / 270° axis. Shortly before the reforms of 'Abd al-Malik a number of unusual or experimental silver types were produced in mints in Syria and Iraq. These can be sub-divided into two groups: the first retain the traditional fire altar design on the reverse but have the legends in Arabic. These were struck in Syria at Damascus and Homs and there is a mintless issue attributed to Damascus.[26] In the second group the reverse design abandons the traditional fire altar in favour of the so-called 'caliph orans', 'standing caliph', and 'mihrab'.[27] None of these survive in large quantities.

The first group has been catalogued by Schindel who noted 13 coins but was only able to record the die axis in five cases.[28] These were all either 90° or 270° with the exception of the Homs coin (*SICA* 305) which is 4h: approximately 100°–110°. This 'irregular' axis could be the result of the turning of the trussel die as explained above. Hodge Malek notes the die axis of three additional specimens, all of which are either 90° or 270°.[29] This horizontal die axis can easily be explained as the work of Persian moneyers transported to Syria who carried on the tradition they were used to.

Arab Islamic Coins Preserved in the National Museum of Qatar, plate 53 coin no. 198. The coin appears perfectly genuine but see the comments on https://zeno.ru/, no. 124187.
[24] Stickel, *Handbuch*, vol. 2, p. 43, no. 34 illustrated on unnumbered plate. The BM specimen (1954,1011.2) is on the web site (https://britishmuseum.org/research/collection_online/search.aspx?searchText=1954,1011.2).
[25] Miles, 'Earliest Arab gold', p. 212, no. 15.
[26] Malek, *Arab Sasanian Numismatics*, p. 142.
[27] In addition there is a type with the *shahada* in Pahlavi on the reverse, Malek, p. 263, fig. 9.10.2; and a standing figure, Malek, p. 329, fig. 9.58.2 on the reverse. These are both from mints in the East.
[28] Schindel, *SNS Israel*, pp. 163–6, pls 27–28. Cf. also pl. 17, no. 225 which is 270°.
[29] Malek, *Arab Sasanian Numismatics*, discussion p. 142, pl. 45, nos 524–526.

Of the second group only the 'caliph orans' type which was struck at two mints in Iraq, Basra and Kufa, survives in any number.[30] Again recorded die axes are either 90° or 270° or in one case '4h'.[31] These again would be the work of local moneyers.

The rare 'mihrab' and 'standing caliph' types are mintless but are assumed to have been struck in Syria. Again one has to resort to estimates but the die axis on the two mihrab coins illustrated by Treadwell, based on the irregular flans, look roughly like 90° and 270°.[32] The 'standing caliph' type is particularly interesting because it involved a clash between two different cultures, Roman and Sasanian, the former with a vertical die axis the latter with a horizontal one. Again there are no precise records, as far as I am aware, but two of the few known 'standing caliph' types have large chips to the flan: the Zubow specimen illustrated by Walker and a coin recently sold by Morton and Eden. The former is 90° and the later 100–110°.[33]

Zubow coin *Morton and Eden coin*

Any conclusion on such limited data has to be very provisional but the evidence points to a conscious attempt to retain a vertical die axis on the gold and a horizontal one on the silver. In the case of the silver this may have been the continuation of traditional practice but the gold was either the work of local goldsmiths or just conceivably co-opted Persian moneyers. What is interesting is that fixed die axes were soon abandoned with the introduction of the reformed coinage though exactly how long the vertical axis was retained on the gold remains unclear. This could have been the result of lack of interest – the Arabs were just not bothered. Or was the volume of coinage such that it was considered impractical? The precious metal post-reform coinage was struck to a very high standard and it is hard to see why attention could not have been paid to the maintenance of a regular die axis. So the alternative hypothesis is that the abandonment of a fixed die axis was a deliberate policy decision. It was another way in which the new coinage marked a conscious rejection of the traditions of both empires.

Copper coins

The Islamic conquest marked a transition in the status of copper coins from being an acceptable fiduciary currency to being a local token currency which, later Islamic jurists insisted, was not really money. So, unlike the die axes on the pre-reform gold and silver, one might expect those on the copper to gradually become less regular as people took less care.

---

[30] The standard monograph by Treadwell, 'Orans drachms', does not discuss the die axis. The coins were well produced on round flans and the axis cannot be reliably ascertained from the pictures.
[31] *SICA*, pl. 8. no. 107 = 90° Basra; *SICA*, pl. 1, no. 5 = '4h', Kufa. Malek, **Arab Sasanian Numismatics**, pl. 2, no. 13 = 90° Kufa and pl. 18, no. 206 = 270° Basra.
[32] Treadwell, 'Orans drachm', p. 269.
[33] Walker, **BMC Arab-Sasanian**, p. 25; *Morton and Eden* auction 54, 23 April 2012, lot 23.

Arab-Sasanian copper

Thanks to the catalogue published by Malek of the coins in the Johnson collection a considerable amount of data are now available. The Arab-Sasanian copper series comprises a multiplicity of types and most are difficult to date. For the present therefore only the broadest analysis is possible. Die axes have been recorded for 266 coins and these are shown as percentages in Fig. 2.[34] The majority have a regular die axis with the largest number being 90° but this is certainly not dominant. The only group which clearly imitates a Byzantine coin, a two bust solidus of Heraclius, which consists of 65 coins, catalogue nos 1541–1605, has been singled out for comparison, partly because it is the largest single type but also because it copies a Byzantine prototype. Curiously the die axis on these coins corresponds closely to those on the main series. All that can be said for the moment is that there does seem to have been an attempt at a regular die axis but this has nothing to do with the prototype selected.

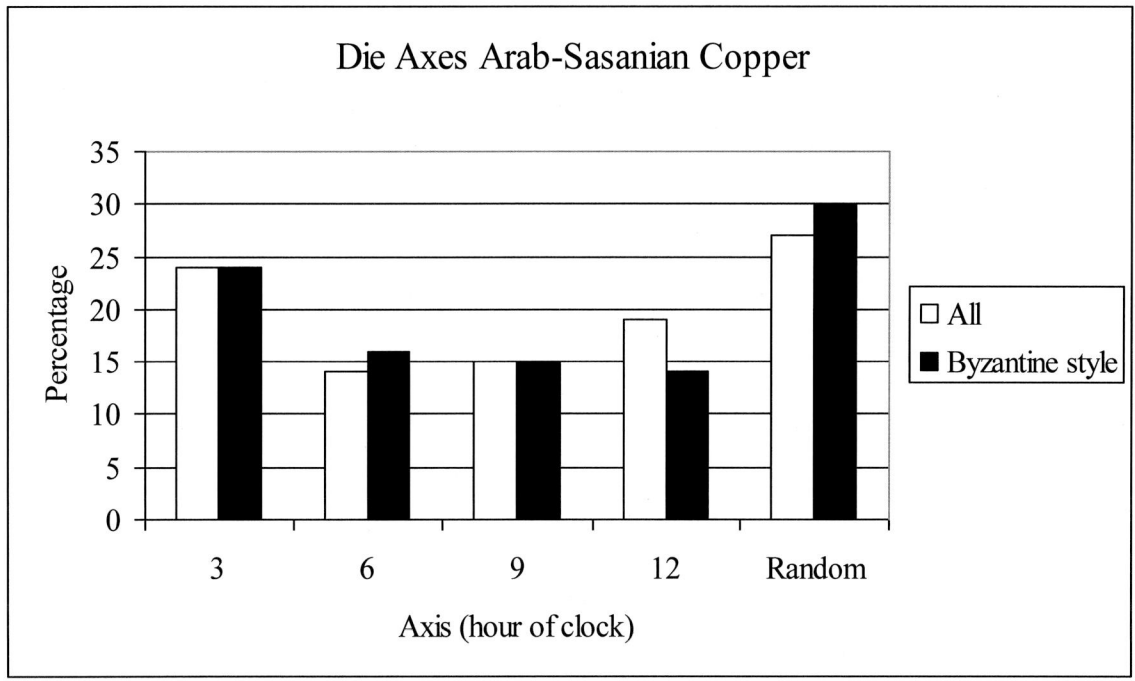

Fig. 2. Die axes on Arab-Sasanian copper coins

Die axes on Syrian copper

Here, there is a succession of groups that can be easily categorised and arranged in roughly chronological order. If the use of a regular die axis was simply the carry over from existing practice ('force of habit') one would expect that it would gradually have died out. That was originally my impression. As already mentioned many of the Phase 1 (Pseudo-Byzantine) coins retain the classical 180° axis but by the time of phase 3 (Standing Caliph) they seemed to be fairly random. A more detailed, though by no means exhaustive, examination shows that the situation is more complicated. I have used two sets of figures in the following statistics. The first records the percentages of coins with an accurate vertical die axis, the second those where the axis is 20° off the vertical in either direction. The expression of coins in percentages applies in all the following tables.

---

[34] Malek, *Arab Sasanian Numismatics*, pp. 656–85, pls 116–130, nos 1353–1616. The Byzantine copper imitations are pls 127–129, nos 1541–1605.

Pseudo-Byzantine (Phase 1)

The first Syrian Pseudo-Byzantine coins are those identified by Henri Pottier as having been issued during the period of the Persian occupation (the 'Syrian Mint'). Unfortunately he does not give die axes so I have used the data given by Steve Mansfield in his catalogue.[35]

No. of coins in sample	180°	160°–200°	0°	340°–20°	Random
76	13	17	11	11	49

Table 2. Die axes on 'Syrian Mint' coins

Surprisingly they are not very consistent. On the ones that are aligned there is some preference for 180° over 0°. There is an interesting contrast with the coins struck at Alexandria under Persian auspices.[36] Long ago Joseph Milne pointed out that, while the die axes on Alexandrian 12-nummi are fairly regular up to the reign of Maurice, the axes on the barbarous folles attributed to the time of Focas are random and even the die axes on the official coins of Heraclius are not consistent.[37] The so-called Persian issues in both modules, on the other hand, are usually 180°, a continuation of Byzantine practice.

The post Arab conquest coins ('Pseudo Byzantine' or 'Phase 1') have been divided into the groups designated by Henri Pottier, Ingrid Schulze and Wolfgang Schulze (abbreviated PSS) because they give information about die axes.[38]

PSS no.	Obverse design
I	Three standing figures
IIa	Two standing figures **M** reverse
IIb	Two standing figures m reverse
IIIa,b	Facing bust (with and without legends)
IV	Single standing figure

For groups II and III I have combined data from PSS and my own collection. For groups I and IV I have used figures kindly supplied to me by Tony Goodwin from his own collection. Goodwin also provided figures for a die liked group of 'dated' coins which has a very clear tendency towards a 180° degree axis.[39] Finally there is a late group published by Andrew Oddy which copy the Sicilian folles of Constantine IV and therefore must postdate 668.[40] I have included coins which are either die linked to his groups or appear to be associated with it. Even at this late date some importance was still being attached to maintaining a vertical die axis.

---

[35] Mansfield, *Early Byzantine Copper Coins*, pp. 278–91.
[36] This attribution has recently been challenged by François Gurnet who argues that, although the coins may be contemporary with the Persian occupation, they were not issued by the Persian authorities. Gurnet, 'Considerations'.
[37] Milne, 'Antinoe', pp. 111–12. This is confirmed by the coins in *DOC*.
[38] Pottier, Schulze and Schulze, 'Pseudo-Byzantine coins in Syria'.
[39] Goodwin, 'Mint striking early dated coins'.
[40] Oddy, 'Constantine IV as a prototype'.

PSS Group	No. of coins in sample	180°	160°–200°	0°	340–20°	Random
1[41]	250	48	4	32	7	9
IIa	42	33	27	12	7	21
IIb	10	10	10	20	0	60
IIIa,b,	63	38	14	8	11	51
IV[42]	250	34	14	18	0	24
'Dated' group	25	60	2	8	2	28
Constantine IV group	65	32	19	9	15	16

Table 3. Die axis (in percentages) of Pseudo-Byzantine coins

It must be stressed that this typological breakdown is misleading. It is not very difficult to find die links between different classes. It is also possible to find die linked coins with different die axes but all we are looking for at the moment is general trends.

There are other ways one can use die axis to try and arrange the very amorphous Pseudo-Byzantine series. For example is there a correlation between regular die axis and good and bad style? This is not as clear as one might have expected. It is remarkably easy to find good style coins on a random alignment. It is more difficult to find really crude examples struck on 180° or 0° but it is not impossible.

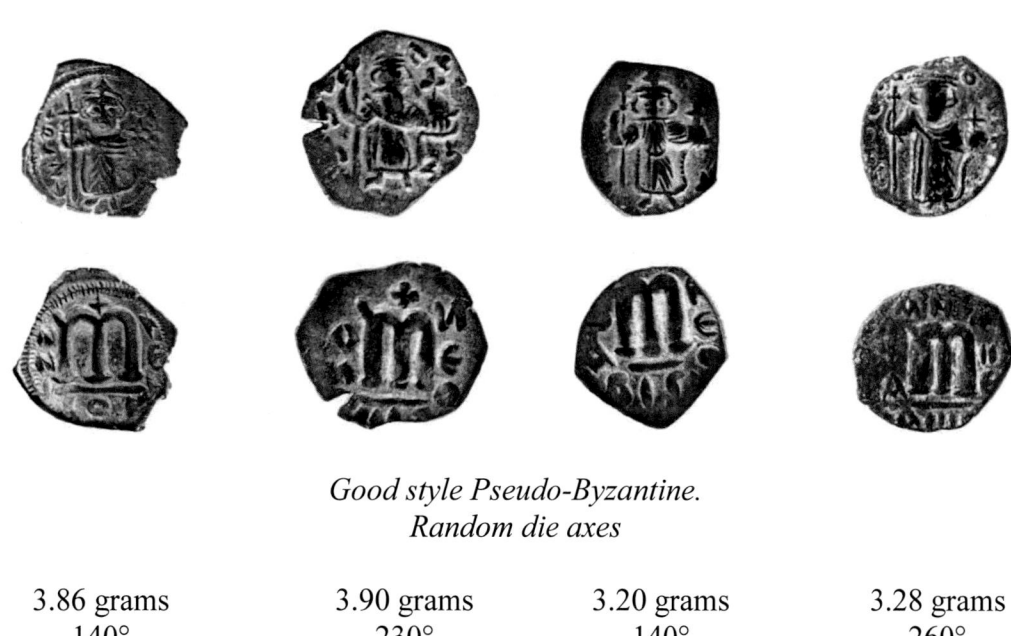

Good style Pseudo-Byzantine.
Random die axes

| 3.86 grams | 3.90 grams | 3.20 grams | 3.28 grams |
| 140° | 230° | 140° | 260° |

---

[41] 'This group comprises mostly 'cut coins' plus some oval coins. I didn't notice any great difference in the incidence of 6/12h between the two flan shapes. It is sometimes more difficult to accurately estimate the die axis on the cut coins, so there may be a slight over-statement of 6/12h'. Email from Goodwin 28 February 2019.

[42] 'These are all 'normal looking' Ps. Byz. - no really crude coins, no highly distinctive coin and none of the types which include certain later features. Also all of them are sufficiently well-preserved to be certain that none are regular Constans II. Provenance so far as I know is Syria/Lebanon. Definitely none known to come from Israel, which I keep separately'. Email from Goodwin 28 February 2019.

Poor style Pseudo Byzantine
Die axis either 180° or 0°

| 3.32 grams | 4.58 grams | 3.53 grams | 5.13 grams |
| 180° | 180° | 0° | 180° |

Umayyad Imperial Image (Phase 2)

Here I only have reasonable samples for two mints: Emesa/Homs (facing bust type) and Jerash.[43]

Mint	Sample (no.)	180°	160–200°	0°	340–20°	Random
Emesa Single bust type	120	86	7	0	0	7
Jerash	65	8	20	9	15	48

Table 4. Die axes (in percentages) of two groups of phase 2 (Umayyad Imperial Image) coins

The contrast is quite stark. At Emesa, for this type at least, only eight coins deviated from 180° or near it. There was no sign of any even approaching a 0° degree axis. At Jerash there are signs of a rather clumsy attempt at a vertical die axis but no preference for 0° or 180°.

A much smaller sample from Baalbek (22 coins) had approximately half the coins with a 180° axis or near it. At Tiberias about half of the nine large module three figures types examined were either 180° or 0° but an examination of 25 small module types showed only two with a clear 180° axis. All the coins examined (large and small module) had the **A** or crescent officina. The dies axis of those with the star or animal officina and those with 'Islamic legends' are random. Unfortunately there is still a major gap in the statistics as far as Damascus / Dimashq is concerned.

The Pseudo-Damascus and associated *al-wafā' lillāh* coins, both of which are clearly of southern origin are well documented thanks to Goodwin and Rika Gyselen.[44] There is evidence of a predilection for a vertical axis but no preference for 180° over 0°.

---

[43] The Emesa sample comes from a dealer's stock. The Jerash are calculated from Oddy, 'Phase 2 coinage of Gerasa'.
[44] Goodwin and Gyslen, ***Irbid Hoard***.

	Sample (no.)	180°	160–200°	0°	340–20°	Random
Pseudo-Damascus	379	16	10	16	12	46
Al-wafa' lillāh	204	6	27	9	24	34

Table 5. Die axes on coins of Ps-Damascus and al-wafa' lillāh expressed as percentages

Taken together these, very provisional, figures seem to indicate a closer attention to maintaining the classical die axis in Syria than in the areas further south. This might be an indication that the classical tradition was stronger in these more northern areas but such an idea would need a far more comprehensive coverage and, in any case seems to be contradicted by the phase three coinage.

Standing Caliph (Phase 3)

In his work on Standing Caliph coins Goodwin argues that on the whole die axes tend to be irregular though for most mints there is limited data. In the case of Halab there is evidence of a predilection for a vertical axis but no preference for 180° over 0°. The regular mint of Ilya Filistin (Jersualem) on the other hand still shows a high proportion of 180° die axis coins. There is no obvious explanation for this except that it reflects the relatively high and consistent metrological standards of the main issue. By contrast there was far less attention paid to die orientation in Schulze's 'special cases' which confirms her opinion that they are not the products of the official mint.[45]

	Sample (no.)	180°	160–200°	0°	340–20°	Random
SC Halab	129	21	12	16	13	37
SC Ilya	236	56	28	10	2	4
Ilya SC Irregular coins	35	14	23	17	0	46

Table 6. Die axes on coins of the Standing Caliph period expressed as percentages

Conclusion

Did the Syrian and Persian moneyers strike coins with a regular die axis out of habit and gradually stop for no particular reason? Or is the abandonment of a fixed die axis part of the Muslim rejection of the whole ethos of ancient coinage like the rejection of images? In the case of the copper, does it also reflect its decline in status? I suggest that it may have been part of the Muslim rejection of the ancient ethos but I accept that this is far from proved. On the present evidence any conclusion has to be provisional. I would ask those fortunate enough to handle and catalogue the rare precious metal coins that they take the trouble to accurately record the die axis. In general it would also help if numismatists, whatever system they use, would indicate how strict their criteria are. In other words is a coin that is not exactly 0° to be recorded as 20° or is some toleration allowed when it seems clear that the mint was aiming at 0°? I would also suggest that the study of medieval die axes should not be regarded as mere numismatic obscurantism, but has the potential to tell us more about the coins and cultural forces influencing the people who issued them.

---

[45] Goodwin, ***Standing Caliph Coinage***, Schulze, ***Standing Caliph Coinage of Jerusalem***.

APPENDIX 1

Obverse and Reverse

There is a remarkable degree of confusion about the definition of obverse and reverse because they can be defined in two completely different ways. Generally the obverse is regarded as the side with the ruler's head or, if there is no effigy, the most important side; a somewhat subjective definition. Numismatists, on the other hand, have tended to regard the obverse as the lower die (pile) and the reverse as the upper die (trussel). Normally the two coincided because the trussel was more prone to wear or break so would be chosen to bear the simpler design which took less time and effort to engrave. In the case of late Roman and Byzantine coinage there is no doubt that the portrait of the emperor was by far the most important feature of the coin as well as being the most time consuming to engrave. With western medieval coins, where portraits were mostly abandoned, it is not always clear which side contemporaries regarded as the more important. Simple dies made with punches took far less work to cut than engraved ones so there may have been less need to worry about the life time of the die.

The annunciation scene on the saluto of Charles of Anjou is most likely to have been the pile since it would have taken more work to engrave. The catalogue of *MEC* regards it as the reverse since it does not bear the ruler's name and title. The coin is always referred to in contemporary documents as a 'carlino'. The annunciation scene with purely religious legends, is probably the most eye-catching feature of the design but there is no evidence that it was called a 'saluto' which is the invention of modern coin people.[46]

In the letter, part of which is reproduced in Appendix 2, even the meticulous Charles of Anjou does not refer to obverse and reverse and does not seem to regard one side as being more important than the other. Attitudes may have been different in the contemporary Byzantine empire since a thirteenth century author, George Pachymeres speaks of the walls of Constantinople protected by the Virgin as being 'on the back' (ὄπισθεν) of the hyperpera of Michael VIII (1261–82).[47]

With Islamic coinages the problem becomes even more difficult. The evidence of later surviving dies is that the mint/date formula was usually the upper die which means it would be on the reverse of Umayyad dirhams and (date only) the reverse of Umayyad dinars. There was certainly some variation even in the 'Abbāsid era. Jere Bacherach *et al.* argued that 'it would be best if scholars (defined) obverse and reverse in terms of the priorities they consider most important and then be consistent in their own work'.[48]

Michael Bates has suggested that the side with the *shahada* was regarded as 'God's side' while the other belonged to the caliph which is why, when the early 'Abbāsid caliphs took the decisive step of putting their names on the coins, they placed them at the bottom of the reverse central legend.[49] The key point is that once the aniconic form of coinage had become established under Islam fixed die axes were abandoned.

---

[46] Lucia Travaini, personal comunication.
[47] Grierson, ***Byzantine Coins***, p. 27.
[48] Bacherach, Awad, Lowick, 'Obverse and reverse in Islamic numismatics', p. 190.
[49] M. Bates, 'Who was named on 'Abbasid coins?'

APPENDIX 2

Charles of Anjou insists on a 0° die axis

Scriptum est Thesaurio Castri ovi etc. Recepimus et diligenter inspexsimus quosdam Karolenses aureos Cusos de novo in Sicla nostra auri Neapolis per vos ad intuendum formam et modum eorum per Rogerium de Camera Celsitudini nostra missos. Quia invenimus quod forma seu Cuneus scuti ipsorum Karolensium ab altera parte eorum non expositus sicut debet. Quia cum debuerit sic ordinatus poni et inprimi. Quod Capud ipsius scuti, Capitibus ymaginum, Beate Virginis et Angeli ex parte altera positis et punta seu pes eiusdem scuti pedibus eorumdem ymaginum equali ordine responderent. Scuto ipso in contrarium posito non concordant. Set verso cudendi ordine predictum Capud scuti cadit in eam partem in quam peded dietarum ymaginum cadunt et punta seu pes eiusdem scuti cadit. In eam partem in quam cadunt Capita eaurumdem ymaginum contra beneplaciti nosti votum.

The original (of which the above is an extract) was in the Angevin Registers, totally and wantonly destroyed in World War II. Since 1950 scholars have carefully reconstituted them from earlier transcriptions, microfilms and notes.[50] Charles' letter seems to survive in slightly different wordings though the discrepancies seem to be of no great significance. I have reproduced the relevant passage from the text in Minieri Riccio which is the one referred to in *MEC* p. 198.[51]

WORKS CITED

S. Album and T. Goodwin, ***Sylloge of Islamic Coins in the Ashmolean* 1 *The Pre-reform Coinage of the Early Islamic Period*** (Oxford, 2002). Abbreviated ***SICA***.

J. Bacharach, H.A. Awad, N. Lowick, 'The problem of the obverse and reverse in Islamic numismatics', ***Numismatic Chronicle***, seventh series 13 (1973), pp. 183–91.

M. Bates, 'Who was named on 'Abbasid coins?', M. Faghfoury (ed.), ***Iranian Numismatic Studies. A Volume in Honor of Stephen Album*** (Lancaster PA, 2017), pp. 89–99.

A. Burnett, 'Die axis in Italy and Rome in the third century BC', ***Nomismata*** 8 (2016), pp. 9–28.

F. de Callataÿ, ***Les monnaies grecques et l'orientation des axes*** (Milan, 1996).

DOC = Grierson, ***Catalogue of the Byzantine Coins in the Dumbarton Oaks Collection***.

R. Filangieri di Candida (ed.), ***I Registri della Cancelleria Angioina ricostruiti da R. Filangieri con la collaborazione delgi archivisti napoletani*** (Naples, 1950 ff.).

T. Goodwin, 'A mint striking early dated (?) Arab-Byzantine coins, ***Spink Numismatic Circular*** (March, 2011), pp. 1–3.

T. Goodwin, ***The Standing Caliph Coinage*** (London, 2018).

T. Goodwin, R. Gyselen, ***Arab Byzantine Coins from the Irbid Hoard***, Royal Numismatic Society Special Publication 53 (London, 2015).

---

[50] R. Filangieri di Candida (ed.) ***Registri***.
[51] C. Minieri Riccio, ***Saggio di codice diplomatico***, vol. 1, pp. 165–6. no. 173.

P. Grierson, 'Pegged Venetian coin dies: their place in the history of die adjustment', *Numismatic Chronicle* sixth series 12 (1952), pp. 99–105.

P. Grierson, *Catalogue of the Byzantine Coins in the Dumbarton Oaks Collection and the Whittemore Collection*, 2: *Phocas–Theodosius III 602–717 AD* 1 *Phocas and Heraclius (602–641)* (Washington DC, 1968). Abbreviated *DOC*.

P. Grierson and L. Traviani, *Medieval European Coinage* 14 *Italy* 3 *(South Italy, Sicily, Sardinia)* (Cambridge, 1998). Abbreviated *MEC*.

P. Grierson, *Byzantine Coins* (London, 1982).

F. Gurnet, 'Some considerations on the Alexandrian copper coinage with star and crescent often attributed to the Sasanian king Khusro II', J.-M. Doyen, C. Morrisson (eds), *Mélanges de numismatique et d'archéologie de Byzance offerts à Henri Pottier* Travaux du cercle d'études numismatiques 20 (Brussels, 2019), pp. 151–65.

G. Macdonald, 'Fixed and loose dies in ancient coinage', G.F. Hill (ed.), *Corolla Numismatica: Numismatic Essays in Honour of Barclay V. Head* (London, 1906), pp. 178–88.

H.M. Malek *Arab-Sasanian Numismatics and History during the Early Islamic Period in Iran and Iraq*, Royal Numismatic Society Special Publication 55 (London, 2019).

S. Mansfield, *Early Byzantine Copper Coins. Catalogue of an English Collection* (Manchester, 2016).

MEC = Grierson and Traviani, *Medieval European Coinage* 14.

W.E. Metcalf, 'Three seventh century Byzantine gold hoards', *American Numismatic Society Museum Notes* 25 (1980) pp. 87–108.

G. Miles, 'The earliest Arab gold coinage', *American Numismatic Society Museum Notes* 13 (1967), pp. 205–29.

J.G. Milne, 'Report on the coins found at Antinoe in 1914', *Numismatic Chronicle* sixth series 7 (1947), pp. 108–114.

H. Nützel, 'Sasanidische Münzstempel', *Amtliche Berichte aus den Königlichen Kunstsammlungen* (Berlin) 31 (1909–10), cols 49–50.

W.A. Oddy, 'Constantine IV as a prototype for early Islamic coins', W.A. Oddy (ed.), *Coinage and History in the Seventh Century Near East* 2 (London 2010), pp. 95–109.

W.A. Oddy, 'The phase 2 coinage of Gerasa under Muʿāwiya and his successors', T. Goodwin (ed.), *Coinage and History in the Seventh Century Near East* 5 (London, 2017), pp. 49–74.

M. Phillips, 'Eastern copies of tenth and eleventh century Byzantine coins. A preliminary survey', J.-M. Doyen and C. Morrisson (eds), *Mélanges de numismatique et d'archéologie de Byzance offerts à Henri Pottier*, Travaux du cercle d'études numismatique, 20 (Brussels, 2019), pp. 293–316.

H. Pottier, I. Schulze and W. Schulze, 'Pseudo-Byzantine coinage in Syria under Arab rule (638–c.670). Classification and dating', *Revue Belge de Numismatique et de Sigillographie* 154 (2008), pp. 87–155.

C. Minieri Riccio, *Saggio di codice diplomatico formato sulle antiche scritture dell' archivio di Stato di Napoli* (Naples, 1878–83).

N. Schindel, *Sylloge Nummorum Sasanidarum. Paris, Wien, Berlin* 3 *Shapur II – Kawad I, 2. Regierung* (Vienna, 2004). Abbreviated *SNS* 3.

N. Schindel, *Sylloge Nummorum Sasanidarum. Israel* (Vienna, 2009). Abbreviated *SNS Israel*.

M. Schlapke, 'Die Münzen und Barren des Erfurter Schatzfundes', Sven Ostritz (ed.), *Die Mittelalterliche Jüdische Kultur in Erfurt*, vol. 3 Mario Schlapke, Oliver Mecking, Robert Lehmann, Carla Vogt, *Der Schatzfund. Die Münzen und Barren* (Weimar, 2011).

I. Schulze, *The Standing Caliph Coins of Jerusalem* (Munich, 2016).

SICA = Album and Goodwin, *Sylloge of Islamic Coins in the Ashmolean*.

A. Smołucha-Sładkowska, 'The first early-Renaissance medals with inverted reverses (6 o'clock die axes)', *Numismatic Chronicle* 178 (2018), pp. 275–80.

SNS = Schindel, *Sylloge Nummorum Sasanidarum*.

W.F. Spengler and W.G. Sayles, *Turkoman Figural Bronze Coins and their Iconography* 2 *The Zengids* (Lodi WI, 1996).

J. Stickel, *Handbuch zur morgänlandische Münzkunde* vol. 2 (Leipzig, 1870).

L. Traviani, 'Il ripostiglio di Oschiri (Sassari)', *Bollettino di Numismatica* 1 (1983), pp. 27–221.

L. Treadwell, 'The 'Orans' drachms of Bishr ibn Marwān and the figural coinage of the early Marwanid period', J. Johns (ed.) *Bayt al-Maqdis. Jerusalem and Early Islam Oxford Studies in Islamic Art* 9 (2) (Oxford, 1999), pp. 223–70.

S. Tyler-Smith, 'The 'year 12: Berlin 2016' hoard of late Sasanian coins', *Numismatic Chronicle* 177 (2017), pp. 419–50.

M. 'Al-Ush, *Arab Islamic Coins Preserved in the National Museum of Qatar* (Doha, 1984).

J. Walker, *A Catalogue of the Arab-Sasanian Coins in the British Museum* Catalogue of the Muhammadan Coins in the British Museum 1 (London, 1941).